SHAKESPEARE OF LONDON

MARCHETTE CHUTE *has written:*

Books for adults

THE SEARCH FOR GOD
GEOFFREY CHAUCER OF ENGLAND
THE END OF THE SEARCH
SHAKESPEARE OF LONDON
BEN JONSON OF WESTMINSTER

Books for young people

AN INTRODUCTION TO SHAKESPEARE
THE INNOCENT WAYFARING
THE WONDERFUL WINTER
STORIES FROM SHAKESPEARE

Books for small children

RHYMES ABOUT OURSELVES
RHYMES ABOUT THE COUNTRY
RHYMES ABOUT THE CITY
AROUND AND ABOUT

SHAKESPEARE
OF LONDON

By

MARCHETTE CHUTE

A Dutton  Paperback

NEW YORK

E. P. DUTTON

Published in the United States by E. P. Dutton, a
divison of New American Library, 2 Park Avenue,
New York, N.Y. 10016.

ISBN: 0-525-48245-8

MARCHETTE CHUTE was born at "Hazelwood," Way-
zata, Minnesota. She attended the Minneapolis
School of Art and graduated from the University of
Minnesota, a member of Phi Beta Kappa. She is a
Fellow of the Royal Society of Arts. One of three
well-known writing sisters, Miss Chute's many books
include GEOFFREY CHAUCER OF ENGLAND (1946),
BEN JONSON OF WESTMINSTER (1953), and STORIES
FROM SHAKESPEARE (1956). Her brilliant style and
scholarship have won Miss Chute national recognition as an outstanding authority on English literary history, and her awards include the Author-
Meets-the-Critics Award for the best non-fiction of
1950, the Secondary Education Board Award in
1954, and the Poetry Chap-Book Award in 1954.

SHAKESPEARE OF LONDON was first published in 1950

Foreword

THIS book is an attempt to bring a very great man into the light of common day. It is an attempt to show William Shakespeare as his contemporaries saw him, rather than as the gigantic and legendary figure he has become since. He was once life size, and this is an attempt at a life-sized portrait.

The book is not a literary biography. It does not concern the part of Shakespeare that was immortal and for all time. It concerns only the part of him that was mortal and belonged to the Elizabethan age. His plays are not discussed as literature, but only as they relate to the working problems of the London stage.

The confusion that surrounds Shakespeare's life has not been caused by lack of information. More is known about Shakespeare than about any other playwright of the period with the single exception of Ben Jonson; and some parts of his life are better documented even than Jonson's. But there has been a tendency to take each aspect of Shakespeare's career separately and brood upon it, instead of setting his career as a whole against the background of his own day. Any man will become incomprehensible if he is isolated from his background.

In Shakespeare's case his background was the theatre. It is unfortunate that so many of the people who have written about him should have had no theatre experience, and even more unfortunate that out of a misplaced reverence they have been unwilling to remember that he was not only a professional playwright but a professional actor also.

It is also unfortunate that the men of the Elizabethan and Jacobean theatre left so few records of their activities. Shakespeare's Stratford is not difficult to reconstruct, since the parish and corporation records were kept with great care. The same thing is true of Shakespeare's London, for the Londoners were proud of their city and made several reports for posterity. But the men who worked with Shakespeare in the theatre did not know how deeply posterity was going to be interested in them, and it did not occur to them to leave a report of what they were doing.

The only man who wrote down a record of contemporary theatre conditions for future readers was Sir George Buck, who was Master of the Revels under James I and therefore in close professional contact with every actor and playwright in London. Buck was an admirer of "the public stages and theatres of this city" and he wrote a treatise on the subject; but the treatise has vanished and nothing remains except Buck's statement that he wrote it.

It may be, after all, that Buck's treatise would not be of much practical value in reconstructing the period. Thomas Heywood, who was one of the most experienced theatre men of the period, wrote a book at about the time of Shakespeare's retirement and gave it the promising title, *An Apology for Actors*. Unfortunately Heywood was so anxious to show the antiquity and dignity of the acting profession that he spent nearly all his time describing the conditions in the Roman theatre and for all practical purposes hardly mentions his own. Ben Jonson, like Heywood, was an actor and playwright and he also put some of his views on paper. They chiefly concern the low state, artistically, of the contemporary stage and his disapproval of audiences who did not like some of his plays. As for William Shakespeare, the greatest actor-playwright of them all, he paid so little attention to posterity that he did not even bother to get his own plays into print.

There is no way to reconstruct the theatre of Shakespeare's day except to piece it together from the scattered references that have been accidentally preserved in everything from account books to sermons. Some of the details have vanished forever, but enough remain to form a reasonable and coherent background for Shakespeare's life.

In dealing with Shakespeare's life, I have taken what seems to me the safest course and have based it entirely on contemporary documents. I have used no evidence that is dated later than 1635; and I have accepted a document as late as this (nineteen years after Shakespeare's death) only because it records testimony given by Cuthbert Burbage, the last survivor of the original group of London theatre men who had worked with Shakespeare.

It was not until the Restoration that anyone was sufficiently interested in Shakespeare's life to begin writing about it, and by that time all the men who had known him were dead and the conditions under which he had worked had completely disappeared. What the men of the Restoration wrote about Shakespeare has had an enormous influence on all subsequent biographies and cannot be altogether ignored. On the other hand, it has no documentary support and cannot legitimately be included in the body of this particular book.

I have put all material of this kind in appendixes. Appendix One is on Shakespeare's *Sonnets*, about which very little contemporary evidence has survived except the name of the publisher and the price of the book. Appendix Two concerns the stories about Shakespeare's life that first became current during the Restoration and have since hardened into accepted fact because so many people have believed in them. Appendix Three concerns the attacks on the authority of the editors of the First Folio and the resulting disintegration of the canon.

A book of this kind is a mosaic, built up of a number of small facts that have meaning only when they are placed in juxtaposition to each other. A single paragraph has sometimes been built up from a dozen different sources of information, and to list these sources would in some cases take more room than the writing itself now occupies. The bibliography lists only a fraction of the books that were used in preparing the text, and I am sorry that lack of space has made it impossible to give individual credit to the thousands of publications, from the middle of the sixteenth century to the middle of the twentieth, that have helped me in writing *Shakespeare of London*.

Nearly all this research was done in the New York Public Library, which is not only one of the greatest repositories of books in the world but has the further and democratic distinction of serving as "a free library for the use of the people." All the books listed in the bibliography are available in the New York Public Library with the exception of the following: Holinshed's *Chronicles*, in the Arents collection in the same building, *Henslowe Papers*, in the library at Columbia University, Stow's *Survey of London*, in the Morgan Library, Ingleby's *Shakespeare and the Enclosure of Common Fields at Welcombe*, in the Boston Public Library, and Stubbes' *Anatomy of Abuses*, in the Folger Shakespeare Library.

All spelling has been modernized. This service is habitually done for Shakespeare, and there seems to be no reason to fail to do it for his contemporaries.

M. C.

Shakespeare *of London*

Chapter 1

THERE were many towns named Stratford in England, but the one that stood on the banks of the river Avon had special reason to be proud of its native sons. John of Stratford had become Archbishop of Canterbury and lay buried in a tomb of alabaster at the high altar, and Hugh Clopton had gone to the great city of London and ended by becoming its Lord Mayor.

By the middle of the sixteenth century these special glories were a thing of the past. But the stone bridge over the Avon that Sir Hugh Clopton had built at great expense for his native town had opened up a year-round traffic with London, and Stratford had become a thriving market community and was now one of the largest towns in Warwickshire. When the young men who were born in the near-by villages decided that they did not want to be farmers, they migrated to Stratford to learn a trade and settle down in one of its well-travelled streets.

Among the young men of Warwickshire who felt the pull of Stratford was one named John Shakespeare. John lived in the pleasant little village of Snitterfield, four miles to the north. His father was a tenant farmer and his brother was a tenant farmer, but John had no intention of following in their footsteps. When he left Snitterfield he probably had no higher ambition than to become a successful business man in Stratford; but before John Shakespeare died he had achieved the highest political office in town, and had been a justice of the peace, a landowner and a gentleman with a coat of arms. He had also become the father of a son named William who had a considerable success on the London stage; and, while this was not in itself a very dignified achievement from the Stratford point of view, John Shakespeare had the satisfaction of knowing before he died that his son was already investing his money in Stratford real estate.

The trade that young John Shakespeare selected for himself was that of making gloves. Everyone wore gloves in the sixteenth century, and since their native manufacture was protected by Act of Parliament, it was a profitable trade. The glovers were one of the most powerful trade groups in Stratford, and on market days they put up their booths and trestles in the most strategic location in town. They did their selling just under the big clock in the paved market square, where most of the customers gathered, and it was not until more than a hundred years later that another powerful trade group, the mercers, managed to take this location away from them. John Shakespeare was a "whittawer," a dealer in the fine white leather from which the best products were made, but like most of his fellow townsmen he sold other commodities, from timber to wool, in his spare time.

The Stratford that John Shakespeare knew was still a medieval town. It had never been walled, which accounted for its unusually straight and broad streets, but in spirit it was a tight, narrow little medieval community. Like every other town in England, Stratford was run on a strict, paternalistic system that had worked well for the citizens' remote ancestors and might be expected to work equally well for them. Every effort was made to protect local industry and keep away outsiders, all trade was strictly controlled and supervised, and every resident was hedged about with rules designed to keep himself and the town in order. An inhabitant of Stratford was fined if he let his dog go unmuzzled, if his duck wandered, if he played cards "or any other unlawful games," if his children were not at home by eight o'clock in the summertime, if he failed to sweep his gutters or if he borrowed gravel from the town gravel pits. If he wanted to bring an outsider into his house he had to have a special license from the High Bailiff, and if from a sense of compassion he gave shelter in his house to "any stranger woman" who was pregnant he was heavily fined.

The natural result of Stratford's strict medieval standards of conduct was that the men of Stratford's governing body were continually obliged to fine themselves and their fellow townsmen for breaking the rules. With so many rules to be enforced it was impossible to avoid breaking a few of them, and there was no citizen of Stratford so virtuous or so distinguished that he escaped a fine for one offense or another.

One of the best sources of revenue was the law that forbade the residents from making private, informal dump-heaps of their own instead of using the four or five official ones. Fines for making a "muckhill at chamber's door" were levied at nearly every frankpledge, for it was one of the commonest offenses in Stratford. John Shakespeare, for instance, makes his first appearance on the town records because he and two of his very respectable neighbors were fined twelvepence each for establishing a refuse heap near their houses instead of using the public one at the end of the street. John Shakespeare must have been a sober, respectable householder for he was very seldom fined for having sinned against the Stratford by-laws, but some of his fellow townsmen were always leaping in and out of the records for having done the wrong thing again.

The dealers in basic food commodities had an especially hard time in Stratford, for the town was operating on the rigid medieval system of price controls and that meant an equally strict supervision of quality. Every year two ale-tasters were elected to see that the bakers and butchers and innkeepers of Stratford were obeying the rules on prices, that the brewers were putting "no hops nor no other subtle things in their brewing" and that the numerous women who retailed beer were not serving it in unsealed pots. In the September elections of 1556, John Shakespeare was made an ale-taster and started his long climb upwards through the various civic offices in Stratford.

The next year John Shakespeare entered the Council, the governing body of Stratford. He was appointed one of the fourteen Capital Burgesses and had the proud obligation of attending the meetings of the Council in the handsome old guild building. John Shakespeare wore a special gown to attend these meetings and there was a fine of twelvepence if he forgot it. There was a further fine of six shillings and eightpence if he left the meeting in any but "brotherly love"; for the citizens in that orderly little town were on the whole a rowdy and opinionated lot and it needed a direct attack on their pockets to keep them in order. More than one Council meeting was broken up for what was politely called "opprobrious words" and occasionally a member had to be expelled for having too excitable a temperament.

The following year, in 1558, John Shakespeare was made one of the constables of the borough, a position that required a strong, healthy and determined man. Physical assaults were a commonplace in a period when every man had a right to wear a dagger but theoretically no right to use it. John Shakespeare happened to get the office at an especially difficult and contentious time, for he had been constable less than two months when Queen Mary died. As long as Mary was ruler, the official religion of England was Catholicism and every Protestant was a potential traitor. When her successor, Queen Elizabeth, came to the throne that November, the state religion became Protestant again. Most Englishmen accepted the change without any special difficulty, but in every town there was a group that did not welcome the new queen and they made the life of a constable a busy one.

The next year John Shakespeare was reappointed petty constable and he was also made affeeror. In this office he was responsible for deciding what penalties should be levied in cases that were covered by no special town statute. He must have done his work satisfactorily, for in 1561 he was given the important position of town chamberlain, and with his colleague, John Taylor, became responsible for administering the borough revenues.

Again John Shakespeare took his post in a busy period. A government order had gone out that all signs of Catholicism in the local churches and chapels were to be effaced, since the one true religion was now quite a different one, and it was the business of the local chamberlains to see that the altars were removed, the images hacked, and the old religious paintings whitewashed. John Shakespeare, for instance, paid a workman two shillings to deface the images that stood in the guild chapel, and it was probably at the same time that all the wall paintings in the chapel were whitewashed. It was rather a pity that the paintings could not have remained for Shakespeare's son to look at, since he would have enjoyed the dragons over the vicar's door, the devils with their tapir-like noses between the nave and the chancel, and St. George warring with the dragon on the other side of the nave while a horse with the horn of a unicorn did his best to be of assistance. The Reformation was responsible for removing a good deal of innocent color from the lives of the people of England, and although St. George was their patron saint he was one of the casualties.

The chamberlains served a two-year term, with John Taylor assuming most of the responsibility the first year and John Shakespeare the second. They collected the town revenues, administered them, and turned in a full report to their fellow members on the Council. The expenditures were miscellaneous, apart from standard ones to the schoolmaster and the vicar, and ranged from seventeen shillings for mending the vicar's chimney to twelvepence for repairs of the much-repaired town clock. When the revenues fell short of the expenses, John Shakespeare made up the difference out of his own pocket. In the end the borough owed him a substantial sum of more than four pounds, but Shakespeare asked no interest and was willing to wait some time for repayment.

It has been repeatedly suggested that John Shakespeare was an illiterate man who could not even write his own name. His handwriting does not appear in the chamberlains' accounts, which were copied out by the town clerk, and when he signed his name to documents he used either a mark or a rather delicate drawing of the compasses he used in his glover's trade. The use of a mark as a signature does not mean anything one way or the other. A close friend of Shakespeare's, Adrian Quiney, made his mark in the Council records on the same page as John Shakespeare and he occasionally used an inverted capital Q for his signature; but there are letters of Adrian Quiney's extant to prove that he could have written his name if he wanted to. Christopher Marlowe's father signed his will with a mark, although he was a clerk in Canterbury with his signature still extant in the church register.

There is no record of a chamberlain in Stratford who did not know how to write, and an illiterate man would be a curious choice for an office that consisted of so much careful bookkeeping. John Shakespeare was such a success in the office that after his two-year term was over and William Tyler and William Smith were acting as the new chamberlains he was retained for another year to draw up their accounts for them. This was not a normal procedure in Stratford, and indicates that John Shakespeare must have been unusually well equipped for the office of chamberlain.

In the meantime John Shakespeare had become a married man, and it is probable that his marriage was quite as gratifying to his relatives in Snitterfield as his steady business and civic advancement must have been. His wife had one of the oldest names in Warwickshire, for the Ardens had been "lords of Warwick" before William the Conqueror came. Just what connection Mary Arden may have had with the Warwickshire Ardens is not clear. When the Office of Heralds in London was obliged to wrestle with the problem they finally linked her with another branch of the family and the actual genealogy has never been straightened out to anyone's satisfaction. At any rate, it is clear that Mary Arden would have been considered a member of the gentry, although she lost that distinction when she became Mary Shakespeare.

But Mary Shakespeare brought her husband a gift almost as good as gentility; she brought him land. Old Robert Arden had no sons, and of all his daughters Mary seems to have been his favorite. He left her in his will not only a substantial cash payment but also a large piece of farm property in Wilmcote. What this land meant to John Shakespeare, son of one of Robert Arden's tenant farmers, can be measured by the tenacity with which he fought to get it back after he had lost it.

Mary was the youngest of Robert Arden's children and yet he made her one of the two executors of his will. It was Mary who was responsible in part for seeing that her father's featherbed and his decorative painted hangings and his colts and sheep and bees and wheat went to their new owners after his death, and that her stepmother did not war openly because she had received only part of the inheritance. Mary was evidently a competent woman, and certainly she married in John Shakespeare an intelligent and competent man.

The year that Robert Arden died, his future son-in-law himself became a landowner. This was the same year that John Shakespeare bought two houses in Stratford, one in Greenhill Street on the west edge of town, and one in Henley Street. He had been living in Henley Street for at least four years past, and he may have bought the house he had already been renting. It was probably to the house in Henley Street that he brought his bride, and it was evidently here that most of the Shakespeare children were born.

The first of the Shakespeare children was born in 1558, the same month John Shakespeare was appointed constable. It was not the hoped-for son who would carry on the family name and inherit the land. It was a little girl named Joan and she died young. It was not until four years later that a second child was born to Mary Shakespeare; this also was a little girl, and they buried her the following spring.

A year after Margaret's burial, in the same month of April, Mary Shakespeare give birth to her third child. This time it was a son, and his father and mother named him William.

The people of Stratford had no way of peering through the mists of the future to discover that the date on which William Shakespeare was born would be of interest to the whole of the civilized world. The Stratford parish register merely recorded the date of his baptism. This was the 26th of April, 1564, and all that can be said with certainty about the day of his birth is that it was a few days earlier.

Tradition and sentiment have united to proclaim that Shakespeare was born on the 23rd of April. This was the date on which he died in Stratford, fifty-two years later. Moreover, the 23rd of April is St. George's Day, and St. George is the patron saint of England as Shakespeare is its patron writer. The pageant of St. George vanished from the streets of Stratford when Queen Elizabeth came to the throne. His dragon no longer snorted through the streets on Holy Thursday, and the two shillings that the men of Stratford had once spent for gunpowder so that smoke and flame could come out of its mouth no doubt went to soberer and worthier objects. Still, it is pleasant to feel that the great master of make-believe was born on St. George's Day, and there is no harm in hoping that he was.

John Shakespeare was still acting as chamberlain the year his son was born, and William must have received a christening worthy of the first-born son of a town official. The ceremony took place in the handsome old Church of the Holy Trinity by the river, and John Bretchgirdle was the vicar who christened the white-clad baby in the presence of his father, his godparents and the assembled congregation so that he could go out into the world as a properly-accredited member of the Church of England. Bretchgirdle was an Oxford graduate who took equal delight in Horace and in carpentering, and when he died the following year he had seen to it that the small boys of Stratford would inherit those of his books they would enjoy reading.

Religion was administered with a firm hand in Stratford, as it was everywhere else in England. Religion and politics were inextricably connected, and every human being in England who was loyal to the Queen was expected to be equally loyal to the Church. Since this loyalty was not in every case quite spontaneous, any citizen of Stratford was fined if he did not present himself, his family and his servants at church every Sunday; and government commissions were constantly on the prowl all over England to make sure that the people were obeying the Act of Uniformity and that those dreaded individuals, religious recusants, were being unearthed and properly punished. The pulpit was a useful outlet for government propaganda, and the special prayers and homilies read from the pulpit by Bretchgirdle and his successors were of great assistance in preventing the people of Stratford from making up their minds independently on any subject whatever.

The religion of John and Mary Shakespeare is not known. Mary's father made a Catholic will, but since he died in the days "of our sovereign lord and lady, Philip and Mary" it would have been odd if he had done otherwise. Little Joan Shakespeare was baptised in the Catholic fashion, in Latin and with the anointing, because Queen Mary was still on the throne; but her brother William, who was born after Elizabeth came to the throne, was baptised in the Protestant fashion, in English and at the font. Nearly two decades later, John Shakespeare's name occurs on a list, drawn up by an ecclesiastical commission, because he had not been going to church. However, his name is not listed among the six suspected of being Catholic but among those who "come not to church for fear of process for debt." In any case, whatever his parents' religion may have been, William Shakespeare was a member of the Church of England. When the Walker family of Stratford named their son William, Shakespeare acted as godfather at the baptism, and he could not have done so unless he were an accredited member of the Church of England.

Three months after William Shakespeare was born, Stratford was visited by the plague. The infection was so serious that the Council could not meet indoors in August and took up a special collection for plague victims at a meeting in the chapel garden. For once the town clerk was not there to record the meetings; his son and his daughter had just died of the plague. In six months there were more than 250 burials, and there must have been many times when John and Mary Shakespeare were frightened for the safety of their only son.

In time the plague wore itself out as it always did. Stratford resumed its normal life, and John Shakespeare continued his steady rise in the town government.

The year after William was born, the town Council found itself obliged to expel one of its members, an alderman named William Bott. Bott had indulged in too many opprobrious words, and John Shakespeare was sworn in as an alderman in his place. In his new dignity as alderman, John Shakespeare wore a black gown faced with fur and on Sundays he had a special seat nearer the pulpit. He was entitled to hang a special lantern before his house on Henley Street during the Christmas season, and above all he had achieved the coveted social distinction of becoming "Mr. John Shakespeare." *

Two years later, Shakespeare's name was suggested for the office of High Bailiff, the highest political office in the power of the town to give. The High Bailiff corresponded to what most towns called the mayor, and the name went back to the days when Stratford had been under the control of a lord of the manor and the lord's bailiff was responsible for administering the town affairs. Stratford had been granted a charter by Elizabeth's brother, King Edward, just before he died and now had its own self-contained government, but the name of "bailiff" instead of "mayor" remained as a sign of the town's origin.

John Shakespeare did not win the election the first time his name was suggested. But it was brought up again the following year and this time his fellow-members of the Council gave him a majority. He took the oath of office on the first of October, 1568, and swore to defend the liberties of the borough and give justice to rich and poor alike. His furred robes were now of scarlet and when he went to preside over meetings in the Council chamber he was given a special escort. When he attended the Church of the Holy Trinity (that great barometer of social prestige) he had a seat in the front pew on the north side of the nave, with Mary Shakespeare and the Chief Alderman beside him, and the lesser aldermen and their wives to his rear.

As High Bailiff, John Shakespeare became also a justice of the peace, and he presided as judge over the Court of Record as well as presiding over the meetings of the Council. The rules laid down in the instruction book of the Office of Heralds stated that he was now eligible for a coat of arms if he should request it, for the office of bailiff was one of those "divers offices of dignity" that made its owner eligible

---

* *Mr.* was pronounced *Master*, as *Mrs.* was pronounced *Mistress*. It was not until later that the syllables were slurred into their present pronunciation.

for admission into the ranks of the gentry. The son of the
tenant farmer of Snitterfield had come a long way.

The son of the High Bailiff, young William Shakespeare,
was now four years old and had a two-year-old brother named
Gilbert to keep him company. The center of his life must have
been at first the house on Henley Street, with its sturdy oak
framework and slanting roof; and he must have known the
premises thoroughly from the pointed gables of the attic to
his father's shop with its leathers and its tools on the ground
floor.

The house was on the edge of town, just south of the gravel
pits that marked the northern limits of the borough, but it
was only a short walk down Henley Street to the intersection
where the real business of town began. Here was the pump
where the Stratford housewives washed their clothes and
hung them, rather improperly, on the Market Cross to dry.
It was here that John Shakespeare had his stall on market
days; and a square wooden structure on pillars not only supported the clock with its gilded dial but had a ledge encir-
cling it from which a small boy could comfortably dangle his
legs and watch the shoppers below.

East of Market Cross was Bridge Street, the thoroughfare
that led towards Oxford and London, and most of the important shops in Stratford were concentrated along its length.
Here were the smithies and the taverns, the shoemakers and
the bake shops, and also Stratford's four excellent inns. An
inn like the Swan could boast of leaded panes and velvet cushions, and its walls were engagingly decorated with pictures
of ancient worthies like Tobias dressed in Elizabethan doublet
and trunk hose.

Beyond Bridge Street a causeway led to the great stone
bridge that Sir Hugh Clopton had built over the river Avon.
In those days the Avon was "a river in summer and a little sea
in winter" and the parapet of the bridge was low enough
so that even the smallest of small boys could see over its edge.
Along the river bank between the town and the bridge was

Butt Close, where the townsmen were supposed to practice their archery, and beyond that was Bank Croft, where the ducks and cattle and sheep of Stratford had their communal pasture. The practice of archery was not only supposed to distract the citizens' minds from "unlawful" games like bowling and cards but also to fit them for soldiering when the Queen needed them, although the development of gunpowder had made archers obsolete and England's own armament industry had reached such proportions that English mariners complained the enemy was destroying them with guns of English manufacture.

Each of the prosperous inhabitants of Stratford had his own barn and his own garden, and the garden that adjoined the guild buildings was noted for its apples and plums. The town was green and leafy in summer, for there were over a thousand elms in its small confines and forty ash—that wood which "being cut down green it burneth green and bright." Around Stratford was farm land, the parallel strips that were still being tilled on the communal system that had served the people well in medieval times. But as a boy grew more adventurous there lay for his delight along the horizon what was now called the Woodland but had been known in ancient times as the Forest of Arden.

As a Stratford boy grew older he found less time for roaming, for school was a serious business in his community. There had always been a free school in Stratford, financed before the Reformation by the Guild of the Holy Cross and since then by borough revenues. The Stratford charter stipulated that the town was to have a "free grammar school for the training and education of children" to be "continued forever," and the boys in Stratford were expected to enter it for a free education as soon as they knew how to read and write.

By the end of the century there was a man in Stratford who taught the children reading and writing while his wife taught needlework, and unless there was a similar arrangement when William Shakespeare was a small boy he probably learned his letters from the parish clerk. The Stratford gram-- mar school was not supposed to handle elementary work of this kind, although it was apparently sometimes forced to assume what it called the "tedious trouble" of teaching the young to read. It was a trouble to the young also, and one weak-minded English uncle of the previous decade spent twenty times as much on sugar plums as on hornbooks before his nephew succeeded in learning his letters.

The hornbook was a slab of wood on which a page full of letters had been fastened and which was covered over with a thin, transparent sheet of horn to protect it from grubby small fingers. Countless generations of children had learned to read clutching the handle of a hornbook and William Shakespeare could hardly have been an exception. From that he probably graduated to *The ABC and Little Catechism,* which gave the youth of England their letters and their religious instruction simultaneously and sold in England at the rate of ten thousand copies in eight months.

Shakespeare learned to form his letters in the way all the little boys in rural districts formed them. The new Italian hand, which corresponds roughly to the modern way of writing, had made great headway in court and city circles, but the medieval way of writing, the one called the secretary hand, was still being used in the country. Some of Shake- speare's fellow-dramatists, like George Peele, used the new Italian way of writing; some of them, like Thomas Kyd and George Chapman, used both fashions interchangeably, and at least one of them, Ben Jonson, worked out an efficient com- promise between the two. The few signatures which are all that remain of Shakespeare's writing are done in the old- fashioned secretary hand he was taught in Stratford, and it is probable that he did not bother to change it after he came to London.

As soon as he could read and write and knew his Catechism, young William Shakespeare was ready to enter Stratford grammar school. He was the son of one of the most prominent men in Stratford, but he received the same education that was democratically open to every boy in town and there was no charge for the instruction.

The curriculum of Stratford grammar school, like that of every other grammar school in England, was serious, thorough and dull. There was no attempt whatever to fit the boys for the ordinary life they were going to find when they graduated, for all school theory in England was based on the medieval system. The purpose of schools in the Middle Ages was to turn out learned clerks for church positions, and therefore what the little boys of Renaissance England learned was Latin, more Latin and still more Latin. About a decade after Shakespeare entered the classroom a London teacher urged that English should also be taught in the schools, but no one paid any attention to so radical a suggestion.

The chief difference between the education given Shakespeare and that given Geoffrey Chaucer two centuries earlier was that Chaucer's comparatively simple instruction book, called the Donat, had been replaced by an authorized Latin grammar written by William Lily. Lily was the first headmaster of the school at St. Paul's Cathedral, and his book must have made him more cordially hated by harassed seven-year-olds than any man before or since. The whole of the English educational system united to pound Lily's Latin grammar into the heads of the young, and if a schoolboy was wise he resigned himself to having to memorize the whole book.

Not one boy in a hundred had any real use for Latin in his subsequent career, and it is sad to think how the young Quineys and Walkers and Shakespeares worked over their construing in the schoolroom, in what one London teacher compassionately called "an unnatural stillness," while the whole of the sunlit world waited for them outside. One of their number was eventually to become an actor and no doubt the strict training in memory-work did him a certain amount of good, but it is hard to see how their work in the schoolroom really benefited most of them.

In the average grammar school the boys worked at their grammar about four years, although an earlier educationalist had urged a little more consideration of the boy's own point of view. "By the time he cometh to the sweet and pleasant reading of old authors, the sparks of fervent desire for learning is extinct with its burden of grammar." Another reformer agreed that it was "cold and uncomfortable" for both teacher and pupil when grammar was taught without an allied course of reading, but he added gloomily that it was "the common way." It was much easier to teach rules than to give boys a real love of Latin literature, and the average teacher took the easier way.

Here and there an imaginative teacher who loved his work triumphed over Lily and kindled a love of Latin writers in the hearts of the young. William Camden, the great London teacher, lit such a fire in the heart of one of his students that Ben Jonson worshipped both Camden and the classics all his life. Somewhere at Cambridge Christopher Marlowe evidently found a teacher who did the same, but there is no indication that any schoolmaster set off a similar spark in young William Shakespeare. Like Geoffrey Chaucer before him, Shakespeare preferred to approach his Latin authors through a translation whenever he could.

Like Chaucer, Shakespeare's one real love among the schoolroom worthies was Ovid, but it was never difficult to arouse a schoolboy's interest in Ovid. The chief difficulty, rather, was to distract his mind from that amorous and delightful storyteller. Nearly all the mythology that Shakespeare knew came from Ovid's *Metamorphoses,* as did that of most of his fellow writers, but it is evident that Shakespeare was much more familiar with the first book or two than he was with the rest of it and even in the case of Ovid he was not above working with a translation.

Apart from learning to read Latin and write Latin, an English schoolboy was also expected to recite Latin, and here again was an aspect of the curriculum that might conceivably be of some use to a future actor. There was considerable emphasis on good public speaking and a controlled, intelligent use of the voice, and many schoolmasters let their boys act out Latin plays by Plautus and Terence to give them experience in handling the spoken word.

Richard Mulcaster, who was head for many years of the excellent school conducted by the Merchant Tailors in London, always kept the spoken word in the forefront of his mind when he taught Latin. When he expounded the mysteries of punctuation to his classes he did it as a singing teacher might, with the emphasis on "tunable uttering." A parenthesis meant the use of a lower and quicker voice, a comma was a place to catch the breath a little, and a period was a place where the breath could be caught completely. This sort of training would have been of great use to William Shakespeare when he started work as a professional actor and had to learn to translate the words written on a cue sheet into the sound of a living voice, and if he did not learn it from some imaginative teacher in the schoolroom it was one of the many things he had to pick up for himself after he reached London.

Apart from teaching him Latin, Stratford grammar school taught Shakespeare nothing at all. It did not teach him mathematics or any of the natural sciences. It did not teach him history, unless a few pieces of information about ancient events strayed in through·Latin quotations. It did not teach him geography, for the first (and most inadequate) textbook on geography did not appear until the end of the century, and maps and atlases were rare even in university circles. It did not teach him modern languages, for when a second language was taught at a grammar school it was invariably Greek.

What Shakespeare learned about any of these subjects he learned for himself later, in London. London was the one great storehouse in England of living, contemporary knowledge and in that great city an alert and intelligent man could find out almost anything he wanted to know. It was in London, for instance, that Shakespeare learned French; and French was taught by Frenchmen who worked in competition with each other and used oral, conversational methods that were designed to get colloquial French into the student's head as quickly as possible.

When French was finally accepted into the grammar school curriculum it was subjected to the heavy emphasis on rules and grammar with which the Latin tongue was already burdened, and Shakespeare was probably very fortunate that no one tried to teach him English by the same system. All the rules, the ritual and the reverent embalming were focussed on Latin, and as a result the writers of the late sixteenth century had a lighthearted sense of freedom where their native tongue was concerned because it had never been laid out in the schoolroom and expounded. Much respect was given to the Latin language, but all the affection, the excited experimentation and the warm sense of personal ownership went into the English. If a writer needed an effective word he could not go to a dictionary for it. There were no English dictionaries, although Richard Mulcaster remarked it would be a praiseworthy deed to compile one. The writer could either reach back into his memory, a practice that forced every writer to be also an alert listener, or else he could invent a new word entirely.

There was still some doubt among thoughtful men whether it was quite respectful to the language to use it in so lighthearted a fashion. George Puttenham apologized for using such "strange and unaccustomed" new words as *idiom, method, impression, numerous, penetrate, savage* and *obscure.* Gabriel Harvey was scolded for using such abnormalities as *theory* and *jovial* and *negotiation;* and Ben Jonson, who could never forget his classical education, was horrified by a fellow playwright who used such outlandish words as *damp, clumsy, strenuous* and *puffy*.

This use of new words could degenerate into complete confusion in the hands of incompetent writers but it gave Shakespeare exactly the freedom he needed. He felt at complete liberty to pick up effective new words and combinations of words wherever he could find them, and a play like *Hamlet* is so full of them that it would have made a schoolmaster turn pale if he had had any responsibility for teaching his charges the English language. Fortunately he had no such responsibility, and young William Shakespeare was free to discover the great reaches of the English language as a freeborn and independent citizen.

Every weekday, summer and winter, from the time when he was about seven years old, young Shakespeare went to school. He walked down Henley Street, turned at the Market Cross and went the two long blocks to the guild buildings. During most of Shakespeare's boyhood the schoolroom was upstairs over the Council room, except for a short period when it had to be repaired, and the same bell that called William to school every morning called his father about once a month to the Council meeting in one of the rooms downstairs.

No single schoolmaster can be assigned the honor of having given William Shakespeare his schooling, since there happened to be a succession of teachers in Stratford during Shakespeare's boyhood. When he entered school the master was Walter Roche, who left because he was given a rectory. Roche's successor was Simon Hunt, who left in 1575 to become a Jesuit. The teacher for the next four years was Thomas Jenkins, and when Jenkins left his post Shakespeare was fifteen and certainly no longer in school. All these men were university graduates, each of them holding a degree from Oxford, for the pay in Stratford was excellent and the twenty pounds a year that went to the schoolmaster was almost twice what he would have received in a large town like Warwick. All three men were presumably competent and well-trained, since there must have been many candidates for the post. It is to be hoped that at least one of them had a spark of Mulcaster's imagination, but they may have been merely the routine pedagogues that the educational system of the time encouraged.

When a boy had completed the curriculum of the grammar school in Stratford, he would have his head well stocked with the principles of Latin grammar and also with a miscellaneous collection of quotations from Latin authors, designed to illustrate the different parts of speech and supply him with a little moral education besides. He had probably been taught to keep a commonplace book, in which he was encouraged to write down any quotations that pleased him in his reading from ancient authors. He had learned how to make a pen neatly, cutting off the goose feathers with his penknife and softening the nib with his tongue. He had learned to sit upright when he was writing so that the humors of the brain would not fall down into his forehead and affect his eyesight, and he had learned how to endure the discipline of long hours of labor.

The school hours for the average English boy were long, usually extending from seven in the morning to five at night, with two hours off in the middle of the day to go home for dinner. The only difference made by the coming of summer was that the school hours were generally longer because there were more hours of daylight. Since curfew was at eight in the summertime, a well-brought-up little Stratfordian had comparatively few hours to play. For the rest, each small scholar was supposed to supply his own books and satchel and pens and ink, with candles extra in the winter; and, as William Lily opened his grammar by pointing out sternly, he was also supposed to come to school with his face washed and his hair combed, and on no account was he to loiter by the way.

It has been suggested that on one hot evening in July, when William Shakespeare was eleven years old, he was taken to the castle at Kenilworth to see part of the show with which the Earl of Leicester was entertaining Queen Elizabeth. On Monday evening the water devices included a dolphin and a mermaid, and the event is therefore said to be the origin of the lovely lines in *A Midsummer Night's Dream* in which Oberon describes the mermaid singing on the dolphin's back. But the Kenilworth water show was grotesque rather than beautiful, since the mermaid was eighteen feet long and the dolphin twenty-four. Both had actors perched on their backs and were propelled by elaborate mechanical equipment, and except for the fact they both appeared in the same show they had no connection with each other. It is very unlikely, in any case, that Shakespeare would have been allowed to leave school in July and make so long a trip. Fifteen miles in those days was a journey of real magnitude; and since no one in Stratford could have known how charmingly suitable it would have been for England's great future dramatist to meet England's great queen, it must remain exceedingly unlikely that he ever made the trip to Kenilworth at all.

In Stratford itself, young William Shakespeare would have had many opportunities to see public entertainments. Stratford was famous for its fairs, and the people of Warwickshire came from miles around to shop at the special booths and stalls that were set up in Market Street in May and again in September. Wherever there were people in England there were entertainers, and no fair would have been complete without its acrobats and performing animals, any more than without its pies.

Stratford also had its share of regular stage productions. The first of the touring companies of actors came to Stratford the year that Shakespeare's father was High Bailiff and they were welcomed by him in his official capacity. After that one

of the large companies stopped there every year or so, showing plays at Stratford in their regular yearly tour through the
provinces.

The acting companies were rigidly licensed under an Act
of Parliament, for nothing could have been more sinister to
the Elizabethan mind than any group of men travelling around
the country without proper credentials. To escape being
listed as vagabonds, each acting company operated under
someone's patronage, the smaller groups under local dignitaries or incorporated towns and the larger ones under
prominent court officials like the Earl of Leicester or the Earl
of Warwick.

When a company of actors arrived in Stratford they first
presented themselves before the High Bailiff and showed their
credentials so that they could be licensed for playing in town.
The first show was put on at the guildhall before the Bailiff
and other members of the Council. Admission to the first
show was evidently free to the public, since the Council was
paying the bill, and there was always an enthusiastic attendance. In Bristol, for instance, when Shakespeare was twelve
years old, part of the iron bar on the guildhall door had to be
repaired because of "the press of people at the play."

Since William Shakespeare was the son of one of the most
prominent of the Council members he probably always had a
good place to see and hear. Perhaps, like a small boy named
Willis of about his own age in Gloucester, he stood between
his father's legs while John Shakespeare sat on one of the
benches. The main room of the guildhall made an excellent
theatre, being long and narrow, with the players acting on a
platform at the south end of the hall and using the smaller
room, at right angles to it, to change their costumes and wait
for their cues.

There must have been a great deal of activity in this im-
provised tiring room, for the touring companies were small
and each actor was expected to play several characters. A

company of six players thought nothing of putting on a play like *Horestes*, which called for a cast of twenty-five, and long practice had made them adept at leaping in and out of their costumes and assuming new parts. In the play of *Cambises*, for instance, two actors handled fourteen roles between them, and in *The Repentance of Mary Magdalene* four men wrestled with fourteen parts that included Carnal Concupiscence, Infidelity, Knowledge of Sin, Mary Magdalen and Christ Jesus. The chief character here was Infidelity, who carried the comedy role known as the Vice; and since vice was always punished in the end while the better and nobler abstractions triumphed, the audience had the comfortable feeling of seeing a play that was "not only godly, learned and fruitful, but also well furnished with pleasant mirth and pastime."

From the point of view of a small boy the whole thing was evidently pure enchantment. The little boy in Gloucester could still remember, seventy years later, every detail of the show he had seen while he stood between his father's legs. He especially remembered the scene in which the wicked hero was transformed into a swine (being a typical small boy he took a deep interest in the way this was handled with a mask and wires) and the splendid climax in which an actor dressed in blue, portraying End-of-the-World, makes the lovely ladies like Pride and Luxury vanish from the stage and the hero is carried off howling by devils. The plots of these morality plays lent themselves to a great deal of violent physical action and to the low comedy that English audiences had been trained to expect ever since the old miracle plays were acted in carts in the town streets.

No reasonable man could object to an entertainment that was full of moral lessons and did not disturb those settled principles that the schools and the parents worked so hard to inculcate. If the plays that went on tour did not deal with moral abstractions, they dealt with equally impeccable and improving stories. The subject might be Biblical, like *The*

Comedy of the Most Virtuous and Godly Susanna, or it might be classical and introduce characters like Menelaus and Clytemnestra to English country audiences. The most careful of Stratford parents would have been willing to let his son see plays like these, and even if the boys acted the plots out afterwards in the elm-shaded gardens of Stratford they could do very little injury to their moral natures.

The effect of these travelling actors on the small boys of Stratford can be measured by the effect of a similar group of English players on another small boy who was Dauphin of France. Louis managed to remain cool and dignified until a moment arrived in the plot when one of the characters had his head cut off. This made a profound impression on the small Dauphin, and for two weeks thereafter his favorite game was playing actor, costuming himself in whatever was handy, taking long strides, and announcing to his mother that he was the whole of the acting company. If the small boys of Stratford played actor for weeks after the players left, they had an advantage over the Dauphin since there were more of them to share the parts, but it is not likely they were any less excited or less impressed than the boy at Fontainebleau.

The actors were made increasingly welcome at Stratford, and soon they were coming at the rate of two companies a year. When Shakespeare was twelve, the companies of both the Earl of Warwick and the Earl of Worcester paid a visit to Stratford. When he was thirteen the Earl of Worcester's men played a return engagement and the town was also honored by a visit from some of the most brilliant actors in England, those under the patronage of the Earl of Leicester.

Chapter 2

THE HEAD of the Earl of Leicester's company was an actor named James Burbage; and when Shakespeare was twelve years old James Burbage built the first theatre in London.

As an actor, Burbage knew how much a theatre was needed in London. The company he headed happened to be the first to get an official license and Burbage was well aware of the difficulties of moving from town to town with a skeleton company, with a constant packing and unpacking of theatrical properties and costumes. The greatest theatre-going population in England was not in the provinces but in London, and there was an excellent profit to be made in London by any company that could establish itself with a permanent base of operations.

At present, the arrangement in London was the same as in other English towns: the companies produced their plays in the open, rectangular courtyards of the inns. The system must have been fairly satisfactory, since an inn like the Cross Keys was still being used by major acting companies when there were new theatres all over London. The shape of the inn-yards made it easy for them to be used as theatres, with the actors working on a scaffold at one end of the inn-yard and part of the audience grouped around them while the more prosperous individuals used the seats in the surrounding galleries of the upstairs rooms; and the stage arrangements must have been elaborate since the Office of the Revels was willing to pay over twenty-four shillings to borrow a property well that had been in use by the actors in the Bell Inn in Gracechurch Street.

Nevertheless the inn-yards had their disadvantages. The actors had to share the yards with the carters, who brought freight and mail to London on weekly schedules. The carters used the inns on definite days of the week, so that their customers would know where to find them, and the arrangement made it difficult for the actors to use the inn-yards more than three days out of seven. It was difficult to collect admissions, the storage of properties was not easy, and since there was no permanent tiring-house the changing of costumes must have been extremely complicated. Moreover the proprietors of the inns charged fairly high rentals, and there was every reason why an intelligent and prominent actor might decide to put up his own building and collect his own rentals.

By good fortune James Burbage had been apprenticed to a joiner in his youth and had practiced the trade of carpenter until he discovered there was much more money in acting. No man could have been better equipped to build the first theatre in England, since as an actor he knew what actors needed and as a carpenter he had the technique to supply it.

Since James Burbage had no model to guide him when he started working out the design for his theatre, he was free to adopt anything that would make for maximum efficiency in the actors and maximum comfort in the audience. One of the ideas that probably suggested itself to him was the system that he and his company used when they acted in guildhalls or in large private residences. This was not unlike the modern theatre arrangement, with a raised stage at one end of a rectangular hall and benches arranged to face it.

This kind of theatre design would have meant a fairly high scale of admission prices, since it left no room for the inn-yard standees who could only afford a penny to see a play. This penny public was treated rather contemptuously by the writers of the period, and when the first Italian theatre was built in the following decade it was probably felt that the designer had done well to design it for a prosperous clientele and supply every member of the audience with a seat. James Burbage was a practical actor and he did not share this point of view. He knew that the penny public, with its willingness to stand long hours to see a production, was the backbone of the theatre business in England, and he was determined to keep his prices within the range of ordinary people.

The advantage of the inn-yard system was that it could accommodate these groundlings, who could pack themselves into the standing room in front of the scaffold and take up comparatively little space. The chief disadvantage of the inn-yard system was the extremely cramped and unsatisfactory working conditions backstage.

In solving this problem there was one other model that Burbage could follow. Near the Thames on the other side of London Bridge were two amphitheatres in Southwark where the public went to see bear-baiting and bull-baiting. These buildings were circular, rather like the old Roman circuses, and built with curving tiers of upstairs seats. An actor was not, of course, a bear. But it might not be impossible to construct a stage that jutted out into the midst of the groundlings, with adequate backstage facilities for costuming and storage, while still keeping to the Bear Garden seating system.

A circular building would give much better visibility than could be achieved in a rectangular inn-yard. Moreover the acoustics would be excellent, for the voices of the actors would be thrown back from the walls almost as though they were acting at the bottom of a padded well. It was a period when the lines spoken by the actors were much more important than the stage effects in building dramatic illusion in the minds of the audience, and people habitually spoke of "hearing" a play rather than of "seeing" it. Burbage wanted his fellow actors to be seen, but even more he wanted every word they spoke to be heard clearly.

An amphitheatre with a jutting stage would not lend itself to intimate effects, but a smaller area behind that front stage could be curtained off and set with movable properties to be used as a bedroom or a cave or any similar scene. The height of the building would make it possible to stage the action of the play on more than one level, a feat that had already been achieved in the inn-yards by using the back galleries. But since the scaffolding itself did not have to be shared with carters, a much more intricate system of trap doors would be possible for the disappearance of devils and the convenience of grave-diggers, and a sturdy contrivance of ropes and pulleys could be fastened to the roof to let down birds and goddesses and other aerial creatures.

A further advantage of the design was that admission money could be collected much more efficiently. The gatherer at the main door could collect the entrance penny, and anyone who could not pay more went and stood in the yard. A spectator who wished a seat went up the stairway and paid another gatherer there according to the location level he wanted. Moreover, the custom of eating and drinking during the performance, which the inn-yard public had come to expect as one of the pleasures of theatre-going, could be apportioned out on a concession system instead of letting the innkeeper get most of the profits.

Although an amphitheatre of this kind was open to the sky, all the seats would be protected from rain by the thatched roof under which they were built. The jutting stage was protected by a stage-cover, a device rather like the sloping penthouse roofs that sheltered Elizabethan store fronts from the rain. The standees were the only ones who ran any danger of getting wet, but this had been equally true under the inn-yard system and by this time they must have been resigned to it.

James Burbage was doing an unheard-of thing in designing a building to be used primarily for plays, and a more cautious man would have planned a fairly small building since he could not be sure he was making a safe business investment. If such a thought passed through the mind of James Burbage he rejected it, for Burbage was a born theatre man and caution was not one of his qualities. He planned his theatre big enough to house a crowd of Londoners on a holy-day vacation, and he did not disturb himself with the thought that attendance on an ordinary working day was going to be very much less. James Burbage had no intention of turning away any potential customer for lack of room.

A building of this kind was of course expensive to erect and it was going to cost a great deal more money than James Burbage had in the world. He signed a lease for the rental of the land on the 13th of April, 1576 (the month of Shakespeare's twelfth birthday) and then financed the payments by mortgaging the lease as soon as he had signed it. But this only paid for the rental of the land and did not bring in any money for the timber and nails and plaster and workmen's wages that somehow had to be financed.

Fortunately James Burbage had a sympathetic wife named Ellen, and Ellen had a brother named John Brayne who had prospered in the grocery business. John Brayne already had a slight connection with the theatre and he agreed to put some money into his brother-in-law's new scheme. This does not mean that James Burbage was an unusually persuasive man. There was no stock exchange in London to drain off the gambling instincts of the London merchants and they speculated informally in every project that was presented to them. Most of the great naval expeditions of the period were financed by London business men, eager to invest ten pounds and see fifty come back, and the great lottery that was held periodically in St. Paul's churchyard might almost serve as a symbol for the attitude of the whole of business London.

Burbage and Brayne between them shared the expense of building the theatre. Later on, the Brayne faction claimed that the venture had made him a poor man; he had poured all his savings into the building, selling even his stock of groceries, and eventually he and his wife had worked as common laborers to save the cost of two workmen's wages, while practically all that James Burbage had done was to profiteer on the lumber. This testimony came at a lawsuit after years of wrangling, and both sides were much more interested in injuring the opposition than in telling the truth. The truth seems to be that both men invested all they could, as a lawyer who worked for them both testified, and that Brayne put in most of the money because he had more to invest. Once the theatre was in operation he got an excellent return on his investment, and most of his financial difficulties arose from the fact that he subsequently went heavily into debt by building the George Inn in Whitechapel and starting a soap-making business there.

The real trouble between the two men was not so much a matter of finances as of temperament. Burbage loved his theatre with the fierce, exclusive affection that a father might lavish on an only son, and it was impossible for him to admit to himself that Brayne had any proprietary rights in the beloved object. The two men quarreled frequently and finally went to a notary to set up a bond that they would refrain from fighting. Brayne started complaining in the notary's office about how much money he had spent and the hot-tempered Burbage struck him, with the result, as the notary reported sadly, that "they went together by the ears" and were with some difficulty finally parted.

When Brayne died in 1586 his widow carried on the feud with Burbage, and the climax came four years later in what might be called the war of the broomsticks. Margaret Brayne armed herself with a court order and some male assistance and went to install her own gatherer in the theatre that Burbage was convinced was his. Accompanying her was a friend named Robert Miles, his son Ralph, and a soap-maker named Nicholas Bishop who was to act as the gatherer. Ellen Burbage was the first to see the little procession and was quite undismayed by it. That redoubtable woman told them to leave at once or her son would break all their heads. James Burbage reinforced this information by putting his head out of one of the windows, improving on his wife's flow of fine Elizabethan invective. He called the respectable Mrs. Brayne a "murdering whore" and said that no court order was going to take his theatre away from him, adding that "if my son come he will thump you hence." At this point his son Cuthbert arrived, on cue as it were, and indulged in what the opposition called "great and horrible oaths," although Cuthbert maintained at the subsesquent trial that neither he nor his father had threatened to beat Miles. The case was otherwise with Burbage's younger son, Richard, who at this point entered the fray. He seized a broomstick and fell upon Robert Miles, who was still clutching the court order, while Mrs. Burbage assisted him with enthusiasm. Nicholas Bishop, the soap-maker, ventured to suggest that Mrs. Brayne was within her legal rights and Richard Burbage threatened to beat him also, "scornfully and disdainfully playing with this deponent's nose" as Bishop later testified. Richard was evidently enjoying himself thoroughly, for when the first of the actors arrived to dress for the afternoon performance he found him still holding the broomstick and laughing. The Burbages were left in full possession of the field and their own gatherers remained in the theatre. Mrs. Brayne brought suit at once, and after a very careful and thorough investigation of the case had been made by two Masters in Chancery, James Burbage was given sole legal possession.

The Braynes were not the only source of trouble, for Burbage was also having a great deal of difficulty with the lease. He had mortgaged it to help finance the building of the theatre, and when the mortgage came due Burbage had no money. He was faced with losing the lease and consequently his precious building with it, especially since the mortgage-holder, John Hyde, was one of that predatory race of grocers and had already made plans to dispose of the mortgage elsewhere. At this time Burbage's elder son, Cuthbert, was in the service of a court official and the official's influence was used to persuade Hyde to let Cuthbert buy up the mortgage. Cuthbert had to borrow a great deal of money to make the payment, and this generous gesture towards his father put him in the theatre business for the rest of his life. Unlike his brother Richard, Cuthbert was not an actor, and he had apparently intended a non-theatrical life for himself. But since he owned the mortgage on his father's theatre he also owned the lease, and for the rest of his long career he was an owner and operator of theatres as his brother's partner.

Apart from his financial problems, James Burbage had another source of trouble when he put up his theatre. There had always been a certain amount of opposition to the acting profession in London, and it crystallized when a whole building was put up with no other purpose but to give plays. The plaster was hardly dry on the walls of the theatre before the London preachers began to wail about the temple of sin that had been erected practically in their midst. Every current disaster that struck London, including the earthquake of 1580, could be traced to God's anger because this heathen development, with its glittering walls and rich costumes, had been allowed to flourish in the otherwise pure air of the city.

These pulpit attacks had a certain promotion value to a manager who was trying to fill a large theatre; for the London preachers depicted the sinful delights of that "gorgeous playing place," as they called it, with such fascinated horror that they must have supplied an excellent advertisement for the place. As the sober journal of Sir Roger Wilbraham indicates, the Elizabethan business man was well aware of the value of this kind of publicity. Wilbraham tells the case of a printer at the turn of the century who found himself loaded with unsold copies of a certain book. "He caused a preacher in his sermon to inveigh against the vanity thereof; since which it hath been six times under press, so much it was in request."

On the other hand, it would be unsafe to underestimate the real fervor and conviction of these pulpit attacks or the effect they ultimately had upon the theatre-going population. The Reformation had done nothing to remove the medieval sense of sin; in fact, it had complicated the matter by putting more responsibility on the individual. An Anglican had more freedom in his search for salvation but he also had more room to worry about possible failure; and the extreme Anglicans, who worried most about their own souls and those of their neighbors, were beginning to be called Puritans.

There were various sects of Puritans, including those who wished to purify the Church of England from the inside and those who wished another kind of state church entirely, but the distinguishing mark of any Puritan was his alarming sense of sin. In his diary he would even reproach himself for his "adulterous dreams" and his waking life was spent in a constant struggle to drown out the temptations of the flesh by hard work and prayer. Dancing was a very unsafe occupation for the godly, since it turned their thoughts in the wrong direction, and even music tended to incline the thoughts of its hearers "to all licentiousness." But nothing was better calculated to kindle the fire of inordinate lust in the tender minds of the young than to let them go to stage plays, and the Puritan opposition to the stage ultimately became implacable.

The Puritans were operating on a perfectly honest conviction. They firmly believed that "horrible enormities and swelling sins" were shown on the stage, with their glittering costumes and men dressed as women, and that the theatre as a whole was a sink of "theft and whoredom, pride and prodigality, villainy and blasphemy." To a Puritan, soberly intent upon the saving of his soul, there could hardly be a worse sin than to indulge carnal desire by going to see a play, and in time the Puritan movement gathered sufficient force to destroy the theatre of England entirely.

This Puritan attitude towards play-going did not find much support in the people of London, but it had the full support of the London Council. The mayor and the aldermen were not at this time Puritans; but they were all business men who were sufficiently prosperous to be able to afford politics, and as business men they took a very unfavorable view of the acting profession. Actors did not sell a legitimate, visible commodity or sell it under the rules of any guild. Consequently they were parasites or, to use a favorite phrase of the period, caterpillars of the commonwealth, strutting about in fine clothes which they got by luring the pennies out of the pockets of simple-minded apprentices who should have been home working. It would even have been better for the apprentices if they had spent their money in taverns; for although the London Council did not necessarily encourage drinking, the taverners were at least selling a legitimate commodity and operating under legitimate rules. Actors, on the other hand, offered no legitimate commodity and really had no place in any well-ordered Christian society.

The opposition of the Puritans and of intense members of the clergy would have made no difference to a man like Burbage, but the opposition of the mayor and the aldermen was a serious matter. Two years before Burbage decided to build his theatre, the London Council put out a series of restrictions on actors, beginning with a stately preamble which pointed out that "the inordinate haunting of great multitudes of people, especially youths, to plays, enterludes and shows" was very bad for the city. From that time forward no plays

could be shown in an inn-yard unless the play had been
licensed, the players had been licensed, the inn-yard had been
approved, the owner of the inn had gone bond that order
would be kept, and the actors had contributed a sum of money
for the poor. The ordinance also stated that no performances
were to be given on Sundays or holy-days, thus removing the
largest part of the potential audience at a single stroke.

The root of the difficulty was what the ordinance called the
"unthrifty waste" of money that was spent in theatre admissions. The Council also had at the back of its mind a dislike
of any arrangement that brought together large groups of
people in a single area, where no one knew what seditious
mischief might be plotted. The only time that any governing
body in England could rest easy at seeing a large crowd of
people gathered together was if they were listening to a sermon. There was a certain amount of justification for this
point of view, since England was never free at this period
from the threat of treasonous conspiracies and even the ulti-
mate disaster of civil war. But it is likely that the Council
would not have accused the innocent and patriotic contemporary theatre of encouraging "seditious matters, and many
other corruptions of youth" if they did not have reason to
dislike, from the business point of view, the thriving trade
that the actors were conducting in the inn-yards.

The result of all this was that James Burbage was naturally
very unwilling to erect his theatre in any district under the
control of the London Council. The fields that lay northeast
of the city walls were under the control of the London government, but just beyond them was a pocket of land that had
once been the site of a monastery. These church lands had
been taken from their owners at the time of the Reformation
and had passed under the jurisdiction of the Crown. The
city had no control over areas like these, which were called
"liberties" and were a constant source of irritation to the
mayor and the aldermen. But they were a great help to

the acting profession, since the Crown approved of plays if the
city did not; and it was therefore in the liberty of Holywell,
east of Finsbury Fields, that Burbage decided to erect his
theatre.

Like most of the surburban property around London,
Holywell was something of a slum area. The land that Burbage arranged to lease from a prosperous gentleman named
Giles Allen consisted of five tenements and a dilapidated
barn that was being used for storage and as a slaughter-house.
Burbage had no intention of pulling down the barn, which he
expected to remodel and rent to tenants. The location he
planned for his theatre was an empty piece of ground surrounded on three sides by the barn, the horse pond, and the
back garden of one of the tenements. On its fourth side his
dream theatre would be flanked by a sewer, which would
have to be bridged before the citizens of London could come
across Finsbury Fields, with its windmills and its picnickers,
to see the plays. Apparently unplagued by any doubts Burbage went ahead with his elaborate plans and signed the
lease. Forty pounds, the price of a whole house, was spent on
the ironwork of the building alone, and Burbage probably
did not lack friends who told him he was making a great and
costly mistake.

It was true that the theatre was very far out of town for a
casual afternoon's entertainment. Quite apart from the half-
mile trip across the fields, a potential playgoer also had to
cross most of London if he lived on the west side of town.
It was much easier to get up a bowling match or go over to
Southwark, outside the city's jurisdiction, to see the bear-
baiting than it was to take the long trip to Holywell, no
matter how much of a novelty the new theatre might be.

Nevertheless, Burbage was an actor of long experience and
he knew his Londoners. He was convinced that no amount
of inconvenience would keep them from seeing a good show,
and he was quite right. They came in droves, beating a path

through the fields, crossing the ditch and pouring their pennies into the waiting hands of the gatherers. "Thither run the people thick and threefold," wailed the London preachers, mourning over their diminished congregations.

Burbage was of course fortunate in having erected his theatre in a prosperous time. Trade was good in London in the 70's and 80's and the people were quite ready to spend their money. Moreover the city was host to a great number of people who came up as tourists or on business from every county in England. Apart from the excellent shops, the great single magnet was the law courts that were held at Westminster four times a year. Nearly every adult in England either had a lawsuit pending at Westminster or was laying the foundations for one; and during each of the law terms, especially the autumn term of Michaelmas, the population of London swelled like the tidal flow of its own Thames. House-hunting in London was never easy at any time of year, for the city was chronically overcrowded; but it became nearly impossible at term time, and every householder on the west side of town could count on an excellent income by renting out spare rooms whenever court was being held at Westminster.

Moneyed visitors like these were a useful addition to Burbage's audience but it was on the average Londoner that he really depended. Instead of making his theatre small and select and roofed-in, with comfortable seats available for a few choice observers, he made it large and rather uncomfortable and available to everyone. The general admission price of one penny was the secret of Burbage's success and the success of the theatre-owners that followed him. In the following century this broad base of a low general admission was gradually destroyed. The theatres became increasingly comfortable and select and protected from the weather, and the entrance fee increased also. This was the end of the Elizabethan theatre and of the men who had worked in it, for it no longer could command the support of the ordinary middle-class London audience.

The nature of this Elizabethan audience has been much misrepresented, chiefly by nineteenth-century scholars, and among those that have been unjustly treated are the London apprentices. They have been pictured as a riotous, noisy group of young clods who, as groundlings, would only appreciate the broadest kind of ranting and horseplay, while their elders and betters in the higher-priced seats were smilingly able to appreciate the finer things that the theatre had to offer.

This point of view can be well documented, but the documentation comes from a rather prejudiced source. It was the London Council that was always viewing the youth of the city with the disapproval that an older generation usually feels for a younger one. It was the opinion of the Council that every young man should spend his time working very hard for an older one, and that any sign of independence or lack of subservience to an employer was a really serious offense. The ideal apprentice was a subservient young man who wore a wool cap and a dark coat and who kept his thoughts from silk embroidery and scarlet stockings and gold rings. He was not supposed to go to a music or dancing school, and some of his employers would have been equally pleased if he had not been allowed to go to plays. "Whosoever shall visit the chapel of Satan, I mean the Theatre, shall find there no want of young ruffians," innocent enough young lads who had become quite corrupted through seeing plays. "Many of nature honest and tractable have been altered by those shows and spectacles and become monstrous," and the Council united with the Puritans in agreeing that nothing could be worse for the morals of an apprentice than going to the theatre.

The apprentices themselves did not think so, and they flocked to the theatre. But a penny was a large sum of money to a boy who was learning a trade and he expected good value for it. Moreover, standing places could not be reserved and he had to arrive at the theatre early to be sure of a good location. From a complaint of the mayor's on the subject, it seems clear that the theatre began filling hours before the show started, and since the groundlings had to stand both during this period and through the whole action of the play, they demanded much more in the way of entertainment than the comfortable citizens in the seats overhead. If the groundlings felt they were being cheated they were not slow to express themselves, and most of the contemptuous remarks about their mental incapacity came from the playwrights whose plays had not had a popular success.

As a matter of fact, the apprentices belonged as a class to one of the most privileged and intelligent groups in London. A landed gentleman did not hesitate to send his son up to London to learn to be a goldsmith or a draper, and in the ranks of the apprentices were all the future aldermen and mayors of London. Each of them was treated by his employer as a member of the household and they belonged entirely outside the ranks of the unprotected, exploited laborers with whom London was unfortunately familiar. They were the future businessmen of London and their only crime was their youth and the fact that they loved the theatre.

Another section of the Elizabethan audience that has sometimes been misrepresented is the women. It was rather arbitrarily decided in the nineteenth century that women seldom went to plays in Elizabethan times. Occasionally a coarse tinker's wife might get in among the groundlings or a fine lady sheltered by a mask might be escorted to one of the expensive seats, but the London housewife stayed home and wove cloth and kept her house clean as a good woman should. This may have been the Victorian conception of womanhood, but it was certainly not shared by the Elizabethans.

From the first the reformers had centered their special attention on the women of London, since it was well known that few "women come from plays . . . with safe and chaste

minds." One writer devoted a whole section "to the gentlewomen citizens of London" and besought them when they
felt nervous and unhappy not to go to plays but to visit a
neighbor or read a good book. Another writer tried to terrify
them with tales of citizens' wives who sinned and then confessed on their death beds that it was the initial mistake of
going to the theatre that had turned their thoughts from a
contemplation of virtue and started them down the slippery
path to perdition.

The citizens' wives paid no attention to all this advice,
for the women of London had always done what they pleased
and expected to go on doing it. England was known as "a
paradise for women" and nearly every foreigner was startled
by the amount of freedom they took as their right. "The
womenfolk of England . . . have far more liberty than in
other lands, and know just how to make good use of it." A
gentleman from Kremzow noted that a throng of spectators
had a great many women in it "for the womenfolk in England
wish to be in at everything," and another foreigner noted it
as "particularly curious" that women went into taverns alone
or accompanied by other women. They evidently went without male companionship to the theatre also, for the mayor and
aldermen spent a great deal of time worrying about the "inveighing and alluring of maids" at the playhouse by young
gentlemen who passed them apples and hoped to escort them
home when the play was over. "They give them pippins, they
dally with their garments . . . they minister talk upon all
occasions, and either bring them home to their houses on small
acquaintance or slip into taverns when the plays are done."
Sometimes this inveighing and alluring was done ahead of
time, and, when John Florio wrote a conversation book in
English and Italian, he included under advice on how "to speak
to a damsel" a useful sentence on how to invite her to go to
to the theatre to see a comedy.

The playwrights themselves were very well aware that a

large part of the success of a play depended on the approval
of the women. There was always an epilogue spoken at the
end of the show, with a request for applause, and although
very few of the epilogues of Shakespeare's plays have survived, three of them are addressed to the women in the audience. For

> if they smile
> And say 'twill do

the play would be a success.

Fortunately for the freedom of the playwrights, the London women took a great deal of pleasure in what would now
be called vaudeville jokes. A girl like Shakespeare's Rosalind
took a lively interest in the subject of sex, which she considered both funny and enjoyable, and so did his Beatrice and
his Portia. To that extent they are echoes of the women in
Shakespeare's audience who sat and laughed comfortably at
dirty jokes. An Englishman who was travelling in Germany
recorded in honest amazement how a mildly off-color joke
was received in a Nuremberg inn: "I observed the women to
blush, and the men also to look one upon another, as if those
words were flat bawdry." He noted that in Germany "the
modesty of the women is singular, and the like nowhere
found." Certainly he had found nothing like it in London.

One reformer of the day rather contemptuously decribed
the average theatre audience as "but an assembly of tailors,
tinkers, cordwainers, sailors, old men, young men, women,
boys, girls and such like," and there is no doubt that it was a
mixed audience of "all sorts, young and old," from carters
to noblemen, that poured across Finsbury Fields whenever
the playing flag of James Burbage's new theatre was hoisted.
The businessmen of London were not slow to realize that
the building of theatres was going to be a very profitable
investment, and within the year a new theatre was built on

the other side of Holywell Lane in what had once been the Prioress' pasture. This second theatre was called the Curtain and in 1585 its owner, Henry Laneman, entered into a seven-year agreement with James Burbage to run the two theatres as a joint undertaking and pool the profits.

Meanwhile another theatre had been erected in the village of Newington, a mile from London Bridge on the other side of the Thames. The theatre of Newington Butts was never completely successful, since it was beyond Southwark and too far out of town for any but the most determined theatre-goer. But in 1587 an expensive theatre was put up in South-wark itself and lavishly redecorated five years later. This theatre was called the Rose and it helped make its owner, Philip Henslowe, a wealthy man. Another Londoner, Francis Langley, also invested in Southwark real estate with the idea of putting up a theatre, and in 1595 he finished the Swan, which was handsomer even than the Rose. When a Dutch priest visited London the following summer, he reported that all four theatres, Burbage's, Laneman's, Henslowe's and Lang-ley's, were buildings of "notable beauty" but he felt that the largest and most magnificent "is the one of which the sign is a swan . . . for it accommodates in its seats three thousand per-sons."

Competition was a healthy thing for the London theatres, and the great thatched amphitheatres flourished and grew strong. In Paris the single indoor hall that was used for plays was operating under a government monopoly that prevented any competition, and when Paris finally built its second public playhouse, London was building its seventeenth.

These London builders were shrewd men who knew a good business investment when they saw it, but none was a real theatre man in the sense that James Burbage was and re-mained. Francis Langley was a goldsmith and a member of the Drapers' Company, and Philip Henslowe was a dyer by trade. Henslowe was a typical Elizabethan businessman and pro-

moter, and he was no more interested in the theatre business
than he was in the starch business or, later on, in bear-baiting.
He was agent for two of the most important acting companies
of the period and spent a great deal of time with actors and
playwrights, financing them and giving them assignments and
occasionally bailing them out; and Henslowe's son-in-law,
Edward Alleyn, was one of the most brilliant actors of the
day. But Henslowe was chiefly in the business to make money,
and he was never a theatre man in the almost violently dedicated sense that James Burbage understood the meaning of
the word.

For twenty years James Burbage warred for his theatre,
protecting it from the encroachments of creditors and mort-
gage-holders and the London Council and anything else that
threatened the object of his tempestuous devotion. His building was called simply the "Theatre," and to James Burbage
it was the one really important structure in England.

His two sons, Cuthbert and Richard, carried on their father's
tradition and like him they were men of the theatre. Richard
was the most famous actor of his day and gave the stage
thirty-five years of his devotion, and his brother remained
his faithful business partner and loyal friend. It was a record
of which their father would have thoroughly approved.

These were the two men with whom William Shakespeare
was associated during almost the whole of his career on the London stage. From 1594 to 1610, at the very least, Shakespeare
was the active working partner of Richard and Cuthbert Burbage. He had part ownership of the theatres they built, and
it was Richard Burbage who acted the leading roles in *Hamlet*
and *Othello* and *King Lear*. Shakespeare saw these men daily,
until in time they were as familiar to him as his own brothers;
and it was his great good fortune that they were not business
speculators like Henslowe but devoted, professional men of
the theatre.

Chapter 3

WHEN JAMES BURBAGE signed the lease for his theatre William Shakespeare was the eldest boy in a fairly large family of children. His ten-year-old brother, Gilbert, had been followed by a seven-year-old sister, named Joan after the little girl who had died. Next came Anne, now five years old, and a little boy named Richard, who was two.

John Shakespeare was a prosperous man as well as the head of a large family, and when William was eleven years old his father took steps to enlarge his Henley Street property. The house in which the Shakespeare family was living on Henley Street was one of a block of three buildings of which John Shakespeare owned the one to the east. In October of 1575 he bought two houses from Edmund and Emma Hall, complete with gardens and orchards, and paid forty pounds for them. The location of the two houses is not identified in the sale itself, but it must have been the two remaining houses of the block of three on Henley Street, since all three are known to have passed into John Shakespeare's hands.

Shakespeare rented the west house to a tenant, but he combined the middle one with his own residence by interior doorways, and it was evidently here that the last of his children, Edmund, was born five years later. This middle house remained in the family for a long time, and it is probably on this account that it was later believed to have been the birthplace of William Shakespeare. But if Shakespeare was born

on Henley Street it must have been in the east house, for John
Shakespeare did not own the other two buildings when his
eldest son was born.

Through this purchase John Shakespeare took his place as
one of the prominent landholders of Stratford, and on a list
of thirty-eight "freeholders" of the town his name stands
sixth. But the son of a tenant farmer had greater ambitions
than this. He wanted to belong to the gentry and the only
way to achieve this was to be granted a coat of arms by the
Office of Heralds in London.

John Shakespeare's desire to rise in the world was typically
Elizabethan. He and his fellows had inherited from the Middle
Ages the theory of "degrees," which meant that everyone was
tucked into a definite social class; and Archbishop Whitgift
was expressing the orthodox view of the period when he
stated in a speech, "Equality of persons engendreth strife,
which is the cause of all evil." Each Elizabethan was supposed
to remain contentedly in the class for which heaven had
designed him, but each Elizabethan interpreted this rule as
applying to his neighbor rather than to himself. There was a
scramble to leave one level of "degree" and rise to the next,
and the determination of the lower classes to belong to the
gentry and of the gentry to belong to the nobility was an
aspect of the period that reformers viewed with special alarm.
The College of Heralds did not object to it, however, since
it brought them a great many fees.

John Shakespeare had a better right than many to apply
for a coat of arms. He had married a daughter of the Ardens,
and whatever her exact connection with the family the name
was a magic one in Warwickshire. Even more to the point,
he had been High Bailiff of Stratford and a justice of the
peace, and this was one of the "divers offices of dignity and
worship" that made a man automatically eligible for a coat
of arms if he could afford to pay the fees that the Heralds
demanded. John Shakespeare was obviously a prosperous man

if he could afford to buy two houses; and a year after this purchase, in 1576, he sent in his application to the Office of Heralds. It was evidently considered acceptable, for Robert Cooke, King at Arms, sketched out a preliminary design for him.*

It was at this point in John Shakespeare's career, when everything seemed to be going so well for him, that something suddenly went very wrong. He attended the meeting of the Stratford Council in the normal way on September 5, 1576, as he had been doing for the past thirteen years. Since his election to the Council he had been absent on only a single occasion, and in the past eleven years he had never been absent at all. But at the meeting of the Council in the following January, John Shakespeare was absent. He was absent at the next meeting, and the one after that, and in fact he never returned again as a regular member. For the rest of his life he only attended one meeting of the Council, and for five years he broke completely with the official governing body of Stratford after more than a decade of devoted, loyal attendance.

What happened to John Shakespeare at this point to make him abandon public life so suddenly and so completely will have to remain a mystery. No evidence survives to show why he left a position that he had filled worthily and that had evidently given him much happiness. It has been suggested that he suddenly became a convert to either Catholicism or Puritanism, but there would have been nothing in this to prevent his attending the regular meetings of the Council. The objection to recusants was a Crown matter rather than a local one; and the Stratford Council had both its sturdy

* The Office of Heralds stated in 1596 that Cooke made this design "in paper twenty years past" which would put the date of John Shakespeare's application in 1576, when William Shakespeare was twelve years old. The accuracy of this date has been questioned, since the Heralds' memorandum goes on to state that John Shakespeare was bailiff "fifteen or sixteen years past," which is obviously incorrect. But the Office of Heralds would be likely to date the business routine of their own office correctly, even if they did not put down correct dates for the internal affairs of Stratford.

Catholics like George Badger and George Whateley and its equally sturdy Puritans like Nicholas Barnhurst. Barnhurst was eventually "expulsed" from the Council, but for his bad behavior and not for his religious convictions. It has also been suggested that John Shakespeare suffered financial embarrassment and it is quite true that he was less prosperous after this date than he was before. But he was never a poor man and he never had to part with the three houses he owned on Henley Street. Nor would it have cost him any money to take the short walk down Chapel Street to attend the Council meetings; the reverse would rather have been true if his fellow-members had followed the usual procedure and fined him for non-attendance.

Whatever John Shakespeare's reason may have been, it did not seem a conclusive one to the other members of the Council and they kept on hoping he would return. At every meeting from that time forward his name appears on the records, although on only one occasion, the fifth of September, 1582, was there a prick after his name to show attendance. In 1586 the members of the Council finally chose another alderman to fill his place, because Mr. Shakespeare "doth not come," but they evidently did it reluctantly. A further evidence of their regard for him is shown by the fact that an alderman was normally fined if he stayed away from meetings, and during these ten years of absence John Shakespeare was never fined.

The best guess perhaps is that some time in the autumn or early winter of 1576 John Shakespeare suffered some sense of personal disgrace that made it impossible for him to show himself at the meetings of the Council. As for the coat of arms he had wanted, it did not come to him. He went on being plain Mr. Shakespeare instead of John Shakespeare, gentleman, and Cooke's design with its spear and its falcon crest went back into the files of the London office of the College of Heralds.

The darkening of John Shakespeare's life at this point is all

the more noticeable in contrast to the increasing brilliance of
Adrian Quiney's. The Shakespeares and the Quineys had
known each other since the days when old Richard Quiney
had been an acquaintance of Richard Shakespeare of Snitterfield, and when John Shakespeare came to live on Henley
Street, Adrian Quiney was one of his close neighbors. It was
together they paid a fine of twelvepence in 1552 for having an
unauthorized muckheap near their houses.

Adrian Quiney was older than his friend and had started
his political climb in Stratford earlier. He was High Bailiff the
year John was made affeeror, and the year that John himself
was elected Bailiff, Adrian Quiney went up with him to London on borough business, their trip being financed for them
by the Stratford Council. When Adrian Quiney again became
Bailiff in 1571, John Shakespeare was Chief Alderman and
therefore his assistant; and the following January the two men
again went to London, to represent Stratford in the law courts
during Hilary term. The two friends evidently worked harmoniously together and for a time their careers were almost
parallel.

When John Shakespeare applied for his coat of arms,
Adrian Quiney was already a member of the gentry. His
coat of arms consisted of a shield of gold with a hand grasping
a sword, and by 1574 he was appearing in the Council records
as Adrian Quiney, gentleman.

Adrian Quiney had another possession that was even more
desirable than a coat of arms: he had a son who was following
in his father's footsteps both in business and in politics. Young
Richard Quiney was a mercer, like his father before him, and
he had the unusual distinction of being appointed a Principal
Burgess when he was still in his early twenties.

Richard Quiney must have been in all respects a thoroughly
satisfactory son. He had evidently been a good boy at school,
applying himself diligently to his studies, for he read Latin
easily and for pleasure and took Tully's *Epistles* on a journey

with him for relaxation. Even his marriage was impeccable, for his bride was Elizabeth Phillips, of a prominent Stratford family, and he married her the same year he became a Principal Burgess.

During the next dozen years, young Richard Quiney's career advanced steadily. He was elected to the office of chamberlain in 1586, at the same meeting in which the Council was reluctantly obliged to deprive John Shakespeare of his alderman's gown. He was elected alderman in 1588, over the heads of four senior members of the Council, the same year in which John Shakespeare was facing failure in a bitter lawsuit over land with one of his wife's relatives. And in September, 1592, he was made High Bailiff of Stratford, with his proud father casting one of the many votes that swept him into office, during the same month in which John Shakespeare's son was being publicly attacked in a London pamphlet as an upstart actor who was trying to become a playwright.

Even back in 1582, when William Shakespeare was only eighteen, it seemed clear that the Quineys were advancing to a much more stable position in the community than the Shakespeares could now hope to attain. On the 27th of November, 1582, Richard Quiney attended the baptism of his first child, with his father, High Bailiff for that year, undoubtedly in attendance; and on that same 27th of November William Shakespeare's marriage license was being issued in Worcester. Young Shakespeare had not chosen his bride with any of the wisdom that Richard Quiney had shown two years earlier. Not only was Shakespeare a minor and in no position to assume the support of a family, but his bride was eight years older than he was and the child was born six months after the wedding.

Young Shakespeare's marriage may have been ill-advised, but there is no special reason to believe that his fellow townsmen considered it scandalous. Anne Hathaway came of an almost stiffly respectable background and it is not likely that a woman of twenty-six found herself caught in a casual liaison and had to demand marriage to protect herself. Nor is it necessary to believe that she trapped an impressionable young man into marriage by seducing him. A more probable explanation is that they had what was known as a pre-contract and that Anne Hathaway felt free to behave as a married woman before the actual ceremony.

A pre-contract was taken very seriously by Elizabethan church law and was nearly as binding as the actual ceremony. If Shakespeare had a pre-contract with Anne and then had married someone else, his marriage would have been in a sense bigamous and could have been declared void by the Ecclesiastical Court; and if he had refused to marry after a pre-contract he could have been excommunicated. Shakespeare's aunt, Agnes Arden, evidently had a pre-contract with her future husband, for when Robert Arden made his will in July he spoke of her as the wife of Thomas Stringer, and Agnes did not actually marry Thomas Stringer until the following October.

Anne Hathaway's own father died a year before her marriage but he left her a marriage portion in his will. Old Richard Hathaway was a landowner in Shottery, one of the small hamlets inside the parish of Stratford, and he left most of the land to his eldest son Bartholomew with the request that he should be "a comfort unto his brethren and sisters." There was a mother-in-law in the Hathaway household, as there had been in the Arden one, and Richard Hathaway's will, like Robert Arden's, specifically requested a quiet distribution of the property. Anne was his eldest daughter by his first marriage and twenty-five years old when her father made his will.* Her brother Bartholomew married almost immediately

* Anne's name does not appear on the Registry of Baptism in Stratford because it was begun in 1558 after she was born. But the brass inscription on her grave says she "departed this life the 6th day of August, 1623, being of the age of 67 years."

after his father's death, and within the following year Anne was married also.

The normal way to get married in Stratford parish was to have the banns proclaimed three separate Sundays or holy-days in the church, so that if there were any objections to the marriage they could be brought forward. If for any reason the banns could not be published, the only alternative was to get a special license from the episcopal court at Worcester and have someone post a bond to indemnify the court if any ob-jections to the marriage were made later. In the case of Shake-speare's marriage this bond was posted by two Shottery farmers named John Richardson and Fulke Sandells. Both men had been friends of Anne's father, but the posting of the bond was a normal part of the arrangement and involved no special gesture of friendship on the part of the two men. At this same time, for instance, Christopher Marlowe's father in Canterbury was acting as professional bondsman for couples who needed a license to get married. The year Shakespeare was married there were an unusual number of these bonded marriage licenses in the Worcester Consistory Court and the following year they reached record proportions. This was the year in which Dr. Whitgift, Bishop of Worcester, became Archbishop of Canterbury and no man could have been more careful than he in seeing that his diocese of Worcester was obeying all the rules.

Marriages of this kind were an extra expense, but there were various reasons why the banns could not be published and a special license was required. As a bishop remarked at the end of the century: "License to marry according to the form set down without banns, are no cause to disordered marriage, but rather the contrary." An allegation normally accompanied the request for a license, explaining why the banns could not be published, but none of these allegations is extant for Worces-ter diocese before 1600 and the one Shakespeare entered has been lost with the rest. In his case the most probable reason why the banns could not be published was that the decision to marry was sudden and there was not time to post the banns before Advent. Between Advent and the octave of the Epiphany was a period known as "prohibited season" during which no marriages could take place, and unless William Shakespeare and Anne Hathaway wanted to wait until the middle of January the only alternative was to go to the expense of a license.

The regular form was used and Dr. Cosin handled the matter in Worcester Consistory Court as part of the ordinary routine of what happened to be an extremely busy day. The clerk made an error, as clerks sometimes do, and wrote down the bride's name as "Whateley," but her name appears with reasonable correctness in the bond, where Shakespeare's name is spelled "Shagspere." * It is not known in what church the marriage took place, except that it was somewhere in Worcester diocese, which included part of Warwickshire, and that it was not in the parish church of the Holy Trinity in Stratford.

John Shakespeare gave his consent to the marriage, since otherwise the license would not have been issued. A minor could not have been married in Dr. Whitgift's diocese unless the father or guardian had given his approval. But John Shakespeare might have felt justified in disapproving of his son's marriage or at least feeling doubtful of its wisdom. When Richard Quiney had married he was twenty-three, with a position in the Council and an interest in his father's business.

---

* In Elizabethan times spelling was still a matter of individual preference rather than rules, and surnames were still being treated almost as casually as they had been in the Middle Ages. One of the Court records under King James gives Shakespeare's name as "Shaxberd," and Christopher Marlowe's name was frequently spelled "Morley" or "Marley." The mistake in Anne Hathaway's name is, however, an outright clerical error as far as can be ascertained. Mistakes of this kind were not unusual, since the year after Shakespeare's marriage the name of a bridegroom was written in the bond as "Robert Bradeley" and on the bishop's register as "Robert Darby."

William Shakespeare was only eighteen and had apparently not settled down to any business at all.

It was the custom in Stratford for the eldest son to bring his bride back to his father's house. Richard and Elizabeth Quiney had followed this custom, and it is likely that William and Anne Shakespeare did the same. His father's property was especially suited to house an extra family, for the middle house had a wing at the back which had its own private entryway, back parlor and kitchen, with its own stairway leading to the second floor.

It was probably in the middle house that the child was born in the following May. It was not the son for whom John Shakespeare must have been hoping. It was a little girl and on Trinity Sunday, 1583, she was christened Susanna.

When William Shakespeare's little girl was baptised on the 26th of May she was the third child that spring who had been given the name of Susanna. It was not a familiar name in Stratford but it was one much favored by the Puritans, following the definite Puritan prescription that children should be given Scriptural names.

It is not surprising that Anne Shakespeare's daughter was given a Puritan name. When Anne's father, Richard Hathaway, made his will he had asked to be "honestly buried," which was a Puritan phrase. Anne's brother Bartholomew was a churchwarden, and all his sons were churchwardens after him. When Bartholomew died he also requested a Puritan burial, "hoping to arise at the Latter Day and to receive the reward of His elect."

If Anne Hathaway had been brought up as a Puritan, that fact alone would constitute a full explanation of the estrangement that evidently arose a few years later between herself and her husband. There were doubtless many people in Stratford who were at least mildly shocked to hear that the son of a reputable man like John Shakespeare had gone into the acting profession, for many people felt that acting was respectacle only when it was done by amateurs who spoke in Latin and that professional actors were little more than tinselled vagabonds. This casual contempt for actors was not shared by the Puritans, who attacked the actors as an actual threat to salvation. It was well known that through their plays they persuaded men and women into the "filthy lusts of wicked whoredom," and even a visitation of the plague could be explained as God's anger against the people for letting so great an evil as theatres exist in their midst.*

It would perhaps be exaggerating to say that it was a tragedy for a Puritan to be married to an actor; but it is not exaggerating to say that it created an insupportable household situation.

If the situation in the Shakespeare household had been normal, Anne Shakespeare would certainly have followed her husband to London once he became permanently settled in his acting career. Shakespeare belonged to one of the great resident London companies and except for the yearly tours of the provinces he spent all his working time in London. But unlike the other actors in his company he had no wife and family in London and for nearly twenty years he lived there in hired lodgings.

An actor's wife in Elizabethan times could be a great help to her husband in his profession. Although there was no actors' guild, the actors used the same system as other business and professional men in London and each of them took a boy into his home to be trained in what was a difficult and exacting art in the Elizabethan period. It was an important part of the apprentice system that the boy should be treated as an actual member of the family, and there is still extant a loving tribute

* The language of some of these tracts is almost unbelievable in its violence. When Shakespeare was twenty-three a book was published in London which described actors as "fiends that are crept into the world by stealth," "sent from their great captain Satan (under whose banner they bear arms) to deceive the world, to lead the people with enticing shows to the Devil." The author also describes them as apes, hell hounds, vipers, minotaurs, painted sepulchres, dogs and of course caterpillars, and his book is most suitably entitled *A Mirror of Monsters*.

to Mrs. Henry Condell and Mrs. Cuthbert Burbage from a boy who had worked with the company. Nearly all the actors in Shakespeare's company were settled householders, with competent wives and a large number of children, and the only exceptions were two or three men who never married, and William Shakespeare.

If Anne Shakespeare was a Puritan she could never have brought herself to go to London and help her husband in his profession. The acting profession, which seemed so normal and natural to Elizabeth Condell or Winifred Burbage, would have been to her one of the snares of Satan. As one anxious reformer put it, actors were "crocodiles which devour the pure chastity both of single and married persons. . . . In their plays you shall learn all things that appertain to craft, mischief, deceits and filthiness." The actors answered these attacks by parodying the Puritans on the stage and laughing at them, but to the Puritans themselves the situation was no laughing matter.

The break between Anne and William Shakespeare evidently occurred within three or four years of his marriage, probably coinciding with his decision to go on the stage. Two years after Susanna was born, Anne gave birth to twins, a boy and a girl, who were christened on the second of February, 1585, by Richard Barton, the "learned, zealous and godly" new vicar. The twins were named Hamnet and Judith, almost certainly after friends of the Shakespeares, Hamnet and Judith Sadler of High Street. After that there were no more children and it seems probable that within the next year or two William Shakespeare had left Stratford and gone to London.

In a general way it might be said that Shakespeare's reason for leaving Stratford was the same as his father's reason for having left Snitterfield: the place was too small for him. The same thing was happening all over England, with the young men leaving the villages for the towns and the towns for the great city of London. When a widow of Stratford wrote

Adrian Quiney, asking him to find a position in London for her twenty-year-old son, she said frankly, "I can get no place for him in the country." London was already so overcrowded and the smaller towns so "decayed" that the Privy Council passed measure after measure in an attempt to reverse the process. But the great city on the Thames remained the magnet that drew every hopeful and ambitious young man in England, and London's own mayors and aldermen had mostly been born in the provinces.

What was true of the ordinary professions was even more true of aspects of the luxury trade like writing or acting or publishing. A tanner named Henry Field was a neighbor of Shakespeare's and one of his eight sons wanted to be a printer. Young Richard Field happened to be the same age as William Shakespeare, but he decided much earlier what he wanted to do; at fifteen he knew he wanted to be a printer. There were no printing presses at Stratford. There were none anywhere in England, except the fifty-three in London and one each, carefully licensed, at Oxford and Cambridge. So Richard Field went to London, apprenticed by his father to a brilliant and scholarly Flemish printer named Thomas Vautrollier. Within ten years Richard Field had married his master's widow and owned the business. Within thirteen years he was able to send back to Stratford for his younger brother Jasper to come up and be his apprentice, and that same year he was the printer and publisher of William Shakespeare's first book of narrative verse. Nothing of the sort would have happened to either Field or Shakespeare unless both of them had been living in London.

It would be pleasant to be able to report that William Shakespeare arrived in London in 1588. A series of books had been announcing that 1588 was going to be a year of special importance, a prediction that the London citizens felt was amply fulfilled by the great naval victory that year over the Spanish Armada. It would have been a graceful contribution on the part of the Muse of History if this had also been the date in which young William Shakespeare first set foot in the city, but the actual date is unknown. All that is known is that Shakespeare was established as a successful actor on the London stage by 1592, and since he was in a difficult and highly competitive profession he must have entered it several years earlier.

Shakespeare came to London at a fortunate time. If he had been born twenty years earlier, he would have arrived in London when underpaid hacks were turning out childish dramas about brown-paper dragons. If he had been born twenty years later, he would have arrived when the drama had begun to lose its hold on ordinary people and was succumbing to a kind of self-conscious cleverness. But his arrival in London coincided with a great wave of excitement and achievement in the theatre and he rode with it to its crest. William Shakespeare brought great gifts to London, but the city was waiting with gifts of its own to offer him. The root of his genius was Shakespeare's own but it was London that supplied him with the favoring weather.

Chapter 4

WHEN William Shakespeare came to London in the 80's, it was still in many ways the medieval city that Geoffrey Chaucer had known. The wall that surrounded the city was still intact, and the only concession the authorities had made to the increased traffic was to open a new gate, called Moorgate, which gave access to the fields to the north. The old monastic foundations had been changed into residences and tennis courts and even into factories, and the beautiful little chapel on London Bridge had become a warehouse, but London was still a city of churches and they dominated the lives of its inhabitants. The service at St. Paul's Cathedral was now given in English, but the building was much as it had been except that its wooden spire had vanished. It had caught fire some twenty years earlier and so many citizens had gathered to watch the blaze and hamper the fire fighters that the famous steeple had burned down to its square stone base. In spite of much talk and several schemes to raise money, the steeple was never rebuilt; but the broad stone base (admission one penny) was a magnet for every tourist in town, who did not leave until he had climbed the crooked winding stairs for a view of the city from the top and who carved his initials in the leads to show he had been there.

The one really new public building in London was the Royal Exchange, which had been erected to save merchants from the inconvenience of having to do business out-of-doors in Lombard Street during the bad weather. Its builder, Sir Thomas Gresham, was as much an optimist as James Burbage, and he made the building very large with a hundred small shops in its upper corridors. At first the shops remained empty, and Gresham frantically offered them rent-free to any merchants who would keep them lighted and full of goods; but the city was growing so rapidly that within the decade Gresham could ask a rent of four pounds a year for each of the little shops and they were full of apothecaries and goldsmiths and sellers of books, armor and glassware.

In every way the tight little medieval city that Chaucer had known was pushing against its confining walls under the pressure of an expanding and increasingly excitable population. The fall of Antwerp had made London a substitute commercial center and the religious wars on the Continent had doubled the foreign population of London in thirteen years. The town historian, John Stow, watched with dismay as he saw the little farm where he had gone as a boy to fetch milk swallowed up in the creeping spread into the suburbs, and the government fought hard to keep the population within bounds by outlawing new buildings and prohibiting the subdivision of old ones. Every few years the government brought out another ordinance on the subject and the penalties were strict; the builder of a new tenement in the crowded suburb of Shoreditch, for instance, was fined twenty pounds and his tenants were allowed to use the building rent-free for the rest of their lives. But in spite of the efforts of the courts, the people went on packing themselves into the overcrowded city, adding to what the citizen of a smaller town bitterly called that "vast, unwieldy and disorderly Babel of buildings which the world calls London."

Meanwhile the city government went on gallantly trying to enforce a medieval code of behavior that had been nearly obsolete in Chaucer's day and was now little more than a wistful ideal. The mayor and the aldermen clung to the conviction that if enough laws were passed it would somehow be possible to turn their sprawling young giant of a city into something small, neat, compact and comfortable. They observed with horror the flouting of their authority in the suburbs, where men like James Burbage put up buildings that had no place at all in a Christian commonwealth, and they still struggled to keep the city in a state of mind of which their great-grandfathers would have approved.

The mayor and aldermen were heavily handicapped in this attempt by the fact they got no support at all from Queen Elizabeth. When a bill to restrict Sunday pastimes was passed by both houses of Parliament in 1585, it was promptly vetoed by the Queen, who herself went to shooting-matches and plays on Sunday and saw no reason why her subjects should not do likewise. It was her opinion that no amount of ordinances would keep a Londoner from enjoying himself, and that the wisest course to pursue was to make a government profit on the money he spent. She gave a patent for licensing gaming-houses to Thomas Cornwallis in 1576, in spite of a strict law against gaming in London, and justified it with the statement that the Londoners "secretly or openly . . . do commonly play and . . . no penalty of the laws or statutes aforesaid hath heretofore restrained them." On the same basis she gave licenses for bowling-alleys and the manufacture of dice and playing cards; and the fencing clubs and theatre owners could always turn to the Queen for protection when the attacks of the city fathers became especially violent. Elizabeth was a true child of the Renaissance, in this matter at least, and her attitude was one that the mayor and aldermen were incapable of understanding.

The truth was that the city authorities were trying to maintain medieval standards in a city that was no longer medieval in spirit. A new spirit of curiosity had developed, an intellectual ferment that made the old ideal of blind obedience almost impossible to enforce. London no longer lived in comparative isolation but was beginning to feel all the influences of Renaissance Europe. Above all, it felt the stirring of new winds from Italy. To the average Londoner Italy was still the place of strange poisons and passionate love affairs, to be mistrusted as the home of the wicked Machiavelli; but English architects travelled in Italy and brought back new designs, English sportsmen did their riding and fencing in the Italian manner, and when a poet wrote love songs he imitated Petrarch. There was a fury of translation from the Italian of novels and plays and poems, and the brilliant Italian actors penetrated England and flourished for at least a season in London.

The people of England, and especially of London, still took a rather provincial view of foreigners. Visitors from the Continent spoke with some bitterness of the self-satisfaction of the English, whose highest praise for any foreigner was that it was a pity he was not an Englishman. A popular English book frankly set out to describe "the misery of Flanders, the calamity of France, misfortune of Portugal, unquietness of Ireland, troubles of Scotland, and the blessed state of England." It was impossible for an Englishman not to feel superior to any foreigner but he was never really rude to him. He did not need to be. As one Englishman put it, "The English, contrary to the custom of all nations, give the higher place and way to women . . . out of a noble mind to give honor and support to weakness, so give they like respect to strangers."

An Englishman knew his own country was the center of the world, but he felt a deep interest in knowing how the men of lesser nations lived. Nearly every young man of birth took a tour abroad and this was also the era of the great explorations, when boys from small English villages came back from long voyages financed by London merchants to tell of the outlandish wonders they had seen. Occasionally these wonders could be seen in London itself, like the gloomy Indians, in brown taffeta, that Walter Raleigh brought back with him. Londoners like Richard Garth and William Cope started collections of instructive curios from other lands, and in Mr. Cope's collection the respectful visitor could see costumes from Java and Arabia, African charms, porcelain from China and a long, narrow Indian canoe hung from the ceiling, to say nothing of such special wonders as an embalmed child, a unicorn's tail, and some little flies "which glow at night in Virginia instead of lights, since there is often no day there for over a month." Some Londoners may have doubted this description of Virginia, but no one would have doubted the unicorn, except what one expert on natural history called a "vulgar sort of infidel people" who believed only in cows and sheep. Unicorns were mentioned even in the Bible and it was well known that the horn of the animal, pulverized and boiled in wine, made an excellent mouthwash.

The gardens of the Londoners echoed their interest in other parts of the world, and a prominent London surgeon like John Gerarde was able to grow tomatoes from Spain, nasturtiums from the Indies and tiger lilies from Constantinople. His ginger plants from Barbary were winter-killed, his cotton frosted, and he accidentally murdered his Dalmatian iris by pouring cold well water on them; but his tobacco and potatoes throve and he succeeded in producing recognizable ears on what he called Turkey corn.

Since London was a great port city and deeply involved in international trading, it was a vital business matter for its citizens to know as much about foreign nations as possible. London had its teachers of almost any foreign language that could be named—Arabic, Dutch, Polish, Turkish or Russian—and a whole colony had arrived from abroad to teach French. They charged a shilling a week and gave a good basic training in colloquial French and pronunciation, concentrating on spoken French rather than on rules of grammar. The emphasis was on business phrases, like weights and measures; but other useful aspects of the language were not forgotten and the beginner learned to say, "Take me about the neck," "You tickle me," and "Do not meddle with her, for she is very ticklish."

This sort of thing was really an effort to supply the deficiencies of a grammar school education, which made no attempt to teach anything but Latin and assumed for all practical purposes that the modern world did not exist. There were also special lectures at Leadenhall in some of the mathematical sciences, which included astronomy, geography and the art of navigation, but the most determined single attempt at adult education was made by Sir Thomas Gresham, builder of the Royal Exchange. Gresham founded a London college to teach law, medicine, geometry, rhetoric and other important subjects, and he specified that the lectures were to be given in English as well as in Latin since "merchants and other citizens" would be in the audience. Emphasis was laid on the practical side of the subject and the professor of music, for instance, was to give half the period to the theory of music and the rest to practical application, using voice and instruments. Cambridge was shocked by what it considered a misuse of money by one of its own graduates and sent Gresham a long Latin letter on the subject, although Cambridge itself did not teach subjects like music and astronomy and had no intention of beginning. When Shakespeare came to London, Gresham College was not yet in operation, but only because Gresham's widow was still inhabiting the mansion on Bishopsgate Street.

In any case, the greatest source of education to the average Londoner was not museums, or language teachers or college endowments. His greatest source of education was books. It was the invention of printing that set the one deep gulf between the Middle Ages and the Renaissance, and the difference between Chaucer's audience and Shakespeare's was the difference between a period when a book was a rich man's toy and a period when it was available to the whole of the middle class.

The average Londoner did not look upon a book primarily as entertainment for an idle hour. The purpose of reading was to tell him something he wanted to know, and books poured from the presses to tell him how to keep accounts, how to survey land, how to play the cittern without a teacher, how to take spots off velvet, or cook, or ride, or write a good hand. There was information on how to graft plants, how to compute interest, and what to do "when the physician is not present," and there were cook books and dream books and books on the art of navigation for amateur mariners.

Elizabethan London was the home of the short-cut, with each of its inhabitants wanting to know as much as possible as quickly as he could. Not for him was the slow, laborious grounding in the classics and rhetoric on which Oxford and Cambridge spent so much time. He could buy a book of classical quotations, conveniently arranged under subject matter, to be used whenever he needed them, and to improve his vocabulary there were books that offered lists of effective similes and other aids to rhetoric. He could buy books that would tell him how to write letters, whether love letters or business communications. So great was the interest in speed and simplification that even the great field of religion was invaded by the short-cut and one book was advertised as "an easy entrance into the principal points of Christian religion very short and plain." If possible, all these books of instruction were written in dialogue, and many of them had little charts appended to help the reader still further.*

* A characteristic example of an instruction book for the London public was Gerard Legh's *Accedens of Armory*. This was a popular book on heraldry, "written down" to the general public, and it included simple drawings that could be colored by the purchaser and useful stories such as that of King Lear. Gerard Legh put the book into dialogue form by calling one of the two speakers "Gerard" and the other "Legh." "Legh" is willing to be instructed indefinitely, but "Gerard" is obliged to leave or his wife will scold him for being late to dinner. A book of this kind could make its owner an amateur expert on the subject of heraldry and amuse him at the same time, and the *Accedens of Armory* naturally had an excellent sale.

If an energetic and restless Londoner could not find time to settle down and read a book, or if he lacked the necessary sixpence or shilling, there was a still quicker and cheaper way of getting information. For a penny a Londoner could buy an illustrated ballad, a single sheet of paper with an engaging woodcut and a vigorous rhyme to be sung to some popular tune. These broadsides occasionally reported bits of history or told stories of Biblical and classical subjects, and a "proper ballad dialogue-wise between Troilus and Cressida" was not unusual. But chiefly they kept the public informed on interesting contemporary news events, especially murders, fires and other public disasters, the death of prominent people and monstrous births both at home and abroad. The passion for recording local events was so pronounced that one wit remarked, "Scarce a cat can look out of a gutter but out starts a half-penny chronicler." In many Elizabethan homes and inns these broadsides were used for wallpaper and must have brightened many an infant mind with their gory details and impeccable moral conclusions. The grown-ups read them out of that frank desire for information mixed with entertainment that was so characteristic of the Elizabethans, and the broadsides even went so far as to supply foreign news occasionally when there had been an earthquake in Italy or a success for English arms in the Low Countries.

A more sober observer of the current scene could pay a little more money and buy news pamphlets that would keep him informed on the state of the wars in Europe--accounts of the exemplary courage of the English, or of the atrocities committed by the wicked enemies of England, or even a book with a special map of France showing all the fortresses. There were more books on news events than on any subject except religion, and the government saw to it that the approach was just as well controlled. When the English navy destroyed the Spanish Armada, one single publisher brought out over twenty pieces on the subject, but when the French king unexpectedly turned Catholic, no one mentioned it at all, in spite of the enthusiasm with which his military career up to that point had been recorded. When battles were recorded from abroad only the Protestant successes were mentioned, and publishers had to be careful even of minor pressure groups when they issued their books. A description of Russia was dedicated to the Queen as the account of "a tyrannical state (most unlike your own) without true knowledge of God, without written law, without common justice" and was then suppressed because some of the London merchants felt it might injure trade relations.

Any of these books and broadsides could be bought in the book stalls that were chiefly clustered together in St. Paul's churchyard. Building space was short in the city and the booksellers had first erected sheds in the area and then changed them into real shops. The book stalls were open by seven in the morning, and here the cheap reprints of plays and the shilling novels jostled for place with translations from the French and Italian and handsome folios on law and medicine and theology.

The Cathedral of St. Paul's did what it could to supply the city's obvious need for the still nonexistent daily newspaper. Its middle aisle was the meeting place for every newsmonger in London, and not only was the news exchanged here but a great deal of informal business was transacted, especially by lawyers. Since the position of the building blocked the road that would otherwise have been used to reach Fleet Street, the Cathedral was used as a short-cut even by delivery men. So many people passed through it every day instead of using Carter Lane that it was treated as an advertising agency. Anyone who was out of work posted the information so that a prospective employer could write his name and address beneath, and the west door of the Cathedral was "pasted and plastered up with serving-men's supplications." Out in the

London streets there were "papers on every post for arithmetic and writing schools," and plays and fencing matches used the same way of advertising themselves.

A young man up from the country would find that London offered a series of opportunities for getting information that were undreamed-of in a town like Stratford, just as he found there the variety of people that only a great port city could offer. He would find also that nowhere in England were people more intent on enjoying themselves, in spite of the twelve hour working day and the repressive theories of the London Council.

Many London shows cost the happy population nothing at all. No one had to pay to see the Lord Mayor's show and cheer the wicker-work giants or to see the water games on the Thames. Queen Elizabeth, that great amateur showman, was given to making sudden, spectacular appearances by torchlight, and when she opened Parliament she was carried through the streets in a red velvet cloak and a gold crown, while twenty-four glittering maids of honor rode in single file behind her. It was an age of the most determined dressing-up, and a knight saw nothing undignified in appearing as Eve in a tilt-yard show, with apples hanging on his armor and long hair attached to his helmet. Seats in the stands for a tilt-yard show cost eighteen pence, but "many thousands of men, women and girls" went to see knights dressed as savages or with moons on their heads, and strange carriages that seemed to be drawn along without traction; and if any Londoner failed to see it he could always buy a pamphlet describing it in detail.

Another source of public entertainment was executions, and the criminals knew what was expected of them by the public. They went to their death like actors, delivering final speeches from the scaffolds, and a hanging at Wapping was made especially impressive because the chief performer wore breeches of crimson taffeta. When there was an important mass execution, like that which followed the Babington Conspiracy in 1586, the government made the scaffold high and railed off the place to keep horsemen away so "the people might plainly see the execution." The idea of the government was to imprint upon the popular mind the horrors of treason and the ghastly death to which it led, but the Londoners treated the occasion like an especially interesting day at the theatre. "There was no lane, street, alley or house in London . . . out of which there issued not some of each age and sex, insomuch that the ways were pestered with people so multiplied, as they thronged and overran one another for haste, contending to the place of death for the advantage of the ground where to stand, see and hear." Londoners who were not good at pushing and therefore missed the actual execution kept arriving at Holborn all afternoon to see the blood on the scaffold; and the unfortunate few who missed it altogether could buy "many rimes, ballads and pamphlets" on the subject.

Important London funerals were also reported in descriptive pamphlets; and if they were further reported in woodcuts the fortunate purchaser could attach the pictures of the various parts of the procession together, making the long strip revolve on pins and "the figures march all in order." One merchant pasted up the pictures of a London funeral of 1586 in this manner and it took up "the length of the room at least," so impressing a nine-year-old boy when the pictures began to move on their pins that he never forgot it.

If a Londoner liked to look at strange animals there was the zoo in the Tower, where four lions, a tiger and a porcupine could be peered at through the wooden lattices after a judicious tip to the keeper; and for a time one of the houses on London Bridge housed a melancholy camel. A traveller from Kremzow reported that he saw in London a cow with six legs and a porpoise. He also saw a woman pigmy six thumbs high, a boy with a head like a pig, and (by an associ-

ation of ideas that would seem normal to any Londoner) the
Earl of Arundel being led to his imprisonment in the Tower.

The Londoners especially liked their entertainment to have
an element of conflict and suspense in it, and they went in
large numbers to the Star Chamber hearings at Westminster.
The final stages of these trials were open to the public and
aroused such interest in the theatrically-minded Londoners
that the audience would start arriving at three o'clock in the
morning to be sure of getting a good seat and the usher of
the chamber made a small fortune in tips.

Betting members of the population spent much of their
time watching cock fights in an arena near Smithfield, where
admission was a penny and the cocks who fought on the
round, straw-covered table were usually well fortified with
brandy. Even more popular were the bear-baitings, which
were patronized by everyone from the lowliest tinker to the
loftiest of visiting noblemen, and a visit to the Bear Garden
was as much standard procedure with the average London
visitor as seeing the tombs at Westminster Abbey. The bears
were lovingly tended by their keepers after their fights with
the dogs and the names of the best warriors among them were
household words in London. As an added attraction in the
80's there was also a mechanical contrivance out of which
leaped a series of performers who danced and sang, and a
rocket which exploded into a rosette and showered the audience with apples and pears.

Best of all, however, there were plays, and whatever a
Londoner's interests might be, there was sure to be a play in
town that would suit him. If he read the gory penny broadsides and went to executions, he could go to the theatre and
see the best contemporary murders re-enacted on the stage,
with property limbs flapping about and real blood flowing.
If he liked processions, he could see kings and councillors at
coronations and in battle order and at other noble events, for
the plays never omitted an opportunity for pageantry "where

the drums might walk and the play ruffle." If he were interested in natural wonders he could see much of zoological interest on the stage, where pigmies warred with cranes, and dragons were as realistic as hoops and painted canvas and gunpowder could make them. If he were interested in foreign lands, he could go to a play like *The Blacksmith's Daughter* at the Theatre and shudder at the treachery of the wicked Turks, and if he were interested in politics he could go to *Pompey and Caesar* or *Catiline's Conspiracies* and mark the danger of treason in high places. There was a whole series of plays on English history for the patriotically-minded; there were plays like *The Jew*, shown at the Bull, indicating the horrors of usury to the grave and thoughtful; and for the young and giddy there were re-casts of Italian comedies and romances about amorous knights and the "wooing of gentlewomen." Any popular story, from Samson to Henry V, found its way to the stage to satisfy the greatest theatre-going public in the world.

Stephen Gosson, a playwright of the period, has described the wholehearted enthusiasm with which a London audience settled down to enjoy itself in the theatre. If the play was a tragedy the susceptible Londoners dissolved into sympathetic tears, "weeping and mourning" with a rich vicarious satisfaction at the woes portrayed on the stage. If the play was a comedy "they generally take up a wonderful laughter, and shout together with one voice," and Gosson admits to having done the same thing himself. "Many times we laugh so extremely, that striving to bridle ourselves, we cannot." Gosson happened to be writing after he had given up making plays and abandoned the theatre, and he added that this kind of enjoyment was very unsuited to a Christian commonwealth. "When such excess of laughter bursteth out that we cannot hold it, there is no temperance. . . . Where no temperance is, there is no wisdom."

Temperance was not a virtue that interested the showmen

of the Elizabethan theatre. Their policy was that anything was justified on the stage so long as it pleased the public. They brought gods and goddesses down from heaven and fiends complete with firecrackers up from hell, their plays roamed the whole world and leaped from Turkey to Babylon as blandly as though time and distance had never existed, and kings consorted with clowns as though there had never been any rigid rules of social behavior to keep each man in his place.

All well-educated men knew that this was the wrong way to do a play. Like everything else, plays had their correct set of rules and every gentleman and scholar knew what they were. A play could never mix comedy and tragedy and it "must always be presented as occurring on the same day, in the same place and at the same time." This doctrine of the unities, which the Renaissance firmly believed in, was an expansion by French and Italian theorists of Aristotle's original theory of unity of action, and by Shakespeare's day its authority among educated men was unquestioned. An Italian critic ranked Homer well below Vergil because he did not understand the importance of such rules and even scolded Euripides because he invented stories about Helen "which were utterly contrary to well-known history."

Out of this grew the theory of "decorum" in writing plays, which meant a judicious balance of the parts to the whole with nothing violent or out of place. Nothing could have been more ill-bred, from this point of view, than for a playwright to descend to the vulgarity of showing violent physical action on the stage, and so many messengers were used to bring in reports of off-stage murders that one otherwise orthodox French critic finally wrote rebelliously, "Much fitter is it for a renowned inn than for an excellent tragedy to be thus frequented by an abundance of messengers."

Well-educated Englishmen believed unquestioningly in these Continental standards for playwrights and tried to produce work that was equally impeccable. When a Mr. Watson of Cambridge wrote a tragedy about Absalom, his standards were so high that he was reluctant to put the play into general circulation because once or twice he had used an anapestic line instead of an iambic one. Mr. Watson could speak learnedly of the writings of Sophocles and Seneca and the precepts of Aristotle, and the young men who followed in his footsteps at Oxford and Cambridge and the London Inns of Court struggled to mount into the same rarefied atmosphere and be worthy of equal admiration. Seneca was the correct model for tragedy, as Plautus and Terence were for comedy, and everything had to be done on a fixed stage and under fixed rules. Even an admired play like *Gorboduc*, the joint product of two young gentlemen of the Inner Temple, was criticized for violating the unities, although everyone agreed that its blank verse was impressively classical and its use of messengers so correct that none of the action of the story took place on the stage at all.

A well-educated Englishman who knew all the rules about writing plays could feel nothing but pain at the wild native growth that flourished on the popular stages. Sir Philip Sidney, who had one of the most intelligent and beautiful minds of his generation, went to the public theatre occasionally but all he could find there was a gross violation of the laws of the unities and of common sense. "You shall have Asia on the one side and Affrick on the other, and so many other underkingdoms that the player, when he cometh on, must ever begin with telling where he is, or else the tale will not be conceived. Now we shall have three ladies walk to gather flowers, and then we must believe the stage to be a garden. By and by we hear news of shipwreck in the same place, and then we are to blame if we accept it not for a rock. Upon the back of that, comes out a hideous monster, with fire and smoke, and then the miserable beholders are bound to take it for a cave."

From Sidney's point of view the plays of the early 80's

may have been ridiculous, with their complete lack of interest in the classical tradition and the heavy demands they made upon the spectator's willing imagination. But the plays made money, as James Burbage of the Theatre or Henry Laneman of the Curtain could testify, and in turn the money began to attract a new group of playwrights.

Most of these young men came from either Oxford or Cambridge, where they had been given a good education in the classics but had not been given any way of making a living. Most of them were the sons of middle-class parents who had ambitiously sent their sons to the university, either through a scholarship or at some personal sacrifice, but with no clear idea of what they should do with their expensive educations afterwards. In Chaucer's day young men like these would have gone into the Church, which still controlled most of the government offices. But even by Chaucer's day the government offices were becoming secularized, and after the Reformation it was no longer the primary duty of Oxford and Cambridge to turn out churchmen. The universities gave their young graduates the education of a gentleman but with no suggestions how to put it to use; and from the practical point of view the only course open to them was either to try for a position as a teacher in a grammar school or with a private family, or else to try to negotiate a position as rector of a parish.

Some of the young men themselves had other ideas. The great city of London beckoned them, and with their excellent classical training they were sure they could make a living in London by writing books. Most of the young men discovered after they arrived that the market for serious young writers in London was not as steady as it might be. A series of plays produced at Cambridge at the turn of the century made a survey of the general problem of how a scholar could earn a living, and there was one scene that must have raised a sympathetic laugh in the audience. The young scholar's last book has not been selling well and the London publisher is extremely unwilling to accept a new one from him until he learns it has the irresistible title, "A Chronicle of Cambridge Cuckolds." This is perhaps a slightly unkind parody of the London bookseller's point of view; but he could not afford to deal in books that his customers would not buy, and if the young gentlemen of Oxford and Cambridge expected to make a steady living they had to turn out the romances and the sensational pamphlets that the public enjoyed.

However, there was one group of paymasters in London who had just as much ready money as the London publishers and were even more in need of material. A successful company of actors needed a great many plays in a year, since they worked on the repertory system, and to keep their positions in the competitive world of the theatre they needed good scripts and were willing to pay for them. The young men from the universities were more than willing to be paid and they had already had some experience with the academic side of playwriting. Both Oxford and Cambridge produced plays at Christmas or to entertain visiting dignitaries, and the refectory at St. John's Hall in Cambridge was famous for "its theatrical apparatus for acting plays."

The greatest of these university men to write for the common stage was Christopher Marlowe. He was the brilliant son of a Canterbury shoemaker and went to Cambridge on a scholarship. There he encountered two fine libraries and the companionship of brilliant and sympathetic minds, and the legendary glories of Greece and Rome became much more real to him than anything in his own century. Marlowe was a true son of the Renaissance in his intense ambition and his love of beauty, and when he wrote a play about a great tyrant king he did it as much to please himself as to please the London public.

Marlowe's *Tamburlaine* was produced on the London stage in the late 80's and was given a very effective production by the Admiral's company. The title-role was played, evidently from the first, by Edward Alleyn, then in his early twenties but already the most brilliant and popular actor in London. The whole city took the play to its collective heart and an equally popular sequel followed immediately.

Part of the popularity of *Tamburlaine* came from the savage effectiveness of its stage devices, for Marlowe was a born theatre man and knew how to make an audience shudder. There was a popular scene in which one of Tamburlaine's captives was carried about in a cage and used as his conqueror's footstool and another one in which the governor of Babylon was hung in chains on the wall and shot at by the besiegers. (The Admiral's company handled this scene with such realism that in a November performance a bullet miscarried and killed a pregnant woman in the audience.) Even more famous was a scene in which Tamburlaine made his entrance in a chariot drawn by two captive kings with bits in their mouths. Alleyn had a whip in his right hand to scourge the actors who played the two kings, and a delighted thrill went over the whole audience when he shouted in his wonderful voice,

> Holla, ye pampered jades of Asia!
> What, can ye draw but twenty miles a day?

A whole generation of theatre-goers went around quoting the scene, and Shakespeare's Pistol was only one of many.

It was not only the stage effects that made *Tamburlaine* so popular; it was Marlowe's poetry. The Londoners loved words and they were capable of getting half-drunk on a really gorgeous flow of rhetoric. Since at least the beginning of the decade the playwrights had been showing "the majesty of their pen in tragical speeches," and the audiences had come to expect poetry with their plays. As one reformer gloomily put it, a few years earlier, "because the sweet numbers of poetry flowing in verse do wonderfully tickle the hearer's

ears, the devil hath tied this to most of our plays." Most of
the verse was probably not very good, but its constant use
produced a series of well-trained listeners, alert and ready to
be moved. Marlowe was a good theatre man but he was a
great poet, and he used blank verse as it had never been used
before on the London stage. The golden rhetoric caught and
held the audience as a new kind of symphony would hold a
musically-trained audience today, and many a London apprentice must have walked home from *Tamburlaine* intoxi-
cated with the lines singing in his head.

Another great popular success of the same period was a
play by Thomas Kyd called *The Spanish Tragedy*. Kyd
never quite belonged with the group of young men who
came down from the universities to write plays; but he
roomed for a time with Marlowe and although he was no
poet he had some of Marlowe's theatre sense and an even
better idea how to construct plays. Kyd had been educated
in London under Richard Mulcaster, and Mulcaster's boys
produced plays so effectively that the general public crowded
to see them until the directors of the school decided that such
performances were undignified and ordered them discontinued. It may have been partly from Mulcaster that Kyd
learned some of the classical theories that were a commonplace at the universities and the Inns of Court, but he could
just as well have found them from his own reading. The ten
tragedies of Seneca, for instance, came out in an English
translation at the beginning of the decade, and Kyd took
some of the bloody devices that Seneca had pictured in ornate rhyme for a Roman audience and put them into action
for an English one. *The Spanish Tragedy* was a success with
a whole generation of theatregoers, and the revenge play,
with its ghosts and its madmen, started on its long career on
the London stage.

Meanwhile, other university men were turning out popular
plays, and although their choice of actual subject matter was

not very different from that of their predecessors in the public theatre, they brought with them a sensitive ear for words and a well-trained mind and some of them were real poets. Most of them knew each other well, and men like Greene and Nashe and Lodge tended to congregate together in what a more academic graduate called a "riming and scribbling crew." All of them drank a good deal and were full of theories about religion and most of them were well acquainted with the insides of the London prisons, either for their religious opinions or for street-fighting or for debt. Tom Nashe gave it as his opinion that going to prison was an experience no writer could expect to miss. "I protest I should never have writ passion well, or been a piece of a poet, if I had not arrived in those quarters. Trace the gallantest youths and bravest revellers about town . . . and you shall infallibly find that once in their lifetime they have visited that melancholy habitation." Even a man's good intentions could get him into trouble with the authorities. When Thomas Watson tried to help his friend Marlowe in a fight in Hog Lane, he ended by killing Marlowe's opponent and spent five months in prison until it was decided he had acted in self-defense.

Marlowe seems to have been the leader of this writing group, if only because he was the only one who was completely in earnest. Some of his companions dabbled in free-thinking because it was currently the fashionable thing to do and they were in instinctive revolt against their conservative, middle-class backgrounds. But Marlowe hated conformity with all the passion of his free-ranging intellect and he felt an actual sense of suffocation under the series of tight religious rules the average Englishman took for granted. In the same way Marlowe's companions respected the classics because they had been taught to honor learning and because they valued their university training as something that set them above the common herd. But Marlowe worshipped the ancient writers because beauty was more to him than life, and even the place-names on a map could give his spirit a lift into another and freer world than London.

Men like Marlowe were, of course, aware that they were working in a perishable medium when they wrote plays. Once a play was sold to a company of actors the author had no control over it at all, and it was only an accident if it got into print. A few of the plays written by George Peele and Robert Greene were eventually printed, but almost none of those written by Tom Nashe or Tom Lodge; and as for Thomas Watson, a member of this group whom his contemporaries ranked with Sidney and Spenser and who had a tremendous reputation in his own day, none of the many plays he wrote has survived at all. Even when a play was printed, it was usually given without the author's name; all of Marlowe's plays that were printed in his own lifetime appeared anonymously, and *The Spanish Tragedy* is known to have been written by Kyd only because of a casual reference by a fellow-playwright more than two decades later. Even when a play succeeded in working its way into print, the text was usually a corrupt acting version and not at all what its author had originally written. Greene's *Orlando Furioso* was printed with its metre dislocated, the Italian quotations misspelled, the classical references shortened or omitted and most of the poetry mangled and apparently quoted from memory. In the case of this particular play some of the cue-sheets of the actor who played Orlando survived and with them Greene's original text; but no other original texts have survived and it is impossible to be sure that the printed versions of Marlowe's plays are exactly what Marlowe himself wrote.

The playwrights knew they were working in a perishable medium and they turned to other forms of poetry to immortalize themselves in the eyes of posterity. Marlowe did not live to finish his classical narrative poem, *Hero and Leander*, but Nashe did an imitation of Ovid in *The Choice of Valentines* and Tom Lodge made a name for himself in 1589 with

Scilla's Metamorphoses. Lodge came of a prominent London family and had been educated at Oxford and at the Inns of Court; and he closed his classical narrative with a firm resolve to be worthy of his upbringing,

> To write no more of that whence shame doth grow
> Or tie my pen to penny-knaves' delight,
> But live with fame, and so for fame to write.

Lodge was unable to keep to this noble ambition since his father's spectacular bankruptcy and his own great gifts for spending money kept him at playwriting in order to earn a living, but he could never quite forgive the penny public for forcing him to debase his art.

All this university-educated group of writers shared the conviction that they were prostituting themselves in writing plays for money and appealing to the base instincts of the "penny-knaves." If they wanted their plays to be popular they had to disregard all the classical precepts they had learned at Oxford and Cambridge and they could never do this without a slight sense of sin. Any of them might have echoed the complaint of Lope de Vega, the popular Spanish playwright: "When I have to write a comedy, I lock up the precepts with six keys, cast Terence and Plautus from my study . . . and I write according to the art invented by those who sought the vulgar applause. For, as the common herd pays for them, it is meet to speak to them like an ignoramus in order to please them." The playwrights consoled themselves slightly by introducing classical references into their plays whenever they could, and a writer like Robert Greene, Master of Arts from both universities, put all his stage directions in Latin to show the excellence of his education. The actors patiently removed them again, since few actors read Latin easily, and the practice survives today only in *exit* and *exeunt.*

It was a constant source of irritation to these university playwrights that the actors who bought their scripts made more money than they did. The first time that Nashe appeared in print it was to express regret that various "sweet gentlemen" of his acquaintance were in the habit of writing plays and had "tricked up a company of taffeta fools with their feathers." If the writers had not done so, the taffeta fools would not have been able to make so much money. They would be forced to go on using old-fashioned plays and would not be strutting around in satin suits in the streets of London. The average playwright was convinced the actors owed all their popularity to the brilliant lines he and his colleagues had written for them, and he was angered to see large audiences drawn to a successful play long after its author had drunk up the whole of the purchase price in the nearest tavern.

Since no playwright had gone to the risk and expense of producing a play himself, he could hardly have been expected to realize that each acting company was carrying a heavy overhead in rentals, costumes and properties. In the early 80's there is a reference to the cost of "these spectacles that scarce last like shoes of brown paper," and by the time Nashe was writing all the expenses had increased. The script was only one item in a series of expenses that had to be assumed by the actors each time a script went into production, and the money that was made on a successful script was of course counterbalanced by the money that could be lost on an unsuccessful one. Although a playwright made less money than an actor he also took fewer risks. Nevertheless, when the playwrights thought of the actors they thought only of the successful ones, and they found it hard to forgive the "taffeta fools" for making so much money when university graduates made so little.

No one felt more strongly on this subject than Robert Greene, for Greene had a very clear idea of the commercial value of his scripts. He was the one member of the university group who was making a satisfactory living by his pen, for Greene was a born journalist and had an almost intuitive idea of what the public wanted. He was very popular with the London publishers, for whom he supplied a series of love stories and slightly fictionized exposés of the London underworld and even a diatribe against the Pope, but he had Lodge's gift for spending money rapidly and he was convinced that the actors did not really understand his worth. He was one of the most popular of all the London playwrights, but the actors neither treated him with proper respect nor paid him enough money, and he broke off in the middle of a prose romance published in 1590 to complain that the actors were "conceited," "covetous" and "insolent." When Nashe had attacked the actors, one year earlier, it had been in a preface to one of Greene's own books, and Nashe's remark about feathers reminded Greene of the fable of the crow who decked himself out in borrowed plumage. This, to Greene, was the perfect image with which to describe an actor. "Art thou proud with Aesop's crow, being pranked with the glory of others' feathers? Of thyself thou canst say nothing. . . . The invention the people applaud for excellent, that comes from the secrets of our knowledge." The actors supplied nothing but "a kind of mechanical labour" which was entitled to a mild respect only so long as the actors did not grow conceited and think they were superior to playwrights. Greene admitted he had made a "long digression" in his novel and returned to the fortunes of Francisco that he had been recounting, but two years later his fury at the actors reappeared and with it the image of Aesop's crow.

During those two years Greene had been a familiar and spectacular figure around London with his red hair and pointed beard, his green cloak and his silk stockings, his mistress from the underworld and her disreputable brother who served as his bodyguard. He was famous for his drinking parties and he had many friends. But in the summer of 1592 he became mortally ill and was suddenly terrified by visions of hellfire. The Bohemian playwright had been soberly reared by devout parents and the teachings of his childhood came back to him with a rush.

It took Greene a month to die and he spent it praying to be forgiven for his sins. He had always taken a deep interest in the repentances that were expected of Newgate criminals and he had evidently written some of their "penitent and passionate" speeches himself. When he came to his own repentance he outdid himself and there was hardly a bookseller in London who did not have on sale one of the pamphlets the great journalist wrote during the month he lay dying in a shoemaker's house near Dowgate. Greene's repentance was completely sincere, for, unlike Marlowe, he was not a nonconformist out of any real conviction. He had been brought up respectably and he tried to die respectably, imploring the youth of England to profit by his example and avoid blasphemy, bad company and drink. He made what was known as a good end, and he shared it with the public only because he was a good journalist.

Of all Greene's repentance pamphlets, the one that stirred the most discussion was *Greene's Groatsworth of Wit*, the last he wrote and the most autobiographical. Calling himself Roberto, he describes his debts, his writing of plays, his desertion of his wife, his taking of a mistress and all his other sins, and supplies a series of rules of good conduct so that others may avoid his unhappy fate. Then Greene addresses himself to three of his friends in a special warning. Greene does not call these three playwrights by name, but the references to atheism make it clear that the first of them is Marlowe. The second playwright is evidently Tom Nashe, who was getting a reputation for clever insults that made more than one writer echo Greene's description of him as "young Juvenal." The third playwright, "in some things rarer, in nothing inferior," is more difficult to identify, but it may be George Peele, whom Nashe warmly praised as "the Àtlas of poetry."

The general purpose of Greene's address to his three friends was to implore them to stop writing plays and working for the actors, "for it is a pity men of such rare wits should be subject to the pleasure of such rude grooms." Greene had already made it clear two years earlier how much he disliked the men who bought plays from him, but the thought of their intolerable prosperity while he lay penniless and dying added a new edge to his fury. By now he has nothing whatever to say in the actors' favor. They are "apes," they are "peasants," they are "painted monsters"; they are puppets "that speak from our mouths" and are "garnished in our colors." Again Greene was reminded of the crow in Aesop who strutted in borrowed feathers, but this time he used the image not to attack actors in general but one actor in particular. "There is an upstart crow, beautified with our feathers, that, with his tiger's heart wrapped in a player's hide, supposes he is as well able to bombast out a blank verse as the best of you; and being an absolute *Johannes fac totum*, is in his own conceit the only Shake-scene in a country."

It is known, from the evidence of a Court document two years later, that William Shakespeare was by this time a prominent actor in London, and he also seems to be the only actor at that time who was also writing plays. The fact that Shakespeare is the actor whom Greene is attacking is further indicated by the pun on his name as "the only Shake-scene in a country," and the identification is reinforced by Greene's phrase about the "tiger's heart wrapped in a player's hide." The phrase is a slanting reference to a scene from a London success that was currently attracting large audiences. The original line reads,

O tiger's heart wrapp'd in a woman's hide!

and the play from which it comes is listed in the First Folio as the third part of Shakespeare's *Henry VI*.

It was hard enough for Robert Greene to tolerate the actors who employed him when they contented themselves merely with buying his plays. When they set up as a rival playwright one of their own number, who thought he could "bombast out a blank verse" as well as Marlowe or Nashe while still continuing his work as an actor, they had produced a *Johannes fac totum*—a Johnny Do-Everything—whose mere existence was more unforgivable than all the rest of their sins combined.

Greene's final repentance pamphlet was a great success on the bookstalls, where it appeared posthumously, but it inevitably had repercussions. The publisher, Henry Chettle, had been obliged to copy the semi-illegible manuscript in his neat hand to prepare it for licensing, and he took upon himself the responsibility of suppressing some of Greene's violence. Chettle was a good-natured man who eventually became a playwright himself, and he modified Greene's attack on Marlowe as an atheist. "Had it been true, yet to publish it was intolerable."

Chettle wished later that he had modified Greene's attack on the author of *Henry VI* also. "That I did not, I am as sorry as if the original fault had been my fault, because myself have seen his demeanor no less civil than he excellent in the quality he professes." The "quality" was the Elizabethan term for the acting profession. "Besides, divers of worship have reported his uprightness of dealing, which argues his honesty, and his facetious grace in writing, that approves his art."

Of all the men writing for the London theatre, Shakespeare seems to have been almost the only one who did not take offense easily. His contemporaries called him "gentle Shakespeare" and he deserved the title. In the short-tempered Elizabethan atmosphere, where a writer almost prided himself on the vigor and variety of his insults and where even gentle scholars like William Camden and John Stow became involved in bitter arguments, Shakespeare stands almost alone for the consistent courtesy with which he behaved. His objection to Greene's attack was apparently the only protest he ever made, and it must have been a mild one or Chettle would not have spoken with admiration of his civility.

The most important thing about Greene's attack is that it establishes the fact that Shakespeare was a successful actor before he became a playwright. This, in turn, explains what he had been doing in the intervening years, since the birth of his twins in Stratford in 1585. It was no easy thing to become a successful actor on the London stage. Acting was a profession that required a long, arduous period of training before a man was capable of appearing professionally before a critical metropolitan audience; and since Shakespeare was a successful actor in 1592, the year of Greene's attack on him, he must have chosen acting as his profession several years earlier.

Chapter 5

ACTING was not an easy profession on the Elizabethan stage or one to be taken up lightly. An actor went through a strenuous period of training before he could be entrusted with an important part by one of the great city companies. He worked on a raised stage in the glare of the afternoon sun, with none of the softening illusions that can be achieved in the modern theatre, and in plays that made strenuous demands upon his skill as a fencer, a dancer and an acrobat.

Many of the men in the London companies had been "trained up from their childhood" in the art, and an actor like Shakespeare, who entered the profession in his twenties, had an initial handicap that could only be overcome by intelligence and rigorous discipline. Since he was a well-known actor by 1592 and Chettle says he was an excellent one, he must have had the initial advantages of a strong body and a good voice and have taught himself in the hard school of the Elizabethan theatre how to use them to advantage.

One of the most famous of the London companies, that of Lord Strange, began its career as a company of tumblers, and a standard production like "The Forces of Hercules" was at least half acrobatics. Training of this kind was extremely useful to the actors, for the normal London stage consisted of several different levels. Battles and sieges were very popular with the audiences, with the upper levels of the stage used as the town walls and turrets, and an actor had to know how to take violent falls without damaging either himself or his expensive costume.

Nearly all plays involved some kind of fighting, and in staging hand-to-hand combats the actor's training had to be excellent. The average Londoner was an expert on the subject of fencing, and he did not pay his penny to see two professional actors make ineffectual dabs at each other with rapiers when the script claimed they were fighting to the death. A young actor like Shakespeare must have gone through long, gruelling hours of practice to learn the ruthless technique of Elizabethan fencing. He had to learn how to handle a long, heavy rapier in one hand, with a dagger for parrying in the other, and to make a series of savage, calculated thrusts at close quarters from the wrist and forearm, aiming either at his opponent's eyes or below the ribs. The actor had to achieve the brutal reality of an actual Elizabethan duel without injuring himself or his opponent, a problem that required a high degree of training and of physical coordination. The theatres and the inn-yards were frequently rented by the fencing societies to put on exhibition matches, and on one such occasion at the Swan a fencer was run through the eye and died, an indication of the risks this sort of work involved even with trained, experienced fencers. The actors had to be extremely skilled, since they faced precisely the same audience. Richard Tarleton, a comic actor of the 80's who was the first great popular star of the Elizabethan theatre, was made Master of Fence the year before he died and this was the highest degree the fencing schools could award.

Not being content with savage, realistic fights in its theatre productions, the London audience also expected to see bloody deaths and mutilations; and it was necessary to find some way to run a sword through an actor's head or tear out his entrails without impairing his usefulness for the next afternoon's performance. This involved not only agility but a thorough knowledge of sleight of hand, since the players were working close to the audience and in broad daylight. Elizabethan stage management was not slavishly interested in realism but it was always concerned with good stage effects and when bloodshed was involved it gave the audience real blood. It had been found by experience that ox blood was too thick to run well, and sheep's blood was generally used. To stage a realistic stabbing one actor would use a knife with a hollow handle into which the blade would slip back when it was pressed home, and his fellow actor would be equipped with a bladder of blood inside his white leather jerkin, which could be painted to look like skin. When the bladder was pricked and the actor arched himself at the moment of contact, the blood spurted out in a most satisfactory manner. Sometimes real knives were used and a protective plate, and a juggler once staggered into St. Paul's Churchyard and died there because he had done the trick when he was drunk and forgotten his plate. In *The Battle of Alcazar* there was a disembowelling scene for which the property man supplied three vials of blood and the liver, heart and lungs of a sheep. Then it was up to Edward Alleyn and his two fellow actors to use skillful substitution in such a way as to create the illusion, before a critical London audience in broad daylight, that their organs were being torn out.

Another test of an actor's physical control was in dancing. Apart from the dances that were written into the actual texts of the plays, it was usual to end the performance with a dance performed by some of the members of the company. A traveller from abroad who saw Shakespeare's company act *Julius Caesar* said that "when the play was over they danced very marvellously and gracefully together," and when the English actors travelled abroad special mention was always made of their ability as dancers. The fashion of the time was for violent, spectacular dances and the schools in London taught intricate steps like those of the galliard, the exaggerated leap called

the "capriole" and the violent lifting of one's partner high
into the air that was the "volte." A visitor to one of these
dancing schools of London watched a performer do a galliard
and noted how "wonderfully he leaped, flung and took on";
and if amateurs were talented at this kind of work, professionals on the stage were expected to be very much better.

In addition to all this, subordinate or beginning actors were
expected to handle several roles in an afternoon instead of
only one. A major company seldom had more than twelve
actors in it and could not afford to hire an indefinite number
of extra ones for a single production. This meant that the
men who had short speaking parts or none were constantly
racing about and leaping into different costumes to get onstage with a different characterization as soon as they heard
their cues. In one of Alleyn's productions a single actor
played a Tartar nobleman, a spirit, an attendant, a hostage,
a ghost, a child, a captain and a Persian; and while none of
the parts made any special demands on his acting ability he
must have had very little time to catch his breath. The London
theatre was no place for physical weaklings; and, in the same
way it is safe to assume that John Shakespeare must have had
a strong, well-made body or he would not have been appointed
a constable in Stratford, it is safe to assume that he must have
passed the inheritance on to his eldest son.

There was one more physical qualification an Elizabethan
actor had to possess, and this was perhaps more important
than any of the others. He had to have a good voice. An
Elizabethan play was full of action, but in the final analysis
it was not the physical activity that caught and held the
emotions of the audience; it was the words. An audience was
an assembly of listeners and it was through the ear, not the eye,
that the audience learned the location of each of the scenes,
the emotions of each of the characters and the poetry and
excitement of the play as a whole. More especially, since the
actors were men and boys and close physical contact could

not carry the illusion of love-making, words had to be depended upon in the parts that were written for women.

An Elizabethan audience had become highly susceptible to the use of words, trained and alert to catch their exact meaning and full of joy if they were used well. But this meant, as the basis of any successful stage production, that all the words had to be heard clearly. The actors used a fairly rapid delivery of their lines and this meant that breath control, emphasis and enunciation had to be perfect if the link that was being forged between the emotions of the audience and the action on the stage was not to be broken. When Shakespeare first came to London, the problem of effective stage delivery was made somewhat easier by the use of a heavily end-stopped line, where the actor could draw his breath at regular intervals and proceed at a kind of jog-trot. But during the following decade this kind of writing became increasingly old-fashioned, giving way to an intricate and supple blank verse that was much more difficult to handle intelligently; and no one was more instrumental in bringing the new way of writing into general use than Shakespeare himself.

Even with all the assistance given him by the old way of writing, with mechanical accenting and heavy use of rhyme, an Elizabethan actor had no easy time remembering his part. A repertory system was used and no play was given two days in succession. The actor played a different part every night and he had no opportunity to settle into a comfortable routine while the lines of the part became second nature to him. He could expect very little help from the prompter, for that overworked individual was chiefly occupied in seeing that the actors came on in proper order, that they had their properties available and that the intricate stage arrangements that controlled the pulleys from the "heavens" and the springs to the trap doors were worked with quick, accurate timing. These stage effects, which naturally had to be changed each afternoon for each new play, were extremely complicated. A single play in which Greene and Lodge collaborated required the descent of a prophet and an angel let down on a throne, a woman blackened by a thunder stroke, sailors coming in wet from the sea, a serpent devouring a vine, a hand with a burning sword emerging from a cloud and "Jonah the prophet cast out of the whale's belly upon the stage." Any production that had to wrestle with as many complications as this had no room for an actor who could not remember his lines.

Moreover, an actor who forgot his lines would not have lasted long in what was a highly competitive profession. There were more actors than there were parts for them, judging by the number of people who were listed as players in the parish registers. Even the actor who had achieved the position of a sharer in one of the large London companies was not secure. Richard Jones, for instance, was the owner of costumes and properties and playbooks worth nearly forty pounds, which was an enormous sum in those days, and yet three years later he was working in the theatre at whatever stray acting jobs he could get. "Sometimes I have a shilling a day and sometimes nothing," he told Edward Alleyn, asking for help in getting his suit and cloak out of pawn.

The usual solution for an actor who could not keep his place in the competitive London theatre was to join one of the country companies, where the standards were less exacting, or to go abroad. English actors were extravagantly admired abroad and even a second-string company with poor equipment became the hit of the Frankfort Fair, so that "both men and women flocked wonderfully" to see them. An actor like Shakespeare who maintained his position on the London stage for two decades could legitimately be praised, as Chettle praised him, for being "excellent in the quality he professes." If it had been otherwise, he would not have remained for long on the London stage.

If Shakespeare had not enjoyed his work as an actor, he could no doubt have given it up when he became a successful writer. Ben Jonson started life as an actor but he gave the profession up as soon as he found he could make a living by his pen. Shakespeare, on the other hand, never gave up his profession. He was a successful actor in 1592, as is shown by Greene's attack on him. He was still an actor in 1598, when he appears on the list of "principal comedians" who acted in *Every Man in his Humour*. He was still an actor in 1603, when he appears on the list of "principal tragedians" who acted in *Sejanus*. He was still acting in 1608 because Cuthbert Burbage names him specifically among the "men players" who arranged to begin using the Blackfriars theatre that year; and since he evidently retired to Stratford two or three years later, it can safely be said that Shakespeare was an actor throughout the whole of his life in the London theatre.

Shakespeare was not, of course, as brilliantly successful an actor as Edward Alleyn, who could make a bad play seem good and whose name was even used on the title page of a printed play because it would increase sales. But Shakespeare's knowledge of people was infinitely greater than Alleyn's, and it is probable that none of the many audiences who saw him on the stage was ever able to deduce his own character and personality from the roles he played.

A busy actor like William Shakespeare did not have much time to write plays. The mornings were probably taken up with rehearsals and there were performances in the afternoon and sometimes special shows in the evening, to say nothing of the strenuous period when the company was on its annual tour of the provinces. A modern writer might feel it was inconceivable that anyone could write plays when he was already working in a full-time profession, but this is an echo of a more degenerate age and was not the Elizabethan point of view at all. The Elizabethans had no patience with any writer who expected to "lie in child-bed one-and-thirty weeks and eight days of three bad lines and afterward spend a whole twelvemonth" trying to improve them, and Ben Jonson, who wrote one play in five weeks, was publicly jeered at because he was so "slow an inventor." Thomas Heywood, like William Shakespeare, was a full-time actor and remained one. Yet Heywood found time, in his limited leisure, to have what he called "either an entire hand, or at least a main finger" in writing two hundred and twenty plays. Shakespeare himself produced less than forty plays during twenty years' work in the theatre, a record that is not remarkable for its bulk, however incredible it may be for its quality.

The fact that Shakespeare was an actor gave him one great advantage over the average playwright of his day. Usually a playwright made a play to order and met the actors in some convenient place where it could be given a reading. Normally an alehouse served as an impromptu office since, as one foreigner remarked, there were "partitions between the tables so that one table cannot overlook the next." Once the play had been read and approved, the dramatist was paid and his contribution was over. Many of the playwrights had so little interest in the finished production that they even did not go to see it acted, and, George Chapman once remarked, "I see not mine own plays." A writer of this kind had no opportunity to judge the total emotional impact of his work on a living audience, and Chapman's plays are unactable today. But Shakespeare was an actor. He was present during every detail of the production of his own plays and when they were acted he almost touched hands with his audience. He was in a position to know exactly what could be achieved from the production point of view, and the quality that has kept him a living force on the stage for more than three hundred years was born in part of his close professional knowledge of his audience.

In the first plays he wrote, Shakespeare shows that he already had a firm grip on the art of manipulating the emotions of an audience. The plays are not masterpieces. Like every other writer, Shakespeare learned by writing. In his late twenties he was not yet ready to write *Hamlet* any more than his audience was ready to receive it. In a sense, Shakespeare and his audience grew up together, and at the beginning of his career as a playwright his approach to stagecraft was as juvenile and crude as the responses of his audience. But the important thing was that he infallibly got these responses.

The most stirring of his early successes, to judge by contemporary reports, was a series of three plays he wrote on the Wars of the Roses. Plays on English history were very popular with Elizabethan audiences, who had not been given any history in their school days and were eager to know about former kings and queens. The Wars of the Roses made an especially good subject for a young playwright, since he could point out the horrors of civil strife and remind the audience by inference how fortunate they were to be experiencing the joys of a settled Tudor monarchy. The next time a Londoner objected to paying a special subsidy or started brooding over the cost of the war with Spain, he could always remind himself how much worse life had been under the inept rule of Henry VI.*

As far as school instruction went, Shakespeare knew no more than his audiences did about the Wars of the Roses. But there were several excellent history books available, of which the most up-to-date was a chronicle history of England, Ireland and Scotland that Raphael Holinshed had compiled from standard sources for a syndicate of printers. Holinshed wrote a brisk, straightforward prose and his conviction that the Tudors were the culmination of English history was an impeccable one. Ten years after the book was published the sales warranted a new edition, and the publishers brought it up-to-date by including the annals of England up to the publication date of 1587. This three-volume edition became the standard history of England and was the one Shakespeare

---

* The three plays on the Wars of the Roses that are being discussed here appear in the First Folio as *Henry VI*, parts one, two and three. In Appendix Three there is a discussion of their relation to the canon, which was questioned by some scholars at the end of the eighteenth century.

used as the general basis of all his history plays; and although it was a rather expensive publication it must have been one of the books he eventually owned.

Only a very self-confident young man would have embarked on the confused mass of quarrels and counter-quarrels recorded by Holinshed and hoped to turn it into manageable stage material; and only a young man who was experienced in the practical problems of the theatre could have succeeded. Occasionally Shakespeare found that the possibilities for drama were smothered under the weight of the material, but in general he managed to manipulate his important scenes in such a way that the audiences nearly choked in an excess of patriotic emotion.

The most successful scene in the first play of the series was the death of Lord Talbot. Talbot was the noblest kind of Englishman and he died on the battlefield at the hands of the perfidious French, clasping within his arms the dead body of his equally noble son. Talbot had a speech that the actor who played the part must have warmly appreciated—the first of a long line of bravura speeches that have made Shakespeare the beloved of actors ever since—and the audience sobbed as one man as the great warrior's soul winged its way to heaven. The play was produced at the Rose on the third of March, 1592, by Lord Strange's company, and played to enormous audiences all season. Only one play in Philip Henslowe's diary records larger grosses in the galleries, and Tom Nashe made a respectful reference to the size of the audiences in a pamphlet he wrote the same year. "How it would have joyed brave Talbot (the terror of the French) to think that after he had lain two hundred years in his tomb, he should triumph again on the stage and have his bones new embalmed with the tears of ten thousand spectators."

The young playwright was not very interested in exact historical facts. He has Talbot's death precede the capture of Joan of Arc, whereas in actual fact Joan died twenty-two years before he did. As for Joan herself, any modern reader is startled by the disrespectful, almost comic characterization that she is given, and it is difficult to remember that to the sixteenth-century Englishman she was a crafty peasant who overturned the brave English only because she was assisted by devils. Even the scholarly Gabriel Harvey saw her as nothing more than "a lusty adventurous wench," and the most that the English could feel was a certain reluctant admiration for her vigor.

The play records a series of battles and sieges that gave Shakespeare an opportunity to exploit all the resources of the stage, and he kept the actors leaping from level to level like the acrobats they were. He even made use of the rarely-used top turret and had Joan ascend it to thrust out a torch, and at one point forced the actors into what must have been a twelve-foot leap from a balcony to the stage when the defenders of Orleans escape from the besieged town.

Shakespeare's second play on the Wars of the Roses gave much less opportunity for battle scenes and processions, but the young actor-dramatist did not forget his audience's love of special effects. In the first act he used three stage levels to have an actor dressed as a spirit rise up through a trap door to confront the Duchess on the balcony, with thunder to mask any noise that might be made by the machinery. Shakespeare also made a lavish use of property heads, for the rebels bring on the heads of Lord Saye and his son-in-law, Jack Cade's head is brought onstage, and Queen Margaret has a special stage direction for "mourning over Suffolk's head." These atrocity scenes were always staged with great care, and whatever company it may have been that produced the play it was certainly prosperous enough to be able to afford four separate heads. It is not unlikely the same system was used that the French used in the Middle Ages, in which a dummy head was carved with the living actor as a model and then realistically colored. A head of this kind could even be made to bleed if a little dough kneaded with bullock's blood was pressed against it and made to look like part of the dead flesh. Suffolk's headless trunk also appears in the play, but this was a property item that even the smallest company could supply as a matter of course. When Thomas Churchyard was hired by the city of Norwich to put on a small outdoor play during Queen Elizabeth's visit, he brought along with him as a matter of course "legs and arms of men (well and lively wrought) to be let fall in numbers on the ground, as bloody as might be."

In the second play of his series, Shakespeare remained equally casual about historical facts and chronology, but this may have been because he was faced with a practical theatre difficulty. The play has nearly fifty characters, not including lords and ladies, aldermen, citizens, soldiers and so on, and this meant that nearly every actor in the company had to play several parts. The action of the play had to be carefully arranged to make all this doubling possible, and if the historical events interfered with practical stagecraft it was history that had to be altered.

In the third play of the trilogy, Shakespeare found himself with a large mass of undramatic material to wrestle with, and the most effective scene occurs not at the end of the play but near the beginning. At the end of the first act the Duke of York's enemies crown him with a paper crown on the battlefield before they kill him, and York turns on them in another of those wonderfully effective speeches that make Shakespeare so loved by actors. The speech is particularly directed against Queen Margaret, "she-wolf of France," and rises in a crescendo of rhetoric to its climax.

O tiger's heart wrapp'd in a woman's hide!

howls the Duke of York, and the audience evidently quivered with delight. The success of this line is shown by the fact it was the one Robert Greene chose to parody when he was at-

tacking young "Shake-scene," and the first printed edition of
the play was given the title, *The True Tragedy of Richard,
Duke of York,* to capitalize on the effectiveness of York's
death in the first act. According to the title page, the play was
acted by the Earl of Pembroke's men, a new company that
appeared for a short time in the early 90's and then collapsed.
Lord Strange's men had presented the first play of the series,
so it would appear that at this time Shakespeare was writing
for more than one company.

The trilogy on the Wars of the Roses is the work of an
ambitious young man, rather uneven in his use of words but
in general deeply impressed by Marlowe, trained in a hard
school of stagecraft and intent upon conquering the emotions
of his audience by every means within his command. He was
fascinated by the technical resources of his stage and knew
exactly what the actors could do with it; and he had the courage to take a large chunk of history out of Holinshed's
Chronicles and transmute it into real theatre material. The
series is unplayable today, if only for its lack of characterization and its jingoistic view of English history, but in its own
day it ranked as one of the best series of productions that the
London theatre had to offer.

Another enormously successful play that Shakespeare wrote
at about the same time was *Titus Andronicus.** In the following century there were playgoers who claimed doggedly that
Titus Andronicus and *The Spanish Tragedy* were the best
plays ever written, and they certainly were if violent and
bloodthirsty action is any criterion. Shakespeare's play was a
severe test of the skill of the actors in staging atrocity scenes,

* The first mention of a production date for *Titus Andronicus* is January
24, 1594, when the Earl of Sussex's men played it at the Rose. But it was
licensed for publication two weeks later and the title page stated that three
different companies had played it, those of the Earl of Derby, the Earl of
Pembroke and the Earl of Sussex. The production date of 1594 applies only
to Sussex's company, so it is evident that both the other acting companies
must have played *Titus Andronicus* earlier than this.

since Titus has a hand chopped off in full view of the audience, his sons' heads are brought onstage, and his daughter Lavinia is instructed by the stage directions to enter with "her hands cut off, and her tongue cut out." Lavinia holds a basin between the stumps of her hands to catch the blood of the men who have raped her, and her father, Titus, serves them up in a pie for their mother to eat.

A modern reader, faced with such a wave of bloodshed, would be likely to conclude that Shakespeare had been carried away by his desire to please his audience and had packed his play with witless atrocities calculated to please the lowest element in the groundlings. As a matter of fact, the exact opposite would be much nearer the truth. Shakespeare was trying to write a "noble Roman history" and conform to the best standards of the classical drama as they were understood in his day.

The model with whom Shakespeare was wrestling at this point was Seneca. To the Renaissance mind Seneca stood for all that was impressive and valuable in ancient tragedy, and although he was unfortunately a heathen writer many useful morals could be drawn from his work. Queen Elizabeth herself had translated parts of some of his plays, and various poets had combined to make the translation of his ten tragedies that was published in 1581. Ever since the cultured young gentlemen of the Inns of Court and the universities had been writing plays, Seneca had been one of their most revered models, and at the violent climax of a Senecan imitation put on at Trinity College, Cambridge, a gentlewoman in the audience "fell distracted and never recovered."

Seneca had written his plays for a rather clever, weary Roman audience who heard them recited rather than acted, and his combination of rhetoric and horror was excellently adapted to keep his audience awake. When his plays were translated into English they were read by a young, excitable public, deeply impressed by the moral maxims and fascinated by the atrocities that were described. When Shakespeare read Seneca, he was especially impressed by the story of Thyestes, in which the hero is served a banquet of his children's flesh. It would not have occurred to him to criticize the revered Seneca, whom even the rigid French classicists took as their model; but for vulgar sensationalism there is nothing in *Titus Andronicus* to match Seneca's description of the cooking of the children, with the chunks of flesh making the broth and the livers sizzling on the spit.

Shakespeare could not transfer Seneca intact to the public stage, since no Elizabethan audience would have been content with six characters, a messenger and a very chatty chorus. On the contrary, Shakespeare loaded his stage for *Titus Andronicus* as thoroughly as he had done for the *Henry VI* trilogy. In the first scene he used the outer and inner stage, the trap door and the balcony, and crowded the area with processions and warriors and all the visual excitement that a crowd of splendidly dressed actors could offer. Nevertheless, when an Elizabethan went to a play like *Titus Andronicus* he would know that he had had a cultural experience. The various quotations from classical authors that Shakespeare had so earnestly imbedded in the text would have told him so. Even the rape and mutilation of Lavinia had classical justification, since it was based on Ovid's story of Philomela.

William Shakespeare was an excited, ambitious young man, eager to succeed as a writer and seizing on every kind of assistance he could get. London was the literary capital of England, and as a Londoner he was bombarded by a series of literary influences from every direction. When Geoffrey Chaucer started to write poetry, more than two centuries earlier, there was only one model he could imitate—the French school of academic love poetry. But William Shakespeare found new models wherever he turned, and the time of his youth, like that of most good writers, was spent in constant, excited experimentation with first one way of writing and then another.*

Having attempted a Roman tragedy in *Titus Andronicus*, Shakespeare attempted a Roman comedy in *The Comedy of Errors*. In the same way that Seneca was the chief model for classical tragedy in the Renaissance, Plautus was the chief model for classical comedy. Nothing in Plautus was more popular than the device of the identical twins in his *Menaechmi*, and for the past fifty years the Italian dramatists had been offering complicated variations on this theme to the Italian theatre-going public. The Italian playwrights operated under fixed rules, for the stage always had to represent a city square, with a series of houses in the background. In the case of a comedy, these houses were usually a church, a home and a brothel. "Especially there must not want a brothel," an Italian stage architect said sternly, for the rules of action in classic Italian comedy were as rigid as the rules of stagecraft. The subject of Ariosto's first comedy "was a most beautiful one of two youths enamoured of two harlots who had been brought from Taranto by a pander," and Raphael himself had supervised the scenery for the first production.

Shakespeare did his best to write a correct Italian comedy in *The Comedy of Errors*. He planned the play as though it were going to be shown on a fixed set, with three doors opening off a market place. One door led to the abbey, one to the house of Antipholus, and one to the house of the courtesan. Shakespeare also kept rigidly to the classical doctrine of the three unities, and all the action takes place in the city of Ephesus in a single day. Both in staging and in construction the play is a neat, tight imitation of academic Italian comedy, which in turn was an imitation of Plautus, and the complicated

* Youth is a comparative term, since Shakespeare was twenty-eight in 1592. But Chaucer was about the same age when he wrote his first important poem, a piece of slavish imitation of the French that shows almost no signs of his future genius. Both men developed comparatively late as writers and both men went through almost exactly the same period of imitation in their twenties.

intrigue is expertly handled. The one characteristically Elizabethan thing about the play is its riot of puns. Shakespeare
never lost his youthful enthusiasm for word-play, and his
audience was so well trained in the art of listening that they
could hear a complicated joke on *hour* and *whore* and set up
a howl of recognition.

During this period of experimentation Shakespeare tried still
another way of writing. Ten years earlier one of the great
figures on the literary scene had been John Lyly, who had
become a playwright after making a great success with a
novel called *Euphues*. Popular novelists like Greene and Munday and Gosson had produced immediate imitations and even
Tom Nashe admitted that he had read *Euphues* devotedly
when he was "a little ape at Cambridge." The rhetorical flour-
ishes and the mannered, ornamental style that Lyly used were
not original with him, and at least one professor of Latin at
Oxford had been training his students to use the same style in
their Latin prose; but it struck the London public, with its
greedy ear for words, as an altogether new and charming way
to write. Lyly had acquired the patronage of the Earl of Oxford and had gone on to write graceful light comedies that
were too slight for the public stages but very well suited to
the boy companies that were acting in small private theatres
at Blackfriars and at St. Paul's.

By the 90's the vein of euphuism was wearing a little thin;
but Lyly's rhetoric was still the model for a good deal of
fashionable writing and Shakespeare was following what was
still one of the main literary currents of the day when he
wrote *Love's Labour's Lost*. The play cannot be dated but
Shakespeare apparently took the names of his three young
lords from the news pamphlets that were coming out about
the wars in France. These pamphlets ceased when Henry of
Navarre became a Catholic in 1593, but before that date
printers like Richard Field brought the public news of men
like the Duc de Longueville, the Duc de Mayenne and Mare-

chal Biron. Shakespeare's little comedy has no relation to actual French history, but he made his hero the King of Navarre and named his three lords Longaville, Dumaine and Berowne.

In *Love's Labour's Lost* Shakespeare gave final proof that he was capable of doing almost any kind of writing and doing it well. The piece is as formal and lively as a galliard and was no more intended to be taken seriously. It is the work of a young man who was beginning to know all the literary angles and how to handle them to maintain a continuous ripple of laughter from his audience. Shakespeare plays a game with words and does a light-hearted parody of most of the literary fashions of the day, from euphuism to sonneteering. He even introduces an engaging sketch of a group of earnest amateur actors trying to present a play while their aristocratic audience makes continuous, gentle fun of them. In his aristocrats Shakespeare presents the first of his lively, mocking young men and his delightful, quick-witted girls, and although they are conventionalized sketches in comparison with what he was to do later, they manage to show the breath of life even in their endless Renaissance discussions on the subject of love. He took the stock Italian comedy figures of the Pedant and the Braggart, and in Holofernes and Armado continued them in their long and honorable tradition. Holofernes is an exact copy of what every comic schoolmaster was supposed to be on the stage, which was already an ancient tradition when Sir Philip Sidney wrote an entertainment to be given at one of the Earl of Leicester's entertainments in 1578 and had the schoolmaster start off, "Let me delicidate the very intrinsecal maribone of the matter."

Love's Labour's Lost is a Londoner's play, written for people who knew all the latest jokes with words. It was written by a man who had been watching and listening even more intently than he had been reading, and who could enter into the aristocratic life of the city with the same ease he could enter into Plautus or the court of Henry VI. But although it is a city play, few Londoners could have written the two country songs that bring it to a close. Nor would anyone but Shakespeare have dared to end his courtly dance of words with a winter song that shows a real country village in cold weather.

All these plays were written in the early 90's and it seems reasonably clear that most of them had been produced before Robert Greene attacked the young actor-turned-playwright in September, 1592. Greene's death happened to coincide with an event that created a chasm in the theatrical world and destroyed the market for new plays entirely. For on the 7th of September, 1592, the London Council put the plague orders into effect and all the theatres were closed until 1594.

The London Council had been attacking the theatres all that year. The mayor and aldermen began with a complaint to Archbishop Whitgift in February in which they asked his help to save the youth of the city, whose manners were being "infected with many evil and ungodly qualities by reason of the wanton and profane devices represented upon the stages." At the end of May there was a riot by some apprentices in Southwark, for which the Council instantly blamed the evil taught by the theatres, and in June all "profane spectacles" were forbidden until the 29th of September. By the 7th of September, however, the plague had made such inroads on the city that the plague orders were put into effect and all assemblies were suppressed within seven miles of London.

This was the same plague that had struck Stratford the year Shakespeare was born, and it had been a frequent visitor in London. The plague orders were invoked whenever the deaths passed a certain number, and represented the best the city authorities could devise. Infected houses were put under a twenty-day quarantine, every householder had to wash his part of the street twice a day, graves had to be six feet deep, two discreet women from each parish were to do the shopping and nursing for the quarantined, with the parish paying for their services if necessary, and the College of Physicians was to designate a certain number of its members to handle infected patients only. Human nature being what it is, the parish nurses were not always discreet and the graves were not always six feet deep, but the London Council had done its best with a problem that was both perennial and insoluble.

A wise and loving citizen of London named John Howes had suggested in 1587 that tax-supported public housing would go a long way to rid the city of the plague. "Let London take example of Augusta in Germany, where the citizens have builded . . . houses for the poor people, in a convenient air, with three rooms, chimneys and privies and little yards." Let London "erect three or four hundred tenements and remove the poor people out of those filthy alleys, and let the alleys be razed down to the ground and converted to open yards and gardens, and so shall the city be . . . delivered of a thousand infections." Such a suggestion must have seemed preposterous to the London Council, since it was already known what caused plagues. As a London preacher aptly phrased it during an earlier visitation of God's scourge, "The cause of plagues is sin, if you look to it well; and the cause of sin are plays; therefore the cause of plagues are plays." The restraint put upon the actors in September was certainly legitimate, since public assemblies tended to spread the infection, but it would have been a good thing for London if the Council had listened more to John Howes and less to the preachers.

The actors did the only thing left for them to do: they went on tour. They continued to hope that the London theatres might reopen shortly, and Henslowe did manage one brief winter season at the Rose. But on the 28th of January the Council repeated its order suppressing all assemblies except for divine service within seven miles of London, and theatre business did not become normal in London again until the 3rd of June, 1594.

The market for new plays was of course destroyed during this two-year period. Touring actors could not afford the risk and expense of trying out new productions. They took with them only plays that they knew would be successful and even these were heavily cut for country audiences, partly because they would not understand London allusions and partly because the companies were smaller and more parts had to be doubled.

To increase their strength, some of the companies amalgamated. Edward Alleyn, for instance, belonged to the Admiral's men, but he joined forces with the actors of Lord Strange's company and sent his wife long letters from the provinces. Like nearly all the other actors Alleyn was a very domestic man and felt his exile from his household in London keenly, one postscript imploring his wife for news. "Mouse, you send me no news of any thing; you should send me of your domestical matters, such things as happen at home, as how your distilled water proves, or this, or that, or any thing what you will. And, Jug, I pray you, let my orange-tawny stockings of woollen be dyed a very good black against I come home to wear in the winter. You sent me not word of my garden but next time you will. But remember this in any case, that all that bed which was parsley in the month of September, you sow it with spinach for then is the time. I would do it myself but we shall not come home till All Hallows tide and so, sweet mouse, farewell, and brook our long journey with patience."

Alleyn was the son-in-law of Philip Henslowe, the theatre owner, and Henslowe wrote that the spinach bed was sown but that a rival company of actors had collapsed. This was Lord Pembroke's company. In spite of a good collection of play scripts, including at least one of Shakespeare's, the company dissolved on tour in August, 1593, and its members had to pawn their costumes to pay their expenses.

Many of the companies tried to help their finances by selling their stocks of play-books to the printers, a practice they normally avoided because it cut down the potential audiences and gave other companies an opportunity to see the texts of their plays. There was an abnormal sale of play scripts during the plague period, and whereas four plays were entered for publication in 1592, twenty-three were entered in 1594. Many of these plays appeared in print with the text in a jumbled, corrupt condition, showing unmistakable signs of having been reconstructed from the memories of the actors. The actors invented where they could not remember or even inserted lines from different plays altogether. But at least a great many plays were brought into print that otherwise would have vanished forever, and it is better to have them in pirated versions than not to have them at all.

Meanwhile the playwrights themselves had fallen on evil days, and one by one the great names were disappearing. Robert Greene had died four days before the plague orders went into effect and was buried in a winding sheet that cost four shillings of his landlord's money. His friend, Tom Lodge, had gone on a naval expedition to make his fortune; the voyage was a disastrous one from the beginning, and Lodge arrived back in England during the plague period, almost penniless, to start a long legal wrangle with his brother William. John Lyly's career as a playwright had ended when the company known as Paul's Boys was dissolved in 1590 and he tried desperately to get some kind of a position at Court for the rest of the decade, living on what he called "dead hopes."

As for the greatest of the university playwrights, his fall was the most sudden and spectacular. On the 30th of May, 1593, Christopher Marlowe was stabbed in a tavern kept by one Eleanor Bull. According to the coroner's report, there had been a quarrel over the bill between Marlowe and one Ingram Frizer. Marlowe seized Frizer's dagger and gave him two head wounds, and Frizer got his dagger back and killed Marlowe instantly with a single stab above the right eye.

The quarrel may have been over the reckoning, as the

coroner's jury decided. It may have been political in origin, since Marlowe had served as a government agent. But Marlowe's own contemporaries were convinced they knew the real cause of it: it was the judgment of heaven on a wicked man who did not believe in the Christian religion. During May an informer had been drawing up a long list of Marlowe's sins as a freethinker, ranging from rowdy remarks about the Holy Ghost to his conviction that religion was only a device to hold men in bondage. Thomas Kyd, who had once roomed with Marlowe, was brought in for questioning by the Privy Council on the subject of Marlowe's "monstrous opinions," and Kyd wrote a letter on the subject of Marlowe's wicked nature and his own pure one that reads unpleasantly today but was a natural Elizabethan reaction to the horrors of atheism. When Gabriel Harvey heard that Marlowe was dead he concluded that the plague had killed him and saw the hand of God in the event, striking him down for "his toad conceit." By the end of the decade a new theory had turned up, that "Marlowe was stabbed to death by a bawdy serving-man, a rival of his in a lewd love." But whatever the exact circumstances, it was generally agreed by Marlowe's smug contemporaries that he was a wicked man and his death was a judgment on him.

Apart from Shakespeare, almost the only playwrights that remained were Thomas Kyd and Thomas Nashe. Since there was no market for plays, Nashe's chief literary contribution to that rainy and dismal year of 1593 was a composition called *Christ's Tears Over Jerusalem*, in which he pointed out with impeccable orthodoxy that the plague was a punishment for sin. "As great a desolation as Jerusalem hath London deserved," reported Nashe to his readers, recognizing a changed literary market when he saw one.

Thomas Kyd's activities as a writer in 1593 were even more peculiar. The author of the popular *Spanish Tragedy* was writing a drama called *Cornelia*, which was not intended to be acted but was designed to assist the Countess of Pembroke in her campaign to raise the artistic level of the English drama.

Mary, Countess of Pembroke, was the sister of Sir Philip Sidney, a charming, forceful, intellectual woman who considered it a duty to her dead brother to try to raise the level of English writing. The theatre-going public in its uncouth way had failed to realize that just across the Channel a great playwright was writing great plays. His name was Robert Garnier and all the best critics in France joined in admiration of his work. Garnier's taste was so civilized that he managed to be a Senecan without any of Seneca's harrowing details, and the Countess of Pembroke was convinced that nothing could be better suited to raise the current low level of English drama than a complete translation of the works of Robert Garnier.

Mary started the movement herself by translating Garnier's play on Marc Antony, which was published in 1592 in a charming little octavo volume, beautifully printed on fine paper. She encouraged her little coterie of poets to do likewise, and perhaps her greatest success was with Samuel Daniel, who did a play on Cleopatra. Daniel was exalted by his mission of helping to "chase away . . . gross barbarism" and he succeeded in avoiding any indecorous action in his play by having a messenger's report that filled nine pages.

Thomas Kyd then undertook to purge himself of the disgrace of having written popular plays for the penny public, and translated Garnier's play on Cornelia. Kyd's French was not quite perfect, but the play itself was impeccable since nothing happened in it at all. The scholars praised the book and Kyd was planning to follow it with a similar work on Portia; but he suddenly died in the winter of 1594, the last of the old popular dramatists and one who had turned his back completely on the popular drama.

A period like the plague, in which all normal theatre activity in London was at a standstill, was a good opportunity for any popular playwright to try his hand at another kind of writing. Especially was this true if he were an ambitious writer and wanted to be admired by a more select and intellectual public than the ordinary theatre-goer. Shakespeare had been growing increasingly ambitious, and both *Titus Andronicus* and *The Comedy of Errors* show an attempt to write in the classical manner. The plague gave him both time and opportunity, for an actor did not go on tour during the winter months, and it was probably late in 1592 that he wrote the classical narrative he called *Venus and Adonis*.

Nothing that Shakespeare had done up to this point counted as real writing. His plays were not his property. They belonged to whatever company had bought them, to publish or not as the company saw fit, and when the first of them began to straggle into print at the end of the plague period they appeared anonymously. No literary man took these cheap little quarto texts seriously, but *Venus and Adonis* was a different matter altogether. It was designed as a conscious work of art and written seriously and conscientiously according to the best models.

There is no mistaking the ambitious frame of mind in which the young poet wrote his first real poem. The correct thing to do was to begin a work of this kind with a Latin quotation, and the motto that Shakespeare chose from Ovid is almost touching in its arrogance.

> *Vilia miretur vulgus; mihi flavus Apollo*
> *Pocula Castalia plena ministret aqua.*

"Let the base mob admire what is vile; golden-haired Apollo may serve me cups filled with water from the Muses' spring." This was the same contempt for the literary taste of the "penny knaves" that was conventional with well-educated young gentlemen and that Thomas Lodge had expressed at the close of his narrative poem on Glaucus and Scilla a few years earlier. Shakespeare used the same metre that Lodge had used in his poem, but his model was not a single narrative so much as the whole flood of ornamental classical narratives in verse in which the young writers of England sought to show that they were the worthy heirs of antiquity. *Venus and Adonis* is steeped in classicism, in the rather limited Renaissance meaning of the word, and is full of the rich imagery and antique rhetorical devices that educated Renaissance readers had been taught to admire.

If *Venus and Adonis* had been written by a gentleman it would probably not have been published at all, for gentlemen circulated their work only in manuscript and did not permit it to be handled by the general public in book stalls. Shakespeare did not belong to this exalted group and like the university writers he was only too anxious to find a reliable printer who would publish the book for him. Whether through friendship or for some other reason his choice was Richard Field, son of old Henry Field of Stratford who had died in the summer of 1591 and whose goods had been appraised by his neighbor, John Shakespeare. Richard Field was living at Blackfriars, where he owned his own press and was one of the twenty-two master printers that were permitted to operate in the city of London.

Richard Field was not only the printer of Shakespeare's poem but its publisher also. On the 18th of April, 1593, he filed notice with the Stationers' Company that he was the owner of "a book entitled Venus and Adonis" which had been duly licensed by Archbishop Whitgift and by one of the wardens of the Stationers' Company, and he paid the usual fee of sixpence to have the information entered on the Stationers' Register. This served as a copyright notice and made it impossible, or at least difficult, for another printer to steal the book and print it himself. Only about sixty-five percent of the books that got into print were registered, but the practice protected the printer's investment and made it possible for him to pay the author a larger sum for the manuscript than if he had to run the risk of piracy. These payments to the author varied from a few free copies of the book, when the printer feared the worst, to as much as forty pounds for a really popular book on theology. It would be a fair estimate that Shakespeare got about two pounds from Field for the manuscript. Certainly he did not get more than that, since from the publishing point of view he was an unknown writer.

Field did not handle much general literature and his publications were mostly books on theology, textbooks and classics. When his master, Thomas Vautrollier, had run the press, his chief contribution to literature had been Sir Thomas North's translation of Plutarch's *Lives*, and Field in his turn had published *The Art of English Poesie* and a very elaborate English version of Ariosto's *Orlando Furioso*. But his books were mostly of the scholarly sort and Field was equipped to set type in both Greek and Hebrew.

Venus and Adonis was a little outside the usual run of Field's printing, but he made Shakespeare's narrative poem into a handsome little volume, with good presswork and careful proofreading. Some extra copies of the title page were struck off, in the usual fashion, to be fastened to various posts around town and used as advertising, and the title page carried the information that the book could be bought "at the sign of the White Greyhound in Paul's Churchyard."

Richard Field had no retail outlet of his own in Paul's Churchyard, so he had arranged for the book to be sold through the shop of John Harrison, senior, who was one of the major London publishers. Field had printed two books in Latin for Harrison, but they would have known each other in any case as fellow members of the Company of Stationers. All the printers belonged to a regular chartered guild, with a hall on the southwest side of Paul's Churchyard and a handsome coat of arms full of books and birds and flowers. The Stationers' Company was one of the most strictly run of the

London guilds, for the government had no intention of allowing seditious printing and the slightest irregularity was severely checked. It was the Stationers' Company that was responsible for tracking down an illegal printer who was trying to do presswork in a tailor's shop while he kept his letters in a nearby hen-house, and it was the Stationers' Company that formally burned all banned books in the Hall kitchen. Discipline was handled through an elaborate organization headed by a Master, two Wardens and a Court of Assistants, and the Master was the highest post in the company that a printer could attain. John Harrison had twice been Master of the company when he accepted *Venus and Adonis* for sale in his shop, the White Greyhound, so that Shakespeare's first poem was launched under the best possible auspices.

Every book needed a patron to whom it could be dedicated, and an experienced man of letters like Gervase Markham could often pack several into a single book. When Markham wrote a poetic narrative on a sea-fight, he opened with a dedication to Lord Mountjoy and announced that he was "eternally" his Lordship's. He then, on the next page, offered his work to the "sacred hand" of the Earl of Sussex. This was followed with a dedication to Sir Edward Wingfield and another "to the right honorable Henry Wriothesley, Earl of Southampton and Baron of Tichfield" whom he implored to favor his work.

> Vouchsafe to sweet it with thy blessed tongue . . .
> So shall my tragic lays be blest by thee
> And from thy lips suck their eternity.

A frenzied obeisance of this kind was correct in addressing a man like the Earl of Southampton, who was one of the most glittering of the younger generation at Court. Even Tom Nashe, who was no courtier, grew almost fulsome in his dedication to Southampton: "A new brain, a new wit, a new style.

a new soul will I get me, to canonize your name to posterity." Barnabe Barnes grew poetic over Southampton's "gracious eyes, those heavenly lamps which give the Muses light," and John Florio said in his dedication, "To me and many more, the glorious and gracious sunshine of your Honor hath infused light and life."

In comparison with the usual dedication to the Earl of Southampton, Shakespeare's address to him is both sober and dignified. "To the Right Honorable Henry Wriothesley, Earl of Southampton, and Baron of Tichfield. Right Honorable, I know not how I shall offend in dedicating my unpolished lines to your Lordship, nor how the world will censure me for choosing so strong a prop to support so weak a burthen: only, if your Honour seem but pleased, I account myself highly praised, and vow to take advantage of all idle hours, till I have honoured you with some graver labour. But if the first heir of my invention prove deformed, I shall be sorry it had so noble a godfather, and never after ear so barren a land, for fear it yield me still so bad a harvest. I leave it to your honorable survey, and your Honour to your heart's content; which I wish may always answer your own wish, and the world's hopeful expectation. Your Honour's in all duty, William Shakespeare."

There is nothing in this dedication to show that Shakespeare knew the Earl of Southampton personally. He merely hoped the poem would please him and offered it in a dignified way that is a pleasant contrast to the average Elizabethan dedication. He called the poem "the first heir of my invention" because it would not have occurred to the young playwright-turned-poet that his stage plays were worth mentioning, as from Southampton's point of view they certainly were not.

Shakespeare probably chose Southampton as his patron because *Venus and Adonis* was a love poem. The Earl was only nineteen years old in that spring of 1593, and the sensuous style and mild eroticism of the poem were the kind a young man would like. The Earl was a newcomer at Court, and some of his contemporaries considered him a rather unstable young man. His father and mother had become estranged when he was a small boy and when his father died, leaving him the bulk of an enormous fortune, he also left a large sum of money to the small Earl's sister on the implacable condition that she was not to live in the same house with their mother. Lord Burghley brought the boy up, and whereas Burghley's own son Robert was a model of industry and propriety, young Southampton was more difficult to manage in spite of the beautifully written exercises he sent his guardian from Cambridge to show his progress. When he left school he was supposed to marry Burghley's granddaughter and refused, and in 1594 a Court lady refused to marry him because he was so unstable and "so easily carried away." The one steadfast emotion in Southampton's life was probably his reverence for the Earl of Essex, whom he worshipped with all the ardor that a young man can feel for a romantic and slightly older one.

At nineteen Southampton was a beautiful figure with his jewels and his laces and his respectful coterie of writing men, a patron young enough to enjoy a love poem and educated enough to appreciate the way it was written. Like all the young men of the day he was brought up on Ovid, and it was to "Ovid's wanton muse" that Nashe had appealed when he wrote an especially outspoken piece of eroticism in *The Choice of Valentines*. Shakespeare's poem is both innocent and dignified in comparison with Nashe's, but it belongs to the same general group and would have appealed to the same kind of reader.

When young Elizabethans read *Venus and Adonis* it was not for its noble thoughts on the danger of lust or for its charming country descriptions, but for the detailed description of an attempted seduction and for the lush, rather overwrought Renaissance imagery. There is a risk in this kind of writing, unless the reader himself is also young and very much in earnest, that the flood of words may give an occasionally comic effect that was not intended. Even Shakespeare did not escape lapses of this kind, as in the scene where Adonis attempts to revive Venus and "wrings her nose." When Venus mourns the death of Adonis, the language gets even more out of control.

"Aye me!" she cries, and twenty times, "Woe, woe!"

As a character in one of Shakespeare's later plays remarked dryly, "This passion, and the death of a dear friend, would go near to make a man look sad." But Shakespeare was not yet at the point when he thought that unrestrained hyperbole was rather funny, and certainly his readers were not.

Venus and Adonis was an enormous success. It went through ten editions in Shakespeare's lifetime and the handsome little book was read and re-read until it fell to pieces. It was lavishly quoted in anthologies, and a Cambridge play written four years later accuses one susceptible young man of keeping the poem under his pillow with a picture of "sweet Mr. Shakespeare" on his study wall.

Shakespeare at once set about writing the "graver" poem that he had promised if the first one was a success. This new poem would not appeal so much to the young and giddy, who liked love stories, but to their more reverend seniors who valued a poem for its moral instruction. It told the story of Tarquin's rape of Lucrece, and was even longer and more ornamental than the first one had been.

Shakespeare had unquestionably met Southampton after the success of *Venus and Adonis,* and Southampton must have shown his appreciation of the poem with a generous gift, since that was what a patron was for. The tone of the second dedication is much warmer and more personal, even though the word "love" had the force in the Renaissance that the word "friendship" has now. "The love I dedicate to your Lordship is without end; whereof this pamphlet, without beginning, is but a superfluous moiety. The warrant I have of your honorable disposition, not the worth of my untutored lines, makes it assured of acceptance. What I have done is yours; what I have to do is yours; being part of all I have, devoted yours. Were my worth greater, my duty would show greater; meantime, as it is, it is bound to your Lordship, to whom I wish long life, still lengthened with happiness. Your Lordship's in all duty, William Shakespeare."

Shakespeare's second narrative poem, like his first one, was in imitation of the best contemporary models. This time his chief model was Samuel Daniel, who had made a great success in 1592 with *The Complaint of Rosamund*. Daniel's poem went through two editions the year of publication, for "everyone passioneth when he readeth the afflicted death of Daniel's distressed Rosamund." Daniel's poem had the further merit of being stuffed with moral reflections, which each reader could copy out in his commonplace book, and Shakespeare could hardly have chosen a more popular model.

Shakespeare used the same metre as Daniel and expanded some of his devices. Daniel gave a brief description of a casket ornamented with pictures from classical legends, which Rosamund connects with her own problem, and Shakespeare gives an extremely lengthy description of a wall painting so that Lucrece can do the same. Rosamund has fifteen stanzas of vocal lamentation before she succeeds in killing herself, and Lucrece's "sad dirge" before her suicide takes almost as long. Shakespeare included the same kind of moral observations that had been admired in Daniel, and in turn his own poem took its place as one of the most extravagantly admired productions of the decade. The narrative was more popular even than *Venus and Adonis*, with four editions called for in six years, and an anthology that was compiled at the end of the decade had ninety-one quotations from *The Rape of Lucrece*.

Richard Field did not publish *Lucrece*. That honor went to John Harrison of the White Greyhound who evidently realized at once that William Shakespeare was going to be a valuable literary commodity. Harrison retained Field to do the printing on the new book, but he took out the copyright himself, entering *Lucrece* in the Stationers' Register on the ninth of May, 1594. He also wanted to publish future editions of *Venus and Adonis*, and arranged with Field to have the copyright transferred to him the following month.

The success of his two poems found Shakespeare in an enviable position in the spring of 1594. No poet, especially a beginning poet, could have asked for more. He had a wealthy, influential and satisfied patron who was one of the highest noblemen in the land. He had a publisher who was one of the most important men in his profession and who was obviously deeply interested in his career. He was beginning to get a chorus of commendation from the critics, especially for "all-praiseworthy Lucretia," and his position in the eyes of posterity, if he kept on as he had begun, was assured. As Richard Barnfield apostrophized him four years later, he was a poet

> Whose Venus, and whose Lucrece, sweet and chaste,
> Thy name in fame's immortal book have placed.

There was nothing in this to prevent Shakespeare continuing with his profession as an actor, but it gave him no special incentive to go on writing plays. The average play did not bring its author more than six pounds, and the approval of Harrison and Southampton would have guaranteed him much more than that for a new narrative poem. Moreover, a poet could not get a reputation by writing plays, which were either not printed at all in 1594 or else flooding the book stalls in cheap, badly printed quartos that were better off anonymous. At its best a play could bring nothing but the uncritical applause of the "penny knaves," while a handsomely printed and successful book that went through several editions brought a poet not only the praise of his contemporaries but a continuing name to generations as yet unborn.

It is no exaggeration to say that the spring of 1594 was the turning point of Shakespeare's life as a writer. *Lucrece* was obviously going to be a success, as *Venus and Adonis* had been, and it was time to fulfill the promise Shakespeare had made in his last dedication to Southampton and write him another poem.

The career of every writer is strewn with various opportunities for destroying himself. If Shakespeare had continued on the course he had planned for himself, of writing for the Earl of Southampton and the better-class Elizabethan reader instead of for the penny public, his genius for characterization would have been permanently blocked. He would have gone on writing handsome ornate poems that were as rich in detail as a well-made tapestry but equally lacked the breath of life. When the special Renaissance cult that produced such poems receded at the end of the decade, Shakespeare's work would have receded with it; he would have become one of the many minor Elizabethan writers whose works interest the literary scholar but have no life at all for the general public.

One of the qualities that make a writer great is his instinct for avoiding a pitfall that can destroy him. Whether or not Shakespeare was consciously aware of the fact, his genius depended on having complete writing freedom. More than any writer in the world's history, Shakespeare needed space around him, space to try anything he wanted without any literary rules to hamper him or any literary specialists to eye his work and pass their small judgments.

There was no space of this kind in Southampton's narrow circle, any more than there ever is in any special literary clique or fashion. The only audience that could give him that kind of liberty was the penny public of the London theatre, the ordinary London citizens who did not judge by Italian rules of the unities or French rules of diction or English rules of decorum but only by what they enjoyed. They did not want words to be treated as masters, to be respectfully arranged according to the best rules. They wanted them to be treated as servants, to bring them real people and real emotions.

In the spring of 1594, when the theatres reopened after the plague, Shakespeare turned his back forever on the literary success he had wanted so ardently when he began writing *Venus and Adonis*. He apparently made no further use of the standing he had achieved with Southampton, and after 1594 there is no document that shows any further connection between the two men at all. He made no further use of his standing with John Harrison and never offered him another manuscript. He wrote some sonnets but he did not want to print them, and they were not published until fifteen years later in what was obviously an unauthorized edition, put into print by a minor figure in the book trade who had neither a shop nor a press. The only poem he ever again wrote for publication was a short piece called "The Phoenix and the Turtle" which appeared at the beginning of the next decade in a book called *Love's Martyr*. Shakespeare was one of four playwrights who contributed verses to the project, which was in honor of Sir John Salisbury, and the contribution seems to have been a good-natured gesture to a friend of his—about the equivalent of a nineteenth-century poet writing some verses for a memory book.

Everything else that Shakespeare wrote for the rest of his life belonged to the company of actors he joined in the spring of 1594. The company controlled the copyright of all his plays, to be published or not as it saw fit, and Shakespeare was content to be merely a working member of the company.

William Shakespeare was like his father in one thing at least: when he decided to do something, he did it thoroughly. Such complete devotion to the theatre was not merely unusual in an Elizabethan writer; it was unheard of, especially when a writer had, like Shakespeare, achieved so lofty a literary eminence in so short a time. Even if he had been unwilling to continue with narrative poems, he might have written court masques, like Ben Jonson and Samuel Daniel and Francis Beaumont. Or, like other playwrights, he might have written city pageants, or verses for special public occasions, or even the complimentary poems that most writers turned out as a matter of course to be printed in the front of their friends' books. Even Thomas Heywood, who spent over forty years in the theatre as actor and playwright, wrote nondramatic works so that his name would not be lost to posterity, and all the other practicing playwrights, from Thomas Dekker to George Chapman, did the same. When the elderly Lady Helen Branch died in the spring of 1594, a writer suggested publicly that an elegy from the author of · *Lucrece* would make a fitting memorial, and when Queen Elizabeth died another writer again called on Shakespeare to write a funeral ode. Shakespeare wrote nothing, nor did he join the almost unanimous chorus of poetical voices that welcomed King James to the throne. He was the one writer of the period who wrote for the stage and for the stage only.

The next sixteen years of Shakespeare's life are of a creative violence unparalleled in literary history. It was as though a great wind had suddenly found its true course and could blow free.

Chapter 6

BY THE spring of 1594 the plague had worn itself out in London. The weather improved, the splendid shops in Goldsmiths' Row were given a new coat of paint, and a goldsmith named Francis Langley began to plan a new theatre in Southwark that would hold three thousand people. The actors who had survived the difficulties of the past two years began to reorganize, and two great acting companies emerged that were to dominate the London stage for the rest of the reign.

One of these two companies was headed by Edward Alleyn and financed by his wealthy father-in-law, Philip Henslowe. During the plague Alleyn had acted in the provinces with Lord Strange's company, but in 1594 he again headed his own company and began a long tenancy of his father-in-law's theatre, the Rose. The patron of the company was Charles, Lord Howard of Effingham, who had commanded the fleet against the Spanish Armada. Since he held the post of Lord High Admiral of England, Alleyn's company of actors was known as the Admiral's company.

Alleyn's chief rivals were the actors with whom he had played in the provinces during the plague. At that time they were under the patronage of Lord Strange, and when he died in the spring of 1594 they found themselves a new patron in Henry, Lord Hunsdon, who was the Queen's first cousin and her closest living relative. Lord Hunsdon was a member of the Privy Council and had succeeded Lord Howard in the important court position of Lord Chamberlain, so that his group of actors was known as the Chamberlain's company.

It is known that William Shakespeare joined the Chamberlain's company when it was formed in 1594 because he is listed as one of the three actors who received payment for that year's Christmas performances at Court. It is not known whether he worked for the company earlier, when it was under the patronage of Lord Strange, since his name is on none of the scattered lists that have survived; but he remained with this group of actors for the rest of his professional life.

The men who made up this company were for all practical purposes closer to Shakespeare than his own brothers, for he worked with them summer and winter, most of the day and often well into the night, for the next sixteen years. They were his fellow craftsmen, his close personal friends, and in one sense as much the tools of his art as the words he used. They were the medium through which he operated as a playwright to reach the emotions of his audience, and it was one of the most fortunate things in Shakespeare's fortunate life that he worked with so able and intelligent a group of men.

An Elizabethan acting company was organized in such a way that each member was heavily dependent on his fellow members, and the economic life of the troupe depended on selfless and intelligent cooperation. There was joint ownership of costumes and properties and scripts, and in the case of Shakespeare's company a hitherto unheard-of step was eventually taken and there was joint ownership of a theatre building.

The success of this kind of thing depended less on legal agreements than on friendship, and each actor had to be willing to subordinate his personal interests to the welfare of the group as a whole. In the next decade a group of shareholders in another theatre company drew up elaborate articles of agreement which covered every possible contingency from the ownership of the costumes to the payment of the gatherers; but the shareholders' only interest was in making money, and in less than two years the organization had collapsed in a flurry of lawsuits. Shakespeare's company had no need of rigid articles of agreement to keep it from quarrelling, and it was not until the actors' shares began to be inherited by outsiders that there were any lawsuits at all.

Even the enemies of the acting profession were obliged to admit that some actors were "sober, discreet, properly learned, honest householders, and citizens well thought of among their neighbors." The description is an excellent one of the men of Shakespeare's company, who lived quietly and worked hard and saved their brilliance for the stage rather than for taverns and dice.

The leading actor of the company was Richard Burbage, who lived all his life in his father's parish of St. Leonard's, Shoreditch. There his seven children were baptised, and when thieves broke into his house on Holywell Street, five children's aprons were among the articles they stole. Richard Cowley was another member of the Chamberlain's company who lived most of his life on Holywell Street, where he and his wife Elizabeth brought up their four children. (Cowley received a posthumous fame by creating the role of Verges in Shakespeare's *Much Ado about Nothing*.) Shoreditch was a theatrical neighborhood, since both the Theatre and the Curtain were located there, and Shakespeare himself lived for a time within easy walking distance of Holywell Street.

Another major theatrical district was Southwark, where the Rose theatre stood already and where Langley was planning to build the Swan. Several members of the Chamberlain's company lived in Southwark. Augustine Phillips and his wife Anne brought up their five children in St. Savior's parish, and Robert Gough, his brother-in-law and fellow actor, brought up another family of five. Thomas Pope, who also lived in Southwark, was unmarried, but that did not mean he contented himself with a childless household. He brought up a series of fatherless children and had help in rearing them from "good-wife Willingson, who is the keeper of my house." Will Sly, who was also a bachelor, lived most of his life in Southwark, but he died in the house of the Browne family in St. Leonard's parish, Shoreditch, leaving Cuthbert Burbage his sword.

The only two important members of the company who did not live in a theatrical district were John Heminges and Henry Condell. These two actors were neighbors in the parish of St. Mary Aldermanbury, a handsome residential district on the west side of town. John Heminges and his wife Rebecca brought up their fourteen children here and had a comfortable home whose cushions were striped with cloth-of-silver. In a near-by house Henry Condell and his wife Elizabeth brought up nine children. The two men were very active in parish affairs, Condell as a churchwarden and both he and Heminges as trustees, and John Heminges in particular had a well-developed business sense and a capacity for leadership. By 1600 he was handling nearly all the financial affairs of the Chamberlain's company, and he kept that position for the rest of his long life. Heminges was the one to whom other members of the company turned when they were in trouble, and he helped execute their wills and care for their children. He ended as a kind of dean of the acting profession, and a quatrain written on the death of Richard Burbage gives an oblique view of his status in the company.

Then fear not, Burbage, heaven's angry rod,
When thy fellows are angels and old Heminges is God.

Heminges and Condell were the last surviving members of the original company and it was these two who were responsible, in 1623, for issuing the First Folio of Shakespeare's plays.

Shakespeare himself had no settled residence in London, since he had no wife and no children in the city. He lived for a time on Bishopsgate Street, which became Shoreditch Road soon after it passed the city walls and was therefore on the direct route to the Theatre and the Curtain. Later he moved to Southwark and became a neighbor of Augustine Phillips and Thomas Pope, and then he took rooms with a private family on the west side of town and lived in the next parish to Heminges and Condell. Like all the other actors, Shakespeare was a London resident and paid regular city taxes, but he was almost the only member of his company who did not have a permanent home.

Since Shakespeare had no household of his own he was probably not in a position to keep an apprentice, since the whole theory of the apprentice system required a woman in the household. The wives of the actors brought up their husband's apprentices as members of the family; and Rebecca Heminges, with fourteen children of her own, had no trouble in making room for the series of boys to whom her husband was teaching the profession. Alexander Cooke was one of Heminges' apprentices and when he grew up he named one of his daughters Rebecca, evidently after Heminges' wife. Another of Heminges' apprentices was John Rice, who acted with Richard Burbage in a city pageant after Heminges had given him special training for the part. Among Augustine Phillips' series of apprentices was Samuel Gilbourne, and when Phillips died he left his "late apprentice" forty shillings, some velvet hose, his white taffeta doublet, his black taffeta suit, his purple cloak, his sword and his bass viol.

All these young men, Cooke and Rice and Gilbourne, stayed with the company whose members had trained them, and all of them are therefore listed in the First Folio as having acted in Shakespeare's plays. Another name that is listed there is that of Nicholas Tooley, who was apprenticed to Richard Burbage and who went to live with Richard's brother after his master's death. Tooley's will emphasizes how much the presence of a motherly woman in the household meant to a

young man. "I do give unto Mrs. Burbage, the wife of my
good friend Mr. Cuthbert Burbage (in whose house I now
lodge) as a remembrance of my love, in respect of her motherly care over me, the sum of £10. . . . I give unto Mrs. Condell, the wife of my good friend, Mr. Henry Condell, as a
remembrance of my love, the sum of £5."

There is a charming survival of the relationship between
an apprentice and his master's household in a letter sent back
to London when the men of the Chamberlain's company
were still under the patronage of Lord Strange and travelling
with Edward Alleyn in the country. Alleyn wrote a letter
for his apprentice, John Pyk, to send back to Mrs. Alleyn.
John Pyk, who was called "Pig" even in the wardrobe lists,
lavishly sent greetings to everyone in the household, from
Dolly who woke him in the morning to Sara who cleaned his
shoes, with a special message to the old gentleman with whom
he used to fight for the best seat in the chimney corner. He
signed himself "your petty, pretty, prattling, parleying pig"
and announced in a postscript that the letter was written secretly "and my master knows not of it." This final piece of
cheerful nonsense must have made the London household
grin, since the letter is in Alleyn's handwriting.

Alleyn had been married less than a year when he went on
tour with Strange's company, but he got complaints from his
wife that the wives of the other actors received letters more
often than she did. Alleyn seems to have been a very conscientious letter-writer, but Philip Henslowe, his father-in-law,
remarked plaintively, "We had no letter from you, when the
other wives had letters sent." Alleyn's companions, like John
Heminges and Augustine Phillips, must have spent a large
amount of their time when they were on tour in writing letters back to their wives, for the actors whose company Shakespeare joined the following year were the most domestic of
men. Henry Condell named three of his daughters Elizabeth
because he was evidently determined to carry on the name of

his "well-beloved wife." It does not need Phillips' reference in his will to "Anne Phillips, my loving wife" or Heminges' "to my loving wife Rebecca" to show the relationship that existed in most of the households of the Chamberlain's company.

The men of the company brought the same atmosphere into their dealings with each other, and the love that Heminges and Condell express in the First Folio for their "friend and fellow" Shakespeare is an inevitable echo of the affection the actors felt for each other. They left each other bequests in their wills, appointed each other as trustees and executors, and left their children and apprentices to each other's care. Any Elizabethan acting company had to practice a reasonable degree of cooperation among its members if it expected to survive as an economic unit, but only in Shakespeare's company is there so constant an expression of trust and friendship.

From a business point of view, an acting company did not of course operate merely on mutual affection. A successful acting company in London required very high professional standards, and the better the acting the more prosperous the company. Here again Shakespeare was fortunate, since his fellow-actors stood high in the profession.

Richard Burbage was still in his twenties when the Chamberlain's company was formed in 1594; but his father, James Burbage, had been a successful actor before him, and Richard was already competing with the great Edward Alleyn for the position of the most popular actor in London. During his thirty-five years in the acting profession he achieved such a reputation that all London went into mourning for him when he died. He interpreted parts as varied as Hamlet, Othello and King Lear, and one admirer went so far as to say that these characters only "lived in him" and died when he did. An actor's work has no testament but contemporary report and cannot be reconstructed, but from the enthusiastic evidence of his contemporaries it seems evident that Richard Burbage was a really great actor.

Another very brilliant member of the company was Will Kempe, who helped Burbage and Shakespeare collect the money for two Court productions in 1594. Kempe was the greatest comic actor of the 90's, and five years earlier Tom Nashe had hailed him in print as the legitimate successor of the great Tarleton himself. This was shortly after Kempe had returned from the Danish court at Elsinore, where he evidently had had a great success. Equally successful at the Danish court were Thomas Pope and George Bryan, both of whom also became members of the Chamberlain's company; and when Pope and Bryan left Elsinore the King of Denmark sent them in a special carriage to their next place of residence, the court of the Duke of Saxony. At least two writers of the period single out Pope as a comedian, and Thomas Heywood, who was himself an actor, classes him with Augustine Phillips and Will Sly, both of whom also belonged to the Chamberlain's company. "Their deserts yet live in the remembrance of many."

Most of the members of Shakespeare's company cannot be traced in individual parts, since the whole principle of a good repertory company lies in the excellence of the performance as a whole rather than in the brilliance of individual members. But it seems safe to say that the Chamberlain's company consisted of an unusually experienced and intelligent group of actors, and that Shakespeare must have had a high standing as an actor or he would not have been asked to join them.

The effect of all this on Shakespeare as a playwright is worth considering. In the first place, when he wrote a play he was sure that it would be given a careful, sympathetic and intelligent interpretation by men who had worked together for a long time and knew their trade thoroughly. The best script in the world cannot survive a bad production and, as a contemporary testified, "A good play sometimes is hissed off the stage, through the fault of the player ill acting it." Shakespeare was obliged to run no such risks with his scripts, since they were all acted by the same group of intelligent men.

In the second place, Shakespeare experienced none of the financial pressure that usually weighed so heavily on any Elizabethan who tried to make a living with his pen. Shakespeare made his living in the same way that Richard Burbage or Henry Condell did—as an actor—and like them he invested in land and was able to leave a substantial sum of money to his heirs. His income was an actor's income, not a writer's, and it came from the pennies that were poured into the waiting hands of the gatherers at the Theatre and the Curtain, and, later on, at the Globe and the Blackfriars.

This money was handled as a lump sum and was divided every week among the actors after the expenses of the productions had been deducted. In the same way that each member of the company shared the expenses of buying costumes and scripts, renting the theatre and paying the wages of the gatherers and other hired assistants, they shared weekly in the money that came in from the audiences. This meant that in bad times the Chamberlain's company had no financial reserves, since they had no wealthy backer such as the Admiral's company had in Philip Henslowe. But it also meant that in good times the members of the company had a great deal of ready cash at their disposal, and ready cash was a scarce commodity in Elizabethan England.

Shakespeare could never have made a living from writing plays. The highest price a playwright could get for a play during Elizabeth's reign was about eight pounds, and a successful writer like Thomas Heywood usually got six. Shakespeare wrote less than forty plays in twenty year's work in the theatre, and that would have meant an average income of less than twenty pounds a year. Ben Jonson once estimated that he had made less than £200 in his entire life from writing plays, and Shakespeare spent more than twice that sum on a single real estate investment. His plays brought him a small additional income but he made his living as an actor, which was "the most excellent vocation in the world for money," as one embittered writer put it. If one of Shakespeare's plays was a success, he of course had the advantage of the increased receipts for that afternoon. But this was equally true of Heminges and Burbage and the rest, since no member of the company could have a success that was not shared by them all.

To realize the enormous advantages of Shakespeare's position, it is only necessary to compare him with the other playwrights of the decade. When any other writer presented a play to the Chamberlain's company or to its rival, the Admiral's, he was paid a flat price for the manuscript and that was the last he saw of it. He surrendered all rights, and since he had no voice in the affairs of the company he had no voice in any of the details of the production.

Nor did he have very much choice in the kind of play he was going to write, especially if the company was in a hurry for a script. It was the custom, in the Admiral's company at least, to divide the plot up and assign it to as many as four playwrights to do an act apiece. Under this system a sound plot constructed by an able craftsman was essential to the play as a whole, and a man like Anthony Munday, who was generally considered "our best plotter," could always find a use for his services. Remarkably good plays were occasionally turned out under this system, but the playwrights themselves apparently did not like it. In the next decade nearly all the good playwrights turned to writing for the boys' companies, which were revived about 1600, because the system under which they operated gave a writer much more room to please himself and much more opportunity to get the play into print.

It is not known if Shakespeare ever took part in this kind of collaboration. There is in existence a play on the life of Sir Thomas More, originally plotted by Anthony Munday and elaborated upon by playwrights like Thomas Dekker and Henry Chettle who were also in Henslowe's employ. The handwriting of one of the collaborators cannot be identified and is believed by many scholars to have been Shakespeare's. But the earliest known specimen of Shakespeare's writing dates from May 11, 1612 and is only the abbreviated scrawl of his signature. Only four other examples of his signature are extant, and the three on his will do not even look like the writing of the same man. An exact identification of his handwriting is therefore impossible, and in any case the probability that Shakespeare ever worked with this particular group of writers is extremely slight.

Men like Thomas Dekker and Henry Chettle were probably not unhappy in Henslowe's employ. Dekker wrote a share in nearly a play a month for four years and was a sufficiently quick writer both as a pamphleteer and playwright not to mind the strain, although he once remarked of his employers that "the player loves the poet so long as the sickness lies in the twopenny gallery" but was less affectionate when there was a full attendance. Dekker was not an especially ambitious man, and neither were his fellow workers for Henslowe, like Haughton and Porter and Wilson and Day.

On the other hand, Henslowe had many writers in his employ who thought of themselves as serious artists, and it must have been hard for men like these to operate under so mechanical a system. Michael Drayton, Shakespeare's fellow poet from Warwickshire, is a case in point. Henslowe noted in his diary in 1598 that he had paid out four pounds in advance on a play called *Earl Godwin and his Three Sons* to "Mr. Drayton and Mr. Dekker, Mr. Chettle and Mr. Wilson." The play was read to Henslowe in a tavern on Fish Street and he paid out five shillings for "good cheer"; but a drink and a pound in advance must have seemed poor pay to Michael Drayton. He had been brought up as a page in an aristocratic household and came to London to be a great poet, beginning his career with a series of Spenserian pastorals. His *Heroical Epistles* were much admired; but literary fame buys no man his dinner, and Michael Drayton turned to writing for the stage. He knew that he would not achieve immortality by collaborating on plays, and in fact the only example of his work that has survived in print was mistakenly attributed to Shakespeare. But Drayton did not forget his literary ambitions and while he worked on Earl Godwin or whatever other subject he was assigned, he dreamed of the masterpiece with which he was going to startle the world. He called it *Poly-Olbion* and after fifteen years of devoted research he got the first section into print. He made no money on it whatever and had great difficulty in getting the next section into print. The printers were reluctant to accept any more of *Poly-Olbion* because, as the normally gentle Drayton said bitterly, it "went not so fast away in the sale as some of their beastly and abominable trash." George Chapman had better luck, and while he was turning out popular comedies for Henslowe he worked on his magnificent translation of the *Iliad*.

Drayton and Chapman had no special incentive to do good work for Henslowe. They wrote plays for him only because they needed the money, and there was no pride in the work or any liberty of action. Their position was exactly the reverse of Shakespeare's, who wrote his plays under no financial pressure at all and had complete freedom in his choice of material. As the enormous variety of his plays shows, he was never under any obligation, if he had a success, to follow it with another play of the same kind. He could range where he wished, experiment as he pleased, and his fellow actors followed him loyally and with devotion.

Shakespeare's company did him one further service as a playwright and this was a vitally important one. They kept the original text of all his plays intact, and in the end saw to it that they were all published. No other playwright of the period had such a service done for him, and three-fourths of the plays written during this period have vanished. When Heminges and Condell presented the first complete edition of Shakespeare's plays to the public they said of their fellow actor and well-loved friend, "His wit can no more lie hid than it could be lost." But many of Shakespeare's plays would have been lost and others would have survived only in corrupt editions if men like Heminges and Condell had never lived, and the survival of plays like *Antony and Cleopatra* and *The Tempest* is directly due to the care that was taken of them by Shakespeare's fellow actors.

All the contemporary evidence about Shakespeare unites to show that in his professional life he was a relaxed and happy man, almost incapable of taking offense. He did not participate in any of the literary feuds of the period, which recur in every century but were particularly numerous in the Elizabethan age, with its delighted talent for invective. As a contemporary of his, Sir John Davies, said admiringly of "our English Terence, Master William Shakespeare,"

Thou hast no railing but a reigning wit.

Part of this dislike of "railing" can be laid to Shakespeare's natural good temper and instinctive courtesy, which earned him the title of "gentle" Shakespeare, but some of it must have been caused by the favorable conditions that surrounded his professional life. He worked for sixteen years without friction and without restraint in the art he had chosen, sure of himself, of his tools and of his results. Professionally he was a fortunate man, and equally fortunate were the men who had the privilege of working with him.

There is only one piece of evidence to show that Shakespeare ever took part in a London theatre quarrel, and in this case he seems to have been trying to assist a friend. A document of 1596 shows that Shakespeare and three others were placed under a bond not to break the peace because one William Wayte had testified that he was in "fear of death and mutilation of his limbs" from them. These bonds were a normal police device to prevent trouble in advance but the customary legal phrase becomes a little comic in this particular case, since two of the four people from whom Wayte feared "death and mutilation" were women. The third was Shakespeare, and the fourth was Francis Langley, owner of the Swan theatre. It seems to have been primarily Langley's quarrel, since earlier in this same month of November Langley had sworn out a similar complaint of his own against William Wayte and against Wayte's stepfather, an unpopular local justice named William Gardiner. The writ against Langley, Shakespeare and the two women was evidently in retaliation, and it seems probable that neither Dorothy Soer nor Anne Lee was any real threat to the peace of London. Shakespeare must have known Langley fairly well to have been willing to enter his quarrel against a rich, stubborn and dangerous man like Justice Gardiner. No professional connection between the two men has been established, but Francis Langley was the owner of the handsomest new theatre in London and William Shakespeare was a prominent member of the Chamberlain's company which may, in 1596, have been using Langley's new theatre, the Swan.

The first theatre that is known to have been used by the newly-formed Chamberlain's company was Newington Butts, a rather unsatisfactory theatre that had been built some fourteen years earlier in the village of Newington on the other side of Southwark. It was too far out of town for any but holiday crowds and the Chamberlain's company used it for only ten days in June of 1594. It looks as though all the large London theatres remained closed for a short time after the plague period, to be cleaned and redecorated for fall reopenings; for the Chamberlain's company was obliged to share Newington Butts with the Admiral's company and only got the use of the stage for six afternoons altogether.

The Chamberlain's company presented two showings each of *Titus Andronicus* and of a Biblical drama called *Esther and Ahasuerus*. *Titus Andronicus* had been played by the Earl of Sussex's men the previous January, evidently to very good houses, and had been published by John Danter with the statement that three different acting companies had presented it. The Chamberlain's company was the fourth, so *Titus Andronicus* was evidently sturdy acting material. A further evidence of its popularity is that Danter also issued a ballad on the same subject, and the misfortunes of Titus were sung on the London streets to the tune of "Fortune my foe," which was normally used to accompany ballads about murders and was consequently called the "hanging tune."

The third play presented by the Chamberlain's men at Newington Butts was *Hamlet*, a popular melodrama of the period which Tom Nashe had jeered at five years earlier as a cheap imitation of Seneca. This *Hamlet* is not extant, but the fourth play put on by the Chamberlain's company had already emerged into print. This was *The Taming of a Shrew*, "as it was sundry times acted by the right honorable the Earl of Pembroke his servants," although it is not known whether the Chamberlain's company acted the same version of the text that Pembroke's did or used the one that appears in the First Folio. The brief season at Newington Butts closed with a second showing of *Titus Andronicus* and after that the company went on its regular summer tour.

By Michaelmas London was back to normal for the first time since the plague, with the town filling for the fall law term and the theatrical season in full swing. The Chamberlain's company decided to use the Cross-Keys Inn for their winter playing, since it was ideally located for the convenience of their audiences. Like the Bull and the Bell, it stood on the great thoroughfare that was called Gracechurch and Bishopsgate Street when it ran through London and Shoreditch Road after it passed the city gate. All three inns had been

used as theatres for many years past, and the carpenter work
that had been done on the Bull and the Cross-Keys to make
them suitable for the actors was still visible seventy years
later.

All these inns were inside the city walls, and the mayor and
aldermen very much disliked having them used as theatres.
But the patron of the Chamberlain's company was the Queen's
first cousin and consequently a persuasive man. He promised
the London Council that his actors would begin their plays
promptly at two o'clock in the afternoon, so that the young
people in the audience would be able to be home before
dark. He also promised that they would forego any attempts
to advertise the play with drums and trumpets through the
streets and that they would make a contribution to the poor
of the parish out of each day's receipts. These were the usual
requirements, and equally usual was the Chamberlain's delicate reminder to the mayor that his company had to be allowed
to exercise its craft before the general public or it would
not be ready at Christmas with any plays to present to the
Queen.

All the discussions between the Crown and the City on
the subject of the theatre ended in the same way. The Queen
wanted to see plays. She had no intention of undertaking the
enormous expense of supporting a private company, and therefore the plays had to come from the ordinary commercial
theatre, since the actors would have nothing to present at
Court in the Christmas season "without their usual exercise"
the rest of the year before regular London audiences. Some
years earlier the Queen had selected a group of the best London actors to be under her special patronage, and although
the Queen's players made no extra money they had so much
extra prestige that the London Council complained bitterly
that every theatre in town was filled with acting companies
calling themselves the Queen's Men. The Queen's company
did not reappear in London after the plague, and for the rest

of the reign the honor of opening the Christmas season at Court went to the Chamberlain's company.

Such an honor might seem inevitable to the eyes of posterity, since Shakespeare was a member of the company, but what really made it inevitable was the position at Court of the company's patron. As Chamberlain, Lord Hunsdon had complete control of the royal household, with full authority over every detail of its maintenance; and this included all Court entertainments, since the Office of the Revels with its staff of officials and workmen was directly under the supervision of the Lord Chamberlain.

Lord Hunsdon was nearly seventy when Shakespeare knew him and famous for "his custom of swearing." Like one of his successors in office he was "extremely choleric by nature, which was increased the more by the office of Lord Chamberlain," a position that involved handling a great many people. Hunsdon was an extremely tactless man and no courtier, but his cousin the Queen loved him for his honesty and faithfulness to her and he was equally faithful "to his friends and servants." Certainly his actors prospered, for they were always given the opening date at Court for the Christmas season and presented more plays before the Queen than any other London company. On the other hand, it is equally true that Lord Hunsdon would not have given them his patronage in the first place unless they had been an exceptional group of actors.

The Chamberlain's company must have started its preparation for the Christmas season fairly early, since an enormous amount of extra work was required before the first play was presented before the Queen on December 26. Sets and costumes and properties could not be planned until it had been decided what plays were going to be given, and the Master of the Revels probably called the various acting companies to his office in Clerkenwell as soon as his summer's work of supervising the airing and sponging and brushing of the costumes had been completed, inventory had been made, and the cobwebs in the workrooms had been cleaned out with the long-handled brushes that were kept for the purpose.

The Master of the Revels was Edmund Tilney, a pleasant, civilized man with some literary pretensions whose only regret when he died was the amount of money he had spent on his clothes. By 1594 Tilney had held the office for fifteen years and had built it up to one of great power and responsibility. His office was in the old palace of St. John's out in Clerkenwell, where he had a suite of thirteen rooms for his own use. Clerkenwell, a suburb north of Newgate, had enjoyed a theatrical reputation in the old days of the miracle plays and when the priory of St. John's was converted into government use much of it was taken over by the Office of the Revels. Tilney was equipped with a garden, a kitchen, storage rooms and a stable in which to keep his horses, and a "great chamber" that could be used for the rehearsal of plays.

Tilney did not choose the plays for the Queen by reading them but by seeing them acted, and the actors brought their musicians, their properties and their costumes out with them. Tilney paid the freight charges out to Clerkenwell, and it cost him ten pounds once for "the charges of the players, the carriage and recarriage of their stuff, for examining and rehearsing of divers plays and choice making of ten of them to be shown before Her Majesty . . . and their sundry rehearsals afterwards." The plays that were finally chosen were supposed to be "the best that were to be had," and were "often perused and necessarily corrected and amended by all the aforesaid officers." In 1594, two of the plays in the stock of the Chamberlain's company survived this rigorous treatment and were selected to be played before the Queen.

Rehearsals were evidently conducted at night, so as not to interfere with the ordinary working day of the London companies. An elaborate lighting equipment was required at St. John's and a bill for one year, which was probably characteristic, included two dozen torches and fifteen dozen candles that were set around the rehearsal hall in a series of plates. Since winter was coming on the fires had to be kept going, and the bill for rehearsals also included four thousand sticks of firewood and two loads of coal. There was also a bill for rushes, which helped to keep the floor of the rehearsal room clean and warm; and a porter and three other attendants got twelvepence each daily "for their attendance and service in the rehearsals."

Once the plays had been chosen, work could begin on the properties and costumes and sets. Some of these were probably supplied by the actors themselves, since the Office of the Revels economized where it could. But the scenic conditions were different at Court, where the players worked in a rectangular hall by artificial light, and the general arrangement was not unlike that of a modern picture stage. Elaborate backgrounds were used, apparently modelled after the Italian system of scenes done in perspective, and there was usually an order placed with some linen-draper for "apt houses, made of canvas, framed, fashioned and painted." The Revels office also used the Italian system of designing small paper models of the scenery in advance, and a typical expense was boat-hire for one of the scene painters who brought the patterns to Whitehall to be approved by the Lord Chamberlain.

The painters were kept hard at work up to Christmas, since they were responsible not only for making canvas houses and castles and villages but also for gilding lions' heads and painting wool-stuffed fishes so realistically that any member of the audience could tell at a glance which was a mackerel and which was a flounder. They worked among paint pots that were a riot of gold and silver and sapphire and crimson, and one of the officers of the Revels kept a stern watch to see that none of the color was wasted and that any of the paint that was left over was replaced in the stores.

Meanwhile the costumes were being designed and executed,

and the beautiful clothes to be worn by the actors were evolving out of piles of taffeta and tinsel and velvet and damask and cloth-of-gold. If old headpieces could be used again, they were cleaned with breadcrumbs and taped to strengthen them, and if not, new ones were designed. Wigs and beards were made and carefully curled, and the chief property maker got out his bowls and rags and brown paper and plaster of paris and started to mold fruits and trees and monsters so that they could be delivered to the painters in time and be dry by opening night.

One of the Revels officers complained bitterly in the 70's because none of these workmen had private places to work. "Tailors, painters, property makers and carpenters are all fain to work in one room, which is a very great hindrance one to another, which thing needs not for they are slack enough of themselves." Apart from the natural inclination of any Elizabethan workman to do as much chatting and as little actual work as possible, the system of a single large room must have made for a great deal of confusion. In spite of baskets and boxes used for storage, and brooms and a dust basket for neatness, the place must have been a wild confusion of properties and costumes and people, with the smell of paint and glue and the sounds of hammering rising above everything else. The actors themselves probably did not mind when they had occasion to be there; the smell was a good theatre smell and they were used to apparent confusion. If anyone was unhappy it was probably the clerk, with his green cloth and his desk and his wax counters. The clerk was responsible for keeping the accounts and the plots of the plays and the models of the settings, and he had to know, when a property maker presented a bill for monsters and holly and horses' tails and guns and moss and "dishes for devils' eyes," that his list matched the one in the harried Revels office.

The life of this clerk was complicated by a series of outside borrowings, all of which had to be returned when the Christmas season was over. Armor was frequently borrowed, since it was an expensive item, and on one occasion at least the armorer's apprentice was also borrowed to help the actors get in and out of the equipment. Once the Revels office borrowed a cloud, presumably from a company of actors since the average London citizen had comparatively little use for a cloud, and then unfortunately they tore it. The Revels office had to go to some expense for the hoop and the blue linen cloth that were needed to mend it, and at that they had to supply their own cord and pulley for the cloud and buy a great many extra nails.

As the Christmas season grew closer, the atmosphere about the Revels office grew increasingly tense. One officer spoke feelingly of "the haste of the preparation," and added that there was "no service more troublesome for the time of the works than the service of the Revels both for the body and the mind." The officers had to be everywhere at once, and the greater the need for haste the more rapidly the expenses mounted. Sometimes the painters had to be fed while they worked because there was no time to stop off for dinner, and one year the headpiece makers had to be given a special bonus because they were still working on Christmas night. There was always some last-minute work, especially in the painting department where final touches had to be made at the Court itself; and one payment was "for coals at the court to dry the painters' work on the rock."

Meanwhile all the other equipment had to be packed in baskets and brought to Court: the scenery, the costumes, the properties and the intricate lighting equipment that the chief wiredrawer and his assistants had to tack and wire and spike into position before opening night. Since the Queen was at Greenwich in the Christmas season of 1594 most of the material went by boat down the crowded Thames, with one hamper for farthingales and another for a frame and probably a whole boat to carry the wire and plates and ropes and branches that were used to set up the torches and candles that lit the hall. Down at Greenwich, Thomas Sheffield, the under-keeper of the palace, was paying eight men extra for night work to make the halls and galleries clean and ready.

The opening date was Thursday, December the 26th, which was St. Stephen's Day, and the performance was due to begin about ten o'clock in the evening. This was the climax of months of hard work, and if the Chamberlain's men managed to remain completely calm and relaxed in that tense atmosphere they were a most unusual group of actors.

All the Revels officers were there, with special attendants at each door, and the seats probably began filling early. Since Greenwich was a small summer palace the seating arrangement was more informal than at Whitehall, where the Chamberlain's men presented most of their plays in subsequent years. Whitehall had a large banqueting hall that had been erected for the sole purpose of giving entertainments, and a foreign visitor who was allowed to peer in reports that the interior was "full of benches and stools ranged one above the other." Unless special scaffoldings were used at Greenwich it is likely that all the seats were on the same level, with a raised stage for the actors at one end of the hall and a throne for the Queen.

The Queen probably made her entrance about the time that the actor who played the Prologue began pinching his cheeks to get some color into them, and when she came in even the most experienced member of the acting company might be permitted the cold clutch of stage fright. For Queen Elizabeth was the golden and glorious sun about whom all of England revolved. Even the greatest lords approached her kneeling, spoke to her kneeling, played cards with her kneeling, and she moved in a glitter of jewels and of homage that made her in many ways the fairy-tale figure that the poets of England said she was.

Queen Elizabeth was in her sixties when Shakespeare's

company faced her from the stage in the Christmas season of 1594, and very little was left of her youth except her straight back and her beautiful hands. She still dressed as a young girl in spite of her wrinkled face and false hair and missing teeth, and occasionally some self-confident male would conclude that her mind was aging also and that she was a conceited and impressionable old woman. The French ambassador who came to her Court three years later began with some such impression, but a few days later he was recording in his journal with reluctant admiration, "She is a very great princess who knows everything." The men of her Court did not altogether like being ruled by a woman, especially a brilliant woman, but most of them both loved her and were a little frightened of her.

As far as her lesser subjects were concerned, Elizabeth had decided early that the only way to get obedience from her turbulent and opinionated countrymen was to be loved. She played the courtier with her people even more than her anxious lords courted her, and the smile that was "pure sunshine" came often enough from England's greatest politician where ordinary English citizens were concerned. This was not a matter of policy alone, for she loved England more selflessly and devotedly than she ever loved anything else in her long and difficult life; but the special grace with which she handled herself before the general public was born of a very clear idea of the value of courtesy in politics. When a schoolmaster at Norwich attempted to deliver a Latin speech to her and lost his head altogether in that glorious presence, the great Queen was as concerned over his stage fright as were any of the sweating Norwich managers of the affair, and when the schoolmaster had finally staggered through to a conclusion she told him, "It is the best that ever I heard; you shall have my hand."

Elizabeth of course expected a much higher standard of performance from a group of professionals like the Chamberlain's company, especially since she had paid for their costumes and properties and was giving them a £10 fee, but in general she was the ideal theatre-goer. She hoped and expected to be amused, and from the actors' point of view it would be difficult to find any more attractive quality in a spectator than that. She and the Londoners shared the same kind of interest in the theatre and liked the same kind of things, for that vigorous woman was far too well educated to play the snob and to give her support to tenuous classical productions only. On her mother's side Elizabeth was descended from middle-class stock and her great-grandfather, Geoffrey Boleyn, had been a merchant of London. The Londoners always felt she was one of them, since she was "descended of citizens" and her ancestor's tomb could still be seen in St. Lawrence's Church; and although her father and her successor had their court fools, Elizabeth preferred to share the great clowns like Tarleton and Kempe with the ordinary London public.

Elizabeth was much more learned than the majority of her subjects, but she did not have the exaggerated respect for learning that plagued so many of the gentlemen of the Renaissance. When the French ambassador expressed admiration at her ability to speak six languages, she remarked "that it was no marvel to teach a woman to talk; it were far harder to teach her to hold her tongue." She made translations from Cicero and Plutarch to relax her lively mind, and read Seneca to calm herself after she had been "stirred to passion" by what she considered the stupidity of her harassed Privy Council; but she was quite willing to stop off and ask the meaning of an unfamiliar word in Latin, "being of the mind of that philosopher who in his last years began with the Greek alphabet."

The actors who played before Queen Elizabeth faced a woman with a lively, critical mind and one who knew a good deal about the details of their trade. The Queen was a poet herself, and as one respectful subject put it, her "learned,

delicate, noble Muse easily surmounteth all the rest . . . be it
in ode, epigram, or any other kind of poem heroic or lyric."
She was an expert musician who could play her own compositions, and an experienced dancer with such a strong sense
of rhythm that when she watched a dance instead of taking
part in it she followed "the cadence with her head, hand and
foot."

In her ideas on comedy Elizabeth leaned towards the same
easygoing humor that her subjects did, and the strict sexual
propriety that she enforced in her Court had nothing to do
with her enjoyment of a bit of Shakespearian plain-speaking
on the stage. Elizabeth had about twenty-eight maids of honor,
for whose welfare she was directly responsible to their parents,
in a Court that consisted otherwise of about fifteen hundred
men, and she had trouble enough with those lively and mar-
riageable young ladies in a Court that was completely mascu-
line down to male cooks and launderers. It is noticeable that
during Elizabeth's reign the dramatists never wrote anything
that condoned or encouraged sexual immorality. Adultery was
a subject for tragedy, not for comedy, and when Shakespeare
went to complicated lengths in *All's Well That Ends Well*
to prevent the hero from committing adultery in his comedy,
he was following the normal practice of Elizabethan playwrights. It was not until well into the next reign that the
situation changed. By then Elizabeth was dead and the influence of her sisters in spirit, the wives of the London citizens, was receding; and it was only old-fashioned dramatists
like William Shakespeare who still wrote the kind of plays
that had once been popular with everyone.

The Chamberlain's company was paid twenty pounds for
the two plays they presented before the Queen that first
Christmas, although it was not until March that "William
Kempe, William Shakespeare and Richard Burbage, servants
to the Lord Chamberlain" were able to collect the money.

The payment was made, in the usual complicated way, by a warrant from the Privy Council, and the warrant states the plays were given before the Queen on the 26th and 28th of December. This must have been a clerical error, however, since the Admiral's company also received payment for a play given on Saturday the 28th.

Moreover, there is evidence that the Chamberlain's company was acting elsewhere on that particular Saturday night. On the 28th of December "a Comedy of Errors (like to Plautus his *Menechmus*) was played by the players" before the young gentlemen of Gray's Inn. This is such an accurate description of Shakespeare's play, *The Comedy of Errors*, that it must be the same; and, since the Chamberlain's company now owned all of Shakespeare's plays, it must have been this company that played at Gray's Inn on the 28th of December.

The Gray's Inn audience was not so very unlike the Court audience at Greenwich, except that the Gray's Inn gentlemen and their farthingaled guests were much younger, much livelier, and had worked themselves up during the Christmas season to a fairly advanced state of foolishness. The whole Christmas season was a golden opportunity for nonsense, and the boys in the various Inns of Court made the most of it.

The Inns of Court were the four resident law schools west of London and trained young gentlemen in that most respectable and profitable of Elizabethan professions. It was an exceptional nobleman who escaped at least a few years' training at one of the law schools, and although it was quite true that not every name entered in the Steward's Book was that of a gentleman, the training was so expensive that a rich father was almost the first qualification for admission. Since most of the boys were at least technically members of the gentry, they were given an education "fit for persons of their station" and were taught dancing, riding and singing, and how to stage theatrical productions. They even staged plays of their own making before the Queen and were quite capable of surmounting the technical complications of showing "Cupid descending from heaven and the Furies rising from hell."

Gray's Inn was the largest of the Inns of Court and it was generally conceded that its members excelled in dramatics; but for their Christmas entertainment of 1594 they hired professional actors. A raised scaffold at the eastern end of their seventy-foot hall was designed for the stage, but the Chamberlain's men had a hard time of it that night. The crowd of spectators at that end of the hall was "so exceeding great that thereby there was no convenient room for those that were actors."

The chief difficulty seems to have been that too many invitations had been sent out and the Elizabethan farthingale took up a great deal of room. But a Christmas revel without "divers ladies and gentlewomen" would have been unthinkable at Gray's Inn, whose members took such a happy interest in the opposite sex that a law had to be passed "that no laundresses or women victuallers should thenceforth come into the gentlemen's chambers of this Society, unless they were full forty years of age, and not send their maidservants of what age soever."

The Revels to which the Chamberlain's company gave their professional services were the first since the plague, and there was evidently a good deal of stored-up enthusiasm to be suddenly released. The evening was spent in "dancing and revelling with gentlewomen" and watching the play; but the mock formality that had been planned for the evening collapsed so thoroughly that the fledgling lawyers, who seized on every opportunity to make fun of the legal procedure they were being taught, held a mock trial the next day to find out who had been responsible for the lack of dignity in "our law sports."

When the young men of the Inns of Court were not putting on shows of their own or hiring professional actors to appear in their halls, they went across London to Southwark or Shoreditch and paid admission like everyone else to see the plays in the regular public theatres. Their presence in London made it for all practical purposes a university town, full of intelligent, well-to-do young men who wanted to be amused. From the actors' point of view, the Inns were a great improvement on Oxford and Cambridge; for the origin of these two universities was monastic and they consistently disapproved of professional actors, while the Inns of Court had originated under the guild system and their governors had no objection to plays. An Oxford boy was punished if he went to see a commercial play, but a boy at Gray's Inn or the Inner Temple could spend his seven-year residence by seeing every new show in London. Since these young men were in close touch with the Court and knew every latest joke and latest fashion, they made an excellent leaven in the average London audience and the actors appreciated them.*

There were no similar schools for girls in London, but their education was not neglected. Even a tax-supported institution like Christ's Hospital taught the little girls in its care how to read before they were sent out in service, and the average girl in Renaissance London could never quite convince herself that she was inferior to a man. In a book written by Edmund Tilney, Master of the Revels, a young lady remarks: "As meet it is that the husband obey the wife as the wife the husband ... For women have souls as well as men, they have wit as well as men." The charming, independent girls in the better-class London households were to a certain extent the models for the delightful heroines of Shakespeare's later comedies, and it was girls of this kind who were the guests of the

---

* Shakespeare's Justice Shallow never achieved the dignity of belonging to one of the Inns of Court, but he attended Clement's Inn, which was one of the preliminary training grounds and run on the same general system. After long years in the country, Justice Shallow still looked back wistfully to those happy days in London. "Jesu! Jesu! the mad days that I have spent."

young men of Gray's Inn the night that the Chamberlain's company presented *The Comedy of Errors*.

A successful acting company like the Chamberlain's would have many calls for special productions. If the occasion was a very important one, the play might be staged in the afternoon, like the performance of Shakespeare's *Henry IV* that his company presented at the house of the Lord Chamberlain when their patron was entertaining an ambassador; but in general the performance was given in the evening so that it would not interfere with the normal daytime schedule. A fashionable supper-party might conclude with a play, like the production of a play on King Richard that was given the year after the Gray's Inn performance and ordered by Sir Edward Hoby. A wedding frequently ended with a play, since whenever there was any special celebration the Elizabethan mind went automatically to its favorite form of amusement, and if the house was not large enough for the production a hall could be hired. "Weddings and other festivities" often took place in rented halls, and the Stationers' Company made a charge of ten shillings when the company hall was used for a wedding. A hall could easily be converted into a theatre by building a scaffolding at one end, and the actors were evidently well paid for their extra productions. Their chief expense was the freight charge for the transfer of costumes and properties, and Philip Henslowe notes that he paid three shillings on behalf of the Admiral's company to "the carman for carrying to and bringing of the stuff back again when they played in Fleet Street private."

It seems reasonably certain that a new play was never launched at one of these private showings. A masque could be composed for a wedding celebration, since a masque consisted of recitation and dancing and it was possible to estimate its effectiveness in advance. But the effectiveness of a play script cannot be estimated in advance; there is no way of measuring its impact upon an audience until it has actually been produced, and the London companies had no way of testing their plays except by presenting them to their regular audience. They risked their own capital when they put a new script into production, and if they had been incorrect in their estimate of the script they shared the financial loss among themselves. If, on the other hand, the script was successful, it became a regular part of their repertoire and was available for special evening productions in the same way it was available for the Christmas season at Court. Queen Elizabeth did not see a play until it had first been applauded by the ordinary London theatre-goers, and the same was probably true of all the special evening performances given by the Chamberlain's company.

Chapter 7

THE PERFORMANCES that the Chamberlain's company gave before the Queen or before private groups were important, but they were still only extras. The basis of the profession was the regular daylight performance that went on about two o'clock in the afternoon before the ordinary Londoners.

A great many of these afternoon performances consisted of old plays that had achieved a permanent place in the company's repertoire, but there was also a steady supply of new scripts in which the actors were investing their time, their faith and their money. Burbage and Heminges and Shakespeare and Kempe hoped that each of these new scripts would be a success, but some of them of course were not. Theatrical production is an uncertain trade, and even the most experienced theatre men cannot be sure in advance of the production values of a script. But in general the Chamberlain's men chose successful scripts, since otherwise they would quickly have ceased to be a successful acting company.

One of the most successful of these scripts was produced in the middle years of the decade, not long after the company had been formed. It was written by one of their own members, William Shakespeare, and called *Romeo and Juliet*. Some of the details may be missing, but it is possible to reconstruct in a general way how the play was made ready for its first performance.

Shakespeare began, as usual, with an old plot in his head.

This was normal theatre procedure, and Shakespeare differed from most of his fellow dramatists only in that he never used a plot from contemporary life. In this case, Shakespeare was using not only an old story but one which the average Londoner of his day must have known very well. In the early days the story of Romeo and Juliet had been a successful play on the London stage. Then a young man named Arthur Brooke, who had seen the stage version, was sufficiently impressed to turn it into a poem just before his unhappy death by drowning. It also appeared in a very popular collection of stories that an officer in the ordnance department, named William Painter, had collected and translated from the Italian in his spare time. Sensational Italian fiction of this type was somewhat old-fashioned by the middle years of the last decade of the century, but Shakespeare never concerned himself about being in the forefront of any literary movement. He was no innovator, and to the end of his career he was willing to take decrepit, old-fashioned stories as the basis for his plays while his colleagues dealt in glossy new inventions of their own.

One of the most curious aspects of Shakespeare as a writer was the way in which he did not seem to consider himself superior to his sources. He was making a serious tragedy out of Brooke's poem and he read the thing carefully and attentively, in some cases following the character's thoughts almost word for word as Brooke gives them. Yet it is no easy thing to read Brooke's version seriously, for his style is strongly reminiscent of Bottom's immortal production of Pyramus and Thisbe. This is the way Brooke's heroine talks to her beloved in the balcony scene:

> What if your deadly foes, my kinsmen, saw you here?
> Like lions wild, your tender parts asunder would they tear.
> In ruth and in disdain, I, weary of my life,
> With cruel hand my mourning heart would pierce with bloody knife.

Shakespeare could read this sort of thing and believe in the story wholeheartedly without being affected in the least by the childishness of the narrator. Brooke's stupidity as a poet did not irritate him in the least, as it might very well irritate a lesser man. Shakespeare's spirit accepted the whole of Brooke's with the same steady, patient courtesy that made it possible for him, as an actor, to appear in so many bad plays in the course of his life without ever becoming discouraged with his profession. His company put on about fifteen new plays a year and Shakespeare, as a regular acting member of the company, must have appeared in most of them. They were not all good plays, and some of them, to judge by the few that are extant, were very bad. For instance, the year that *King Lear* was first produced at Court another play given on the same occasion by Shakespeare's company was *The Devil's Charter* by Barnabe Barnes. Barnes' play had an abnormally large cast and Shakespeare could probably not have avoided acting in it, even if, as a working member of the company, such a thing had crossed his mind. A good actor cannot start rehearsals by privately considering himself superior to his material and Shakespeare must have given Barnes' play what he had given scores of similar plays in the course of his career, the courteous attention of a good professional who is anxious to make a success of the production. Barnes tenderly saw his own play into print, and the contrast between that childish melodrama and *King Lear* is probably characteristic of the gap between the plays Shakespeare himself had written and the plays in which he was only an actor. A more self-conscious artist would have been angered by such a situation. Shakespeare was as untroubled by it as he was by the childishness and vulgarity of many of the sources he chose for his plays.

Almost as irritating as Arthur Brooke's style to a modern reader is his dogged determination to point a moral. This was the normal Elizabethan practice, although it was not Shake-

speare's, and the reading of stories could only be justified if
they taught some useful lesson. William Painter justified translating a story of unlawful love like Romeo and Juliet's by
pointing out it would teach readers "how to avoid the ruin,
overthrow, inconvenience and displeasure that lascivious desire and wanton will doth bring," and Arthur Brooke was even
more concerned for the moral welfare of his reader. "To this
end (good reader) is this tragical matter written, to describe
unto thee a couple of unfortunate lovers, thralling themselves
to dishonest desire, neglecting the authority and advice of
parents and friends, conferring their principal counsels with
drunken gossips and superstitious friars . . . abusing the name
of lawful marriage to cloak the shame of stolen contracts,
finally, by all means of unhonest life, hasting to most unhappy
death."

Shakespeare's eye passed over all this moralizing without
his mind accepting any of it. If he noticed anything it was
Brooke's one word, "hasting," since neither Brooke nor Painter
had suggested any motivation for the tragedy except due
punishment for sin. Shakespeare's mind did not move in this
particular pattern, however normal it may have been in his
own day, and instead he made the story a tragedy of haste.
The tragic flaw in the characters is that they are all in too
much of a hurry, and Shakespeare made some changes in the
original story to emphasize this. He cut down the action of
the story from several months to less than a week, and then
made it a week of "hot days" in which everything comes
quickly to flower and equally soon fades. He made Juliet only
fourteen, although Brooke said she was sixteen, and her love
for Romeo is "like the lightning."

Brooke had done almost nothing with characterization, and
in his version Mercutio appears briefly and is hardly more
than a name. He made a slightly more determined effort
with the Nurse, who was a stock character in fiction of this
type, and he gave her a long passage describing how she nursed

Juliet, which Brooke himself had to admit was a "tedious long discourse." Shakespeare also gave the Nurse a passage describing how she had nursed Juliet, and the shout of delighted laughter that went up on the opening day of the production has been echoing in audiences ever since.

Heminges and Condell made a report on Shakespeare's writing habits after they had been handling his manuscripts for nearly thirty years and they said that their fellow actor was a very rapid writer. "His mind and hand went together; and what he thought, he uttered with that easiness, that we have scarce received from him a blot in his papers." That is to say, Shakespeare was one of those writers who works everything out in his head before he puts any of it down on paper. His company later had another playwright, John Fletcher, who worked in the same way. As Fletcher's publisher said, "Whatever I have seen of Mr. Fletcher's own hand is free from interlining; and his friends affirm he never writ any one thing twice; it seems he had that rare felicity to prepare and perfect all first in his own brain." It was fortunate that Shakespeare was able to "prepare and perfect all first in his own brain," since his profession was not one that supplied him with long hours of leisure to cross out and laboriously improve his lines. Since a play is not in any case a collection of lines but an organic, swift-moving whole, Shakespeare had good use for his actor's memory, which could keep the whole gathering structure intact in his mind until it was finished and ready to be recorded on paper.

When a play was finished, the usual procedure was for the playwright to read it to the assembled actors to see if they wished to buy it. Since Shakespeare was already a prominent member of his own group of purchasers, and one of the most popular playwrights of his day, this part of the transaction was probably already a foregone conclusion. Once the average writer had been paid, his connection with the script was ended and it was left to the company of actors to produce it in any

way they saw fit; but in Shakespeare's case the problem of
transferring the printed words to the stage and bringing them
to life was only just beginning.

The first thing that had to be done with *Romeo and Juliet*
was to get it licensed. No play could be produced on the
London stage until it had been certified that no seditious
material had crept into it that might corrupt the susceptible
public. The Crown was not concerned with suppressing indecorous or blasphemous material in the theatre and it was
not until the following reign that oaths were outlawed on the
London stage. It merely wished to make sure that one of the
greatest popular mediums of communication, the theatre, did
not lend itself to any propaganda against the dignity of the
government or of the Queen.

The licenser was Edmund Tilney, Master of the Revels.
Tilney had originally censored the plays that were shown
before the Queen, but he had gradually extended his control
to all the plays in the London area. His post was rather a
profitable one, since a fee of seven shillings had to accompany
the manuscript of *Romeo and Juliet* when it was sent out to
his office in Clerkenwell.

Once the script had been licensed nothing could be added
to it, but the actors were free to make the abridgements that
would fit it into the normal playing time of two hours. In
general, Shakespeare seems to have offered rather lengthy
manuscripts to his company. He was not an economical writer,
and he did not husband his strength or indulge in mathematical
computations over a few extra words. He evidently wrote
at white heat, once he had the paper in front of him, and he
could not be expected to pause at intervals, with his pen in
the air, to check back over his material and make sure that the
play was not running too long. Many of his finished scripts
needed an acting time of more than three hours and could
not have been brought to an end during the brief daylight
hours of a winter afternoon. The necessity for cutting a script

of Shakespeare's must have been a routine part of the general problem of getting it into production, and although no evidence remains on the subject it seems likely that the cuts were worked out at rehearsals and by general agreement. The men of Shakespeare's company all had years of practical experience in the theatre, and they could be trusted to cooperate with him intelligently in the cutting of his scripts. Nor did these theatre cuts affect the original version, since the full-length play as Shakespeare had written it was available to the printer whenever the company authorized its publication.

Shakespeare's original script, with its suggested cuts in the margin and with Tilney's signature at the end, was apparently not copied out for the prompter. It seems to have been used just as it was, except that the loose sheets were stitched together and enclosed in some kind of wrapper. Any kind of wrapper would do, from a medieval manuscript to an expired law paper, just so that it was capable of standing hard wear. Once the play had been produced this "book" was carefully stored, since it was the only official copy of the play the company had and the only proof that it had been properly licensed.

The next expense, after the payment for the licensing, was probably the payment to the copyist who wrote out the actors' parts for them to memorize. The only document of this kind that has survived is one made for Edward Alleyn, with corrections in Alleyn's handwriting, but they were probably more or less alike. An ordinary sheet of paper was divided lengthwise to make six-inch widths and pasted to form a long continuous strip that the actor could roll back as he worked. The closing lines of the previous speech were indicated to give the actor his cue, and directions for action were put in the left-hand margin.

The casting of *Romeo and Juliet* probably did not take very long. The actors knew each other's work intimately and could talk the problem over among themselves instead of bowing to the decree of an outside manager. Casting was controlled by a single consideration, the good of the production as a whole, and an actor's private ambitions had very little to do with the matter. Through a printer's error, one piece of casting in *Romeo and Juliet* has been preserved, and it shows that Will Kempe played Peter. The best comedy role in the play was of course that of the Nurse, and Peter, her servant, has very few effective lines. Will Kempe was the most popular comic actor of the period, but the Chamberlain's company did not use the star system. The company as a whole evidently felt that Kempe could be used to best advantage in a small role, and that was the one he played.

There is no reason to believe that the Elizabethans had any special respect for type-casting and always gave the most elderly member of the company the oldest role or the same man the low-comedy lead. Thomas Pope was famous as a clown, but the only role to which he can definitely be assigned in his long career is the dignified part of Arbactus, while the actor who played the comedy role in the same play is not identified anywhere else with a comedy characterization. Nor is it necessary to suppose that Shakespeare was always given dignified roles. He did not have his present reputation then, and like everyone else in the company he played whatever part would most clearly benefit the production as a whole. The basis of any good repertory company is intelligent, varied acting, and the Chamberlain's was a good repertory company.

Once the major roles had been cast, the minor parts like the townsmen and the guests at the ball could be handled through doubling; and if there were not enough actors in the immediate company to fill all the parts, outside actors would be hired for the occasion. There were always more actors in London than there were parts, waiting hopefully for a call from one of the theatres, and they were paid a flat rate that was usually a shilling a day.

Regret has sometimes been expressed by modern writers

that there were no actresses to be cast in Shakespeare's plays and he had to undergo the grief of seeing Juliet played by a boy. But this shows a misunderstanding of the period, for a Renaissance boy was not brought up in the least like a modern one. The average man of Shakespeare's day did not consider it effeminate to write poetry or play the lute or load himself with jewels and silks and perfumes. Shakespeare's Rosalind was speaking for the normal Renaissance point of view when she said she would be "changeable, longing and liking . . . full of tears, full of smiles . . . as boys and women are." It was not until the Puritan Commonwealth that the convention was established that men were supposed to have an entirely different life to women and many of a boy's natural qualities were choked out of him as "unmanly." The situation was different in Shakespeare's day, and the boys of his company understood perfectly what moved a young girl to laughter or to tears.

In addition, these boys had daily training by masters in the profession; and a boy who lived and worked under the watchful eye of a brilliant actor like Richard Burbage knew a great deal about acting by the time he was ready to be cast for a leading feminine role. He had been trained as a singer and dancer and in every aspect of handling his body gracefully. Above all, he had been trained in the use of his voice, since it was through the voice that the illusion could be most completely maintained. Shakespeare had this point clearly in mind when he wrote *Romeo and Juliet*, and in his great lyric tragedy of young love he lets the lines carry the illusion and keeps his actors away from much physical contact. The famous balcony scene, with the two young voices reaching out and caressing each other, would be a less useful device to a modern dramatist who could trust to the physical contact of the actors to convey the idea of sudden love. When the two lovers first meet in Brooke's poem they sit silent, dumbly holding hands at the ball; Shakespeare has them speak a sonnet. Throughout the play he had to trust to words instead of action in the love scenes, and every reader of the play should be deeply grateful to the boy actors.

A certain number of musicians were required at the ball to obey Capulet's command, "Come, musicians, play," but it was no special casting problem to find an actor who could play a musical instrument. When Shakespeare's fellow actors like Pope and Bryan appeared at the Danish court of Elsinore, part of their business was to "attend with their fiddles and instruments." After more than a decade as a successful actor Edward Alleyn was still being styled "musician," and Kempe was listed as an "instrumentalist." When Augustine Phillips died he willed his various musical instruments to his apprentices as a natural part of their equipment as actors, and they were certainly expected to know how to use them. It was a period in which music was so vital a part of the life of the average Londoner that even a charity school like Bridewell taught music to its charges, and the right to sell ruled paper on which to copy songs was a valuable and profitable patent. The knowledge of music that Shakespeare shows in his plays was normal for the period, and was in part the result of the same knowledge and enthusiasm on the part of his audience.*

* With the single exception of *The Comedy of Errors,* music was used in all of Shakespeare's plays. The percussion and brass instruments were used extensively in the history plays, and the actors had to be experienced in handling military music both on and off stage. The stringed instruments were too light in tone for general use in the large public theatres and mainly supplied a delicate musical background to the songs, in which the music was kept subordinate to the words. Shakespeare's songs were usually accompanied by the lute, which the actor would handle in much the same way as the modern guitar. Group singing was unusual, except for the use of choristers in *Henry VIII,* but Shakespeare introduced music to accompany group dancing at every reasonable opportunity. The chief wood instruments on the stage were the cornet and the hautboy—the Elizabethan cornet being a kind of horn and the hautboy the ancestor of the modern oboe. Shakespeare used hautboys under the stage to give an effect of supernatural music in *Antony and Cleopatra,* and he used them to supply a "lofty strain" of dance music in *Timon of Athens. The Tempest* calls for an especially intricate series of musical effects, but by that time Shakespeare and his colleagues had had a lifetime of experience in handling musical

If the Chamberlain's company was like the Admiral's, they had an extraordinary clutter of properties stored away, from which they could choose whatever they needed for a new play. *Romeo and Juliet* required very few properties and most of these would be easy to get, like the ladder of cords for the Nurse to bring in, the basket for Friar Lawrence and the wrenching iron for Romeo. There had to be a bed for Juliet, and the other large movable property would be the Capulet tomb. The Chamberlain's company already had the tomb they had used in *Titus Andronicus*, but the Elizabethan public evidently did not expect to see the same tomb twice unless it had been refurbished, and Henslowe's property account for 1598 lists three of them.

There was no attempt at realistic settings in *Romeo and Juliet*, since the scene changed so often that it would only have slowed up the action. Nor did a well-trained Elizabethan audience need this kind of assistance. When Romeo and his friends entered with torchbearers, the audience knew it was a street scene and that they were seeing Romeo on his way to Capulet's ball. When this group of actors left the stage and another group came on with napkins over their arms, the audience knew at once that the scene had changed and that preparations for the ball were being made in Capulet's house.

This was the sort of stagecraft that Sir Philip Sidney had once ridiculed, but Sidney was underestimating the creative power of the audience's imagination. Shakespeare never underestimated it. He knew that the imagination of the audience could build Capulet's house more quickly and effectively than all the lathe and pasteboard in London. When Shakespeare wanted to give the illusion that his two lovers, standing on the bare boards of a theatre in the glare of an afternoon

cues. Music was so important in the theatre that in *Cymbeline* "solemn music" is heard in the wilderness; and this unlikely event is justified by the fact the owner of a cave possesses an "ingenious instrument" that can play mechanicall;

sun, were in an orchard at night, he turned like the excellent stage technician he was to the magic and power of his poetry; and his audience, who were the best-trained listeners in the world, saw the moonlight silver the tops of the fruit trees as they listened to Romeo's voice.

Up to this point the Chamberlain's company had not incurred any unusually heavy expenses, but an unavoidable item in any new play was the cost of the costuming. All the actors wore contemporary fashions on the stage, but they could not be expected to get up on the bare boards in their street attire and recreate the mood of legendary Verona. The splendor of the costumes gave the illusion of remoteness and glamour that a modern production can achieve through clever lighting, and the costumes were a heavy item on any company's expense account.

The Chamberlain's company did not, of course, buy a completely new set of costumes for each production. They had a fairly large stock on hand and a little ingenuity could give the illusion of a new outfit, especially for some minor actor who was only filling in as background at the ball. Old costumes were always being reused, or, as the Revels office put it, "translated." If the Revels office started with eight jerkins of purple cloth-of-gold for mariners, the jerkins made their next appearance translated into six costumes for Hungarians and then into four kirtles for Diana's nymphs, and so on down until the final note was made, "not now serviceable," and they vanished out of the wardrobe department. All the London companies used old materials as far as they could, but there was a limit to this kind of economy in the case of costumes for the leading actors. Romeo and Juliet were members of the nobility and had to be costumed accordingly.

Philip Henslowe kept two tailors working for him, as well as several people who did supplemental sewing, and his bills for costuming were enormous. He spent nine pounds on taffeta for the two feminine leads in a play of Henry Porter's, and it would have taken a hired actor thirty weeks to earn as much as that. A flame-colored satin doublet cost forty-five shillings, and even the facing of a cloak cost nine. Although cheap material like buckram could be used for stiffening, the fabrics that the audience saw had to be velvets and satins and taffetas. They had to be in the brilliant colors that the London public had grown to expect, and bore imaginative names like goose-turd green, pease-porridge tawny, and popinjay blue.

From the point of view of a costumer, everything about contemporary fashions was designed to give the actors as much trouble, discomfort and expense as possible. The basic idea of Elizabethan tailoring was a smooth, unbroken fit, and the clothes were curved with whalebone or padded with buckram to make them stand out from the body as though they had no relation to the wearer. Both men and women strove for extremely narrow waists, flaring hips and broad shoulders, and many men were not above wearing corsets to get the desired effect. Even the sleeves were sometimes stiffened with whalebone and the doublets were so stiff their wearers could hardly bend. All tailors depended heavily on "bombast," which was a stuffing made of cotton or horsehair or even of bran or rags, to give their customers the correct bulges that fashion demanded, and the problem of how to combine this rigid shape with the violent action that was demanded on the stage, especially in duelling scenes, was one that each tailor had to solve for himself.

A quick change of costume could not have been easy, since all the clothes were held on by an intricate system of fastenings. The stockings were fastened to the doublets by a series of laces or points that must have been tiresome to fasten or small boys would not have been scolded for leaving them undone, and yet the seams of the stockings had to be as straight as though they were "set by a plumb-line." The cloak was held to the shoulders by concealed cords in the lining that were knotted under the armholes, and the jerkins had extra slits that could be buttoned to ensure a smooth fit. The costumes of the women were even more complicated because of the lavish use of pins. The various parts of a woman's costumes were made detachable so that she could use different color combinations, and the pins were called "great farthingale pins," "middle farthingale pins" and so on, according to what part of the costume they were holding together. Wire pins cost about a penny a hundred and costumers depended on them heavily, although by great good fortune hooks and eyes were also in general use.

Ruffs were a whole problem in themselves. Everyone wore them above a certain social standing, and in Shakespeare's plays even the prostitutes wear ruffs. They were complicated to make, since they had to be stiffly starched and the pleats set in with a hot setting-stick; and the larger ruffs required an underpropping of pasteboard and wire to be fastened around the owner's neck underneath. The amount of discomfort involved seems to have made no difference, and the size of the ruffs grew, as a contemporary remarked, "every day worser and worser."

The Elizabethan costume seems to have been tenderly designed to be both as unflattering to the wearer as possible and as unsuitable to the climate. A sudden rain could mean ruin, for the starch in the ruff would dissolve and leave it a limp rag around its owner's neck, and for all their brilliant colors the English dyers had not yet achieved the certainty of fast dyes. Perhaps one of the reasons for the popularity of orange-tawny as a color was that it was one of the few dyes of the period that could be trusted to keep its color.

In addition to all his other problems, the costumer had to wrestle with the shopmen. He had to know if twelve shillings a yard was a fair price for satin, and be able to test velvet to make sure it was not gummed. Moreover he had to get prompt deliveries in spite of the notoriously unreliable nature of "tailors' and silkmen's promises." But in due time Romeo and Tybalt and Mercutio had costumes that were not only handsome but would hold together in the strenuous duelling scenes Shakespeare had supplied for them. In the case of lesser actors the fit of the clothes was of less importance and much could be done with pounds of copper lace sprinkled about with a liberal hand. One of the merits of *Romeo and Juliet* from the costumer's point of view was that at least there were no battle scenes requiring armor. Armor was expensive, difficult to get on and off, and even required special underwear, and although much could be done with painted imitations it is not likely they were ever worn by the principals.

To make sure that all the properties were ready when they should be and that the actors would remember all their cues for entrances, a large sheet of paper was pasted on a board and hung on a peg at some conspicuous point backstage to carry all this information. This action sheet was called a "plot," and it listed in two columns when each actor came on and in what character and noted the general line of the action. Notes were also made in the margin of the prompt book when new properties had to be ready backstage, and careful timing was arranged on all the technical details.

Some companies kept strict order at rehearsals by a system of fines. If an actor was late to rehearsal he was fined twelvepence and if he was absent, two shillings. If he was not ready in costume on the actual day of the show at a specified hour he was fined three shillings, if he was drunk ten shillings, and if he was absent altogether unless by "just excuse of sickness," he was fined twenty shillings. A shilling was the price of a day's wages for a hired actor, but no company could afford lazy or unreliable performers.

The most important thing achieved at the rehearsals, apart from the smooth efficiency that comes from experienced teamwork, was the gradual creation of the reality of the characters in the minds of the actors. The men who were rehearsing *Romeo and Juliet* not only had a great deal of acting experience and an increasing knowledge of how to work effectively as a unit, but they had the final advantage of working with the man who had invented the characters and knew them better than anyone else in the world. The rehearsal period must have been one of enormous satisfaction to the Chamberlain's men, with the play coming slowly to life before their eyes and their sense of excitement deepening.

The final expense was to advertise the play, since even the most receptive London audience could not be expected to rush to a new play unless they had some idea of what it was going to be about. The advertising was done on single sheets, called playbills, which were posted up about the city wherever a potential member of the audience might see them. These playbills cost the actors a fair amount of money, but they had no choice where they placed their order. It had to go to James Roberts, who had married the widow of the printer who had previously held the monopoly and who consequently possessed, by decree of the Stationers' Company, the right of "the only imprinting of all manner of bills for players." The Elizabethan age was a period of monopolies, and the practice tended to keep prices high where a more competitive system might have lowered them.

It is not known how many bills were printed to advertise a single play, but a fencer who was promoting a private match put in an order for more than a hundred. Only one playbill of the period has survived and it may not be a characteristic one, since the play was not produced and its unethical promoter evidently never intended that it should be. But if the playbill for *England's Joy* represented normal procedure, it was the custom to advertise each of the big scenes in rich and detailed language that would have done credit to a circus.

A new play always attracted a large audience and was evidently not presented on a holiday when a full house could be expected whatever was played. A new production like *Romeo and Juliet* was probably given in the middle of the week, and the silk flag that had cost the company about thirty shillings was run up on the turret to show that the playhouse was open for business. The men who distributed the drinks and fruit that were sold to the audience had their stock ready, the gatherers took up their various posts, and the men with the trumpets waited for the actor who played the Prologue to give them their cue that the play was ready to begin.

The Elizabethan theatre was not based on the element of surprise but on the gratification of expectation. If anyone did not know the general plot of *Romeo and Juliet* before he entered the theatre, the speech of the Prologue solved the matter for him. The actor who played this part cannot be envied, since it was up to him to capture the attention of an excitable, individualistic audience, most of whom had been waiting for a long time since the places were not reserved and many of whom were probably busy chewing. Shakespeare's Prologue did not go in for mystification. He stated clearly and at once that the play was about two unlucky lovers who were eventually going to die because their parents were having a feud. Then the two minor actors who played Capulet's men came on with swords and bucklers, and the play began. If it was a success with the audience, it would be put in the regular repertoire of the company and probably played again some time the following week. If it was a failure it would be quietly forgotten and another play would go into rehearsal immediately.

Romeo and Juliet was an instant success. Everyone liked it, but the young people liked it especially, for it put their own dreams into poetry and gave them back again. When a satirist at the end of the decade described various young men in London—the one who collected jokes, the one who knew everything about fencing, the one who made a hobby of dancing and had "dreams of toe-turns," and so on—the young man with the craze for play-going had just seen Shakespeare's play and was able to speak "naught but pure Juliet and Romeo." This young man's idea of making love was to quote from the latest success at the Curtain, and other young men of the period were like him in jotting down lines from the play in their commonplace books. When Robert Allot published his popular anthology, *England's Parnassus*, in 1600, he quoted more lavishly from *Romeo and Juliet* than from any other of Shakespeare's plays and most of Allot's contemporaries would probably have agreed with his choice.

Popularity of this kind was too valuable to ignore, and a printer named John Danter, who had brought out the play and the ballad of *Titus Andronicus* in 1594, brought out the play and the ballad of *Romeo and Juliet* in 1597. Danter made the special point on the title page that the play was a popular one, showing to "great applause." The Londoners who had seen the play wanted to relive their experience, and the Londoners who had missed it wanted to see what the play was about, and Danter's edition probably sold well.

It did not deserve to. It was one of those corrupt editions that occurred whenever the company would not release the official text for publication and the printer had to pick up whatever version he could. This happened with the quarto editions of six or seven of Shakespeare's plays, and the text of *Romeo and Juliet* is by no means the worst. But it shows throughout what happens when a second-rate mind tries to follow a first-rate one.

The pirate who supplied Danter with his text invented his own lines of verse when he could not remember the original, and achieved such a misfortune as:

> Ah, Romeo, Romeo, what disaster hap
> Hath severed thee from thy true Juliet?

He was evidently working with the shortened stage version and yet he managed to make Juliet's closing speech longer than in the original because he lacked Shakespeare's gift for condensation. He had no ear for dialogue, and where Shakespeare has Capulet demand drier logs:

"Call Peter, he will show thee where they are,"

the individual who pirated the script was moved by vague memories of Will Kempe, who played the part of Peter, and produced a line that would turn any actor's hair grey: "Will will tell thee where thou shalt fetch them." His ability to spoil Shakespeare's stage effects shows up especially well in the balcony scene. The Nurse has been shouting "Madam" while Juliet calls Romeo back again in a whisper. The pirate has Romeo also answer "Madam," a line which he could not deliver on the stage without giving the effect that he was parodying the Nurse. The text is not only inaccurate but badly printed, with an entirely new printer's type emerging suddenly in the middle of the second act, and the whole thing is a stupidly second-rate version of a great play.

Shakespeare was not the only writer whose plays were subjected to this kind of abuse. At about this same date the Rose theatre was showing a very popular play by George Chapman called *The Blind Beggar of Alexandria*. Chapman was telling the story of a tragic queen named Aegiale but it was the comedy disguises of the blind beggar that pleased the public, and when the play was published, a year after *Romeo and Juliet*, the serious parts of the play were so heavily cut they were almost unintelligible. This mutilation may already have occurred in the stage version that was presented at the Rose, for the Admiral's company felt no responsibility for nsuring a correct version of the text. The Chamberlain's company evidently felt otherwise about *Romeo and Juliet*, for a new text, "augmented and amended," was published two years after Danter's corrupt version. This script was evidently the one that had been used as a prompt copy, since Will Kempe, instead of "Peter," appears in the fourth act.

The success of *Romeo and Juliet* was partly due to the brilliance of the stagecraft and the luminous beauty of the lines, but the greatest force of the play lay in its characterization. Nothing quite like Shakespeare's ability to create real people had ever appeared before on the English stage. He had shown occasional signs of it in his earlier plays, where for a moment the characters cease to be types and become individuals, but it was not until he joined the Chamberlain's company that he began peopling the stage with that incredible succession of human beings who are as real today as when the first excited audience listened to them. This power of characterization had of course lain dormant with him, but it could not have flowered unless conditions were favorable. If the actors who interpreted Romeo and Juliet had failed him, he might not have had the heart to go on to Hamlet and King Lear.

The support that Shakespeare's company gave him was not limited to *Romeo and Juliet*. The same care and intelligence must have gone into the production of each of the scripts he brought them, since they were unquestionably the best group of actors in London. Shakespeare had what every playwright needs, sympathetic and intelligent interpretation, and his genius for characterization was given the space it needed in which to grow. Even in the unpromising field of the history play Shakespeare was able to find real people among the wars and the trumpets, and before he had spent four years with the Chamberlain's company he had lifted the history play to such a height of reality that Falstaff himself was at home in it.

The first history play that Shakespeare wrote for his company was probably *King John*. As he often did, Shakespeare worked from an old play and in this case he followed the general line of the action so closely he must have had the original before him as he worked. Nevertheless, he used only one line from the original play in his own version, for Shakespeare did not rewrite old plays; he transformed them. The original play had no characterization in it, but Shakespeare saw an opportunity for one and seized upon it, creating what was possibly a predecessor of Mercutio in the chatty and delightful Bastard of Faulconbridge.

In another history play, Shakespeare went to his well-thumbed copy of Holinshed's *Chronicles* to conclude the Wars of the Roses that he had been recording in the *Henry VI* trilogy. The trilogy had ended with the future King Richard promising himself that he would "snarl and bite" as soon as he had the chance, and *Richard III* gave it to him. Shakespeare did not usually use Marlowe's device of building a whole play around a single, towering villain, but Richard of York made a splendid villain with his crippled body, his bloody plots and his violent love-making. Richard Burbage was famous for the role and evidently played it to the hilt. In the final scene of Richard's downfall he had a wonderful moment for any actor when he shouted, "A horse! a horse! my kingdom for a horse!" and he did it so well that the line became a kind of byword in the theatre and was freely parodied. There was a story of a host, "full of ale and history," who took his guests over Bosworth Field and solemnly showed them the very place where Richard Burbage had cried out the famous lines, before he had died in the battle.

Richard the Third was a very popular villain with Englishmen, and a popular anthology on the lives of prominent people called *The Mirror for Magistrates* had already celebrated his "fine and fatal fall." *The Mirror for Magistrates* devoted itself almost exclusively to the collapse of the great, with suitable accompanying morals, and no career lent itself better to moralizing than that of another King Richard, Richard the Second. Shakespeare found no moral in Richard II's career, but he was deeply interested in the temperament of that dreamy master of self-dramatization. Shakespeare's Richard II was the kind of man who could even take a certain aesthetic pleasure in his own downfall, and his tragedy is not quite a tragedy because the king is more interested in his reactions to events than he is in doing anything about them. The part is not a bravura part, like Richard III, but if Burbage played it he must have found the development of the characterization even more interesting.

Richard II was destroyed by his practical cousin, who became Henry IV, and in the two parts of *Henry IV* Shakespeare deals with the problems he encountered by usurping the throne. Shakespeare knit his history plays very tightly to each other, so that most of them form an uninterrupted sequence, and at the end of *Richard II* the new King Henry indicated that he was having difficulty with his son, who had taken to going about with "unrestrained loose companions." When Shakespeare started his new play he found himself less interested in King Henry than in Prince Hal and his loose companions. An old play by the Queen's Men called *The Famous Victories of Henry the Fifth* had spent some time on Hal's youth and had named the leader of his disreputable followers as one Sir John Oldcastle.

The more Shakespeare thought about Sir John Oldcastle the clearer he became. There were a great many opportunities to observe old soldiers in London, since the city supplied a fourth of the men in the entire kingdom, and Shakespeare knew the elaborate army grafts on which many an old captain had retired. He knew the cheating and the lying and the cadging of these disreputable old codgers, and he combined it with the Italian tradition of the braggart soldier; and out of this unpromising material leaped one of the greatest comedy creations in the history of the world.

As soon as Sir John Oldcastle appeared on the stage in the Chamberlain's company's production of the first part of *Henry IV*, a howl of unregenerate joy went up from the audiences

who at once took the disgraceful old gentleman to their collective hearts. The notoriety given the respectable name of
Oldcastle was quite unjust, for in real life Sir John had been
a renowned warrior, and someone evidently objected. The
name of this individual is unknown, but it was probably
Henry Brooke, eighth Lord Cobham, who was descended on
his mother's side from Sir John Oldcastle. Shakespeare oblig-
ingly changed the name to Sir John Falstaff, and went on to
use that name in part two of the play. There were those who
objected to this name also, since it sounded too much like
Sir John Fastolf, another respectable warrior of the 15th century, but there is no way of pleasing everyone.

Shakespeare was thorough in altering "Sir John Oldcastle"
to "Sir John Falstaff", and the only sign in the play that Oldcastle had ever existed is a line in the second act that requires
a three-syllable name to scan. The reference to Falstaff as
"my old lad of the castle" was not necessary to omit, since
that was a common slang phrase for a roisterer; Gabriel
Harvey, for instance, spoke of Greene and his companions as
"old lads of the castle." But many people were still calling
the play *Sir John Oldcastle* at the end of the decade, and the
Admiral's company capitalized on the situation by producing
a play about the historical Sir John. They announced smugly
that their play was not about a "pampered glutton" but
about a virtuous peer, and closed the prologue by hinting
pretty strongly that the Chamberlain's company had basely
betrayed history.

Let fair truth be graced
Since forged invention former time disgraced.

Michael Drayton was one of the four writers who did the
play for the Admiral's company, but it is to be hoped he was
not the one responsible for the prologue.

Meanwhile Shakespeare had also been writing comedies;

and in the comedies, as in the history plays, he came to mastership by degrees. The first romantic comedy he wrote for the Chamberlain's company was probably *The Two Gentlemen of Verona*, an elaborate study on the theme of love and friendship that was in some ways as artificial as *Love's Labour's Lost*. But this time Shakespeare did not lack for plot complications, and he packed into the play all the routine Italian devices that he was later to lift to such radiant heights. He used the device of the girl disguised as her lover's page who is obliged to plead his suit with his rival, and later he made the scene one of the most delightful in *Twelfth Night*. He used the device of the noble band of outlaws in the forest that he later transformed in *As You Like It*. He used various devices that reappeared in *Romeo and Juliet*, like the friar, the ladder of cords and the exile from court. The exchange of rings and the girl dressing as a man reappeared in *The Merchant of Venice*, and so did a whole scene in which the lady talks over her suitors with her maid. Shakespeare's willingness to use old material extended to material he had used himself, and he was just as capable of improving old devices as he was of improving the plays and books he used as his sources.

Shakespeare was never very interested in innovations and he even found a place in his heart for that shopworn relic of medievalism, the clown. Men like Christopher Marlowe and Ben Jonson very much disliked making a concession to popular taste by thrusting a clown into one of their carefully-wrought plays, but the London audiences had been accustomed to this sort of thing for centuries and William Shakespeare saw no reason for depriving them of anything to which they had been accustomed. He thrust the usual clown into *The Two Gentlemen of Verona*, although there is no real place for him in the story and Launce and his trick dog are not much more than a vaudeville interlude to get a laugh. But Shakespeare continued to use the clown as he continued to use the cheap plot devices of Italian fiction, and Launce is the ancestor of wonderful creations like Dogberry and Bottom. Shakespeare never considered himself superior to the ordinary popular stagecraft of the period. He used it, and in using he transformed it.

Another romantic comedy that Shakespeare wrote in the same general period was *The Merchant of Venice* and again he used the dream background of an imaginary city. Shakespeare's Venice is just as unreal as Shakespeare's Verona, and Antonio's troubles with his ships would have raised a shout of laughter in a city that had been insuring cargoes for generations. Even more unrealistic is the way the characters discuss usury, which was not only a commonplace in Venice but equally a commonplace in Shakespeare's London. A government decree at the beginning of Elizabeth's reign stated firmly that usury was a sin but it also went on to state that ten per cent was a legal rate of interest. Half the members of Shakespeare's audience had either lent or borrowed money at high rates of interest, and they knew perfectly well that Shakespeare's *Merchant of Venice* was a folk play that had nothing to do with current economic conditions. As one contemporary remarked, "He is accounted but for a fool that doth lend his money for nothing," and although in theory the average Englishman still held to the medieval conception of usury as a wicked occupation fit only for Jews, in practice every Londoner made it a part of normal business procedure.

Shakespeare's portrait of Shylock is as unrealistic as his portrait of business conditions in Venice. It is a folk portrait, for Shakespeare had no opportunity to see any real Jews. They had all been exiled from England in the Middle Ages and the law that kept them out was in full force. A typical incident in the 80's involved a mining expert from Prague who was working at Bristol. It was discovered he knew Hebrew and further questioning showed he was a Jew. He was arrested by the local magistrate, sent up to London for questioning by the Privy Council, and at once deported.

The crime of Joachim Gaunz was not his race but his religion, and if he had been baptised into the Christian faith he would have been welcome in England. There had even been a home for converted Jews established in London at the time of the expulsion, and although the building in Chancery Lane was eventually annexed for government offices any Christian of the Hebrew race was welcome in London. The point is illustrated in *The Merchant of Venice* by Shylock's daughter, who is perfectly respectable from the audience's point of view in spite of her ancestry because, as she says, "I shall be saved by my husband; he hath made me a Christian."

The only "Jews" that Shakespeare could have met in London were baptised Christians of the Hebrew race, and none of these would have served as a model for Shylock. The model was medieval Christian tradition, and this tradition was so strong that even the greatest of writers had been unable to shake themselves loose from it. When Geoffrey Chaucer described a "cursed Jew" it was to show him murdering a little Christian boy as part of his normal behavior, and when Christopher Marlowe wrote *The Jew of Malta*, Barrabas tries to poison a whole city-full of Christians and is finally plunged, to the delight of any contemporary audience, into a boiling cauldron. This was the only tradition that was available to Shakespeare when he created Shylock, and the degree to which he was able to break loose from this tradition is astonishing. Less and less as he continued his career was he able to simplify—to look at his characters through half-closed eyes and record only a few effective characteristics. Even in his folk portraits he was unable to prevent himself from seeing real human beings, and where his audiences expected only a comic villain they got Shylock. "I am a Jew. Hath not a Jew eyes? hath not a Jew hands, organs, dimensions, senses, affections, passions? . . . If you prick us, do we not bleed?"

The varying elements that go to make up *The Merchant of*

Venice are not handled in a single key, and for a modern audience especially the play often seems to pull apart. Yet Shakespeare was able to take an even more varied group of characters and turn them into a perfect whole in *A Midsummer Night's Dream*, that irresistible combination of moonlight and moonshine. Again Shakespeare was economical, for he had already used the device in *Love's Labour's Lost* of the stage-struck amateurs who try to put on a play; and the production of Holofernes and the curate is a pale forerunner of the inspired nonsense of Bottom's production of Pyramus and Thisbe. The fairies were all played by children, and their rigid training as dancers must have been useful to them; but Puck, who was not technically a fairy, was played by a grown man. Incidentally, Shakespeare completely changed the character of the English fairy for future generations of readers, for they were rather malignant, earth-bound little country folk before Shakespeare housed them in flowers.

All these plays were produced in the first four years of Shakespeare's association with the Chamberlain's company and can be dated as having been written before September, 1598. Attempts to find internal evidence for dating the plays are extremely risky in dealing with a mind like Shakespeare's, with its casual, gigantic leaps and its occasional carelessness. But by great good fortune a book was entered for publication in September of 1598 in which the author had written a list of Shakespeare's plays.

The book was called *Palladis Tamia* and its author was Francis Meres. Meres was an Oxford graduate who had been mildly successful with a religious book and had been commissioned to contribute to a series of cultural handbooks called *Wits Commonwealth*. These short-cuts to erudition were always popular with the London public, but, while most of the compilers kept to useful quotations from the classics, Francis Meres was more ambitious and set out to show his knowledge of the contemporary literary world of London.

Meres' knowledge of the literary world was not very extensive and he was under the impression that Marlowe had been stabbed by "a bawdy serving-man," a description of himself that would have surprised Ingram Frizer, who ended up as a churchwarden. But when Meres came to Shakespeare, whom he mentions in five different connections, he shows himself to be remarkably well informed.

It is not surprising that Meres knew about *Venus and Adonis* and *The Rape of Lucrece*, since these two narrative poems were still going into edition after edition; but unless Meres was acquainted with someone in Shakespeare's own circle he could not have known that he was circulating "sugared sonnets among his private friends." Still less could Meres have known about Shakespeare's plays, since only a few of these were in print and most of them anonymously, and yet Meres was able to produce a long list of the plays that Shakespeare had written. "As Plautus and Seneca are accounted the best for comedy and tragedy among the Latins; so Shakespeare among the English is the most excellent in both kinds for the stage; for comedy, witness his *Gentlemen of Verona*, his *Errors*, his *Loves Labours Lost*, his *Loves Labours Won*, his *Midsummer Night's Dream*, his *Merchant of Venice*; for tragedy, his *Richard the Second, Richard the Third, Henry the Fourth, King John, Titus Andronicus*, and his *Romeo and Juliet*." If *Loves Labours Won* is another name for *The Taming of the Shrew*, this is practically a complete list. The only omission is the *Henry VI* trilogy, which can be identified as Shakespeare's from other contemporary sources.

This is the only list of its kind that was ever given for an Elizabethan playwright, just as it happens to be the only case in which all a playwright's texts have survived. It is extremely fortunate that the greatest of Elizabethan playwrights should also have been the best documented, and that Meres should have performed a service for Shakespeare that he denied to all of the rest. Meres mentioned a great many playwrights in his book, from popular playwrights like Greene and Kyd to noblemen who practiced the art like Lord Buckhurst and the Earl of Oxford, and he was sufficiently well informed to include even a newcomer like Ben Jonson. But William Shakespeare was the only one he singled out for extended comment, and the evident reason was that he admired him. "The Muses would speak with Shakespeare's fine filed phrase, if they would speak English."

Shortly after Meres wrote *Palladis Tamia* he retired to Rutland as the rector of a small parish, and it is to be hoped that he was happy there. He may not have been an important writer or made a great success of his literary career in London, but few men deserve more gratitude from any biographer of Shakespeare.

Chapter 8

BACK in Stratford the Shakespeare family had been involved for the past eighteen years in a difficulty over land that resulted in two bitter lawsuits. Going to law was a normal part of Elizabethan existence, and there was hardly a family in England in that argumentative age that did not have at least one lawsuit pending. John Shakespeare had a normal number of suits during his lifetime, mostly over the collection of debts, and won or lost as the case might be. But there was a special bitterness in the lawsuits that involved his wife's inheritance at Wilmcote.

A short time after John Shakespeare left the Council so abruptly, he found himself in need of money and borrowed forty pounds from his wife's brother-in-law, Edmund Lambert, with a mortgage on some of Mary Shakespeare's land as security. Forty pounds was a comparatively small sum for what was a fairly large piece of property, but since the transaction was kept in the family, John Shakespeare no doubt felt he was safe enough in taking out the mortgage.

The payment of the money was due in 1580, which happened to be a difficult year for John Shakespeare. He was concerned in a case involving a breach of the peace at the Court of Queen's Bench at Westminster, and when neither he nor a Nottingham hat-maker put in an appearance on a stipulated date he had to forfeit twenty pounds for himself and another twenty for the hat-maker. Nevertheless, John

Shakespeare had another forty pounds in cash for Edmund Lambert, and on Michaelmas Day he took the fifteen-mile trip south to the village where his wife's brother-in-law lived to pay off the mortgage. Lambert refused to accept the money, saying that Shakespeare owed him more than that, and when he died seven years later Edmund Lambert was still in possession of the property.

John Shakespeare happened to be under heavy extra expenses the year Edmund Lambert died. He was being sued for ten pounds that his brother Henry owed someone and had failed to pay, and he had lost another ten pounds because he had gone surety for a Stratford coppersmith named Michael Price who had failed to make a stipulated appearance at the court in Coventry. Nevertheless John Shakespeare was ready to shoulder the extra burden of an expensive lawsuit, and in Michaelmas term of 1588 he and his wife and his son William presented a bill of complaint against Edmund Lambert's son and heir in the Court of Queen's Bench at Warwick. The hearing was set for the following year and the Shakespeares lost the case, since the Elizabethan law in regard to mortgages was unyielding.

John Shakespeare refused to admit failure and eight years later he brought suit against John Lambert again. This time he tried the Court of Chancery, an informal court that really attempted to get to the rights of the case where a strict interpretation involved special legal hardship. The outcome of the case is unknown, but there is no evidence that John Shakespeare got back his land.

Five years after the failure of his first suit, John Shakespeare lost another of his possessions. There was a bad fire in Stratford in September, 1594, and in spite of the fire ladder and the collection of buckets at Market Cross, the fire succeeded in getting as far as Henley Street. The two houses in which the Shakespeares were living were not affected, but the third house, which John Shakespeare had been renting out, was either destroyed by fire or pulled down by fire-hooks. It was the opinion of the vicar of Stratford that the cause of the fire was the unwillingness of the citizens to observe the Sabbath, which was an entirely orthodox conclusion. His predecessor in the Stratford pulpit had read a prayer of thanksgiving, after the repulse of the Spanish Armada, which officially attributed the attempted Spanish invasion to God's punishment of various English sins, including "excess in meat and drink." Every disaster in Elizabethan England, from the greatest to the least, was always attributed to the hand of God.

Two years after the loss of a house by fire there was a tragedy in the Shakespeare family that was perhaps the most heartbreaking blow John Shakespeare ever sustained. His grandson Hamnet, the only boy in the family and the only heir of the family name, died in August, 1596. Of all the hopes that must once have centered around William Shakespeare's only son there remain only two brief entries in the Stratford register, one giving the date of his baptism and the other, eleven years later, giving the date of his burial. The two surviving children were the boy's twin, Judith, and her thirteen-year-old sister, Susanna.

When Hamnet was buried in Stratford on the 11th of August, his father's company was playing at a town in Kent, forty-seven miles on the other side of London. If the boy's illness was a long one there may have been some way to get word to his father in time, so that he could at least have reached Stratford in time for the burial. But once the actors were on tour there was no way to reach them except to send a letter by carrier to some town on the route, with instructions to hold it there until the playing company arrived. This was not a reliable arrangement even when the letter went from London and the sender knew the company's route. Philip Henslowe knew every detail of his son-in-law's profession and yet when Alleyn was on tour Henslowe wrote to him, "We would write oftener to you than we do, but we know not whither to send to you." Unless word of Hamnet's illness reached his father before Shakespeare left London for the regular touring season of 1596, it is not likely that anyone in Stratford was able to get in touch with him until the company was back in London again.

From that time on there seem to have been no more tragedies in old John Shakespeare's life. The remaining five years of his life were not only undisturbed but must have been actually triumphant. The increasing splendor that spread over the Shakespeare family in Stratford was the reflected glow from the eldest son who had left the previous decade to join a despised profession but who had since become a rich and consequently respected man.

The first outward sign of the changed position of the Shakespeares in Stratford came in 1596, the otherwise tragic year of Hamnet's death. On October 20, a new draft of the Shakespeare coat of arms was made in the London office of the College of Heralds. This draft was in John Shakespeare's name, since it was he who became the gentleman, but it seems almost certain that it was William Shakespeare who arranged to have the matter reopened.

This time the grant went through and John Shakespeare received the coat of arms that had been designed for him twenty years earlier. Robert Cooke had made him a handsome, simple design: a gold shield with a band of black across it that bore a spear of gold tipped with silver, and for a crest a silver falcon with outstretched wings standing on a silver wreath and supporting a spear. John Shakespeare and his heirs could blazon the arms on their "rings, signets, edifices, utensils, liveries, tombs and monuments," and from that time forward he walked the streets of Stratford as complete and accredited a gentleman as his friend Adrian Quiney. In 1599 there was a move to get his wife's arms, those of the Ardens, impaled with his. The Heralds' Office went into the matter carefully and finally established her connection with the Ardens of Cheshire, but this impalement was never actually made.

After John Shakespeare's death in the next decade, when his son William had succeeded him as the "gentleman" of the family, there was a discussion in the Heralds' Office over the suitability of this grant of a coat of arms to the Shakespeares. There was nothing improper in the grant itself. John Shakespeare had been a bailiff and a justice of the peace and he had married into the great family of the Ardens. He was probably not worth the £500 attributed to him and he may not have had a great-grandfather who fought under Henry VII and thus won lands in Warwickshire, but amiable fictions of this kind were considered legitimate. What was wrong with the Shakespeare coat of arms was that it had been granted by Sir William Dethick, that brilliant, bad-tempered thunderhead of an official who so maddened some of his colleagues in the Office of Heralds that they would have gone to almost any lengths to prove him in the wrong.

Dethick's co-official in the grant to the Shakespeares was William Camden, a kindly gentleman and great scholar who had succeeded Robert Cooke; but Camden was also unpopular in the Heralds' Office because he was an outsider who had been given a high post over the heads of various experienced officials who were in line for the honor. The situation particularly maddened the York Herald, Ralph Brooke, who had a temper of his own and who had already attacked Camden's learning. In 1602 Brooke drew up a list of the mistakes Dethick and Camden had made in office and these included the granting of arms to "Shakespeare the player." The Shakespeares did not come from the upper walks of life and in any case the coat of arms that had been granted them was too close to Lord Mauley's.

The reply that Dethick and Camden made to Brooke still exists in its original manuscript form, written out between a drawing of the Shakespeare coat of arms on one side of the page and that of Lord Mauley on the other. The two chief Heralds maintained that the two designs were not the same because the "spear on the bend" in the Shakespeare one made an obvious difference. Moreover, John Shakespeare had been worthy to receive arms. "The man was a magistrate in Stratford-upon-Avon. A justice of the peace, he married a daughter and heir of Arden and was of good substance."

This defense of the Shakespeare family made by Camden is especially interesting because of Camden's position in the literary world of his day. His *Britannia* had made him the most admired writer in England on learned matters, and since he habitually wrote in Latin his fame was even greater on the Continent than it was in England. It was chiefly because of his fame as a writer and antiquarian that Camden had been elevated to so high a post in the Heralds' Office without previous experience in the work, and if Camden said the Shakespeares were eligible for a coat of arms, the family could not have had the backing of a more learned authority. Camden was an admirer of Shakespeare as a writer, and he once made a list of contemporary English poets, starting with Sidney and Spenser and ending with "William Shakespeare, and other most pregnant wits of these our times, whom succeeding ages may justly admire." Camden was one of the few men of the period who had connections with William Shakespeare from both the Stratford and the London end; he knew him both as John Shakespeare's son and as a writer, a fact that makes his testimony of special interest.

Less than a year after the new draft of the coat of arms had been made, the prestige of the Shakespeare family in Stratford took another enormous step forward. On the fourth of May, 1597, William Shakespeare bought the second largest house in town.

New Place was much more than just a house. It was a symbol of high social standing in Stratford and its owner had a special pew in church called the Clopton Pew. The house had been built by Sir Hugh Clopton, onetime Lord Mayor of London who also gave Stratford its great stone bridge. Sir Hugh had hoped to retire to Stratford before he died and he built what he called "my great house" opposite the Guild Chapel that his money had already beautified.

As late as 1543, in the century after Sir Hugh's death, New Place was described as "a pretty house of brick and timber." But brick was an unusual building material in Stratford, and the thin bricks of the period did not prove to be very durable. New Place was still a fine house when one of Henry VIII's physicians lived in it and collected silver, but it had a succession of tenants and when the Underhill family took it over in Shakespeare's boyhood it was already badly in need of repair. It was probably for this reason that Shakespeare was able to buy it for only sixty pounds, a low price for a house of this kind, especially since there had been two recent fires in Stratford and good houses were scarce. Shakespeare must have made extensive alterations, for he sold the Corporation a load of stone the following year, when the bridge was undergoing one of its frequent repairs, and since the sub-soil of New Place is gravel the stone must have come from some alterations that were being made in the foundations.

The property had its own ancient garden and included an orchard and two barns. There was nothing wrong with New Place that money could not cure, and in return its owner was assured a position of unquestioned prominence in the community. The Shakespeare family had come a long way since the previous decade, when they had been so completely outdistanced in Stratford by the Quineys.

It was almost a case of poetic justice that when Richard Quiney was in London in 1598 he tried to borrow money from William Shakespeare. Quiney was there on town business, trying to get a remission of taxes because of a depression and two fires in Stratford, but before he hurried off to Court on the 25th of October he sat down in his inn, the Bell in Carter Lane, and wrote a letter to Shakespeare in his small, swift, lawyer-like hand. Quiney wanted his "loving good friend and countryman, William Shakespeare" to lend him thirty pounds and was willing to advance excellent security.

What Quiney wanted the money for is not quite clear. He told Shakespeare he wanted to pay off "the debts I owe in London" and that these were disquieting him because he did not like to be "indebted." Since he was raising more money to do it, it would seem that Quiney did not consider a debt to Shakespeare as coming within this category. On the other hand, Richard's father, old Adrian Quiney, wrote his son that if he got any money from Shakespeare there was an excellent bargain in knit stockings at the nearby town of Evesham and that twenty pounds invested there would bring in a good return. Probably Richard Quiney wanted part of the money to pay off old debts and part of it to make some business investments as a mercer; and since he was successful at Court in getting a remission of Stratford taxes, it is to be hoped he was equally successful in his attempt to borrow money from his "loving good friend."

By 1598 William Shakespeare had become one of the major householders in Stratford, but unlike Richard Quiney he never showed any interest in the welfare of the town or how its affairs were conducted. The town records are almost blank where his name is concerned, and Shakespeare's chief activity in Stratford, apart from the growing number of his real estate purchases, seems to have been his lawsuits with fellow townsmen over debts. The London actor seems to have been rigidly on his dignity in his native town, in contrast to his easy, relaxed relations with his colleagues in London. He was deeply interested in the fortunes of the Shakespeare family but not in the fortunes of Stratford, and even when he finally retired to New Place to live he sided against his native town in the great enclosure controversy. Shakespeare had many friends in Stratford, such as Hamnet Sadler, and kept them as friends all his life; and it is quite possible that he loved the town of his birth as he certainly loved the countryside around it. But it seems undeniable that he had very little interest in Stratford's welfare and very little sense of local responsibility.

One of the few occasions in which Shakespeare's name appears in the local records was in February of 1598. A survey was being made in England to see how much barley was being held in private hands, and the returns from Stratford showed every major householder in town on the list, including the owner of New Place.

For the past few years there had been an alarming succession of bad harvests in England and the Privy Council was keeping a close eye on the local price of wheat and barley, or, as the Elizabethans called it, corn and malt. To offset any tendency toward profiteering, the Privy Council ordered a survey of every barn in England, so that if the owner had any extra grain he could be forced to sell it to the general public at a set price.

The real trouble in the Stratford area was the fact that the normal flow of grain from the neighboring counties of Worcester and Gloucester was being diverted because better prices could be obtained elsewhere, and the Privy Council sent a stiff letter to both counties on the subject. But there was also a survey made of the Stratford area to make sure that no one was illegally holding grain.

The survey showed that everyone in Stratford was being illegal, or at least as illegal as possible. William Shakespeare of Chapel Street Ward had about ten quarters of malt stored in his thatched barn in Chapel Lane; ten quarters would be about eighty bushels and well over the legal limit. Shakespeare's respectable neighbor in the same ward, Alexander Aspinall, the schoolmaster, had eleven quarters. His equally respectable neighbor, Thomas Dixon, had seventeen. About a dozen residents of Stratford, many of them with smaller households than the Shakespeare family, had more malt in their barns than Shakespeare did, and the truth was that everyone in Stratford had as much barley stored away as possible and held on to it as long as he could.

The medieval idea that prices could be controlled legally and that everything should be shared was still strong enough in England so that the Privy Council had the approval of the general public. But occasionally there was an individualist who thought otherwise, like the grain holder who announced defiantly in Star Chamber, "My goods are my own . . . I will do what I list with them." For this he was fined a hundred pounds and obliged to wear a paper cap, like a schoolboy's, which described his misdeeds.

The depression of the late 90's did more than affect the malt supply in Stratford and its roots were deeper than a few years of heavy rains and bad harvests. Ever since the Spanish Armada was overthrown, England had been paying for the war with Spain with increasingly heavy taxation and a draining-off of her natural resources. Many of her European markets were closed by the war, and privateering on the high seas had raised freight costs and made a stabilization of trade almost impossible. There was a trade war with Germany and a dangerous rebellion in Ireland. Prices had been climbing steadily, with wages and rents lagging far behind, and when food began to run short it added the final touch to the increasing gloom of the decade. Everything was "exceeding measure in price, such was our sins deserving it," and the only thing the Privy Council could suggest was that the Londoners ought to eat less.

The acting companies in London were fully aware of the depression, since they all depended on the free spending of their customers. But in 1596 they experienced a further, private disaster in the death of the Lord Chamberlain, who worked with all the companies since he controlled the Office of the Revels but who was particularly vital to the welfare of the Chamberlain's company. Henry, Lord Hunsdon, died in July, in his seventy-first year and was buried in Westminster Abbey; and the office of Chamberlain went to William Brooke, seventh Lord Cobham, a man who disliked plays. The mayor of London, who never missed an opportunity to harry the players, rushed to the attack as soon as their powerful protector was dead; and Tom Nashe found there was no market for new plays in London because the actors "are piteously persecuted by the Lord Mayor and however in their old lord's time they thought their state settled, it is now so uncertain they cannot build upon it."

Nevertheless, Shakespeare's company maintained its position at court, giving all six of the plays produced before the Queen at Whitehall that year, and in the spring their prospects brightened. Lord Cobham died in March and the Office of Lord Chamberlain went back into the Hunsdon family. It was given to George, second Lord Hunsdon, who had already taken over the patronage of his father's company of players and who received in April his father's position at Court. Shakespeare's company had been known since the preceding August as Lord Hunsdon's company, but now it became the Chamberlain's company again. It was during this interim that *Romeo and Juliet* was first published, since the title page stated that it had "been often (with great applause) played publicly by the Right Honorable the Lord of Hunsdon his servants."

In spite of the sympathy the new Lord Chamberlain had for the players, the mayor of London did not give up his efforts to purge the city of that sink of iniquity, the London theatre. On the 28th day of July, 1597, the mayor and aldermen wrote a long letter to the Privy Council, making a list of all the misfortunes the City was enduring by having actors in its midst. Even the heathen, the mayor said plaintively, only saw plays occasionally but Londoners saw them all the time.

"They are a special cause of corrupting youth, containing nothing but unchaste matter, lascivious devices, shifts of cosenage and other lewd and ungodly practices," which is a fair description of a play like *Romeo and Juliet* from the Puritan point of view. In addition, they brought together thieves and whoremongers and contrivers of treason who would certainly corrupt by their presence any members of the audience who were not already hopelessly ruined. They attracted people who should have been in church, to the profanation of religion, and they "drew apprentices and other servants from their work," to the hindrance of trade. Moreover, if there was a plague the Londoners tended to go to plays to comfort themselves and thus the theatres were a threat to health as well as to everything else.

It is impossible to say what effect this powerful document might have had upon the Privy Council, for the Privy Council had just taken measures of its own to suppress the theatres. On the same day the letter was sent, the Privy Council issued a government order to have all the plays in London discontinued and every theatre in London pulled down.

The Privy Council was not interested in plays like *Romeo and Juliet*, however they might corrupt the young or hinder honest trade. The Council was interested only in the possible spread of sedition through the theatre, and it had been informed that the newly organized company of Lord Pembroke had produced a play at the Swan which contained "very seditious and slanderous matter." Three of the actors were at once sent to prison in the Marshalsea, and although the author could not be sent to join them since he had wisely left town, his lodgings were ransacked for further examples of suspicious writing.

The play was called *The Isle of Dogs* and its author was the irrepressible Tom Nashe, who had found an incautious buyer for his latest play in Pembroke's company. Nashe was the last of the old, excitable, brilliant group of university men that had once gathered around Marlowe and Greene, and he was still in spirit the impish mocking undergraduate who had once been nearly expelled from Cambridge for writing an indecorous school play.

According to Nashe himself, he wrote only the induction and the first act of *The Isle of Dogs*. The rest of the play was written by an actor in Pembroke's company, a young man in his twenties named Benjamin Johnson who had come back from the wars in what was evidently a restless state of mind and was hoping to graduate from acting to writing plays. When Johnson and his two fellow actors were packed off to the Marshalsea, the Privy Council reported of him that he "was not only an actor but a maker of part of the said play." He continued as a maker of plays, many of the best of which he wrote for Shakespeare's company, and after a time the spelling of his name altered to "Ben Jonson."

The Privy Council usually threatened much more than it actually performed where the London theatres were concerned. In spite of its grave pronouncements, no theatre in London was pulled down. But playing was discontinued for a time and all the acting companies took to the road. Summer was the normal time for touring, in any case, and the Chamberlain's company had probably planned a brief tour in the wealthy and populous counties of Sussex and Kent, very much like the one they had taken the previous year. But this year's tour was not a brief one, thanks to *The Isle of Dogs*, and the Chamberlain's company took the most extended tour of the provinces that they made in all of Elizabeth's reign.

Touring was not as comfortable or as profitable as playing in one of the large London theatres. The company acted in a series of local halls or inn-yards, and when they moved on to the next town all their musical instruments and properties and costumes had to be stored in the play-wagon, carefully making sure that the costumes were "folded up with the thread, not against the thread." The leading actors rode on horseback, with "their luggage and some part of their company" in the wagon, but each of them had once had the experience of being a hired actor, such as those who trudged alongside the wagon with shoes full of gravel. These hired actors were paid less than their London wages in the provinces, since the receipts were usually smaller, and Philip Henslowe paid a hired actor ten shillings a week in London and only five when he was on tour. The standard of the performances had to be kept high, since the London companies were in direct competition with excellent provincial companies, but the work was not as stimulating as in London. No new plays could be launched and the ones already in existence usually had to be cut for country playing.

On the other hand, every member of Shakespeare's company had learned to expect the annual tour of the country as a normal part of his existence as an actor, and since they liked and respected each other as human beings they probably derived a good deal of enjoyment from travelling about the countryside. The English method of forming an acting company showed to special advantage when it came to touring, since a group of experienced men and carefully trained boys could travel cheaply and live together amicably with a minimum of emotional friction. The Italian actors used women in their companies, and although some English travellers agreed that these women were almost as good as men in the parts, their presence complicated the lives of the troupe as a whole. Apart from the trouble and expense of housing the women, there were fierce rivalries between the *prima* and *secunda donna* of the company and even more savage wars between the leading actresses of rival companies. Since the whole existence of these travelling companies depended on the unity of the troupe as a whole, the great Italian actress, Vittoria, was justified in complaining bitterly when a rival whom she called simply "that woman" tried to lure her company away from her. Occasionally this rivalry resulted in furiously brilliant performances by the actresses, but it did not contribute to the economic stability of the company as a whole.

The Chamberlain's company was untroubled by any internal dissension and must have travelled very comfortably, especially since they were an unusually prosperous company and kept to well-travelled routes. The accommodations along the route were excellent, for, as one enthusiastic traveller declared, England had "the most commodious inns of all the world." The inns in cities like Bristol and Bath were actually much better than those in London, and they competed briskly for the patronage of the traveller with signs out front that cost as much as forty pounds. Some towns had a dozen inns, a few of them able to accommodate as many as three hundred travellers and their horses. Each horse was cared for "very diligently" by one of the hostlers, in wistful expectation of a large tip, and its owner was "sure to lie in clean sheets, wherein no man hath lodged since they came from the laundress." Unlike the Continental custom, the English inns did not charge a flat rate and each man was given as much food and service as he wished to pay for. The one rule laid down by the government was that each innkeeper was responsible for seeing that all his guests went to church on Sunday, for not even on the road was an Englishman free from the paternal eye of the Anglican religion.

The Chamberlain's company began their tour of 1597 by travelling through Kent toward the Channel port of Dover. Dover had its regular local audience and was also full of travellers who stayed at its numerous inns on their way to or from the Continent. They travelled abroad under a careful system of regulations, for the Privy Council did not approve of people "flying beyond the seas without license."

Dover had its own attractions for the tourist, for the castle on the hill above the town had been built by Julius Caesar, and his soldiers had left flour there that was now as hard as lime. There were cannons piled up in the port, and English warships riding at anchor, and in August the visitor could

watch the samphire being gathered from the steep cliffs along
the sea. The fat leaves of the samphire were gathered to be
pickled and sold in the London streets as a sauce for meat,
and Shakespeare has described what the gathering of it looked
like:

> . . . half way down
> Hangs one that gathers samphire, dreadful trade!
> Methinks he seems no bigger than his head.
> The fishermen that walk along the beach
> Appear like mice . . .

Shakespeare visited this district more than once with his
company and had many opportunities to see the samphire
gathered in August before he described it in *King Lear*. It
grew at Rye, and the Chamberlain's company also visited
Rye in August of 1597. Rye was an old walled town along
the coast and had once had a good harbor, but its position as
a port town was being gradually destroyed by the encroach-
ment of the marshes behind it. It had a good inn but its chief
distinctions were its twenty brass cannons and the fact there
had just been a fascinating local murder. A London bookseller came out the following year with a full account of the
deeds of one "Henry Rabson, fisherman of Rye, who poisoned his wife in the strangest manner that ever hitherto hath
been heard of." Rabson used ratsbane and powdered glass
and thus passed into temporary renown.

Another town that was famous for a murder was Faversham, which the Chamberlain's company had already visited
at the beginning of August on their way to Dover. It was
nearly half a century since Mr. Arden had been murdered in
Faversham, but it was one of those striking sex murders that
everyone enjoys and even the historians gave the event their
respectful attention. An excellent play called *Arden of Faversham* had been drawing large audiences, since it had the ad-

vantage of being able to show the "dissimulation of a wicked woman, the insatiable desire of filthy lust and the shameful end of all murderers." Apart from this distinction, Faversham was a flourishing town famous for its oysters, and it had a market building with a clock that must have reminded Shakespeare very much of the one in his native Stratford. It was in May of this year that Shakespeare had bought New Place, and his thoughts must have been in Stratford oftener than usual that summer.

If the season had been a normal one, the Chamberlain's company would probably have turned back to London after touring through southeastern England. But the London theatres were still tight shut under the watchful eyes of the Privy Council and the mayor, for once in agreement, and the Chamberlain's company went west towards Bristol and Bath, which housed some of the best theatre audiences in England. On their way they stopped at Marlborough, which lay on the route. Marlborough was a market town in Wiltshire whose chief distinction was that Merlin Ambrosius, the builder of Stonehenge, may or may not have been buried there. More interesting from the actors' point of view was a local bylaw stating that "the chief officers of the borough shall not give license for the players, or using of any stageplays or interludes in the Guildhall."

The situation was very different at Bath, where every acting company was welcome. The old town had been seeing an average of fifteen to twenty plays a year for the past two decades, and the Chamberlain's company was only one of five that played there in 1597. The Guildhall, east of High Street, was not much of a building now that the cloth industry had decayed, and the actors probably preferred the inn-yard of one of the town's large and excellent inns.

After the collapse of its cloth industry, Bath had found a new source of revenue in its medicinal baths, which were owned by the city but brought prosperity to everyone. People flocked from all parts of England to be cured of various diseases or to participate in what was a very pleasant social season. The town had two bowling greens and a tennis court, the latter judiciously located next to the largest and most centrally located bath in town, which was called the King's Bath. There was also the New Bath and the Hot Bath, all three discreetly walled and supplied with dressing rooms. The town rented the baths out on a concession system, and each one had a bath keeper with a succession of bath guides under him. The guides manned the pumps and supplied linen for the bathers, and since they depended largely on tips they took a deeply affectionate interest in their patrons.*

Bath was a fashionable town, and many of the nobility owned houses there which they rented or loaned to friends when they were not in residence. The patron of the Chamberlain's company, George, second Lord Hunsdon, "kept the most honorable house that ever was kept there," and he had such faith in the curative powers of the waters that his sovereign wrote him, "I cannot but wonder, considering the great number of pails of water that I hear have been poured upon you, that you are not rather drowned than otherwise." Queen Elizabeth did not believe in anything but a careful diet and much exercise, and in another letter to the Lord Chamberlain she again expressed her doubts of the virtues of Bath's water. "I somewhat still doubt that there hath been too great abundance of the same squashed upon you."

Sometime in September the Chamberlain's company played in Bristol, another city upon the Avon that also loved the theatre. It stood northwest of Bath, on a hill, and was one of

---

* According to Elizabethan theory, these hot baths had been established in Bath in pre-Roman times by a British king named Bladud. King Bladud was not content with this distinction and "by vain trust of the art of necromancy took upon him to fly in the air, from whence he fell down and brake his neck." There were still relics in Bath of the Roman occupation, including stone images at intervals in the town wall, but Shakespeare would have seen no relics of the unlucky King Bladud, whose son was the equally unfortunate King Lear.

the chief cities of England. In some ways Bristol was a miniature version of London, with its Cathedral and the beautiful houses that had been built by its merchants. Its stone bridge over the Avon was nearly as good as London Bridge over the Thames, for it was lined with houses in the same way and even had a chapel on it. The Avon at this point was tidal, and the ships could be brought "under sail into the very heart of the city." The merchants prospered and their place of exchange, which was called the Tolzey, was covered over for protection from the weather like the Royal Exchange in London. The fair of St. James, where actors were especially welcome, was a near rival to the great St. Bartholomew fair in London, and Bristol could lay claim to being the second city of the realm. Its citizens must have been unusually literate, since in Shakespeare's lifetime the first free public library in England was established there. The Guildhall was always open to travelling companies, and in September of 1597 the Corporation paid thirty shillings "unto my Lord Chamberlain's players playing at the Guildhall."

When the Chamberlain's company arrived that autumn the city was not at its best. The years of depression and bad harvests had hit Bristol hard, and 1597 was the year in which the mayor decreed that all the citizens must "keep as many poor persons in their houses as their income would permit, for fear of an insurrection." Wheat was selling that year for twenty shillings a bushel and matters might have been even worse if one intelligent alderman had not imported rye from Danzig and made it available to the people of Bristol at half the local price.

By October the Chamberlain's men had probably returned to London, a hundred and fifteen miles away. Ben Jonson had been released from the Marshalsea the eighth of October and Henslowe's theatre, the Rose, was open by the eleventh. The Swan seems to have been the only theatre that remained closed, and the winter season was probably fairly normal.

Nevertheless, the luxury trades must all have had a hard time of it, for London was much more intricately organized than Bristol and felt the dislocation of high prices and shortages much more intensely. Moreover, the depression of the late 90's brought with it a general sense of gloom that was in noticeable contrast to the kind of light-heartedness that Shakespeare had seen in the city when he first came up to London.

The first people to register this change in the mental climate were the writers, although the *fin de siècle* mood of disillusionment that attacked literary London was of course due to more than the depression. The young writing gentlemen at the Inns of Court were not especially interested in what was going on at the Royal Exchange. Their gloom was a reaction from the over-excited optimism that had characterized London in the 80's. Men like Sidney and Marlowe had seen the world in a golden, conquering light that could hardly have been sustained indefinitely, the temperament of the average man being what it is.

The pendulum of literary fashion usually swings violently once it begins, and the disillusioned young moderns of the late 90's turned their backs on their elders under the impression that they had made a completely new discovery about the world they lived in. For that great Renaissance characteristic—love of action—they substituted the conviction that the world was a pit of iniquity and the only thing worth doing was to sit down and point out its sins. For that other great Renaissance characteristic—love of beauty—they substituted a kind of horrified fear of sex coupled with a fascinated interest in its abnormalities. And for vigor they substituted cleverness.

A young writer like John Marston might almost stand as a symbol for this new generation. His father had sent him to the Inns of Court hoping he would be a lawyer like himself, but young Marston had other dreams; he was going to be a writer. Half-Italian, emotional, ambitious and still in his early twenties, he wrote a long, lush, erotic narrative poem and used the meter of *Venus and Adonis*, since that was still the model for hopeful young men to follow. There seems to be no doubt that Marston wrote *Pygmalion's Image* in sober emulation of a respected elder and it was not until he finished it that he realized that no advanced young man took that sort of thing seriously any longer. So Marston promptly announced that his erotic tale had been a parody.

> Deems't that in sad seriousness I write
> Such nasty stuff as is Pygmalion?

Having turned his back on *Pygmalion's Image*, with its typically Renaissance glorification of physical passion, Marston launched on a series of satires in the new modern temper. The satires were very successful and Marston followed them the next year with *The Scourge of Villainy*. In his new book Marston undertook "to purge the snottery of our slimy time," and since this ambition gave him the opportunity to make a detailed study of the "slime," especially in relation to sex, he had a production for which the booksellers must have loved him well. Other young writers also started to point out the sins of the "sin-drowned world" and the craze for satires had reached such a height by 1599 that Archbishop Whitgift forbade their publication and ordered some of them burnt in the yard of Stationers' Hall. Marston's book was among those that were destroyed. He turned instead to writing for the stage, and his disappointed father in Coventry was finally obliged to admit that his son would never be a lawyer. Marston had a colorful and violent career as a playwright, with several excursions into prison, and finally ended up, as so many writers did, by entering the church.

Another young man who was deeply interested in the new fashion of writing satires was Ben Jonson, the actor who had been imprisoned for his share in writing *The Isle of Dogs*. Jonson was a boy in his teens in the great days of Spenser and Marlowe, and when he began writing there were very few links remaining with that romantic past. Nor was Jonson in the least interested in the past, although he had been hired by Henslowe in 1597 to write conventional, old-fashioned plays and was even paid ten pounds for some "new additions" to that popular old melodrama of Kyd's, *The Spanish Tragedy*.

When Ben Jonson published a complete edition of his plays, he ignored all the work he had done for Henslowe. The first play he was willing to call his own was a satirical comedy which he wrote in the new style and which was produced by the Chamberlain's company in 1598. Jonson called the play *Every Man in his Humour*, and the changed literary atmosphere in London assured its instant success.

Jonson wrote his play as a strict Roman comedy and in the classical manner. He kept rigidly to the three unities but even more he kept to the spirit of the old classical comedy. Its purpose had always been to chastise vice, which fitted in well with the current Elizabethan craze for satire, and it never attempted to show real people but only simplified character types. This fitted in well with Jonson's natural tendency toward abstraction and simplification, for he was interested in people only for their oddities and did not have Shakespeare's gift for seeing them in the round.

Jonson's attitude towards the classics was almost one of worship, and no man in England had a greater respect for learning. He had been brought up to be a bricklayer and was still officially listed as "citizen and bricklayer of London." But he had gone for a time to Westminster School, before his stepfather took him away to lay bricks, and there he had come under the influence of the great William Camden. That gentle, wise and learned man had a profound influence on Ben Jonson and kindled a love of learning in him that nothing ever succeeded in quenching.

The Chamberlain's production of *Every Man in his Humour* brought Jonson into close contact with William Shakespeare, who was one of the actors in the play. Shakespeare's name heads the list of "principal comedians" in the play, with Burbage, Phillips, Heminges and the rest of the company following. Thus began the long, although frequently interrupted, association between Ben Jonson and the company, and the long and frequently exasperated association between Ben Jonson and William Shakespeare.

Shakespeare was one of the very few writers with whom Ben Jonson never had a public quarrel. But they must have had several private arguments on the subject of how to write plays, for Ben Jonson still had the subject on his mind years after Shakespeare's death. He kept returning to it the way a man will when he feels he has not had the last word.

In his younger days Shakespeare himself had written a classical comedy in *The Comedy of Errors*, in which all the characterizations were simplified and the unities strictly obeyed. He had found that way of writing too formal and constricted for him, and since he was not comfortable in the tidy atmosphere of Plautine comedy he saw no reason to continue with it and started instead down the road that led to Falstaff. He and Jonson had a completely different approach to the art of writing, and since Shakespeare saw no reason why everyone should be alike he probably had no wish to discuss the matter. But Ben Jonson was a walking bundle of theories and he was never content to let differences be.

Jonson was convinced that the correct way to write poetry was first to lay the idea out in prose. This was the way writing was taught in the schools, and the way William Camden had taught it to him. Shakespeare had apparently never heard of this rule, judging by the way his pen raced across the paper with what seemed to Jonson disgraceful ease. Jonson remarked acidly that Shakespeare "flowed with that facility that sometimes it was necessary he should be stopped," and he never quite forgave Shakespeare's fellow actors for boasting that his plays reached them without a blot or erasure in the lines. "Would he had blotted a thousand."

Jonson put a great deal of careful research into his plays, and it disturbed him deeply that his fellow playwright had so little respect for facts. Three years after Shakespeare's death Jonson had still not forgotten that he had put a seacoast in Bohemia, when "there is no sea near by some hundred miles." Shakespeare had found the seacoast in a piece of popular fiction by Robert Greene with which he was working at the moment, and it had not occurred to him to investigate the matter. What he was watching was the story. But Jonson would have gone at once to the nearest map or the nearest geographical expert and thrashed the matter out thoroughly before he added another line to his play. Moreover Shakespeare paid no attention to the unities, mixed comedy and tragedy disgracefully in the same play, and in general seemed incapable of realizing that literary rules had been made to be obeyed.

Yet in spite of all their differences Jonson loved Shakespeare and called him "my beloved." He was not a man who gave his affections lightly but he said of Shakespeare, "I loved the man, and do honor his memory, on this side idolatry, as much as any." The highest praise Jonson could give a man was to call him honest, for the phrase had high connotations in the Renaissance and Jonson carefully saved every letter in which the word was applied to him. It was a word which in turn he applied to Shakespeare: "He was, indeed, honest, and of an open and free nature." Several men had said so, but the praise has a special force coming from a man as tempestuous as Ben Jonson.

While Jonson labored over his correctly classical lines he was living a life of violent extremes. He had already seen the inside of a prison the previous year for helping Nashe write *The Isle of Dogs*, and within a month of the production of

Every Man in his Humour he was back in prison again for killing a fellow actor of Pembroke's company. He was in and out of prison during the reigns of both Elizabeth and James. He upset the authorities by turning Catholic during a prison sentence and then after twelve years turned back again with such enthusiasm that he drank all the wine in the communion cup. He had feuds with men as inoffensive as Samuel Daniel, beat John Marston and took away his pistol, frightened Michael Drayton, and insulted the great Inigo Jones for a time with such vigor that he almost made a trade of it. He loved practical jokes, preferred to have married women for his mistresses because they had more experience, and told as conceited a man as King James to his face that he had no ear for poetry. He was a very heavy drinker, "a great lover and praiser of himself," and a man both well loved and well hated. "Passionately kind and angry; careless either to gain or keep; vindictive, but if he be well answered, at himself."

His friend, William Shakespeare, was almost Jonson's complete opposite. As far as all the available evidence goes he was never in prison, never fought a duel with anyone, never bore a grudge, was very careful with his money, and lived and worked for twenty harmonious years with the same group of men. Yet while Jonson labored for the classic ideal of decorum in his plays, Shakespeare went to such violent extremes in his writing that Jonson said that some of it was "ridiculous" and "could not escape laughter." Jonson would probably have agreed that real life was occasionally ridiculous, but he saw no reason to tolerate real life on the stage.

Chapter 9

WHEN the Chamberlain's company produced Ben Jonson's successful new comedy in September of 1598, they acted it at the Curtain. The Theatre was not available, for the Burbage family was at the climax of a series of difficulties over its ownership.

Ever since he built the Theatre, James Burbage had had difficulty with the owner of the land on which the Theatre was built. Giles Allen did not want the building on his land indefinitely, and when Burbage applied for a ten-year extension of the lease that would have assured him ownership until 1607, Allen refused to give it to him. This meant that the lease on the land would expire on April 13, 1597 and that the Burbage family would automatically lose the building also.

James Burbage did not have the temperament to sit down and wait helplessly for the fatal date to arrive. He was already in his sixties, but he decided that he would build a new theatre and it would be even finer than the one he was about to lose. He bought a piece of property on the west side of town for six hundred pounds, with a down payment of a hundred and a mortgage for over two hundred more. The property consisted of the major part of an old building that had once been used by the monks of Blackfriars, and although it was within the city walls it was outside the city's jurisdiction.

Burbage spent several hundred pounds converting part of the interior into a theatre, probably using the second floor which could be reached by a huge flight of steps from the yard. In the previous decade the owners of a boys' company had maintained a theatre in Blackfriars, but it had since been reconverted into gentlemen's residences. This was in any case a select, private theatre, so that James Burbage was the first man in England to make a roofed-in, lighted interior hall into a public theatre and was again a pioneer in theatre building.

He was perhaps too much of a pioneer. From his own point of view the liberty of Blackfriars was merely a locality where the city of London could not stop him from building a theatre, and he forgot that Blackfriars might have its own objections. The liberty was an exclusive residential district of about five acres, inhabited by "noblemen and gentlemen," with a special porter to shut the four gates of Blackfriars every night. Tennis courts were permissible, bowling alleys could be tolerated, but a public theatre was clearly insupportable. Not only would "the noise of the drums and trumpets" disturb the ladies who worshipped at the fashionable little upstairs church of St. Anne's, but the people who attended the plays would probably be "vagrant and lewd persons" who would ruin the district.

It is possible that if Burbage had planned his theatre anywhere in Blackfriars but on the higher slopes of the hill in the most exclusive section, he might have been left in peace. But as it was, the hammering and carpentering for the new theatre went on in the center of the most elegant part of Blackfriars, and George, Lord Hunsdon, was actually going to be obliged to use the same passageway.

By November, 1596, the new theatre was nearly finished and it was then the residents of Blackfriars went into action. They sent a petition to the Privy Council for the suppression of the theatre that was signed by thirty-one prominent residents beginning with Lord Hunsdon and that redoubtable dowager, Lady Russell, and including such estimable citizens as the printer, Richard Field. There was never the slightest doubt that such a petition would be granted, and the Privy Council promptly agreed that a public theatre would not be permitted in Blackfriars.

It may have been this that killed James Burbage, for he had put all his hopes into the new theatre. He died less than two months later and was buried in Shoreditch. He left the now-useless Blackfriars theatre to his younger son, Richard, by deed of gift, as he left his personal property to Cuthbert, and both the sons combined in an attempt to save the Theatre in Shoreditch.

The lease on the Theatre land expired in the spring of that year, and for a year and a half following Cuthbert Burbage wrestled with Giles Allen to try and persuade him to sign a new lease. At about the time his brother Richard was acting in Ben Jonson's successful new comedy, Cuthbert got Giles to the point where he might sign if he were paid the enormous bonus of a hundred pounds. Cuthbert hopefully drew up the lease, neatly engrossed on parchment and with the wax all ready for the sealing, and when Allen came up from his country house in Essex to collect his quarter-day rents at Michaelmas, there was a final conference at the George Inn in Shoreditch. Allen had never intended to sign, for he had already planned to tear the Theatre down and use the land for his own purposes. He suddenly refused to accept Richard Burbage as security, there was a quarrel, and all negotiations were broken off. Cuthbert's year and a half of patient diplomacy had gone for nothing.

Cuthbert and Richard Burbage were their father's own sons and they did not accept defeat easily. They might have lost the lease to the land, but they still owned the building that was on the land. There was a clause in the original lease that granted James Burbage the right "at any time or times before the end of the said term of one and twenty years, to have, take down, and carry away to his own proper use" the building he had erected, and although it was true that the twenty-one years had expired, the two Burbage brothers saw no reason why this should stand in their way.

A more serious question was how an expensive operation like the tearing-down and rebuilding of a theatre could be financed, and to solve it they turned to the five actors whom Cuthbert called "those deserving men"—William Shakespeare, John Heminges, Augustine Phillips, William Kempe and Thomas Pope. A group of actors had never before been asked to help finance the building of a theatre, but the men of the Chamberlain's company were an unusual group of actors.

The arrangement that was finally worked out between the Burbages and Shakespeare and the others was that all seven of them should join together as a syndicate and finance the undertaking by purchasing shares. The two Burbages would hold a half-interest in the new building, and the five actors the other half-interest, making Shakespeare's share, for instance, one-tenth of the total. So that the actors could pass on these shares to their descendants, they turned them over to two trustees who regranted them as shares held in common. One of these trustees was William Levison, a churchwarden of John Heminges' parish, and he must have been an excellent businessman since he handled the details for one of the largest and the best-run of all the London lotteries. This regranting of the shares turned out to be a mistake, since a great deal of trouble arose as the actors died and left their shares to people who were not in the theatre. But as long as the actors held the shares themselves there was no friction whatever. William Shakespeare and the rest assumed the various expenses of a theatre landlord, from the rental of the land and the maintenance of the building to the annual fee that had to be paid to Tilney for a theatre license, and in return no longer had to pay any rent for the theatre in which they acted. This was a completely new arrangement in the history of the London theatre and must have attracted a great deal of interested attention from other actors. It worked perfectly, but that was only because the members of the Chamberlain's company were already close friends and knew how to trust one another.

The next problem was where to find a piece of land to use for the theatre. It had to be near enough London so that audiences could get home before dark, but it could not be anywhere in the city's jurisdiction. Henslowe had built the Rose in the Liberty of the Clink, which was on the Southwark side of the Thames and in the jurisdiction of the Bishop of Winchester; and near the Rose there was a piece of land that had a few shacks on it but was chiefly being used as a dumping ground. The ground was marshy and would have to be reinforced, but all the land in that district was riddled with ditches and Henslowe had to maintain a series of bridges over them to give the public access to the Rose. One site in Southwark was no worse than another, and the location was an excellent one from the point of view of the theatre-going public.*

The owner of the property was a London lawyer named Sir Nicholas Brend who again lived in the same parish as John Heminges. Brend had come into the ownership of the land through the recent death of his father and he was willing to rent it on a thirty-one-year lease at an annual rental of fourteen pounds and ten shillings. There must have been a complete meeting of minds between Brend and the new syndicate, for the lease was not signed until the following February but the new owners of the land took possession on Christmas Day.

Three days after Christmas, a small but determined company assembled in Shoreditch on the land where the Theatre was standing. The chief figure was an experienced London carpenter named Peter Street and he brought with him a crew of men armed with wrecking tools. Richard and Cuthbert Burbage were there, accompanied by their indomitable mother who "liked well" the whole idea; and along with the Burbages was a friend from Waltham Cross named William Smith who

---

* There is a difference of opinion as to the exact site of the Globe. It was near Maid Lane, but whether north or south of it is uncertain.

had lent them some money to help with their share of the financing.

Giles Allen was in Essex but he had left two agents to keep an eye on the Theatre for him. One of these agents, a silk-weaver named Henry Johnson, later testified in court that Cuthbert Burbage and Peter Street assured him they were only taking the building down to replace it on the same site and pointed out "the decays about the same as it stood there, thereby coloring their deceit." Giles Allen's own version of the affair was that he had intended to pull down the Theatre, "to convert the wood thereof to some better use," but that the Burbages and Peter Street and William Smith had come with swords and daggers and axes and in spite of the protests of all the neighbors had in a "very riotous, outrageous and forcible manner" pulled the building down. Allen went to law immediately, even suing Peter Street for the grass his men had trampled, but in spite of his money and influence he lost the case.

Peter Street had his own wharf down by the Thames, and the lumber from the Theatre was taken there and freighted over the river to its new destination in the Liberty of the Clink. Wood was scarce and expensive in England, largely because coal had not yet come into general use in the rapidly expanding industrial plants and logs or charcoal were still being used. Richard and Cuthbert Burbage had good reason to be grateful to their father for the heavy, valuable timber he had used in the original building. They had to buy new foundations and fittings and pay the wages of carpenters and plasterers, but all this cost only about four hundred pounds, which, of course, was much less than the price of a new building. James Burbage had evidently built better than Philip Henslowe, who put up the Rose in 1587 and had to pay more than a hundred pounds for repairs five years later.

Some of the syndicate's money had to go into heavy piles for the foundation, for a network of ditches ran into the

Thames, rising and falling with the tide, and the new theatre was, in Ben Jonson's phrase, "flanked with a ditch and forced out of a marsh." The yard of the theatre must have been paved or it would have been unusable in wet weather.

There were no major changes in James Burbage's original design and the new building was still arranged with tiers of seats around a jutting stage, with a thatched roof on top and the center open to the sky. But Peter Street was able to avail himself of all the latest improvements in theatre construction and nothing was omitted that would help the comfort of the audience or the convenience of the actors. There was probably much more room for the storage of the Chamberlain's company's large stock of costumes than there had been in the old Theatre and all the latest devices in backstage machinery were installed. There was a system of trap doors through which the three apparitions in *Macbeth* would eventually rise, and one trap door must have had a platform that could be held a foot or so below the stage so that Richard Burbage could leap into Ophelia's grave and impress the scene on a whole generation of theatre-goers. Equally intricate machinery was installed at the top of the building, just below the roof, waiting for Jove to descend on his eagle in *Cymbeline;* and there the stage crew produced the thunder and lightning that Burbage defied as King Lear.

The syndicate called its fine new theatre the Globe, and the emblem they evidently used was that of Hercules carrying the world on his shoulders. At first the alley behind the theatre was still known as Brend's Rents, but it began to be called Globe Alley and within fifteen years that became its official name. William Shakespeare was paying only one-tenth of the rent to Brend, but in the eyes of Brend's lawyers he seems to have been the major member of the syndicate; the year after the Globe was built, a survey of Brend's property described the Globe as a new building in the possession of "William Shakespeare and others."

Peter Street worked quickly with the rebuilding of the theatre, and the Globe was able to run up its playing flag and be ready for public performances by the summer of 1599. It was the handsomest theatre in London and gave the Chamberlain's men a decided advantage over their nearest rivals, the Admiral's company.

The Admiral's company was quick to adjust the balance and before the year was out they had a new theatre of their own which was called the Fortune. It was financed by Philip Henslowe and Edward Alleyn, and the contract with Peter Street stipulated that in nearly all the construction details it was to resemble "the late erected playhouse on the Bank." Even the proportions of the stage were to be the same as at the Globe, except that the posts that supported it were to be square, with carved satyrs at the top. The one great difference between the two theatres was that Alleyn wanted the Fortune to be square instead of round, a new idea that was apparently not successful since after the building was destroyed by fire it was rebuilt circular. The new theatre was erected in the suburbs north of town, after some delicate adjustments had been made with the local authorities; and although it attracted part of the theatre-going public northward, instead of south to the Bankside, it left the Globe the undisputed title of the finest theatre in Southwark. It remained for a generation "the glory of the Bank" and all of Shakespeare's plays from that time forward were produced in it.

One of the first of these productions was evidently *Julius Caesar*, since, in September of the year the Globe opened, a German tourist named Thomas Platter crossed the Thames to the Bankside with a party of friends "and there in the house with the thatched roof witnessed an excellent performance of the tragedy of the first emperor Julius." Platter did not understand English, and he was chiefly impressed with the way the actors danced together after the performance. He got more real enjoyment out of another play he saw during his visit to London, which had a great deal of dumb show and tussling and a comic servant who threw shoes at his master's head. But Platter thoroughly approved of the seating arrangements in all the English theatres, which were built "so that everyone has a good view." He liked the system that charged a penny for standing room in the yard, with higher prices for "the most comfortable seats which are cushioned," just as he also liked the custom of selling food and drink during the performances, and he was full of admiration for the handsome costumes of the actors. He could at least enjoy the costuming of Shakespeare's new play, even if he could not understand a word that was being said.

Shakespeare was trying something new in *Julius Caesar*. Most of the sources of his plots had been cheap fiction or old plays, but in *Julius Caesar* he wrote the first of a series based on the great classic, Plutarch's *Lives*. Plutarch was greatly respected in the Renaissance, and Robert Garnier had used him as the source of all the Senecan dramas that the Countess of Pembroke had tried to transplant into England. Shakespeare had no interest in this kind of restricted closet drama and he did not read Plutarch with respect but with delight. His attitude was very like that of Sir Thomas North, the English country gentleman who had captained three hundred men against the Armada and who had translated Plutarch's *Lives* into English. North knew no Greek and frankly admitted he was working from a French version, but he had no difficulty in recognizing Plutarch's heroes as friends and contemporaries. He explained to his readers that while most classics were "fitter for universities than cities," Plutarch's work was "fit for every place" and could "reach to all persons, serve for all times." Shakespeare himself was a city man, the product of no university, and he felt very drawn to Plutarch.

It is possible that Shakespeare wrote *Julius Caesar* more slowly and with more conscious care than most of his other plays; for he restricted himself to a vocabulary almost as limited as the one for *The Comedy of Errors* at a time when most of his plays were a riot of new words. He seems to have been deliberately making an experiment in classical control, but he did not let the experiment interfere with his knowledge of people and the results failed to please that determined classicist, Ben Jonson. Jonson was so annoyed by *Julius Caesar* that he still had it on his mind years later. One of Shakespeare's characters had said, "Caesar, thou dost me wrong," and Caesar had replied, "Caesar did never wrong but with just cause." Which was "ridiculous," said Jonson hotly. Nor was he appeased by the fact that Shakespeare evidently removed the offending lines, since they do not appear in the printed version of the play.

Jonson believed in reason and logic in the treatment of character and, unlike Shakespeare, he did not realize that dictators are not subject to reason and logic. Twentieth-century history has confirmed Shakespeare's portrait of a dictator, but it belongs to a realm of the creative imagination that Jonson could never enter. Jonson's characters were filtered through his careful mind, as his poetry was filtered through his prose. Shakespeare's characters were filtered through nothing and seem to have been born of gigantic lightning flashes of intuition. Shakespeare could describe the country of minds he had never seen as though he had been born there. Jonson cautiously required a map and even then he did not stray from well-defined paths.

During this same year of 1599 the Chamberlain's company produced the second of Jonson's comedies, this one called *Every Man out of his Humor*. Jonson called it a "comical satire" and said that "the happier spirits in this fair-filled Globe" would not be offended by it. But in spite of a good cast headed by Richard Burbage and John Heminges the play was not popular with the Globe audiences, although it did well in book form, and Jonson rather snappishly suggested it was too realistic. No doubt the audience would have preferred a play showing "a duke to be in love with a countess, and that countess to be in love with the duke's son, and the son to love the lady's waiting maid; some such cross-wooing, with a clown to their serving-man, better than to be thus near and familiarly allied to the time."

The operatic and unreal plots that Jonson is describing were common enough on the London stage, but Jonson may have been thinking specifically of his friend Shakespeare. It was at about this time that Shakespeare was writing his string of romantic comedies, *Twelfth Night*, *As You Like It* and *Much Ado About Nothing*. Will Kempe and Richard Cowley played the two comic constables in *Much Ado About Nothing*, and Kempe left the Chamberlain's company soon after the Globe was built, so that 1599 must be the date of that one comedy at least.

All three of Shakespeare's comedies are full of dukes and comic serving-men and examples of cross-wooing, and neither Illyria nor the Forest of Arden was "near and familiarly allied" to the problems of the contemporary world. Shakespeare had chosen his three plots with that same easy-going lack of dignity that maddened Jonson whenever he thought about it. Two of the plots evidently came from anthologies of cheap Italian fiction and the third one, *As You Like It*, came from a popular prose romance called *Rosalynde* that Tom Lodge had written when he went on a voyage to the Canaries in the 80's. Shakespeare had no objection to using all the plot devices he had already found serviceable—the girl dressed as a boy, the forest outlaws and so on—and the relaxed, giant hand took up this shoddy material and raised it into the golden light of comedy and romance. The audiences at once recognized Rosalind and Beatrice and Viola as real and delightful people, and Malvolio was so popular that *Twelfth Night* was once called by his name instead. This intimate relationship between Shakespeare and his audience was incomprehensible to an orderly mind like Jonson's, and he once remarked gloomily that "the beast, the multitude . . . love nothing that is right and proper. The farther it runs from reason and possibility, with them the better it is."

A special production of *Twelfth Night* was put on by the Chamberlain's company for the young gentlemen of the Middle Temple on the second of February, 1602. The Middle Temple had a new hall that could be used by the actors for their production, a hall so "large and stately" with its beautiful carved roof that it took its proud owners years to pay off the debt that was incurred in building it. One of the young lawyers who saw *Twelfth Night* was especially amused by Malvolio and noted in his diary all the details of that section of the plot. His name was John Manningham and being a well-educated young man he also jotted down the play's sources. In his estimation, *Twelfth Night* was "much like the Comedy of Errors, or *Menechmi* in Plautus, but most like and near to that in Italian called *Inganni*." *Twelfth Night* does not have the remotest resemblance to a Plautine comedy, and its chief relationship with *Gl' Ingannati* is that a disguised girl is sent by her lover to further his suit with another woman, a situation that was a commonplace in popular comedy and which Shakespeare himself had already used in *Two Gentlemen of Verona*.

John Manningham's diary was really a collection of odds and ends of information he had picked up in the Middle Temple and around London, interspersed with anecdotes and with the texts of sermons he happened to admire. Later on in Manningham's diary, somewhere between notes on a new surgical instrument called a catheter and on Dr. Turner's new compound, laudanum, he jotted down an anecdote about two of the actors in the Chamberlain's company. In the days when Richard Burbage was such a success as Richard III, a citizen's wife had arranged an assignation with him before she left the playhouse. Shakespeare overheard this and went

to her house instead, and when Burbage arrived and said that
Richard III was at the door, Shakespeare sent down word
that William the Conqueror came before Richard the Third.
To this anecdote Manningham kindly added the note, "Shakespeare's name William," in case anyone missed the point.

When Manningham recorded an anecdote of this kind, it
was his custom to jot down the name of the man who had
given it to him, such as Mr. Curle or Mr. Chute. In this case
the name is unfortunately not legible, making the anecdote
of even less value since the source is unknown. It is not unlikely that Shakespeare had been nicknamed "William the
Conqueror," considering his unbroken string of triumphs
in the theatre, and it is certainly true that many women went
to the theatre, both in England and on the Continent, and
fell in love with the actors. But this does not mean that two
close friends like Richard Burbage and William Shakespeare
spent their evenings cavorting in rivalry with stray members
of the audience. The anecdote is an echo of the contemporary
theory that all actors were a race of painted butterflies, given
to fornication because they really had little else to do with
their time. In the eyes of many otherwise intelligent Elizabethans, actors led "an idle loitering life" and anyone could
easily imagine all the wicked things they undoubtedly did in
their spare time.

Another of Shakespeare's plays that can be dated as belonging to the early history of the Globe theatre is his chronicle
play of *Henry V*. The Chorus at the beginning of the last
act hopes that the Earl of Essex will soon be returning from
Ireland with the rebellion crushed and asks the audience to
imagine an even greater welcoming crowd waiting for Henry.
Essex left for Ireland the 27th of March, 1599, and returned the 28th of the following September, so that *Henry V*
was evidently produced in the summer of 1599, shortly before Thomas Platter crossed the Thames to see *Julius Caesar*.

Henry V was one of the great popular heroes of English

history, and the London audiences had frequently seen him acted on the stage. Knell had played the part in the 80's with the Queen's Men, and the Admiral's company had also produced him on the stage, complete with a satin doublet laid with gold lace. Shakespeare had a well-worn subject but one that could not fail to appeal to his audiences, and he made his King Henry everything that an English monarch should be. He had completely reformed since the days when he was Falstaff's companion and had instead become the noblest of England's warriors.

Shakespeare for once seems a little conscious of the limitations of his stage in *Henry V*. It must have been hard on any writer of history plays to see a mighty battle blazing along the horizon of his imagination and to know that when it was transplanted into the theatre it was going to be a matter of a few drums and trumpets, some property swords, and a group of actors on foot chasing each other in one door and out another. Perhaps it was the building of the new theatre that had set Shakespeare to brooding a little on the limitations of his stage.

> May we cram
> Within this wooden O the very casques
> That did affright the air at Agincourt?

Yet Shakespeare knew that he was dealing with one factor in the Globe that had no limitation, the imagination of the audience, and it was this factor to which he appealed steadily through the actor who played the Chorus. "Piece out our imperfections with your thoughts." Shakespeare knew he could trust the imagination of his audience, and it was because he took it into full partnership that he got such remarkable results.

In *Henry V*, Shakespeare supplied the last link in his series of history plays that covered more than a hundred years in

English history from the last of the Plantagenets to the first of the Tudors. The series was not written in chronological order, and since he started writing it when he was a comparatively young man the quality is very uneven. But each is carefully linked to the play that precedes it and the play that follows it, and all of them have the same approach to English history.

This approach was the one that had been laid down by the Tudor historians and encouraged by the Tudor monarchs, to wit, that nothing contributes to a kingdom's welfare like a strong and duly accredited monarch. The last of the Plantagenets, Richard II, was a duly accredited monarch but he was not a strong one. Henry IV, who usurped his throne, was a strong monarch but he was not an accredited one. His son, Henry V, was everything that was admirable in a king, but his premature death brought his weak son to the throne and *Henry VI* records the chaos that a weak ruler can bring. The crown is finally seized by Richard III, who was strong but not duly accredited, and the kingdom is a welter of blood until the houses of York and Lancaster are united in marriage and the new house of Tudor is born.

Shakespeare wrote the second half of the series first, but the political philosophy was not one that required any special planning. He was following the chroniclers like Hall and Holinshed, and the chroniclers were following the general temper of the times. Shakespeare was not a man to embark on detailed independent research when he was writing a play, and he could not have foreseen that his way of writing was so persuasive that future generations of Englishmen would take their views of history chiefly from him.

Shakespeare had brought Sir John Falstaff into both parts of *Henry IV* and had evidently intended to go on using him in *Henry V*. "Our humble author will continue the story, with Sir John in it," promised the actor who spoke the final lines of *Henry IV*, but Falstaff nevertheless did not appear in the new play. He dies offstage and there is only that wonderful prose piece, with its unsurpassed mixture of comedy and tragedy, describing his death.

It has been suggested that Shakespeare was unable to keep his promise because the actor who played Falstaff, presumably Will Kempe, had left the company. But there is no proof that Kempe played Falstaff, no proof he had left the company when *Henry V* was written, and certainly no proof that so competent a repertory company had only one actor who could do a certain kind of part. A more probable explanation is that Shakespeare found it would be difficult to keep the attention of the audience on his noble and warlike king as long as Sir John was on the stage to pull the eyes and the hearts of the audience in the wrong direction. That fat and altogether reasonable coward stood for everything that was disgraceful (however delightful) and could have succeeded in making ridiculous even the glories of Agincourt. There are plenty of comic characters in the play but none of them fails to take the war with France seriously. This would have been quite beyond the powers of Falstaff, the darling of the London audiences, and so he died at the turning of the tide and went to Arthur's bosom.

However, Shakespeare did not find it as easy as that to dispose of the irresponsible old gentleman and he evidently yielded to public demand in giving him a play of his own. This was *The Merry Wives of Windsor*, which makes no attempt to be historical and is the only middle-class domestic comedy that Shakespeare ever wrote.*

The setting of the play is not the castle of Windsor but

---

* John Dennis stated at the beginning of the eighteenth century that Queen Elizabeth had ordered the play to be written, but he seems to have had no authority for the story and was trying to arouse interest in his own version, which he called *The Amours of Falstaff*. Shakespeare's play needed whatever aristocratic connections it could get, since by that time it was not considered a very gentlemanly piece of work. "The plot is good, but the characters and persons of the play so mean, the wit and conversation so plain, that 'tis scarce worth reading."

the town of Windsor, and the chief characters are not aristocrats but townspeople. Shakespeare knew the sprawling little town well and he used it with unusual thoroughness as the background of his play. He used the Garter Inn, which stood on High Street near Peascod Street, as Falstaff's headquarters. He used Herne's Oak, which stood on the right of the footpath from Winsdor to Datchet, for Falstaff's rendezvous. And he used the creek in Datchet Mead near the ferry, where the laundresses in town took their clothes, as the place where Falstaff was dumped into the Thames along with a bundle of dirty linen. The town sets the atmosphere of the play, since at every point it is the court characters that are duped and the town characters that are successful. Queen Elizabeth unquestionably enjoyed the play when she saw it, since she had something of a middle-class background herself and shared the play's brisk contempt for the average husband. The heroines of the play are two lively and intelligent townswomen of Windsor who have a tolerant liking for their husbands but are extremely fond of each other, and the average London housewife must have given the Chamberlain's company an extra handclap when the play was over.

During this period a great many of Shakespeare's plays got into print and were available for sale in the various book stores. Occasionally they appeared in corrupt, pirated copies, like *Henry V* and *The Merry Wives of Windsor,* but in general they were good texts that must have been authorized by the company. Thirteen of Shakespeare's plays were in print by 1601, and most of the quartos were no longer anonymous but had his name as part of the advertising matter on the title page. When *Much Ado About Nothing* was registered for publication in August of 1600 it was listed as "Written by Master Shakespeare," which is the earliest appearance of his name in the Stationers' Register; and when Shakespeare's company stopped authorizing the publication of his plays, later on in the decade, the publishers began issuing plays by

other writers and announcing that they were written by
Shakespeare. This happened with company productions like
The London Prodigal and *A Yorkshire Tragedy*, which the
London booksellers felt should have been written by Shake-
speare though they obviously were not.

Even a respectable publisher like William Jaggard was not
above using Shakespeare's name to promote sales. The year
the Globe was built, Jaggard got hold of a collection of verses
copied out in manuscript which included five sonnets of
Shakespeare's in its twenty love poems. By a judicious use of
wide margins and ornamental borders and many blank pages,
Jaggard managed to produce a thirty-two page booklet and
called it "*The Passionate Pilgrim*, by W. Shakespeare."

The makers of anthologies also found that Shakespeare's
name helped their sales. There were a great many of these
anthologies around the turn of the century, and William
Shakespeare was one of the writers they leaned on heavily.
One of the best of the anthology editors was John Bodenham,
who issued *Belvedere* and *England's Helicon* in 1600 and included Shakespeare's work in both. *Belvedere, or the Garden
of the Muses* was really a dictionary of poetical phrases, help-
fully divided into sub-headings, "Of Virtue," "Of Patience,"
"Of Tyrants" and so on, and the reader could find poetical
thoughts for all occasions from Shakespeare and other writers. A similar anthology that came out the same year was
called *England's Parnassus* and advertised itself as containing
"the choicest flowers of our modern poets," including nearly
a hundred quotations from Shakespeare. Most of these quotations came from Shakespeare's two narrative poems, which
were still felt to have more literary value than his plays. Moreover, they were more usefully occupied with noble thoughts,
and it was noble thoughts that any Renaissance anthologist
was after. For generations no one in England had questioned
the doctrine that the chief end of literature was to improve
conduct, and the tendency to divide up poetry into "thoughts"

was characteristic of a period that read Geoffrey Chaucer chiefly as a purveyor of moral maxims.

It was a literary fashion of the period, when praising Shakespeare's work, to emphasize its "sweetness." A literary judgment, once formed, travels for a long time on its own momentum, and in the same way that Chaucer's contemporaries went on praising him as the writer of pretty love songs long after he had become a vigorous realist, Shakespeare's contemporaries united to eulogize the writer that William Covell called "sweet Shakespeare." Richard Carew compared him to Catullus, and Francis Meres was echoing the general opinion of the period when he praised him as "mellifluous and honey-tongued Shakespeare." In the same year Richard Barnfield spoke of Shakespeare's "honey-flowing vein," and in the following year of 1599 John Weever wrote an epigram on "honey-tongued Shakespeare." Weever made the usual mention of *Venus and Adonis* and *The Rape of Lucrece*, but distinguished himself by being aware of the fact that Shakespeare had also created someone named Richard and someone named Romeo. He added frankly that there were "more whose names I know not," but he was quite sure they must all be "saints" with "sugared tongues" since Shakespeare begat them.

The somewhat idiotic way in which Shakespeare's admirers were praising him for one of the least of his talents tended to make the youthful intellectuals of the period look down on his work as rather old-fashioned. Some clever youngsters at Cambridge wrote a series of three plays, around the turn of the century, for university production, and the undergraduate who wrote part one of *The Return from Parnassus* included a direct attack on "sweet Mr. Shakespeare." The butt of the play is a "known fool" named Gullio who insists upon quoting *Venus and Adonis* and announces to all and sundry the virtues of his favorite poet. "Let this duncified world esteem of Spenser and Chaucer. I'll worship sweet Mr. Shakespeare." It seems hardly necessary to say that Gullio was an Oxford man, which alone would be sufficient to explain the unsoundness of his literary judgment to any young gentleman of Cambridge.

The second part of *The Return from Parnassus* was produced at Cambridge in 1601 and takes a somewhat more lenient view of Shakespeare as a poet. *Belvedere, or the Garden of the Muses* had just been published and the characters of the play have a thorough discussion of all the poets that had appeared in the popular new anthology. The chief objection to Shakespeare, incredible as it may seem, was that he always did the same kind of work.

> His sweeter verse contains heart-throbbing line,
> Could but a graver subject him content,
> Without love's foolish lazy languishment.

The butt of the play is not any special writer but the Chamberlain's company as a whole. The plot concerns two Cambridge scholars who are trying to make a living after they leave school, and at one point in the play they try to hire out as actors in Shakespeare's company. Burbage and Kempe appear onstage, and Kempe is a complete illiterate who is opposed to "that writer Ovid and that writer Metamorphosis" and believes that "our fellow Shakespeare" can turn out a better play than any university-trained man. Burbage tests out one student's acting ability with a speech from *The Spanish Tragedy* and the other's with a play that evidently ranked as the equivalent of Kyd's old melodrama, Shakespeare's *Richard III*. After Shakespeare's two fellow actors leave the stage, the two Cambridge scholars decide to become fiddlers instead, since anything would be better than joining up with a company of "mimic apes."

There is an element of exaggeration here, as in most good

comedy, but the Cambridge plays do mirror the contempt that most young university intellectuals felt for a popular professional writer like William Shakespeare. The plays written by the students of Oxford and Cambridge, or by their teachers, were in every way superior to the crass London product. They were quite untainted by commercialism, they appealed to educated gentlemen instead of London tinkers, and it was undeniable that they were beautifully staged. When Oxford entertained a Polish dignitary with a play, it experienced no difficulty in showing "Mercury and Iris descending and ascending" or producing an artifical snow that was "strange, marvellous and abundant." And when Cambridge needed costumes to represent "sundry personages of greatest estate" they made a direct appeal to Lord Burghley for the loan of some of the gorgeous robes that were housed in the Tower of London.

This superiority of the university gentlemen over the common London players was generally acknowledged, and in 1593 the Privy Council informed both universities that "common players" were not to be permitted any longer within their jurisdiction. The students of Oxford and Cambridge were the future hope of the nation and it was not fitting that their minds should become corrupted by watching these vulgar productions. There was already a university statute providing for the punishment of students who attended plays given by professionals, and throughout the last years of Elizabeth's reign the London companies were paid not to perform at the universities.

The unauthorized first edition of *Hamlet*, which was ready for publication in July, 1602, and published in a very bad text the following year, announced on its title page that it had been many times acted "in the City of London, as also in the two Universities of Cambridge and Oxford." It must have been in the towns of Oxford and Cambridge, rather than in the university section, that *Hamlet* was acted, and the students who went to the inn-yards to see it must have gone very quietly.

Since the hero of Shakespeare's play was himself a university product, his views on the drama were those of any well-educated young intellectual of the period. Hamlet had nothing but scorn for the groundlings, and his idea of true theatre was to hear the sorrows of the characters described at secondhand in dignified and interminable blank verse. Nothing could be more distasteful to any well-educated Renaissance gentleman, from Sir Philip Sidney down, than to have an actor play Hecuba by running about the stage in indecorous agony, with a blanket about the queen's hips and Troy burning behind her. The proper thing to do was to describe her from afar, and the play from which Hamlet quotes so admiringly represents the best practices of university stagecraft, with Hecuba's agony filtered to the audience at second hand through Senecan blank verse. It was the penny public, the groundlings, who demanded a full view onstage of Hecuba's agony and who encouraged the sprawling, violent dramas of which the universities so thoroughly disapproved. It is a sobering thought that Hamlet the playgoer would not have approved of *Hamlet* the play, with its mixture of comedy and tragedy, its failure to observe the unities, and all its other sins against decorum that any young gentleman from the universities would have noticed immediately.

The plot into which Shakespeare inserted his intellectual young student from the university of Wittenberg was a shabby old melodrama that had been in the repertoire of the Chamberlain's company for a long time and had evidently been written about the time when Shakespeare first came up to London. The ghost who went around wailing, "Hamlet, revenge," was a byword in the late 80's, and a play that Shakespeare's company produced the year the Globe was built managed to be very amusing at the expense of this kind of antiquated drama.

A filthy whining ghost
Lapt in some foul sheet, or a leather pilch,
Comes screaming in like a pig half sticked
And cries, *Vindicta*—Revenge, Revenge!

Shakespeare, as usual, knew what he was doing. It was not the first time he had used shoddy material as the springboard for a play, and in this case his actor's eye saw the special uses of the situation. The bloody, barbaric old plot gave him a dark backdrop for the unhappy young modernist who was his hero, and his hero's temperament in turn gave him a solution for the chief difficulty confronting any dramatist who worked in the field of revenge tragedy. Unless there was some reason why the revenge was delayed, the play would be over in the first act; and a revenge hero like Hamlet, caught in the general backwash of gloom and indecision that characterized the final years of Elizabeth's reign, was exactly the sort of man who was incapable of working himself up to a single course of action until he had succeeded in ruining the lives of everyone in the cast.

Hamlet was born in part of the young men who had been glooming about the universities and the Inns of Court in the *fin de siècle* atmosphere of the late 90's and passing remarks on the hollowness of life, the futility of heroic action and the degrading nature of sexual intercourse; but he was also the product of a more specialized group that was interesting the doctors of the period. A competent London physician like Timothy Bright would have diagnosed Hamlet as a melancholic and put much of his "internal darkness" down to physical causes. Melancholics, as Dr. Bright explained, "be not so apt for action." They are "given to fearful and terrible dreams," are "exact and curious in pondering," are "sometimes furious and sometimes merry," and are "out of measure passionate." They have frequently studied too much, they mistrust their memories, and they dislike color in their clothes.

This sort of information was useful to Shakespeare as a kind of springboard, but it was no more than that. He was not like George Chapman, who was very learned in Elizabethan theories of psychology and loaded his heroes with them. Shakespeare did not work from theories but from people. He knew that Hamlet's dilemma, between the flesh and the spirit, was at the heart of every human being's private tragedy, and he made Hamlet so terrifyingly real, with his courtesy and his violence, his intelligence and his self-hatred, his inconsistencies and his terrors, that every generation since has been able to recognize in him its own image.

The actors of the Chamberlain's company must have realized, sometime during rehearsals, that they had been given the script of one of those astonishing plays that please everyone. If they did not, the reaction of the audience would have told them soon enough. Even at its lowest level, *Hamlet* is a magnificently constructed piece of melodrama, with enough blood and pageantry and swordplay to please the sleepiest ten-year-old; and at its highest it travels so far into the secret countries of the heart that even the wisest should be able to see a new landscape unfolding in front of him.

Echoes of the play's success in the contemporary theatres still exist. Anthony Scoloker introduced a book of his by remarking that any piece of writing should ideally be like Sidney's *Arcadia*, which was still the most admired work of the period. "Or, to come home to the vulgar's element, like friendly Shakespeare's tragedies. . . . Faith, it should please all, like Prince Hamlet." Gabriel Harvey, who had once argued literary theory with his friend Sidney and was still respected as a scholar, used a blank space in his copy of Chaucer to jot down in his neat handwriting a few comments on the current literary scene. He noted that "the younger sort take much delight in Shakespeare's *Venus and Adonis;* but his *Lucrece,* and his *Hamlet, Prince of Denmark,* have it in them to please the wiser sort." *Lucrece* was in its fourth edition and was

generally conceded to be the best thing its author had ever
written; to link it with a common play from the boards of
the Globe theatre was an almost unheard-of concession for
a literary man to make.

Shakespeare poured a kind of lavishness into *Hamlet* that
is in direct contrast to the spareness of his *Julius Ceasar*. *Hamlet* is the longest play he ever wrote and has by far the largest
vocabulary of new words, and the cutting of the play for
normal stage production must have posed a difficult problem.

Even at the risk of being obliged to omit something important, the actors who shortened the play probably did not
cut Hamlet's remarks about the "aery of children" who were
"most tyrannically clapped." The rivalry between the children's companies and the adult actors was very much in the
public eye at the moment, and the theatregoers enjoyed any
reference to it on the stage.

It was really the Burbage family that had accidentally started
the boys' companies on their current cycle of prosperity.
Richard Burbage still owned the empty theatre in Blackfriars his father had built, and Henry Evans offered to rent it
from him in 1600. Evans had himself produced plays in the
Blackfriars in the 80's, working with John Lyly under the
patronage of the Earl of Oxford, and since the actors were
boys and their plays were geared to attract the better class of
patrons, the residents of Blackfriars had made no objection.
The upper rooms in which the boys acted had since been
turned back into private residences but Burbage's theatre was
still available; and in 1600 Henry Evans signed a lease with
Richard Burbage to rent the theatre for forty pounds a year.

The boys' company that Evans originally managed had been
a product of the Tudor custom of maintaining singing boys
who occasionally put on Court plays under the guidance of
their singing master. This particular company had been known
as the Children of the Chapel Royal, and when Evans organized
his new company in 1600 he was careful to keep the old name

with all its courtly connotations. Nevertheless, the new company did not have Court patronage. It was a straight commercial proposition, run not by a single singing master but by a board of directors, and it hoped to make its money direct from the London public, as the adult companies did.

By charging more for their seats the Chapel company was able to appeal to a more cultured and wealthy clientele than the public theatres. There was no standing room and none of the crude amphitheatre atmosphere of a large theatre like the Globe or the Fortune. There was a much greater emphasis on music, and a duke who was travelling in England reported that for an hour before the comedy began there was a performance on "organs, lutes, pandores, mandolines, violins and flutes." He said that he had never heard better singing "except perhaps the nuns of Milan," and he was also deeply impressed by the use of artificial light, "which produces a great effect."

At about the same time that Henry Evans revived the Children of the Chapel, Edward Pearce revived the singing school of St. Paul's Cathedral, which had also produced Lyly's plays in the 80's. Both companies evidently tried at first to produce the old plays that had once been in their repertoires; but Lyly's gentle little Court pieces were hopelessly out of date and the boys' companies turned to more modern dramatists.

The new crop of playwrights like Marston and Jonson and Chapman soon found that the boys' companies gave an author much more liberty to write as he pleased than he could find under the sternly commercial eye of a man like Philip Henslowe. Henry Evans was even willing to encourage their current interest in satire and in sensationalism, and for the next seven years the Children of the Chapel at Blackfriars steered a delicate line between full houses on the one hand and entanglements with the censor on the other.

Ben Jonson quite frankly used the boys' companies to pay off old scores. Henry Evans produced his *Cynthia's Revels*

late in 1600 or early in 1601, and Jonson dragged into the
text a private quarrel he was having at the time with John
Marston and Thomas Dekker. Marston, who loved a fight,
apparently wrote a play for Paul's Boys in which he pilloried
Jonson, and Jonson embarked on a new production which he
called *Poetaster*. In this play he managed to insult a great
many professions, but kept his chief violence for John Marston and for some of the actors of the Chamberlain's company.
The Chamberlain's company then leaped into the fray by
producing a play written by Thomas Dekker and called
Satiromastix, or The Untrussing of the Humourous Poet. The
"humorous poet" is of course Jonson, and Dekker's caricature
of him is rather clever, if allowance is made for the usual bad
manners of the period.

Within a year or two, the protagonists themselves had lost
interest in what Dekker called the "merry murdering" and
what was later called the "war of the theatres." Jonson offered
his important new tragedy to the Globe, and Marston dedicated his own new play to Jonson as one of his dearest
friends. He and Jonson collaborated with Chapman on a
charming comedy for Henry Evans, and the temporary violence between the Children of the Chapel and the men of the
Globe was forgotten.

Although Shakespeare mentioned this warfare in *Hamlet*,
he did not take any sides. One character in the play said
there had been "much to-do on both sides" and another that
there had been "much throwing about of brains." Hamlet himself made the sensible suggestion that the boy actors ought not
to encourage their playwrights to attack the men actors
since they would some day be men actors themselves. This
prophecy turned out to be correct. The boy actors who played
the chief roles in Jonson's *Poetaster* were Nat Field, John
Underwood and Will Ostler, and within ten years all three
of them had joined Shakespeare's company at the Globe.

During the first decade of the new century nearly every

playwright of consequence wrote for the boys' companies and in general did his best work for them. The two exceptions were Thomas Heywood and William Shakespeare, both of whom were shareholders in men's companies and consequently remained faithful to their own organizations. But even if the case had been otherwise, it is doubtful if Shakespeare would have felt any interest in working for a private theatre. Unlike Jonson, he had no contempt for the average London playgoer and no wish to write plays that would appeal to a small, select audience that was relaxed and receptive after listening to an hour of good music. Shakespeare was used to a large, excitable, restless audience that had worked hard for its pennies and did not hesitate to show its feelings if it became bored. Shakespeare's audience was not bored by him, and it seems equally certain that Shakespeare was not bored by his audience.

Chapter 10

DURING these years of working with the Chamberlain's company, Shakespeare had no settled place to live in London. Unlike most of the other members of the company he had no household of his own, and he moved from one part of London to another in what were apparently always hired lodgings.

When Shakespeare first joined the Chamberlain's company he was living in St. Helen's parish on the east side of town. This might be called a theatrical neighborhood, since it extended along the length of Bishopsgate Street, the great thoroughfare that ran under various names from London Bridge to Shoreditch and had three inns that were used as theatres along its length inside the city walls. But St. Helen's was one of the most aristocratic parishes in London and was famous for its "many fair houses." The most famous was Crosby Place, which had once lodged the future Richard III and was currently the home of the Lord Mayor. The beautiful residence of Sir Thomas Gresham was also on Bishopsgate Street, and just after Shakespeare left the parish the handsome mansion was turned into a school for London merchants.

Shakespeare worshipped on Sundays at the church of St. Helen's, whose graceful Gothic spire could be seen from the river and whose tombs and monuments were second only to those in Westminster Abbey. Sir Thomas Gresham and Sir John Crosby both had marble tombs, but even more magnificent was the one of Sir John Pickering, who lay life-size under a canopy with his ruff and his trunk-breeches and his noble Roman nose. Shakespeare could not avoid being familiar with the tombs of the titled dead, since he was a resident and taxpayer of the parish and was obliged to go to church on Sundays. A parish church like the one in Southwark had a system of passing out metal tokens to each member of the parish, which he had to deliver up to the communion table on Sunday or face severe consequences; for if any adult male taxpayer did not go to church regularly, his politics were immediately suspect.

All collection of taxes was handled through the unit of the parish, and Shakespeare went on the lists of St. Helen's for the subsidy that had been voted by Parliament in 1593. There were seventy-three taxable residents in his parish when the second assessment was made in 1596, and the value of Shakespeare's goods was rated at five pounds. This does not sound like much for a successful actor, but the most prosperous resident in St. Helen's was given an evaluation of only three hundred pounds, and in St. Leonard's parish both Richard and Cuthbert Burbage were rated as having fewer possessions than Shakespeare.

It was the policy of the government to keep the property evaluation low but the tax rate high, and when another subsidy was voted by Parliament in 1597 Shakespeare was taxed thirteen shillings and fourpence on his goods, a rate of about thirteen per cent. The two tax collectors in Shakespeare's ward were a skinner named Thomas Symons and a draper who bore the delightful name of Ferdinando Clutterbook. Their problem was not an easy one in a shifting population like London's, and about a fifth of the tax collections in St. Helen's could not be made. Shakespeare already owed five shillings on the last installment of the previous subsidy because he was among those who were either dead or "departed and gone out of the said ward," and the petty collectors of Bishopsgate ward naturally discovered they could not collect the new tax from him either.

Government offices always move slowly, but by 1599 it was decided that Shakespeare was within the tax jurisdiction of the Sheriff of Surrey and instructions were sent to the Sheriff to make the collection. Then it was finally discovered that Shakespeare's residence was in the Liberty of the Clink, which was not under the Sheriff but in the jurisdiction of the Bishop of Winchester. The Bishop of Winchester evidently included Shakespeare's back taxes in a lump sum that the Bishop accounted for in 1600, since nothing more was heard of the matter.

It is not known when Shakespeare moved across the Thames to the Liberty of the Clink, since he may not have gone there directly from St. Helen's parish, but he was evidently living there when the Globe opened. The Liberty of the Clink was a true theatrical district, and although it was not as aristocratic as St. Helen's parish it was certainly much livelier.

The Liberty of the Clink was one of the three areas into which the ward of Southwark was divided; and although London persisted in treating Southwark as a kind of appendage across the Thames, Southwark thought of itself as an independent and extremely important borough and, in fact, did supply more soldiers than any city in the realm except London. The Liberty of the Clink had a rather unfortunate reputation in the early days of the century, since most of the brothels in London were in the Bishop of Winchester's jurisdiction; and the parish church had even been obliged to set aside a special burying-ground which was courteously known as the Single Woman's Churchyard.

When Shakespeare moved to the Clink the stews of Winchester no longer had any official sanction, but the area was still considered a doubtful one by many Londoners, if only because so many theatres had been built there by that time. The Bear Garden, the Rose and the Globe all stood close to

Maid Lane in the Liberty of the Clink, and the only really respectable building in the area was the Bishop of Winchester's handsome palace which formed the eastern boundary of the Liberty. The area was heavily built up, but mostly in a series of tenements called "rents," and the whole district was riddled with a series of large and small ditches that had to be crossed by bridges.

The water in the ditches was stirred by the tide and reminded the residents of the Clink that theirs was a watery district controlled by the Thames. More than a third of the householders in the district were watermen, who owned the hundreds of small boats that crossed and recrossed the Thames, and owed their whole living to the river.

The watermen supplied the main traffic link between London and Southwark, since London Bridge was too far down the river to be of much practical use and in any case it was quicker and cheaper to go by boat. It cost only a penny to ride from the London side of the river to the Clink or to Paris Garden, and there were many landing stairs on the Southwark side to accommodate the stream of customers. A visitor who came to London at the turn of the century said that the boats were "charmingly upholstered" and had "embroidered cushions laid across the seats, very comfortable to sit on or lean against." He added that "generally speaking the benches only seat two people next to one another," which must have seemed an extra advantage to young couples going over to Southwark to see the latest play.

The public might be well served, but the watermen felt that their life was a difficult one. About two thousand boats were engaged in a fiercely competitive business, and much time was spent in jockeying for the best position at the landing stairs or trying to appeal to the better nature of potential customers. The watermen were licensed, as everyone had to be in Elizabethan England, and they resented the set fare which prevented their charging more than a penny to go straight across the river and more than sixpence for distant parts of town against the tide. They pointed out bitterly that the rate had been set by statute in the days of Queen Mary and that both rents and the price of food had more than doubled since. As a result, the watermen depended chiefly on tips to make a living and warred briskly with their customers on the subject. The Watermen's Company did its best to control the behavior of its members, but it was impossible to deny that there was a tendency in the ranks towards "abusive and unreverend speeches." Many of these watermen were old sailors who had once served under Drake or Frobisher, and a contemporary expert on mental diseases concluded it was the nature of mariners to be "tempestuous and stormy." If a customer tried to leave a penny tip with a waterman who had expected twopence, the waterman's language was vigorous even by Elizabethan standards; and Elizabethan standards of invective were very high.

The watermen and the theatre people not only combined to give Southwark much of its color, but economically they were dependent on each other. A theatre like the Globe could not have operated at a profit unless the trip from the London side of the river was quick, easy and inexpensive, and in turn the watermen found they made their chief living from the theatre customers. A handsome new building like the Globe multiplied the customers, and more and more sailors went into the business, "hoping that this golden stirring would have lasted ever." When Philip Henslowe decided to build the Fortune on the London side of the river, his decision must have seemed like black treachery to the Watermen's Company; and in the following decade there was a desperate petition to the government to force the actors to stay on the Southwark side of the Thames if it did not want all the watermen to starve.

The watermen themselves estimated that between three and four thousand people crossed the Thames every day to visit the Globe, the Rose and the Swan, and they further estimated that nearly forty thousand people in Southwark were directly involved in the prosperity of the watermen. This may be an exaggeration but there is no doubt that the watermen formed a large part of Southwark's population. One list of baptisms in the parish church shows the names of four bakers, four glovers, one innkeeper, one actor, one schoolmaster and seventy watermen.

The parish church of Southwark stood east of the Globe on the other side of the Bishop of Winchester's palace. The building had once been the old priory church of St. Mary Overy, and Chaucer's friend, the poet John Gower, was buried there with a coronet of roses around the head of his stone image. After the Reformation, St. Mary's amalgamated with another parish church to serve the whole of Southwark with a single building and the old church was renamed St. Savior's. The handsome building was still too large for the needs of a single parish, and churchwardens like Philip Henslowe found it was always needing money for repairs.

The parish of St. Savior's might almost be called the actors' parish. Both Philip Henslowe and his son-in-law, Edward Alleyn, served as vestrymen in St. Savior's, and it was the following year that Henslowe became a churchwarden. Shakespeare's fellow actor, Augustine Phillips, lived at Horseshoe court near the Globe and brought three of his children to be baptised at St. Savior's, and Thomas Pope had been on the token books of the parish since the days when he had been acting under the patronage of Lord Strange. A later member of Shakespeare's company named Lawrence Fletcher was buried in the parish church of St. Savior's, and another actor to be buried in the church was Shakespeare's youngest brother, Edmund, about whom nothing else is known. Edmund died in Southwark in 1607 when he was twenty-seven years old and his burial is listed in the parochial accounts for that year: "December 31. Edmund Shakespeare, a player, buried in the church with a forenoon knell of the great bell." The bells of St. Savior's were famous, with their own special warden, and it cost twenty shillings to ring the great bell for Edmund Shakespeare where the lesser bell would only have cost twelve-pence.

Apart from the beauty of the parish church and the dignity of Winchester House, Southwark was chiefly noted for its fine inns and for its many prisons. There were five prisons in Southwark, the Clink, the Counter, the Marshalsea, the King's Bench and the White Lion, and since a great many Elizabethan Englishmen went to prison at one time or another in their lives the prisons of Southwark were usually well filled. Shakespeare was living in Southwark in the winter of 1601 when the Marshalsea prison had its population increased suddenly by some of his friends and neighbors from Stratford. A group of the leading citizens of Stratford had been indicted for riot, which was a serious offense in the Elizabethan period. The group was headed by the High Bailiff himself and included such friends of Shakespeare as Richard Quiney and Henry Walker; and since all the men were well-to-do, they were immediately released on bail.

The men of Stratford had acted in defense of the town, for an attempt had been made to enclose some of the public pasture land so that it could be used for private grazing. All the leading citizens had at once seized shovels and mattocks, gone down to the river bank, and personally uprooted the hedges that had been planted to fence the cattle in. They had also gone off with six loads of willows, said the aggrieved plaintiff in his complaint.

The plaintiff was Sir Edward Greville, Lord of the Manor of Stratford and a curious man even in that age of outstanding eccentrics. His father had been sent to the Marshalsea for trying to kill a man and was eventually executed for murdering one of his tenants for his money. Young Edward started on his own career by accidentally killing his brother at target

practice, and his father assured him it was the best shot he had
ever made. He bought the manor of Stratford after the death
of the Earl of Warwick and was unable to convince himself
that his position as lord of the manor was largely an honorary
title. Stratford had its own charter and was self-governing,
but Sir Edward Greville took his position so seriously that in
the previous decade he had blocked the election of Richard
Quiney as High Bailiff until Quiney finally asked one of
Greville's influential relatives, Sir Fulke Greville, to intervene.

The war that was raging between Sir Edward and the citizens of Stratford in 1601 also involved the Stratford charter,
since Sir Edward insisted that he controlled the appointment of
the toll-gatherer at the Stratford fair. Having been promptly
released from the Marshalsea, Richard Quiney returned to
London in Trinity Term to present the town's case at Westminster, and he brought with him a document that had been
drawn up in consultation with four of the town's oldest inhabitants, all of whom remembered back to the days when
the charter had originally been granted to Stratford.

One of these four men was John Shakespeare, who had
lived in Stratford for half a century and could remember the
days when young King Edward had given the town its charter just eight days before Queen Mary came to the throne.
John Shakespeare had been living on Henley Street in 1553
and he was probably living there still, for he had not sold
either of his two houses. Although he was now an old man
in his seventies he was still interested in his rights. Two years
before he testified in regard to the charter, he had brought
suit in the Court of Common Pleas against a Wiltshire man
who had bought some wool from him over thirty years earlier
and had failed to pay for it.

It is satisfactory to know that after his many years of political isolation from Stratford, John Shakespeare was able to
do the town one final service. It was in the spring of 1601
that he helped the town steward and his old friend Adrian

Quiney draw up the case against Sir Edward Greville, which was finally submitted to arbitration. A few months later he died, and he was buried in Stratford on the eighth of September, 1601.

It was now William Shakespeare who bore the title of "gentleman" after his name, who was the head of the house and the one responsible for the welfare and dignity of the Shakespeare family in Stratford. He inherited the two houses in Henley Street from his father, and rented the east house to a man from Welcombe named Lewis Hiccox, who shortly after converted it into an inn called the Maiden-Head. The other house he rented to his younger sister Joan, who had married a hat-maker named William Hart and had already given birth to the first of her three sons. Shakespeare always thought of the house as belonging to Joan and he gave her life residence of it in his will, at an annual rent so small as to be only a token payment.

When John Shakespeare died, William Shakespeare had been the owner of New Place for four years, but his father's bitter experience over losing his wife's land had evidently made William Shakespeare doubly careful when it came to any real estate transactions. New Place had been bought under somewhat peculiar circumstances, for William Underhill died shortly after he sold the house to Shakespeare and it was later discovered that his elder son had poisoned him. The son was hanged and his estates were forfeit to the crown, from which the younger son, Hercules Underhill, recovered them by paying a fee when he came of age. Hercules came of age on the sixth of June, 1602, and Shakespeare at once set out to get confirmation of his purchase of New Place. Hercules was too unwell to come up to London and a special commission was sent to him in Northamptonshire to get his ratification. The confirmation of Shakespeare's title to New Place must have cost a great deal of money and may not have been legally necessary, but William Shakespeare, gentleman, was not a man to take any chances when it came to the ownership of land.

Shakespeare received the conveyance from Underhill during Michaelmas Term of 1602, and by that time he had made a new and even more extensive purchase of Stratford real estate. On the first of May he had bought a hundred and seven acres of land in the Stratford area and had become one of the largest property holders in the district.

The owners from whom Shakespeare bought this large acreage were a prominent local family named Combe. At one time or another Shakespeare had dealings with several members of the family, but the two men who were involved in this particular transaction were a distinguished Warwick lawyer named William Combe and his nephew John, who was a wealthy bachelor and lived near Stratford in the village of Welcombe. William Combe had invested in the property only nine years earlier, and it was typical of the purchases that had made the Combe family such prosperous and influential members of the local gentry.

It was this group of landed gentlemen that was entered by William Shakespeare, grandson of a tenant farmer. The land he bought was the kind that his grandfather Richard had been farming when John left to make his fortune in Stratford, and that was still being farmed by his uncle Henry until he had died six years earlier. The farmland that surrounded Stratford was laid out on the old medieval system in a series of long, narrow strips that were worked side by side by various tenant farmers, and the one real difference from the medieval period was that the rent was now paid to various private owners instead of to the lord of the manor. The system of dividing the land into strips was a wasteful one, since it made it almost impossible to improve the condition of the soil. The same difficulty applied to the communal pasturing of cattle, which made it impossible to improve the breed. But the medieval system had the sanction of all antiquity, and any effort to make a change in it met with almost hysterical local opposition.

Shakespeare's purchase from the Combes consisted of over three hundred of these farming strips, and he bought them in a single cash payment of three hundred and twenty pounds. Since Shakespeare was not in Stratford his brother Gilbert handled the transaction for him, and the document was signed and delivered to Gilbert in the presence of witnesses. The document itself was vitally important, since in this case Shakespeare had no other proof of legal ownership. Since the deed was not recorded in the manor court, clear title was guaranteed in the deed itself in an impressive tangle of legal verbiage; but Shakespeare took the further precaution, when he bought twenty more acres from the Combes nine years later, of having his title to the original acreage confirmed.

Shakespeare made one more real estate purchase in Stratford in this same year of 1602, but it was a comparatively small one. At the end of September he bought a cottage and about a quarter of an acre of land in Chapel Lane, just across the street from New Place. The purchase itself was simple enough but it was conducted in an atmosphere of pure medievalism, for the owner of the property, Walter Getley, held it on a copyhold tenure from the Manor of Rowington, which was in the possession of the widow of the Earl of Warwick. Walter Getley was obliged to appear at the court "of the noble Lady Anne, Countess of Warwick" and restore the cottage to her, and when William Shakespeare appeared in due time and swore fealty to her he would receive the cottage from her hand. Getley appeared through his attorney, but Shakespeare evidently had to go through the formality of appearing in person and he also assumed the obligation of paying the manor a token rent of a little over two shillings a year as long as he owned the property. These relics of medievalism were familiar enough to the men of the Renaissance, and the laws that governed property rights were born of such an overlapping of ancestries that the situation was a source of great profit to the legal profession.

Shakespeare's position in the community was probably a great satisfaction to his family in Stratford, but it was not an unusual one for an Elizabethan actor to achieve. Most of the leading members of Shakespeare's company, Heminges and Burbage and Phillips and Pope, were granted coats of arms and were classified as gentlemen, although both Phillips and Pope claimed the designs of ancient houses to which they were not really entitled. All the actors in Shakespeare's company were well-to-do, and most of them made the usual Elizabethan investment and bought property. Thomas Pope owned three houses in Southwark when he died, and Richard Burbage left real estate worth over three hundred pounds. Augustine Phillips bought a country estate at Mortlake in Surrey, and Henry Condell, who already owned two houses in London, eventually retired to a home in the Cotswold Hills that was only fifteen miles from Stratford.

There were several contemporary attacks on the actors who grew wealthy "by penny-sparing and long practice of playing," and especially on the ones who "purchase land and now esquires are made." An especially violent attack was made in 1603 by Henry Crosse, who blamed the situation on the "witless and brainsick multitude" who went to plays and thereby enriched the actors. "These copper-lace gentlemen grow rich, purchase lands by adulterous plays," and by lording it over better men than themselves threaten the very life of the commonwealth. Crosse describes the plays of the period with the reluctant devotion of a man who must have once been a playgoer himself. "They do not only feed the air with sweet words, equally balanced, the eye with variable delight, but also with great alacrity doth swiftly run over in two hours' space the doings of many years, galloping from one country to another, whereby the mind is drawn with expectation of the sequel, and carried from one thing to another . . .

when as at a lecture and holy exercise all the senses are morti-
fied and possessed with drowsiness, so that by this we may
see our corrupt nature." Crosse said that "at a play the whole
faculty of the mind is altogether bent on delight," which is a
fair description of the way the members of the audience felt
when they saw a play like *Hamlet*, and an explanation of why
the actors of Shakespeare's company made money.

None of the members of the Chamberlain's company grew
as rich as Edward Alleyn of the Admiral's company. Alleyn
became almost the Elizabethan equivalent of a millionaire,
leaving two thousand pounds in his will after he had spent
five times that amount in building Dulwich College and en-
dowing a series of almshouses. Alleyn also acquired a coat of
arms, the heralds having finally decided that he had some
vague connection with the Townleys of Lancashire; and the
childless man was so anxious to immortalize his name that he
decreed the master and warden of Dulwich College must always be someone who bore the same name as himself. But
Alleyn did not make all his money in the acting profession,
since he had successful real estate investments and a series of
miscellaneous activities that ranged from starch-making to
bear-baiting; and the other actors in the Admiral's company
did not become as wealthy as he or even as well-to-do as the
men in the Chamberlain's company.

No group of actors in London was quite as steadily respectable as the men who made up Shakespeare's company.
Home-owners, taxpayers and hard-working professional men,
they were exactly the sort of people that the mayor of London would have approved of thoroughly if he could have
brought himself to approve of actors at all. Although such a
record was almost inconceivable in Elizabethan London, no
members of the Chamberlain's company seem to have been
sent to prison. The usual reason an actor went to prison was
for debt or because the play he had been appearing in dis-
pleased the government, but the men of the Chamberlain's

company did not get into debt and they were politically conservative.

Only once did the Chamberlain's company come close to
disaster on a matter of politics. This was in February of 1601,
a month after the group of prominent Stratford men had been
imprisoned in the Marshalsea for riot; and it was fortunate
that Shakespeare's company had a reputation for not med-
dling in politics or the Privy Council would have been obliged
to take a very grave view of their offense.

The difficulty had its origins back in the days when Shakespeare had written *Richard II*. The political point of view
was irreproachably correct as far as the series as a whole was
concerned, but Shakespeare was faced with a special dilemma
in the case of Richard II. Richard had been deposed by Henry
of Lancaster, who fathered that glorious monarch, Henry V;
but on the other hand Richard was an anointed king of an
ancient line, and there was no greater sin in the Tudor lexicon
than to attempt to depose an anointed king. Shakespeare tried
to minimize the problem by laying special emphasis on Richard's unfitness to rule, but this did not agree with the Tudor
theory that all rulers were divinely appointed by God. "All
power is of God. And therefore, whether the man be good or
bad, he must be obeyed." When *Richard II* was published in
1597 the scene in which King Richard is deposed was omitted,
and although there were three printings of the play in Elizabeth's reign, it was not until five years after her death that
the deposition scene was finally included in a printed text.

This omission of part of the text was probably not so much
a piece of voluntary discretion on the part of the publisher as
of outright censorship on the part of the Crown, for Elizabeth
was developing a fixed idea about the last of the Plantagenets.
"I am Richard II, know ye not that?" She was convinced
that some of her noblemen might see in that unlucky ruler an
historical precedent for trying to depose her, and the gentleman she had especially in mind in that connection was the

Earl of Essex. When an inoffensive lawyer from Cambridge
wrote an account of King Richard's fall he succumbed to a
kind of mad innocence and dedicated the book to Essex. "No
book ever sold better," remarked its publisher, who with
something less than innocence had apparently suggested
the dedication in the first place. Everyone involved in the
book was summoned at once before the Privy Council for
questioning, and the dedication to the Earl of Essex was removed in the next printing. This was in 1599, when Essex
was still high in the Queen's favor and was just setting out
for Ireland to crush the rebellion.

Elizabeth was an astute politician, and her estimate of Essex
was politically correct. That spoiled and sulky young nobleman knew how much the people loved him, and he found it
impossible to believe that there was any reasonable limit to
his ambitions. Essex was an extremely handsome young man
who was convinced that he knew how to handle a doting and
fading old woman, and it seems never to have occurred to
him that Elizabeth had ten times his brains and twenty times
his resolution. Having mismanaged everything he touched,
Essex was by 1601 in one of his periodic states of disgrace,
and he conceived the unfortunate idea that in a general up-
rising he might destroy his enemies at Court and force the
Queen to favor him.

Essex was extremely unlucky in his circle of advisers, of
whom the adoring Earl of Southampton was probably as intelligent as any, and Sir Charles Percy suggested an idea that
was characteristic in its impractical melodrama. It was evidently Sir Charles' theory that the population of London was
a tinderbox that any spark could ignite, and he proposed that
the spark should be applied by a production at the Globe of
Shakespeare's *Richard II*. This evidently seemed quite reasonable to the rest of the group, and six members of the Essex
group went to the Chamberlain's company and told the actors
what they wanted. The Chamberlain's company tried hard to

find a reasonable excuse and said that the play was so much out of date they could not afford to produce it for the small audiences that might be expected. Sir Charles and his friends removed this excuse by offering the actors an outright sum of forty shillings, and Shakespeare's company agreed to produce *Richard II* on Saturday, the seventh of February.

The Essex faction had a Saturday dinner at Gunter's and then were rowed across the Thames to the Globe where they arrived early and saw the play of the "killing of Richard the second." It was expected that by Sunday the population would be in a state of seething emotion; and just as the sermon at St. Paul's was finished, the Earl of Essex at the head of two hundred young men, whose swords were wrapped in their cloaks, rushed through the streets of London calling on the citizens to arm. Essex was heading for the house of Sheriff Smith, who had promised him support, and when Smith saw him coming he withdrew by the back door. There was no man the Londoners loved more than the Earl of Essex, and yet, as Camden says, "in all the city, then well exercised in arms, full of people, and most devoted unto him, not so much as one man of the meanest sort took arms for him." Essex had overestimated the devotion of the Londoners if he thought they would side with him against the Queen. By ten o'clock that night everyone involved in the abortive rising had surrendered. Essex and all his party were imprisoned and a searching questioning began of anyone who had any connection with the affair.

The men of the Chamberlain's company were for once in their careers in a really serious position. If the examiners had found evidence that any of them sided with Essex or that they had produced *Richard II* deliberately, it would have gone hard with them. Sir Fulke Greville destroyed the manuscript of an inoffensive closet drama he had written about Antony and Cleopatra, for fear that someone might interpret it as an account of Elizabeth and Essex, and even in the following reign Samuel Daniel got into trouble with the government because it was thought his play of *Philotas* might be a study of the fall of Essex instead of a general study of the fall of ambition.

Augustine Phillips, who had been chosen to represent the Chamberlain's company, was searchingly questioned by the two government examiners, and according to Phillips he "and his fellows were determined to have played some other play" and only yielded with reluctance because of the extra forty shillings. Popham and Fenner were skilled examiners, and if Phillips had not been telling the truth they would have discovered it.

Fortunately, the men of the Chamberlain's company had a spotless political record and they were Elizabeth's favorite group of actors. The government was willing to concede their innocence, and Shakespeare's company played before Elizabeth a fortnight later as though nothing had happened. The play they presented at Whitehall on Shrove Tuesday closed their regular Christmas season at Court. This was the same day that Elizabeth signed the death warrant of the Earl of Essex, and he was beheaded the following morning.

Essex died as Mary Queen of Scots had died, in black and scarlet and with great gallantry. But Elizabeth had loved him as she never loved her cousin of the north, and she never quite recovered from the final choice she had to make between her emotions and political necessity. The execution of Essex was the final climax of a long series of political murders that she had been obliged to countenance, and it must have seemed to her sometimes that her throne was built on blood.

Elizabeth was now nearly seventy and she had never had any life of her own except her life as queen. She had built her country from an insular little Protestant community, bankrupt and frightened, into one of the great powers of Europe, and she had loved her country with a devotion that was almost fanatical in its intentness. She had never set foot outside

England and it probably had never occurred to her to do so. England was her world, the one great reason for her existence, and she served her country with a singleness of purpose that very few nations are fortunate enough to command. In turn she expected the same service from her own ministers, and those underpaid, overworked officials could get what satisfaction they might out of the fact that she honored them with such a burden.

Of all her ministers, Lord Burghley had been the most loved and the most trusted, for he had worked with her from the beginning. "God bless you," the Queen wrote him, "and long may you last." He had struggled gamely against old age and gout and increasing deafness, and had at last quietly died in 1598 when he was nearly eighty years old. His son Robert became Secretary of State, but although he was clever enough he had none of his father's tact and experience. He managed to antagonize the Queen's last Parliament, that of 1601, so thoroughly that Elizabeth herself was obliged to take a hand. The Queen had lost none of her old magic. She summoned the hundred and forty members of the House of Commons into her presence at Whitehall and made one of the most charming and politically astute speeches of her career. "Though God hath raised me high, yet this I count the glory of my crown, that I have reigned with your loves. . . . It is not my desire to live nor reign longer than my life and reign shall be for your good."

For nearly half a century Elizabeth had played the intricate game of politics and her enemies on the Continent waited hopefully for her death. The news-letters of Europe announced periodically that she was suffering from cancer or some other fatal disease, and the Papal Secretary stated that any loyal Catholic who tried to kill her "not only does not sin, but gains merit." But what killed Elizabeth in the end was apparently pure weariness. She had outlasted her age, and the world she had known had vanished. The men who filled her Court were the sons and grandsons of the men she had once known, and in her heart she was a stranger to them.

Elizabeth had always been a good actress, and the last years of her reign were as lively as any. She rode horseback and went on long progresses, dragging the reluctant members of her Court behind her, and a duke who saw her in 1602 said that she still walked like an eighteen-year-old. But in December of that year she told one of her godsons that she felt "creeping time" at the gate, and when Shakespeare's company played before her at Richmond, two months later, they must have noticed a great change in the Queen. She had come to Richmond on the last day of January, in a torrent of wind and rain, and she never returned to London again.

By the 19th of March it was known that the Queen's illness was mortal, and all the theatres were closed. Elizabeth sat on cushions, staring ahead of her and not speaking. All her life she had scorned medicines, and none of the twelve hovering physicians could persuade her to take any. Finally she went to bed and lay with her face to the wall, speaking to no one. Her last gesture was to keep Archbishop Whitgift on his knees beside her in prayer when the old man hoped to rise. Then she went to sleep, and at three o'clock in the morning of March 24, 1603, the great Queen died without waking, "called out of the prison of her body into an everlasting country in heaven."

The greatest of England's rulers was dead, and the Age of Elizabeth was ended.

Chapter 11

THE NEW ruler of England was James the Sixth of Scotland, henceforth to be known as James the First of England. Londoners found it a curious experience to be waiting to greet a king, since no one under fifty could remember a time when there had been a man on the throne of England. There had been fear of disorder or even of civil war when Elizabeth died, since she had refused to name her successor, and when the throne went peaceably to her nearest relative, the son of Mary, Queen of Scots, the relief of the Londoners was enormous. "Every man went about his business, as readily, as peaceably, as securely, as though there had been no change, nor any news ever heard of competitors, God be thanked!"

The Londoners did not know what to expect of James, for pictures of the new king and queen were not published until after their arrival. When James had married Anne, thirteen years earlier, his journey to Denmark to get his bride had been reported to the London public in two ballads and a "thing in prose." Another ballad had come out to describe the christening of his eldest son, but the Londoners' chief acquaintance with James came through his own writings.

James was a determined author and he had already produced a great many poems, as well as a book of advice to poets, a study of the Apocalypse, a translation of some of the Psalms, a translation of *Lepanto*, a treatise on demonology and a book of advice to his son on how to be a king. Unlike Queen Elizabeth, who wrote poems but in a gentlemanly way never permitted them to get into print, King James saw to it that his work was published. Even after he came to the throne of England he continued his writing career, just as he continued his love of books. When he was restless at night he could go to sleep only if someone read to him, and his idea of a pleasant way to spend the morning with a young favorite was to teach the boy Latin.

On the seventh of May, 1603, the king was met on the road to London by all the city's dignitaries and by such a crush of uninvited spectators that anyone with a cart to rent made a small fortune. Any Londoner who achieved a view of his new ruler over the heads of his neighbors saw a youngish-looking man in his late thirties, with sandy hair and a thin, feminine skin. He had none of the beauty of his mother, or even the straight-backed grace of Queen Elizabeth, for his legs were so weak he could not walk without assistance and part of his love of hunting may have come from the fact he needed no help when he was on horseback. His forehead was too big for his face, his tongue was too big for his mouth, and he spoke with a broad Scots accent that must have sounded strange to his new subjects of the south. He was not a kingly man, for he was emotional, prying and lacking in dignity. But he gave England twenty-two years of unbroken prosperity, "lived in peace, died in peace, and left all his kingdoms in a peaceable condition."

From the point of view of Shakespeare and his fellow actors, the most important question about the new king was how he felt about the theatre. The pressure of the Puritan bloc was increasing steadily in London, and none of the acting companies would be able to remain in existence unless they had the support of James as they had once had the support of Elizabeth. James had been brought up under the shadow of the Scottish kirk, which strongly disapproved of plays, and in his book of advice to his son he had mentioned actors only once. "Delight not to keep ordinarily in your company comedians."

Fortunately for all Shakespeare's as yet unwritten plays, the new king thoroughly enjoyed the theatre and his point of view towards actors was quite unaffected by the way he had been brought up. His favorite actor in Scotland had been an Englishman named Lawrence Fletcher, and four years earlier there had been a brisk battle on Fletcher's account between King James and the city of Edinburgh. The deacons and elders of the city had tried to prevent Fletcher from taking a house in town and giving plays, and the King had not only forced them to withdraw the ban but had made them announce the fact from their own pulpits. Fletcher had been one of the King's favorite actors since 1594, and when James became the new king of England he set the actor at the head of the company that was henceforth to be known as the King's Men. The warrant for the patent of the new company was dated the 17th of May, ten days after the King's arrival in London, so that no time was lost.

The new company that was called the King's Men was merely the old Chamberlain's company with Lawrence Fletcher added to it. The second name after Fletcher's was William Shakespeare's, and the other actors listed in the patent were Richard Burbage, Augustine Phillips, John Heminges, Henry Condell, William Sly, Richard Cowley and Robert Armin.

Robert Armin had taken Will Kempe's place with the company as their major comedian when Kempe turned in his theatre shares shortly after the Globe was built. Armin must have been an excellent comedian, since according to a story in *Tarleton's Jests*, Richard Tarleton himself had singled him out as his successor. The story went that young Armin chalked up some verses on a wainscoting and Tarleton capped them with the doggerel:

My adopted son therefore be
And enjoy my clown's suit after me.

According to the story, Armin at once resolved to be Tarleton's successor. "Private practice brought him to present playing, and at this hour performs the same where, at the Globe on the Bankside, men may see him." Whether the story is true or not, it reflects the current opinion of Armin as a comedian and was also a good piece of advertising for the Globe.

Besides Kempe, two other members of the company had left it before the royal patent was issued. George Bryan had become a member of the Court, and he served as a groom at the elaborate funeral ceremonies for Queen Elizabeth. Thomas Pope had evidently retired by 1603, for he died the year following, leaving a special sum so that a monument could be erected to him in St. Savior's.

Two years after the patent was granted Augustine Phillips also died, and the love he bore his fellow actors is shown by the fact that he included them all in his will. Heminges and Burbage and Sly were three of his executors, and he left a silver bowl to each of them. He left thirty shillings in gold to Shakespeare and Condell; and Cowley, Armin and Fletcher got twenty-shilling gold pieces. Although Fletcher is included in Phillips' will as one of his "fellows" he does not seem to have been a very active member of the company. He does not appear on any of the lists of working actors, although these are admittedly scattered and incomplete, and his name is not included in the First Folio list of all the actors who appeared in Shakespeare's plays.

The royal patent made Shakespeare's company the most prominent group of actors in England, and they kept that position, unchallenged, for the rest of the reign. The patronage of the Lord Chamberlain had been valuable enough, since he headed the royal household and controlled the Office of the

Revels; but it was even more valuable to be under the direct
patronage of the king himself. King James saw an average of
five times as many plays a year as Queen Elizabeth had done,
and more than half of these were presented by Shakespeare's
company.

The whole royal family were ardent playgoers, and the second most important company in London was put under the
patronage of James' wife and given a patent as Queen Anne's
Men. This was a new company that had made an elaborate
start towards the end of the previous reign under the patronage of the Earl of Worcester, with Will Kempe as its chief
actor, Thomas Heywood as its chief playwright, and Philip
Henslowe to give it financial backing. The Admiral's company, which had once been the chief rival of the Chamberlain's, was now considered the third company in London and
was put under the patronage of Prince Henry, the king's eldest son. In actual practice, the three companies performed interchangeably at Court and Shakespeare's company did many
plays before Queen Anne and Prince Henry just as the
other two companies performed before James. Each company
had its own set of plays, and the royal family wished to see
them all.

Queen Anne in particular was an indefatigable playgoer.
In Scotland she had found a certain amount of entertainment
in dabbling in politics until her husband, who had a horror of
women concerning themselves in men's affairs, put a stop to
it. Anne was a thoroughly stupid woman whose chief assets
were a pleasant manner and a good complexion, and in the
twentieth century she could have spent her time quite happily in a round of motion pictures, bridge games and beauty
parlors. Living as she did in the early seventeenth century she
went to plays, and a letter is still extant that Sir Walter Cope
wrote to Viscount Cranborne in 1604. "Burbage is come, and
says there is no new play that the queen hath not seen, but
they have revived an old one, called *Love's Labour's Lost*,

which for wit and mirth he says will please her exceedingly."
Shakespeare's early comedy had pleased Queen Elizabeth at a
Whitehall showing, and there was no reason why it should
not please Queen Anne at a private production in the house
of a nobleman. The house used was either the Viscount's own
residence in the Strand or that of the Earl of Southampton,
who had finally been pardoned for his part in the Essex conspiracy and was back in favor again.

The plans for the new king's coronation brought a rush of
visitors up to London in the early summer of 1603. Scaffoldings were built for the triumphal procession, speeches were
written, and new arrivals every day filled the inns and the
theatres. "The streets were plumed with gallants, tobacconists
filled up whole taverns, vintners hung out spick-and-span new
ivy bushes," and so much money was being made that everyone tried to ignore the fact that the plague was again creeping into the overcrowded city. There had already been signs
of trouble in Southwark when Elizabeth died in March, and
as the hot weather came on the plague increased with it until
the city authorities could ignore it no longer. On the 13th of
July the plague orders were sent out to all the parish churches,
and when James was crowned on the 25th in a ceremony to
which the general public was not admitted, over eleven hundred people a week were dying in the London area.

By the middle of the summer London was almost a ghost
city. Anyone who was forced to stay in town took care to
walk in the middle of the street, chewing orange peel or
smoking tobacco; and the price of rosemary, which was considered a preventive, soared from twelvepence an armful to
six shillings for a small bunch. Among the many who died
was Ben Jonson's seven-year-old son, and among the many
who were heroes was Dr. Thomas Lodge, one-time playwright and man about town, who was now a physician in
London and working selflessly in the quarantined and desperate households of the city.

All the London theatres were of course closed, and the King's Men went on an extended tour that reached as far north as Coventry and as far west as Bath. By the end of November they were nearer home again, at Mortlake in Surrey, and word reached them there that their royal patron wished his company to perform for him. King James was at the moment in Wiltshire, staying in the great square stone house that the Earl of Pembroke's grandfather had built near Salisbury; and it was here at Wilton House on the second of December that Shakespeare's company acted for James the first play he is known to have seen in England.

Wilton House already had its literary associations, for the uncle of the present earl was Sir Philip Sidney and it was here that he had written his greatly admired *Arcadia*. The earl's mother was the Countess of Pembroke, that redoubtable woman who had tried to save the English theatre from "barbarism" in the 90's by transplanting the correct French dramas of Robert Garnier. Her son William, third earl of Pembroke, was himself a famous patron of poets and his intelligent gift to Ben Jonson, of twenty pounds a year to buy books, was characteristic of him.

The production at Wilton House may have marked the first association of the Earl of Pembroke with Shakespeare's company, but it was certainly not the last. He became a warm friend to them all, especially to Richard Burbage, and when he himself was appointed Lord Chamberlain he was able to do a great deal for them in his official capacity. It was fitting, when Heminges and Condell brought out a complete edition of Shakespeare's plays in 1623, that the Earl of Pembroke and his brother the Earl of Montgomery were the "incomparable pair of brethren" to whom the book was dedicated.

James rewarded his company for the performance at Wilton with thirty pounds, which was a large sum even allowing for the expenses of the journey from Mortlake. James was giving money about with a right royal hand, and he later remarked that his first two and a half years in England were a "perpetual Christmas." The facts of life caught up with him and there were spasmodic attempts at economy, such as fewer meat dishes at Court. But James could never recover from the delight of spending money, after his impoverished reign in Scotland, and Parliament was always arguing with him over the huge sums of money he and his wife managed to spend.

The King celebrated Christmas that year at Hampton Court, and the handsome brick palace was the home of masques and feasting very much as it had been in the old days of Henry VIII. The Earl of Pembroke danced in a masque, and Queen Anne showed her legs freely in the costume of Pallas. Shakespeare's company had their usual opening date of December 26th and they had a particularly heavy schedule their first week. They played four times before King James and twice before Prince Henry, giving two performances on Sunday.

Prince Henry was nine years old, a grave, beautiful, self-possessed child who grew up to be adored by the people of England and the very model of a prince. Both King James and Queen Anne had endured sickly childhoods, and James still had no real control of his body; but their two eldest children, Prince Henry and Princess Elizabeth, were as beautiful as the figures in a fairy tale. The younger son, Charles, was something of a misfit after so handsome a pair, since Charles was like both his parents and could not walk unaided when he was a child. Henry was not above teasing his younger brother about his crippled legs, but Charles made no objection since like everyone else he adored Prince Henry. "Sweet, sweet brother . . . I will give anything that I have to you." Henry died young and Elizabeth made an unhappy marriage and Charles was beheaded by his own subjects; but when the King's Men played before them that Christmas at Hampton Court they were everything that a royal family should be.

By March the plague was over in London and the postponed triumphal procession was scheduled for the 15th. The city had been presenting these pageants to their new rulers for centuries, and few people knew more about the art of welcoming kings. The scaffolds for the arches were completed and given their elaborate finishing touches, the speeches of welcome were written and rehearsed, and Edward Alleyn, who was to play the Genius of the City, was fitted for his purple buskins and tried on his long white wig.

The whole show cost the city four hundred pounds and the crowds were enormous. In spite of the railings there was a "strong stream of people," and there was so much shouting that the carefully written odes of Ben Jonson and Thomas Dekker and Michael Drayton could scarcely be heard. It was the kind of celebration Queen Elizabeth would have enjoyed thoroughly, but the new ruler of England bore it politely and without enthusiasm. James hated crowds and he never felt any temperamental affinity with his emotional Londoners. He once remarked on a visit to Oxford that he would like to "be a University man" and spend all his time in the Bodleian Library, and his idea of real pleasure was to engage in an intricate theological discussion on some minor point of doctrine. It is probable that he enjoyed nothing more thoroughly in his whole reign than his Hampton Court conference with the churchmen of England in 1604, and the English-speaking world may be glad that he did since out of this conference was born the King James Version of the Bible.

James had none of the vigor and flamboyance of his great predecessor, but he shared one quality with her: a love of peace. James was convinced that all wars were both expensive and useless, and he bent his energies to avoid them. It was an unusual point of view for the period, and a comedy was played at Brussels that parodied the English king's faith in ambassadors. As one of James' own subjects put it, the King would "rather spend £100,000 on embassies, to keep or procure peace with dishonor, than £10,000 on an army that would have forced peace with honor."

James was especially anxious to bring to an end the long, dragging, expensive war with Spain, and as soon as he was crowned he set the peace machinery in motion. In the same March that the Londoners were shouting at his triumphal procession, the costumers of Spain were occupied with the new clothes that the Constable of Castile had ordered for his suite so that they could accompany him to England with as much splendor as possible. The English plans to receive the Spanish envoy were equally elaborate, and Queen Anne gave up Somerset House, which was her town residence and the finest palace in London, to be filled with the best furniture and the most beautiful tapestries that the royal family possessed to honor the Spanish ambassador.

Although the Constable of Castile was bringing his own suite, it was also desirable for him to have as many English attendants as possible, "people chosen for their good disposition and nobility" and also, no doubt, for their excellent carriage and general impressiveness. Among those who were chosen to be attendants were the twelve actors who made up the royal company, and John Heminges and Augustine Phillips were paid over twenty pounds "for the allowance of themselves and ten of their fellows, his Majesty's Grooms of the Chamber and players, for waiting and attending on his Majesty's service, by commandment, upon the Spanish Ambassador at Somerset House, for the space of eighteen days."

It was not a new thing for royal actors to be Grooms of the Chamber. The same posts had been held by Richard Tarleton and his fellow actors when they had been appointed the Queen's Men, and James was merely continuing the precedent she had established. When livery was granted to all the members of the King's household at the time of the coronation procession in March, the King's actors were issued livery with the rest. (This time Shakespeare was first on the list and Lawrence Fletcher third.) This livery consisted of the cloth for red doublets and cloaks, and by ancient custom it went to everyone in the royal service, even down to the perfumers and basket makers.

If the Constable of Castile had understood English, the King's actors would probably have been used to present plays before him. Since he did not, Tilney supplied bear-baiting and acrobatics for his entertainment, and the actors became attendants at Somerset House, dressed in scarlet with the King's cypher embroidered in gold. The twelve actors probably had very little to do except look decorative, since the Spanish ambassador had brought three hundred of his own attendants with him. In return, they received board and lodging at the royal expense during their period of service, as well as nearly two pounds apiece that Phillips and Heminges collected for them.

Shakespeare was not the first major English poet to wear this kind of livery. Geoffrey Chaucer wore the royal badge as a member of the household when Richard II put on one of his greatest tournaments, and, like Shakespeare, he wore it for reasons that had nothing to do with his poetry. Chaucer wore the king's livery because at that time he was Clerk of the Works and was responsible for erecting the scaffoldings for the tournament; Shakespeare wore it because he was a professional actor in a company that was under royal patronage. It is quite probable that Juan Fernandez de Velasco, Duke de Frias and Constable of Castile, never knew that the attendant who served him for eighteen days at Somerset House was a playwright also, much less that posterity was going to be interested in the Constable chiefly because William Shakespeare had once been paid to attend him.

The Spanish envoy had an excellent time in London, doing the usual sight-seeing around the city and buying so lavishly that the London jewellers beat a path to Somerset House. After a final grand banquet at Whitehall he went to bed with an attack of the gout, and the King visited his bedside to wish him a final farewell. He recovered sufficiently to leave London on the 25th of August, after having given "very bountifully unto all that attended him," and since the treaty had been signed in the course of the festivities England and Spain were at last at peace.

Shakespeare and his eleven fellow actors were in service at Somerset House from the 9th of August to the 27th, and this seems to have been the first and last time they served the King in their technical capacity as Grooms of the Chamber. For the rest of the reign their services were evidently confined to acting. Two years later, for instance, the King of Denmark came over in the summer to see his sister Anne and was lavishly entertained by his royal brother-in-law. The Danes paused long enough in their drinking and feasting to see a few plays and the King's Men acted for them both at Greenwich and at Hampton Court.

The Constable of Castile had no sooner left England in the summer of 1604 than the preparations for the Christmas season began to take shape in the Office of the Revels at Clerkenwell. The King was so eager to see plays that it was decided to break with precedent and start the Christmas season on the first of November instead of the normal date of the day after Christmas. The honor of opening the season went of course to the King's Men, and the play that was assigned for the opening was Shakespeare's *Othello*.

Tilney was now Sir Edmund Tilney, for he had been knighted by James the previous year, just before the coronation. During the first excited months of his reign James had passed out knighthoods with an almost comically lavish hand, and three or four hundred knights were made the same day as Sir Edmund Tilney. A notice was posted inside St. Paul's offering a memory course so that Londoners could remember the names of the new knights, and so many jokes were made on the subject that King James himself apologized for all the knights he had made. Nevertheless, Tilney deserved the honor if some of the others did not, for he was a hard-working, intelligent official and was kept even busier in the reign of James than he had been in the reign of Elizabeth.

Tilney and four of his assistants in the Office of the Revels worked twenty days that summer overhauling the theatrical costumes that were stored at Clerkenwell, airing them and having them repaired. Richard Prescott, the porter, was kept busy earning his twelvepence a day attending to all the rehearsals and must have grown very familiar with all the actors of the King's company. Shakespeare and his group were presenting nearly all the plays that were produced at Court that Christmas. The Queen's Men were putting on one play by Heywood, the boys' company at Blackfriars was putting on one play by Chapman, and the Prince's Men had not been asked to perform that particular year at all.

Two amateur groups of actors were also busy rehearsing, for a masque was to be presented by the Earl of Pembroke and seven other gentlemen of the Court, and Queen Anne was planning to appear in a similar production with eleven of her ladies. Ben Jonson got the important assignment of writing the masque for the Queen and decided to have them appear as Moors in azure and silver costumes with feathers and pearls in their hair. Inigo Jones designed the stage machinery for the masque and it was staged at an initial cost of three thousand pounds, which was not a large sum for a woman with Anne's talent for spending money. Lady Hatton failed to get a part in the masque and Lady Hertford got the measles and the Queen was so bent on being realistic that she had everyone's arms painted black up to the elbows. The officials who were responsible for training the twelve lady-Moors in the use of their fans must occasionally have thought wistfully of the happier lot of the King's Men, who only had a single Moor to deal with in their opening production of *Othello* and had Richard Burbage for the part.

Othello was to be produced in the great Banqueting Hall at Whitehall, and Peter Wright, who was responsible for all the lighting equipment, had a complicated problem. His assistants fastened pasteboard around the columns of the hall to protect them from the wires that anchored the lights, and six men were required to haul up the great branches that held a huge array of candles and to wire them into place. Plates were set into the roof above the lights to lessen the danger of fire, for the Banqueting House was old enough and rickety enough without any added complications. It had been built in 1581 of wooden boards with a painted canvas roof, and although it was charmingly decorated it was growing rather unsafe. King James had the building pulled down a short time later and a new Banqueting Hall, "very strong and stately," put up in its place. Even in the Christmas season of 1604, the Banqueting Hall evidently was used for *Othello* only and the rest of the plays were produced elsewhere.

When James and his Court saw *Othello* on the first of November they saw what had once been a cheap melodrama exalted into great poetry. At the end of Elizabeth's reign, Shakespeare had been reading a group of stories that had been collected by Giraldi Cinthio, and in it he had found an ugly story of a woman whose husband went mad with jealousy and ordered her to be murdered. The casual Titan who worked with the King's Men had lifted up the bloody, old-fashioned tale, made what structural changes he thought were necessary, and added the greatness of his poetry and the reality of his people. The basic plot has been called unreal, but it never seems so when Shakespeare's version is given a good production, and it can safely be said that the production which Burbage and his fellow actors gave before King James was a good one.

The King's Men gave a Sunday production of *The Merry Wives of Windsor* and then followed it on St. Stephen's night with *Measure for Measure*. This was another rather ugly plot that had been taken from Cinthio's collection, and it had been somewhat softened when it was turned into an English play a quarter of a century earlier. The heroine of the play is forced to surrender her honor to save her brother's life, and Shakespeare manipulated the plot so that she is able to avoid the bargain and the play can end happily. The play is wonderful in sections but not very successful as a whole, since a rather complicated, mechanical plot of this kind did not give Shakespeare the space he needed for his characterization. At about this same time he turned another Italian story of this kind into a play and called it *All's Well That Ends Well*, and here he was even less successful and for the same reason. The casual manner in which Shakespeare persisted in picking up his plots occasionally betrayed him, especially when it involved routine situations from medieval folk stories and blocked what was one of the greatest of his gifts, the gift of characterization.

After the King's Men had presented *Measure for Measure* in the palace hall, there was an interval while the Earl of Pembroke and his fellow performers presented their masque with music. Then, on Innocents' Night, the King's Men reappeared with that hardy old perennial of Shakespeare's, *The Comedy of Errors*. The plays of Heywood and Chapman followed, and then the King's Men returned with another old favorite by Shakespeare, *Love's Labour's Lost*. By this time it was Twelfth Night, and the twelve lady-Moors were ready to appear in the complicated cockleshell that Inigo Jones had designed for them.

The King's Men had the rest of the Christmas season, and among the various plays they produced were two more by Shakespeare. On the 7th of January they presented his *Henry V*, and on Shrove Sunday they did *The Merchant of Venice*. James was so pleased with *The Merchant of Venice* that he ordered a repeat performance, and it was played the following Tuesday, "again commanded by the King's Majesty."

When King James was bored by a play he did not hesitate to say so. The following summer he attended a series of stage

productions at Oxford into which the university had poured
an enormous amount of time and money, even including
special movable scenery and the expensive services of Inigo
Jones. At the first play, James tried to leave before it was finished and only stayed because of the personal entreaty of the
Chancellor. At the second one he "spoke many words of dislike" in a tone that was evidently all too audible. At the third
he frankly went to sleep, for he had none of Queen Elizabeth's
determination to be gracious to her subjects at whatever cost
in boredom to herself. James could not have been an easy man
to please, being intelligent, critical and very restless, and it is
a tribute to Shakespeare's company that they evidently
pleased him enormously.

The new ruler of England was not temperamentally in
sympathy with his London subjects in the way that Queen
Elizabeth had been, but at least he had one characteristic in
common with the thousands who flocked to the Globe playhouse each week. Neither he nor they could resist the plays
of William Shakespeare.

Chapter 12

THE KING'S MEN reopened the Globe on Easter Monday, 1604, after the plague had closed the theatre for the better part of a year. The Prince's Men returned to the Fortune, and a short time later the Queen's Men, who had been using the old Curtain, got a theatre of their own out in Clerkenwell and called it the Red Bull. This left Shakespeare's company the one major group of actors in Southwark, and for the rest of the reign they were the undisputed lords of the Bankside.

The company's royal patron had given Richard Burbage thirty pounds in February "for the maintenance and relief of himself and the rest of his company . . . till it shall please God to settle the City in a more perfect health." The company must have needed the money, for the rent on the theatre had to be paid whether the Globe was open or closed. Moreover, there is some evidence that one of the last plays that the King's Men presented before the plague closed the theatres had been an elaborately staged and expensive failure.

The play was Ben Jonson's *Sejanus*, acted by an enormous cast that was headed by Richard Burbage and William Shakespeare as the "principal tragedians." The production had evidently been planned to attract the crowds that had come up to London to see the coronation, but Jonson's play was too learned and pretentious to please the average member of the theatre-going public.

Jonson had planned a Roman tragedy in the strict Senecan

model and he apologized for not having observed the unity of time, a failure that was unavoidable "in these our times, and to such auditors." He did not need to apologize for his research and was able to cite in detail an impressive array of sources, "being all in the learned tongue, save one." He wrote *Sejanus* as his first important tragedy, to fulfill all the true "offices of a tragic writer," and it was almost as though he were trying to show the rather casual author of *Julius Caesar* what could be achieved by a learned and conscientious playwright who was willing to obey the rules.

The author of *Julius Caesar* was one of the principal actors in *Sejanus*. It is not known what part Shakespeare took in Jonson's play but it makes very little difference, since all the characterizations are equally wooden. Shakespeare was accustomed to acting in pretentious plays, just as he was accustomed to acting in bad ones; and he accepted his roles in the same relaxed way he accepted the plots for his own plays and made the best of them.

It was this easy-going temperament of Shakespeare's that made him occasionally irritating to an intense and theoretical nature like Jonson's. Jonson once told a friend of his that Shakespeare lacked "art," and since by art Jonson meant the rigid, pseudo-classic theories of the Renaissance, he was quite right. Shakespeare had no special respect for theories. In his 'prentice days there had been a brief period when he tried to follow classical models, but since then he had paid no attention to rules and had used whatever dramatic technique happened to suit the story on which he was working.

The word that comes to mind in connection with Shakespeare is not "art" but freedom. He went his own way and made his own laws. By the time King James came to the throne, Shakespeare was the master of every resource of stagecraft, just as he was the master of every art of language, and a torrent of such force makes its own channels.

This is not to say that Shakespeare failed to be interested

in Jonson's theories. He was interested in everything, and during this period he must have been seeing a good deal of Jonson. The year after the Globe reopened, the King's Men produced *Volpone*, which was Jonson's first real success in classic comedy. For the first time he managed to bring to life on the stage his theory that each character should have a single dominant trait or "humour," and Burbage and Heminges headed the cast in what must have been an excellent production.

It may have been at about this time that Shakespeare experimented with a play that had a classical background and in which each character symbolized a single quality. The play was *Timon of Athens* and the "humour" of the hero was misanthrophy. "Hate-man Timon" was a familiar name to the Renaissance, and his "strange and beastly nature" had been frequently described. It is not clear why such a stiff and unnatural figure should have attracted Shakespeare in the first place, but he evidently grew bored with the idea so quickly that he was never able to give the play the careful attention it needed.

Shakespeare made another experiment with what might be called the "well-made play," again taking his story from Plutarch, and this time he made a brilliant and almost chiselled study of the danger of pride. A good actor in the title role can make a very effective play out of *Coriolanus*. The writing is magnificent, much of it in that clipped, vivid shorthand that well-trained theatre audiences at the Globe could follow as easily as their predecessors at the Theatre could follow the rolling periods that imitated Marlowe. But Shakespeare's hero is too rigidly simplified to achieve the humanity and reality of most of his people, and *Coriolanus* is one of those plays that an audience can admire but cannot take to its heart.

Shakespeare found still another story in Plutarch, and this time his imagination took fire. The result was *Antony and Cleopatra*, which Jonson must have disapproved of even more thoroughly than he disapproved of *Julius Caesar*. No one could call *Antony and Cleopatra* a "well-made play" from the Renaissance point of view. It has thirty-two changes of scene and ranges over the whole of the ancient world with a technique not unlike that of the old-fashioned plays of the 80's at which Sir Philip Sidney had once laughed. As for Cleopatra, her creator ignored the theory of the dominant "humour" with which he had been experimenting in *Coriolanus,* and he made her almost as complicated and as unpredictable as Hamlet. Cleopatra is not a consistent characterization; she is instead an enchanting woman, who cannot be held to respectable laws on paper and insists in walking off the page and into reality.

Shakespeare gave the King's Men an extremely difficult production problem in *Antony and Cleopatra* since for once the major role in a tragedy was given to a woman instead of to a man. For someone in the Globe company, the part of Cleopatra must have been the most severe test of his acting career. Shakespeare gave the actor his full assistance and let the Queen's passion for Antony be carried to a great extent by her lines or by the comments of the other players. In turn, Shakespeare trusted the capacity of his colleague at the Globe so completely that he dared to put into the mouth of Cleopatra a slighting reference to the "squeaking" boy actors of Rome. He must have known that by that time the audience would be so convinced of the reality of the story that they would have forgotten a male actor was playing the Queen and be conscious only of the Queen herself. The great magician knew what he was doing, and the magic did not fail him.

Shakespeare's interest in Plutarch during this period did not make him forget his old favorite, Holinshed's *Chronicles.* Shakespeare never considered himself superior to that rather old-fashioned historian, and, not long after James ascended the throne, he found in the *Chronicles* a story of a Scottish king that he transformed into the wonderful tragedy of *Macbeth.*

The mood of the play was Shakespeare's own, for he found no special hint of it in his source. Holinshed's Macbeth reigned for seventeen years and most of these were given over to "worthy doings and princely acts." Although there are as many murders as in the play, Holinshed relates them in a singularly matter-of-fact fashion and he even manages to flatten out the three witches, who are either "the goddesses of destiny or else some nymphs or fairies endued with knowledge of prophecy by their necromantical science." It was out of such unpromising material as this that Shakespeare made a tragedy that is the color of blood and moves as steadily as the coming of darkness.

It has been repeatedly suggested that *Macbeth* was written as a compliment to King James, who once wrote a treatise on demonology. It might as well be said that the play was a compliment to Londoners, since it would have been difficult to find anyone in the audiences at the Globe who did not believe in the powers of darkness. A hard-headed businessman like Philip Henslowe could place in his diary, between notes on buying costumes and paying playwrights, the information that if a man wrote certain words on parchment with the blood of a bat and tied it around his left arm he would get whatever he wanted. This might be an especially useful formula in a chancy business like that of the theatre, but it was not theatre men only who trusted to bat's blood and incantations.

Like most normal people, King James believed in witches; but unlike most normal people he was intelligent enough to know that some of their accusers were hysterics who faked their seizures. He exposed one such case just after he came to the throne, and before the end of his reign he saved a whole group of his subjects in Leicester, who were waiting to be hanged in the regular way as witches, by proving that the boy who accused them of witchcraft had been faking. James was so completely a sceptic that he did not even believe in the curative power of the royal touch, the "healing benediction" that is described at some length in *Macbeth*. He refused to continue the ceremony when he first came to the throne, because all healing was in the hands of God and not in the hands of a king; and he only consented to it finally as a matter of policy because the French kings still kept up the custom.

Shakespeare was not a man given to complimenting royalty, and when the King ascended the throne he was almost the only writer in England who did not break out in sobs of poetical joy because so beneficent a royal sun had come to shine over England. But if he ever had wished to compliment King James, he could certainly have devised a more graceful tribute than the bloody Scottish tragedy of *Macbeth*, whose only reference to the current ruler was in the "treble sceptres" that would be carried by some of Banquo's descendants.

In the winter of 1604 the King's Men produced a play that was a direct compliment to King James. The play was called *Gowry*, and told the story of a conspiracy against James by the Earl of Gowry that had occurred four years earlier. The story included a cache of gold pieces, a loyal falconer and a melodramatic fight on the stairway of Gowry House, and its dramatization by the King's Men attracted an "exceeding concourse of all sorts of people." One of their number played the part of King James himself, and although the King did not object, some of his Council felt it was improper to show the royal person on the stage and the play was evidently discontinued.

The custom of showing real people on the stage was common enough in the reigns of both Elizabeth and James. When Shakespeare's company presented in 1599 a drama based on the Battle of Turnhout, which had taken place two years earlier, they gave the real names of all the men who had taken part in the battle and presented Sir Francis Vere to the life with his beard, his satin doublet and his hose trimmed with silver lace. When a breach of promise suit was tried in the

London courts in the winter of 1603, one of the principals paid an outright sum to George Chapman to put the whole situation in a play, with the chief characters only faintly disguised, so that the suit could be won by ridiculing the opposition. It was a usual practice for a playwright to present someone he disliked upon the stage, ridiculing his "red beard" or his "little legs," and Lord Burghley once suggested that the best possible punishment for two cheats was to "have those that make the plays to make a comedy thereof," using their real names.

It was this custom that prompted Hamlet to tell Polonius that he should treat the actors carefully, "for they are the abstracts and brief chronicles of the time; after your death you were better have a bad epitaph than their ill report while you live." Shakespeare was almost the only playwright of the period who saw no need to comment on contemporary Londoners in his plays, and he did not share Hamlet's view that a playwright should chronicle his own times.

Hamlet was expressing a familiar opinion when he said that a play should show "the very age and body of the time his form and pressure." Nearly all the playwrights of the period, like Chapman and Middleton and Dekker, were locating their plays in contemporary London; and although Jonson's first satirical comedy, *Every Man in his Humour*, was ostensibly located in Florence, the Italian settings were only a thin disguise for real places in London and he changed the names to English ones when the play was printed in his collected works.

Shakespeare, however, did not write any play in the reign of James that had a setting in contemporary London. Instead he ranged from ancient Scotland to ancient Egypt and when he wrote a play about England he set it in prehistoric Britain and called it *King Lear*.

Shakespeare was a writer who was incapable of settling down mentally, and after having tried every other effect that could conceivably be achieved on a stage he set out to orchestrate a storm. *King Lear* opened the Christmas season at Court in 1606, and if the rambling palace of Whitehall did not blow down that night it was certainly not the fault of Shakespeare's lines. It is extremely difficult today to find an actor with the voice and the physical endurance to measure up to the part of Lear, but the Whitehall production had Richard Burbage. Burbage and Shakespeare had been growing up together, and when Shakespeare had written his youthful melodrama of *Richard III* it was Burbage who had created the lead. They had worked for more than a decade in intimate, daily association with each other, and the actor who had already had a great success as Hamlet and Othello was able to measure up to the titanic lines of King Lear.

Like *Hamlet*, an earlier version of *King Lear* had already been a success on the London stage, but unlike *Hamlet* the earlier version of *King Lear* is still extant. The original *King Lear* is a dull, respectable sort of play that is neatly motivated and follows the original story in Holinshed very closely. There are no disturbing characters like the Fool and everything comes out well in the end, for Lear and Cordelia do not die and the two wicked sisters are routed. Shakespeare merely used the original play as a springboard for the action and produced a play that is not well-motivated, that does not follow the chronicles and in which all the good characters are destroyed. The action of the characters is as senseless as life itself, and the appalling picture it conveys of the uselessness of old age, the stupidity of most mortals and the cruelty of living would be almost unendurable to the average spectator if the greatness of its poetry did not exalt it. *King Lear* is the one play of Shakespeare's that seems to have no basis at all in any kind of Christian dogma, and it is significant that he chose a pre-Christian era and wrote of events that took place "in the days when Jeroboam ruled in Israel."

It has sometimes been said that Shakespeare's plays mirror

his life. But *King Lear* was written at a time when the country was prosperous and at peace and Shakespeare himself seems to have had no troubles of either a business or a personal nature. It was in the difficult years of the late 90's, when a depression had gripped England and his only son had died, that Shakespeare wrote his radiant series of light lyric comedies.

During these successful years of working with the King's Men, Shakespeare moved his residence again and returned to the London side of the Thames. The exact date when he left Southwark is unknown, but it may have been at about the time of James' accession that Shakespeare left the Liberty of the Clink and took lodgings on Silver Street.

Silver Street was in St. Olave's parish, an aristocratic neighborhood on the northwest side of town that stood next to the parish in which John Heminges and Henry Condell had their homes. It was a district of handsome houses, and Shakespeare lived there as a lodger in the home of a French family named Mountjoy. Christopher Mountjoy was one of the many Huguenots who left France after the Massacre of St. Bartholomew and he had prospered in London as a maker of headdresses for women. For a long time Mountjoy had lived in St. Olave's parish as an alien and then he had finally become a naturalized citizen.

The Mountjoys had an only child, Mary, whom they had educated in the intricacies of silver wire and the art of using a twisting wheel until she knew almost as much about the business as they did. They also had an apprentice, Stephen Belott, who completed his seven years' service with them and in 1604 had just returned from a trip to Spain. A marriage between the two young people seemed both obvious and desirable, and Mrs. Mountjoy turned for assistance to her friend and lodger, William Shakespeare.

A marriage agreement was a serious matter because of the property settlement involved, and it was Shakespeare's responsibility to work out an arrangement on the dowry that would be agreeable to both sides. A married couple who were friends of Belott went formally to Shakespeare to discuss the size of the marriage portion that Mountjoy had offered, and as Shakespeare himself testified there were "many conferences" on the matter. The family servant, Joan Johnson, remembered eight years later how the lodger, "one Mr. Shakespeare," had made the arrangements whereby Stephen Belott consented to marry Mary Mountjoy, and on November 19th Mary and Stephen were married in the little church of St. Olave's across the street and came back to Christopher Mountjoy's house to live. The wedding took place in the midst of the Christmas season at Whitehall, just nineteen days after the King's Men had opened the season with a performance of Shakespeare's *Othello*.

The middle of the following summer, Shakespeare made another of his major investments in Stratford. On July 24, 1605, he spent the largest single sum of his lifetime, so far as the records go, and paid £440 for a lease on some of the Stratford tithes.

The purchase was one that involved a great deal of local prestige, for a holder of the tithes was an important man in Stratford. Seven years earlier, when Richard Quiney was in London, a Stratford business man named Abraham Sturley had written him to suggest that, since Shakespeare had money to invest, the matter of the tithes ought to be discussed with him. "We think it a fair mark for him to shoot at, and not impossible to hit. It obtained would advance him indeed, and would do us much good. Do no fail to urge this," Sturley continued, soaring into Latin. "This would be a labor, this a work, of surpassing honor and credit."

When Shakespeare finally bought the tithes Richard Quiney was dead, killed tragically in trying to stop a fight that had been started by some of Greville's men. But the ownership of the tithes was still a matter of surpassing honor and credit—

"*et gloriae et laudis*"—and the purchase symbolizes the lofty position that the Shakespeare family had attained in Stratford.

The tithes had originally been a tax collected by the church, but even before the Reformation the church had fallen into the habit of selling or leasing the tithes to secular owners. In 1544 the Collegiate Church of Stratford had rented them to the Barker family on a ninety-two year lease. The Barkers sold their lease to the Hubands, retaining an annual rental fee, and the complicated holdings were gradually divided among various people who wanted to sub-lease them. By the time Shakespeare made his purchase from Ralph Huband there were forty-two people who held various rights under the original ninety-two year lease, and Shakespeare's purchase consisted of about one-eighth of the entire property. The purchase gave Shakespeare the right to collect one-half the tithes on "corn, grain, blade and hay" from the three villages of Old Stratford, Welcombe and Bishopton, and also a one-half right to various lesser tithes, such as that on wool, from the parish of Stratford as a whole.

In exchange for his £440, Shakespeare had the right to collect these tithes until the whole lease expired thirty-one years later and the property went under the control of the Stratford Corporation. In the meantime, he was obliged to pay an annual fee of £17 to the Corporation and one of £5 to John Barker. Even when these payments were deducted, the investment was an excellent one; Shakespeare was able to get a return of about ten per cent on his investment, and within twenty years the value of the property had almost doubled. Moreover, the investment carried with it additional social prestige; for in the same way that his purchase of New Place had given him a special pew in church, the purchase of the tithes gave him a special place of burial. Shakespeare was now a lay rector and had the right to be buried within the rails of the chancel.

As the position of the Shakespeares became increasingly dignified in Stratford, it is likely that most people managed to forget that the head of the family was an actor. He did no acting in Stratford. He was William Shakespeare, gentleman, and the way he was making his money in London could be conveniently forgotten.

The acting profession had never been considered a dignified one in Stratford, although there had been a time when the people of Stratford enjoyed plays as much as the Londoners did. In Shakespeare's boyhood the acting companies had been welcome, but they were not welcome any longer. The year before Elizabeth died, the Stratford Council decided formally that no more plays were to be given in the Guild hall, and that any member of the Council who licensed the actors to perform should be fined ten shillings. Ten years later the Council decided that sterner measures should be taken in Stratford, considering the wickedness of plays "and how contrary the sufferance of them is against . . . the examples of other well-governed cities and boroughs." Therefore the Council decreed "that the penalty of ten shillings imposed in Mr. Baker's year for breaking the order shall from henceforth be ten pounds."

Like so many other towns in Warwickshire, Stratford was changing into a Puritan community, and every year the change in it became more pronounced. Within three years after Shakespeare's death, the Puritan faction had grown so strong that it was able to install a new vicar to replace the easy-going John Rogers. This set off a riot against the "sucking Puritans of Stratford," and two of Shakespeare's close friends, John Nashe and William Reynolds, ended up in the court of Star Chamber for leading an attack against Stratford's Puritan "rulers."

What had happened in Stratford was to a certain extent happening all over England, especially in the south and east. The Puritan doctrine, with its emphasis on hard work and independence of thought, made a strong appeal to the respectable middle classes; and since there is no pleasure in being respectable if someone else refuses to be, each Puritan set out vigorously to convert his neighbor to his own austere doctrine. Cambridge University and the Inns of Court produced dozens of ardent young men who had seen the light and who set out as travelling lecturers to spread the doctrine all over England.

By the time James came to the throne the Puritan party had a majority in Parliament, and one of the early signs of their influence was a bill passed in 1606 "for the preventing and avoiding of the great abuse of the Holy Name of God in stage plays." Instead of passing a bill that called for a ten-pound fine for every oath that was permitted on the stage, the Puritan party would have liked to pass a bill outlawing the stage entirely. But too many people, from the King down, loved the English theatre, and it was not until the middle of the century that the Puritan party gained enough power to destroy its enemy, the stage.

Puritanism had of course many merits, even apart from the great contribution it made to political thought by affirming the dignity of the individual conscience and denying the old doctrine of the divine right of kings. But from the point of view of the English theatre, Puritanism was an unmitigated disaster, and if the movement had taken hold in England any earlier than it did, none of the plays of Shakespeare could have come into existence.

Shakespeare had the great good fortune to be born in a period in which he could address an audience that had no special bias; and among the many kinds of freedom that Shakespeare possessed this freedom was by no means the least. Two centuries earlier, Geoffrey Chaucer had wrestled with the church's disapproval of love stories and of realism, and half a century later, Milton sacrificed the richness of his gifts on the altar of Puritan austerity. But in the sunny time when Shakespeare began to write, a man could say almost anything he pleased so long as he did not encroach on political matters. What have been called the spacious days of Queen Elizabeth were in many ways not spacious at all, but they did give the average Englishman a great deal of freedom when it came to the question of enjoying himself.

At the end of the 80's the playwrights had a brief skirmish with the Puritan party, during the Marprelate controversy, and had shown Martin Marprelate on the stage in what they considered a suitable costume—"a cock's comb, an ape's face, a wolf's belly." But in the next decade, the controversy died down and the attitude of the playwrights towards the Puritans was amused rather than angry. The actor who played Falstaff could be sure of a laugh when he raised his eyes heavenward and said in the Puritan sing-song: "Hal, I prithee, trouble me no more with vanity." The playwrights considered the Puritans a small, distempered portion of the population, and they took much the same point of view towards them that Sir Toby Belch took towards Malvolio: "Dost thou think, because thou art virtuous, there shall be no more cakes and ale?" But in another ten years Puritan virtue was spreading over the whole land, and some of the playwrights began to be frightened. The old note of tolerant humor begins to disappear and a kind of savageness takes it place.

Meanwhile the Puritans could legitimately retort that the playwrights had lost the respect for simple morality that they had once shown in their plays. The old plays of the 80's, with their clear-cut distinctions between virtue and vice, had been replaced in the reign of James by a newer kind of drama. Although George Chapman's dramas had an ethical basis, his heroes insisted that they and their passions were above the law.

> Be free, all worthy spirits,
> And stretch yourselves.

John Marston was a savage moralist, but some of his morality consisted in presenting violent pictures of the sin he claimed to be attacking, and a play like *The Insatiate Countess* gave many normal Londoners who were not good Puritans a reason to stay away from the theatre. The final result of such an atmosphere was the plays of Beaumont and Fletcher, which have no moral base at all and are merely designed to be sensational and entertaining.

Unlike the earlier dramatists, neither John Fletcher nor Francis Beaumont was a member of the lower middle class. John Fletcher was the son of a former bishop of London, a lively, unclerical individual who was fond of horses and fine clothes and who died suddenly after a disastrous second marriage leaving eight children and a great many debts. His son was evidently given a good education, and he started his writing career in a rather lofty manner by giving the public what he felt the public ought to have. The play was a pastoral in the classical manner called *The Faithful Shepherdess*, and it was published with high praise for its "elegant propriety." But it was a complete failure on the stage, since, as Fletcher said in his arrogant preface to the printed edition, the public evidently expected to see a lot of shepherds, "sometimes laughing together, and sometimes killing one another," and were incapable of recognizing a classical tragi-comedy when they saw one. The failure of *The Faithful Shepherdess* confirmed Ben Jonson's opinion that the London theatregoers were a collection of illiterate fools, and he assured Fletcher that his work would be immortal when time had destroyed "what all these fools admire."

Another writer who hastened to assure John Fletcher that the public did not understand true art was Francis Beaumont. Francis was the third son of Mr. Justice Beaumont, a prominent member of the Inner Temple, and since he was also a gentleman born he could sympathize with the select atmosphere that Fletcher was trying to encourage on the English stage.

Moreover, Beaumont himself had written a play that was a failure because the audience could not understand it. *The Knight of the Burning Pestle* was a satire on the citizens' audience, and tells the story of a Londoner and his wife who stray into one of the private boys' theatres and suggest that their apprentice be allowed to play the lead. Their innocent and straightforward notions of dramatic art are very skillfully parodied by Beaumont, and the chief object of parody is a play that Thomas Heywood wrote in honor of the London apprentices and which Heywood himself admitted was now out-of-date. But Heywood is not the only popular, old-fashioned writer to receive Beaumont's attention, for although the apprentice in Beaumont's play has won acclaim as an amateur actor in such reliable old melodramas as *Mucedorus* and *The Spanish Tragedy*, when he is asked to recite some lines from a "huffing part" he embarks on Hotspur's speech on honor from *Henry IV*. Beaumont evidently considered Shakespeare's work of the 90's sufficiently old-fashioned and sufficiently popular with a citizens' audience to ensure a laugh when it was quoted direct in the more select atmosphere of a private theatre.*

It seems almost incredible to a modern reader that two writers as dissimilar as Shakespeare and Heywood could be chosen as joint objects of parody, but it was natural enough in Beaumont's day. Shakespeare was the major playwright of the King's company, and Heywood was the major playwright of its chief rival, the Queen's company. Both men had been successful writers in the 90's, which was now considered a

---

* It is hard to know exactly what Beaumont thought of Shakespeare. In a rhymed letter to Ben Jonson, Beaumont said he hoped to use simple language,

> And from all learning keep these lines as clear
> As Shakespeare's best are, which our heirs shall hear
> Preachers apt to their auditors to show
> How far sometimes a mortal man may go
> By the dim light of Nature.

But just before this Beaumont has already announced what this unlearned style is to be:

> . . . if this equal but the style which men
> Send cheese to town with, and thanks down again
> 'Tis all I seek for.

period of comparative barbarism, and both of them had consistently been pleasing the general London public ever since. The companies they worked for both appealed to the same group of playgoers, for when two plays of Heywood's required larger casts than a single company could produce, the King's Men and the Queen's Men united to present them at Court.

If anything, Heywood had shown himself to be a man of more ambition and more learning than Shakespeare. He had already made a good translation of Sallust, and in 1608 William Jaggard published his long and ambitious poem in the Spenserian tradition called *Troia Britannica*. Most of its seventeen cantos were devoted to a retelling of the stories in Ovid's *Metamorphoses*, and since the book did not sell particularly well Heywood thriftily turned the same material to stage use. Both *The Golden Age* and *The Silver Age* were among the stage successes of the period, and they had the special merit of combining sensation with spectacle. Jove ascended on his eagle, Ceres and Proserpine danced with the country maidens, and so many devils filled the stage that the Queen's Men must have paid a large bill for fireworks. The cast of *The Silver Age* was an enormous one, including thirteen actors just for centaurs and planets, and this was one of the two plays that the King's Men and Queen's Men presented jointly at Court. The one other play they produced in this way was also Heywood's, and although he called it a "true Roman tragedy" *The Rape of Lucrece* was a blurred mixture of farce and of Shakespeare's youthful version of the story.

Both of these plays had been first produced at the Red Bull, where they were extremely successful, but not every play that the Queen's Men produced there was a success. Their production of John Webster's brilliant tragedy, *The White Devil*, was a failure, and Webster blamed the lack of "a full and understanding auditory." Webster did not like the atmosphere of the public theatres and complained that if a man wrote the most magnificent tragedy that was ever conceived, "observing all the critical laws," yet it would be destroyed if it were presented before the general public. "The breath that comes from the uncapable multitude is able to poison it."

Webster did not want anyone to think that his failure to please the "uncapable multitude" had made him envious of his fellow playwrights. "I have ever truly cherished my good opinion of other men's worthy labors, especially of that full and heightened style of master Chapman: the labored and understanding works of master Jonson: the no less worthy composures of the both worthily excellent master Beaumont and master Fletcher; and lastly (without wrong last to be named) the right happy and copious industry of Mr. Shakespeare, Mr. Dekker and Mr. Heywood."

Here is another case of an intelligent writer of the period linking Shakespeare with Heywood. It seems nearly incredible today that Shakespeare could be classed with a writer like Heywood and praised chiefly for his "copious industry," but from the contemporary point of view the chief playwright of the Globe and the chief playwright of the Red Bull belonged to a different and slightly lower classification than the learned gentlemen who did most of their best work for the private theatres.

The truth of the matter was that most of the writers of the period were too close to Shakespeare to recognize his greatness, in the same way that an object held too close to the eyes cannot be seen clearly. Michael Drayton could find no higher praise for his fellow writer from Warwickshire than to say he had "as smooth a comic vein" and "as strong conception . . . as any one that trafficked with the stage." An Oxford man named Thomas Freeman wrote an enthusiastic epigram on "Master W. Shakespeare" and praised the "wit" of his plays, but his chief proof of Shakespeare's versatility seemed to consist of the fact that his Venus was lustful and his Lucrece was chaste. Heywood included Shakespeare's name in a rhymed account of the nicknames of all the playwrights he had known, from Kit Marlowe and Tom Kyd to Jack Fletcher and Frank Beaumont. His remark on Shakespeare's nickname is charming.

> Mellifluous Shakespeare, whose enchanting quill
> Commanded mirth and passion, was but Will.

But the lines themselves are no more flattering than those he wrote on Jonson or Beaumont. Another Oxford student ranked Shakespeare with Chaucer and Spenser but included "rare Beaumont" as one entitled to equal honor.

There is only one piece of contemporary evidence remaining to show that any man of the Elizabethan or Jacobean age realized that a giant was walking among them, and that is the wonderful poem that Jonson wrote on Shakespeare for the First Folio. For once Jonson was able to suppress his own private theories and realize of Shakespeare,

> He was not of an age, but for all time.

As a result, Jonson's magnificent lines still seem intelligent today, while the opinion of Shakespeare expressed by most of his contemporaries seems merely fantastic.

This achievement is all the more remarkable because, in general, Jonson followed the doctrine that was held by all the learned men of his period and believed that anything the penny public loved was automatically worthless. Although Jonson and Chapman and Beaumont all wrote plays that were successful with the general public, they kept repeating in print that a really good piece of writing could attract the attention only of a chosen and initiated few. Shakespeare's plays consistently attracted enormous and enthusiastic audiences, so it seemed clear to the literary theorists of the period that there must be something wrong with them.

One of the few publishers who succeeded in getting a play of Shakespeare's into print during the reign of James followed this literary fashion and praised the play for not having been applauded by the worthless multitude. The play was *Troilus and Cressida*, which had been entered in the Stationers' Register in the previous reign as having been "acted by the Lord Chamberlain's men," but had not been published then. The editor who finally printed it in 1609 believed, rightly or wrongly, that it had never been acted, and he congratulated his readers on getting a play of unsullied purity. It had "never been staled with the stage, never clapper-clawed with the palms of the vulgar," and he bade his readers thank fortune that it had never "been sullied with the smoky breath of the multitude." This was the kind of statement that would have made the actors of the King's company smile, since they were all actively engaged in bringing as many members of the "multitude" as possible into the Globe.

The great difference between Shakespeare's point of view towards his audiences and that of writers like Jonson or Webster or Fletcher came from the fact that Shakespeare was not a writer only. He was an actor also, in constant touch with the public and closely interlocked with the economic life of his company. Shakespeare worked in a healthy, practical atmosphere in which there was little emphasis on theories and much on results. Moreover, he had no interest in any private, personal fame of his own, and while Chapman and Fletcher and Jonson and even Heywood saw their plays into print for the public to admire, Shakespeare did not. His plays belonged to his company and Shakespeare was a working member of that company, subordinating his own personal prestige to the welfare of the group as a whole.

In 1608 the group that was fortunate enough to have Shakespeare as a member took over another theatre in joint ownership. The system they had inaugurated with the Globe had worked so harmoniously for the past nine years that when the Blackfriars theatre fell empty the men of the King's company became its joint operators.

Richard Burbage owned the Blackfriars, and Henry Evans had leased it from him in 1600 for forty pounds a year. The boys' company that Evans had installed in the theatre had been prosperous from the first, but from the first there had been trouble also. The Blackfriars theatre opened to the accompaniment of a lawsuit that had forced Evans to leave town for a time and since then the company had plunged from crisis to crisis. In 1605, the boys of the Blackfriars presented a comedy by Jonson, Chapman and Marston that spoke slightingly of the king's Scottish knights, and all three of its distinguished authors went to prison. The next year the Blackfriars boys put on a play of John Day's called *The Isle of Gulls* and again "sundry were committted to Bridewell." Henry Evans spoke with a resigned melancholy of what happened when the playhouse was closed, "some of the boys being committed to prison by order of his Highness, and . . . a continual rent of £40 to be paid." In 1608 the Blackfriars boys presented a play by George Chapman in which the Queen of France not only appeared on the stage but gave another lady a box on the ear. The alert French ambassador lodged a protest and succeeded in having three members of the company imprisoned, although to his regret "the principal person, the author, escaped." This final disaster proved to be too much for the company. It was dissolved, leaving a trail of lawsuits in its wake, and by August Richard Burbage was able to buy back the lease.

Burbage saw no reason to rent his theatre to another boys' company, which would be operating in direct competition with the Globe. Instead, to use Cuthbert Burbage's words, "it was considered that house would be as fit for ourselves, and so purchased the lease remaining from Evans with our money, and placed men players, which were Heminges, Condell, Shakespeare, etc."

The actors came into the syndicate on shares, as they had with the Globe, except that the rent was paid to Richard

Burbage instead of to Sir Nicholas Brend. The seven shares were divided equally between Richard Burbage, Cuthbert Burbage, William Shakespeare, John Heminges, Henry Condell, William Sly, and an outsider named Thomas Evans who was evidently some relation of Henry Evans and had to be included before Henry would surrender the lease. Each of them was responsible for one-seventh of the annual rent of forty pounds, and Richard Burbage drew up a lease with each of the six men on the 9th of August, 1608.

The new syndicate was not able to open the Blackfriars theatre immediately, since it was in "decay for want of reparations" and evidently had to be extensively repaired after it was taken over. Moreover, there was a heavy visitation of the plague that winter, and even the Globe apparently had to be closed. The King's Men were on tour as late as October, and were again on tour the following spring as early as May, and for both that year and the next the King paid John Heminges for the private practice of the company, "being restrained from public playing within the city of London in the time of infection." The exact date when the Blackfriars theatre was opened is unknown, but it does not seem likely that Shakespeare acted in it for more than a year or two before his retirement.

The residents of Blackfriars had evidently grown resigned to having a theatre in their midst, and they did not present a petition on the subject until 1618. Even then, it was merely the popularity of the theatre to which they objected. The coaches of the theatregoers clogged Ludgate Hill, blocked the entrances to residences and broke down the stalls of the tradespeople; and the petition asked the Star Chamber to force all future theatregoers to come by foot or by the water-stairs. The petition does not necessarily imply that all the audiences were aristocratic, for it makes a special point of stating that many of the coaches were "hackney coaches bringing people of all sorts."

The aristocratic nature of the Blackfriars theatre under the King's Men has been overestimated, for there is no evidence that they altered the kind of plays they had been showing at the Globe in order to conform to a new audience. The King's Men went on producing the kind of plays that had already pleased the public and the Court at the Globe and at White-hall, and although they were able to charge higher prices at their new winter theatre there is no evidence that they made any other changes in their general policy. The three plays that Beaumont and Fletcher wrote for them in collaboration have been described as being characteristic of a more aristocratic policy at the Blackfriars, but one of the most successful of these plays, *Philaster or Love Lies A-Bleeding*, was advertised when it was put into print as having been "acted at the Globe."

It has frequently been stated that the more select atmosphere of the Blackfriars influenced Shakespeare's last group of plays: *Cymbeline*, *The Winter's Tale* and *The Tempest*. But these were not at all the kind of plays that Henry Evans had been presenting at the Blackfriars before he lost the theatre. If anything, Shakespeare's plays are much closer, from the point of view of stagecraft, to the series of plays that the rivals of the King's Men were presenting at the Red Bull. The elaborate, masque-like staging that was required for Jove's eagle in *Cymbeline* and the pastoral dances in *The Winter's Tale* are much closer to similar devices in Heywood's current series of plays than they are to anything in the productions of the children's companies.

The plot devices in Shakespeare's last group of plays are on the whole old-fashioned. He used the device of the headless corpse in *Cymbeline*, which he had once used so lavishly in *Henry VI*, and he also used the motif of the girl disguised as a page that had appeared in so many of his early comedies. In *The Winter's Tale* he was using the plot of a popular novel that Robert Greene had written in the 80's and that probably caught his eye in a reprint of 1608. *The Winter's Tale* leaps over seas and years with such a complete disregard for the classical tradition of the unities that it might almost have inspired the stern condemnation of the English drama that George Whetstone had voiced thirty years earlier. "The Englishman . . . is most vain, indiscreet and out of order; he first grounds his work on impossibilities; then in three hours runs he through the world, marries, gets children, makes children men."

A Dr. Forman saw both *Cymbeline* and *The Winter's Tale* produced at the Globe, and with the usual efficiency of the period he was able to find a moral in *The Winter's Tale*: "Beware of trusting feigned beggars." This seems to be the only thought that Dr. Forman was able to derive from the delightful Autolycus, and it is all too probable that he never noticed the golden poetry in which the play is written. Dr. Forman also saw a production of *Macbeth*, and jotted down a long synopsis of the plot very much as young John Manningham had once jotted down the plot of *Twelfth Night*. Forman was impressed by the sleepwalking scene and the blood on Lady Macbeth's hands, but in his uninspired prose the dismal nature of most of Shakespeare's sources for his plots becomes apparent. The question of how any man could take these limp and uninteresting tales, keep most of the story intact, and yet transmute the whole thing into enduring art, is one that can be explained only on the basis of alchemy. William Shakespeare had some formula for white magic that could take any kind of dross and turn it into gold.

It is generally believed that *The Tempest* was the last play Shakespeare wrote before he retired from the stage. It can be given a tentative date of 1610, because the year before there had been a spectacular shipwreck in the Bermudas and a shipload of Englishmen was obliged to spend ten months on "that dreadful coast" which was "supposed to be enchanted and inhabited with witches." Accounts of the shipwreck could be obtained in London the following year and apparently gave Shakespeare a few details for his own enchanted island. The play was certainly written by 1611, since it was chosen to open the Christmas season at Whitehall in the Banqueting Hall, and it does not seem improbable that this was the last play Shakespeare wrote while he was still an actor on the London stage.

For his last play Shakespeare returned to a device he had not used since *The Comedy of Errors;* he observed the strict dramatic unities, for all the action takes place on a single island in a single afternoon. When he wrote his first comedy, Shakespeare was an ambitious young man trying to do the right thing by imitating Plautus; when he wrote his last comedy, he was the complete master of every detail of his craft and only adopted the revered theory of the unities because for once it happened to suit his purpose.

Shakespeare also used some of the most intricate stagecraft he had demanded of his company since the early days of the history plays, and gave the stage crew this kind of direction to translate into action: "Enter Ariel like a harpy; claps his wings upon the table; and, with a quaint device, the banquet vanishes." Shakespeare was not asking anything unreasonable of the King's Men, for at about the same time Heywood was expecting the Queen's Men to show onstage the death of Hercules from a thunderbolt hurled by Jove and his soul descending as a star into the firmament. What was abnormal, or rather supernatural, about the production of *The Tempest* was the magic of the lines. The greatest of England's poets had never written more beautiful poetry.

It is a temptation to see Shakespeare himself in his fellow magician, Prospero, and it has even been suggested that when Prospero throws away his magic wand and returns to Italy it is an image of the playwright leaving the theatre and returning to Stratford. It is doubtful, however, that anything so pretentious would have occurred to Shakespeare in connection with himself, especially since he was an objective artist and not in the habit of suddenly inserting pieces of autobiography into his plays.

Shakespeare had good reason to retire. He had been an actor for twenty years, and it was a profession that called for strenuous and unremitting physical activity, with no rest even in the summer or at Christmas. He had also spent twenty years of intense mental activity, creating the greatest series of plays and the most wonderful procession of people that one man ever fathered in the history of the world. If any single consideration made him decide to leave the theatre it may very well have been sheer weariness. He had worked long enough and hard enough and he was entitled to a rest.

Chapter 13

THERE had been several changes in the Shakespeare family in Stratford during Shakespeare's last years on the London stage, and one of the most important had been the marriage of his elder daughter Susanna.

On the fifth of June, 1607, Susanna married a prominent Puritan physician, Dr. John Hall. The marriage was socially satisfactory, for Dr. Hall was an Oxford graduate and a member of the local gentry. He had a large and fashionable practice in the neighborhood of Warwick and eventually numbered the Earl of Northampton, more than forty miles away in the next county, as one of his patients. In the following reign he was offered a knighthood, which he refused, and he left a medical diary in Latin which a Warwick surgeon considered sufficiently valuable to expand in English and print.

A Puritan like Dr. Hall did not normally have so large a practice in the upper classes, but, as a fellow doctor remarked, he was "in great fame for his skill both far and near . . . Such who spare not for cost, and they who have more than ordinary understanding—nay, such as hated him for his religion often made use of him." Susanna was twenty-four when she married her distinguished Puritan husband, and Dr. Hall was eight years older.

It is likely that Susanna was not so ardent a Puritan as her husband. When she was living as a widow at New Place during the Civil War, her house was chosen as the one in which to lodge the Queen. On the other hand, her epitaph says that she was "wise to salvation," and in 1649 that approving phrase in Stratford would normally have been used of a Puritan. She was, in any case, not an unduly grave and rigid member of the sect, for the epitaph calls her "witty above her sex" and adds,

> Something of Shakespeare was in that.

If Susanna had something of her father in her, Dr. Hall was a fortunate man.

The married couple went to live at Hall's Croft, a house near the parish church and within easy walking distance of New Place. A daughter was born the following year and c the 21st of February was christened Elizabeth. There were no more children.

The next event in the Shakespeare household was a sad one. Little Elizabeth Hall was six months old when her great-grandmother died. Mary Shakespeare, wife of John, had outlived her husband and four of her sons and daughters, and before she died she had seen the Shakespeare family become one of consequence in the district. There had been many changes since Mary Arden married the son of a tenant farmer and bore him the first of his children on Henley Street.

It can be assumed that William Shakespeare returned to Stratford for his mother's burial, which took place on the 9th of September, 1608, since he was still in Stratford the following month. On the middle Sunday in October he stood in the parish church as godfather to a child named William Walker. The Walkers were a prominent family in Stratford, and Henry Walker had just finished a term as High Bailiff of Stratford when he asked Shakespeare to serve as godfather to his son.

Earlier in this same year of 1608 another Stratford child was christened William, but little William Greene had the further distinction that his family was actually living at New

Place. He was the son of Thomas and Letitia Greene, who had been making their residence in Shakespeare's house, and he already had a four-year-old sister who had been named Anne. The father and mother of Anne and William must have been on excellent terms with Anne Shakespeare, since it was evidently her household they were sharing.*

Thomas Greene was a prosperous local lawyer who had been educated at the Middle Temple in London, where John Marston and his father had gone surety for him. He came to Stratford in 1601 and stayed for fifteen years; and although he ended as a prominent barrister in London, he always spoke affectionately of the "golden days" he had spent in the service of the men of Stratford.

Thomas Greene was living at New Place the year of Susanna's marriage, although he had bought a home of his own called St. Mary's House, just beyond Hall's Croft. Two years later he began negotiating for occupancy with the current tenant, one George Browne, and finally decided to let Browne stay another year and sow his garden. Greene noted the arrangement in his diary in his thin scrawl, making the entry on Sept. 9, 1609: "Seeing I could get no carriage to help me here with timber, I was content to permit it without contradiction; and that rather, because I perceived I might stay another year at New Place."

Greene's diary suggests the probable time of Shakespeare's retirement. Greene asked Browne to have the house vacant by the 25th of March, 1610, so that he could use the timber he mentions in the extensive alterations he was planning, and he hoped to move into his new house by September 29th. This would indicate that he expected to leave New Place by that date, and the most natural reason for Greene's planning

---

* Thomas Greene speaks of Shakespeare as "my cousin Shakespeare." But no relationship has been traced between them, and since Greene also speaks of "my cousin Graves" and "my cousin Baker" he may have been using the word only as a term of affection.

to leave was that the master of New Place was coming home to live.

During the next six years, Greene spent the enormous sum of four hundred pounds on his new residence, converting it into what he himself called a "gentlemanlike" home, but it could never have had the social connotations that were attached to New Place.

It is not possible to reconstruct the appearance of Shakespeare's home, for it was torn down at the beginning of the eighteenth century and rebuilt in another style. But it is known from the statements on the deeds and the original foundations that the house had a sixty-foot frontage, ten fireplaces, and a bay window on the side facing the garden. A boy who had played in the original house in his youth remembered, when he was an old man in the next century, that there had been a brick wall separating New Place from the street, with a grassed court between the wall and the house, and that the building itself was fronted with brick and had plain leaded windows. The property had two barns on the side that fronted Chapel Lane, and two orchards. The original garden that dated from Sir Hugh Clopton's day was still in existence and must have been a fine one. Fifteen years after Shakespeare's death, Sir Thomas Temple was asking for shoots from one of its vines. The house was large enough to be used for a Queen, but there is only one record of the hospitality of New Place during Shakespeare's lifetime. This is an entry in the Chamberlains' accounts for 1614, "for one quart of sack and one quart of claret given to a preacher at the New Place." It has been said this was a Puritan preacher, as there were many such travelling around Warwickshire. But it may equally well have been one of those who delivered an annual lecture before the Stratford corporation, through an endowment. There were three such endowments by 1614, and the same year John Combe died and left provision in his will for a fourth.

William Shakespeare took very little interest in the affairs of the town, in spite of the fact that he was now a permanent resident of Stratford. The only time he concerned himself in town affairs seems to have been in 1611, when a group of local householders pledged themselves to help finance a bill for improvement of the highways that was coming up in Parliament. The seventy-two names on the subscription list include all the major householders of Stratford, from Dr. John Hall at Hall's Croft to Thomas Greene at St. Mary's House, and only William Shakespeare of New Place does not appear on the list. His name is added by itself on the right-hand margin, evidently as an afterthought.

It may be that Shakespeare was out of town when the subscription list was made up and asked to be included after he returned, but his frequent trips to London do not quite explain his lack of interest in the welfare of Stratford. His name is so conspicuously lacking from the Stratford records that it can only be concluded he felt no interest in the problems that were so important to fellow townsmen like Thomas Greene and Henry Walker. These men were his friends, but their interests were not his.

Before his retirement, Shakespeare's name appears twice in the Stratford records, in each case because he was bringing action for the recovery of debts. In 1604 he sued an apothecary named Philip Rogers who had run up a debt of over thirty-five shillings on some purchases of malt, with William Tetherton acting as his attorney. In 1608 he sued a member of the gentry named William Addenbrooke over a debt of six pounds. This case went to a jury, with Henry Walker presiding at the trial and Thomas Greene acting as town clerk, and Shakespeare was awarded damages. This is an abnormally low number of lawsuits for a Stratford resident, since there was no machinery for the monthly or quarterly collection of bills and a suit in the Stratford Court of Record had come to be regarded as a normal way to collect a debt.

Shakespeare was a careful man where money was concerned. He was not in the least like Ben Jonson, who was "careless either to gain or keep," and he went to some expense to hedge his investments in after he had made them. In 1611 he bought the twenty more acres of pasture land from the Combes, and had a special legal document drawn in Trinity Term to confirm his title to the acreage he had bought from the Combes nine years earlier, so that there could be no possible question of his full legal ownership of the land.

The same sense of caution made him join with some of the other owners of the lease on the tithes to present a bill of complaint to the Lord Chancellor. An annual fee to Henry Barker was being paid by forty-two people, of whom Shakespeare was one, and if any of them failed to contribute his share Barker could theoretically foreclose on the whole property. The suit was really a friendly one to get the apportionment on a businesslike basis, and its chief target was Shakespeare's good friend William Combe, who owned the lease on the other half of Shakespeare's special group of tithes. Shakespeare was joined in the suit by Richard Lane, who had the largest single holding, and by Thomas Greene, who had a reversionary interest in Combe's part of the tithes. William Combe answered the bill of complaint by saying he was already paying five pounds a year to Barker but was willing to increase his contribution slightly, and he joined Shakespeare and the two others in requesting the court to make a fairer distribution of costs among the holders of the tithes.

The suit was a friendly one and Shakespeare remained on good terms with the Combes. He knew three generations of the family, starting with old William Combe, who had become High Sheriff before he died. It was William and his nephew, John Combe, who sold Shakespeare the acreage in 1602, and when John Combe died twelve years later he remembered Shakespeare with a substantial bequest in his will. In turn, Shakespeare remembered Thomas Combe, John's nephew, in his own will. He must have known him very well, for he left Thomas Combe his sword, an intimate piece of personal property that would have gone to Shakespeare's own son if he had lived.

Most of Shakespeare's friends seem to have been among the landed gentry, like the two Nashe brothers who witnessed the Combe sale. Shakespeare left memorial rings to both of them in his will; and the wealthier of the two, Anthony Nashe, had a son Thomas who eventually married Shakespeare's granddaughter. Another county friend was Thomas Russell, Esq., a distinguished man in the district whom Shakespeare made one of the overseers of his will.

In spite of his retirement to Stratford, Shakespeare was a frequent visitor in London. He had business and personal ties in the city that he could hardly have severed even if he had wished to.

In Easter term of 1612, Shakespeare was called to London on a rather unhappy business—a family quarrel that had turned into a lawsuit and in which he was one of the chief witnesses. The marriage of Mary Mountjoy and Stephen Belott had encountered difficulties, and most of them originated in Mary's peculiar father. Gentle Mrs. Mountjoy had died two years after Shakespeare arranged her daughter's marriage, and after she was buried in St. Olave's church her husband's relations with his son-in-law became increasingly strained. Christopher Mountjoy refused to pay the marriage portion that he had promised, announced publicly he would leave his daughter nothing in his will, and would not even have his son-in-law "at his table." Finally Belott brought suit in the Court of Requests to force him to pay the marriage portion, and a long line of witnesses testified to such vital matters as whether Mountjoy had given Belott money to go to the barber when he was his apprentice and who had paid for the young man's stockings during the same period.

"William Shakespeare of Stratford-upon-Avon in the

county of Warwick, gentleman," was given a list of only five questions to answer and was called only once. He testified he had known both men for about ten years, that Stephen Belott had been a good and faithful apprentice, that Mrs. Mountjoy had asked him to arrange the marriage and that there had been many conferences about it. He said that Stephen had been living in Mountjoy's house at the time, but he did not recall the exact terms of the marriage settlement and he knew nothing of what Mountjoy may have promised Stephen in his will.

At Trinity Term a new set of questions was presented and finally the court decided the case was not in its jurisdiction and referred it to the French Huguenot church in London of which both men were members. Mountjoy was ordered to pay his son-in-law twenty nobles and refused. He was twice summoned by the church elders and failed to put in an appearance, and eventually he was suspended with a request that the members of the church pray for his soul. The suspension had nothing to do with Belott's lawsuit but was caused by the fact that Mountjoy had a mistress and the French Huguenot church would not tolerate what it called *"ces scandales."* As for Stephen Belott, whom Shakespeare had described as "very good and industrious," his daughters married well and he eventually came into an inheritance from a brother who had been a schoolmaster in Holland.

It is possible that Shakespeare was in London some of the time during the winter following the trial, for the Princess Elizabeth was being married and the King's Men were involved in a heavy schedule of plays as their part in the celebration. The treasurer paid John Heminges the very large sum of £153 6s. 8d. for the plays that were produced during the season, and these included more plays by William Shakespeare than by any other writer. The Revels Office had been shifted from Clerkenwell to Blackfriars, and Sir Edmund Tilney had been succeeded by a relative by marriage, Sir George

Buck; but there were no changes otherwise, and the plays were selected and rehearsed as carefully as ever.

The King's Men produced a variety of Shakespeare's plays, ranging from *Othello* to *The Winter's Tale* and from *The Tempest* to *Much Ado About Nothing*. They gave *Julius Caesar*, and two plays called *Hotspur* and *Sir John Falstaff* which must be the two parts of *Henry IV*. They also gave a play called *Benedict and Beatrice*, which was evidently a repeat performance of *Much Ado About Nothing*.

Outside of Shakespeare's plays, the King's Men presented Jonson's excellent comedy, *The Alchemist*, which they had first produced in 1611 with Richard Burbage and John Heminges playing the leads. They also gave several popular plays like *The Merry Devil of Edmonton*, whose authorship is now unknown. But most strongly represented, next to Shakespeare, was that succesful new team of writers, Francis Beaumont and John Fletcher.

The King's Men presented during the wedding festivities all three of the plays that Beaumont and Fletcher had written for them: *Philaster*, *The Maid's Tragedy* and *A King and No King*. The new playwrights worked very well together, for they had a gift for taking a subject like sadism or incest and being able to turn it by a last-minute twist into a comedy, clothing the story in such charming language and such a variety of incidents that the spectator could forgive the artificiality of the situations and a certain lack of reality in the characterizations. The team had also written for the children's companies, but they did their best work for the King's Men, and it was a well-deserved compliment when John Heminges' grandson was named Beaumont.

Francis Beaumont was still writing at the time of the Princess Elizabeth's wedding, for he wrote the masque that was presented by the Inner Temple and Gray's Inn. It was "fraught with art, state and delights," and when he retired to the country at about this time, having made a very correct marriage, he took with him a resplendent reputation as a writer. John Fletcher went on writing plays for many years to follow, collaborating with various writers like Massinger and Field and Rowley, but he and Beaumont had been such close friends and worked so successfully together that their names became inextricably associated with each other. When an edition of the plays was published in 1647, it came out as the joint work of Beaumont and Fletcher, in spite of the fact that Beaumont had a hand in very few of them, on the publisher's sentimental plea that since they were "never parted while they lived, I conceived it not equitable to separate their ashes." John Fletcher was not even credited with the sole authorship of *The Faithful Shepherdess* in his own lifetime, although it was a play to which Beaumont had contributed nothing but some admiring verses in the front; and very few of the plays in the folio edition can be safely attributed to both of them except the three plays that the King's Men produced during the celebrations for the Princess Elizabeth's wedding.

The King's only daughter was marrying Frederic, Elector Palatine of Bohemia, a sober, polite young Calvinist of the same age as herself. The marriage had been scheduled for the previous November, but Elizabeth's adored brother, Prince Henry, had been taken ill. He had a game of tennis one Saturday with a member of Frederic's entourage, and tennis was a game the Prince took much too seriously. He played in his shirt and contracted a chill, and the next day he began to shiver violently. From then on followed the horrible tragicomedy of a royal death, with the terrified physicians trying everything from cupping-glasses to a slit cock. The dying Prince endured their efforts patiently and said his prayers "quietly by himself," since he had no privacy otherwise, until he finally lapsed into a delirium and died on the sixth of November. The last conscious words he spoke were, "Where is my dear sister?" But they would not let her come to him and she had gone without food for two days when they finally brought her word of her brother's death. The two of them had been so close to each other that he had secretly promised to go part of the way with her to her new home.

Elizabeth's wedding was finally held in February, on St. Valentine's Day. It was a fairy-tale wedding, with the princess clad in white with a gold crown on her head and all her attendants glittering with jewels like the Milky Way, but the chief figure could have had very little satisfaction from any of it.

The next Court event that followed Elizabeth's wedding in February was the anniversary of the King's accession day on March 24th. A large tournament was always held on this occasion, but the tournament of 1613 has a special interest since William Shakespeare made a contribution to it.

It had been the custom for about a century for the knights who took part in the tournaments to carry paper shields called *impresa*, which were collected afterwards and hung on permanent display in a room in Whitehall. Each knight was supposed to have on his shield a picture and a motto that united to hint at his identity or his state of mind, and the guessing of these little courtly riddles was part of the fun of going to a tournament. A knight who had fallen in love could show Venus in a cloud, and one who was having difficulties at Court could show a man climbing a mountain and being pushed back by contrary winds. One knight who could think of no device at all appeared with a blank shield, except at the base there was a painter's pencil, a little shell of colors, and the motto: "Make of me what you will."

A great deal of thought and attention was lavished on these shields, and each knight tried to be more clever than his fellows. One of those who was especially anxious to distinguish himself in 1613 was Francis Manners, the new Earl of Rutland. He spent twenty-four shillings for gilt stirrups, twenty-four pounds for plumes and feathers, and four pounds, eight shillings in payment to William Shakespeare and Richard Burbage for designing a shield for him.

Shakespeare invented the motto for the Earl of Rutland's shield and Richard Burbage painted the design that went with it. Apart from his great gifts as an actor, Burbage evidently had a contemporary reputation as a painter, and for a long time a portrait he made of a woman hung in a gilt frame in Dulwich College. Each man was paid in gold, and the amount was noted in the accounts of the Earl of Rutland's steward.

A shield devised by two such talents should have made a profound impression on the spectators at the tournament, but unfortunately it did not. The only member of the audience who left a record of the event says that none of the emblems was a success except the two carried by the Earl of Pembroke and his brother, and that some of the rest were so confused "that their meaning is not yet understood." Moreover, it rained, and the Earl of Rutland's expensive plumes were very limp and wet before the tournament was over.

During this same month of March, 1613, Shakespeare made another of his real estate investments, but, for the first time, not in Stratford but in London. Shakespeare bought a house and yard in Blackfriars that stood within six hundred feet of his company's theatre. He paid £140 for it to a musician named Henry Walker, which was forty pounds more than Walker himself had paid for it at the beginning of the reign. Values were rising in a residential district as fashionable as Blackfriars and Shakespeare could expect a good income from the property, which he had not bought for his own use but as an investment. He rented it to John Robinson, who was evidently the man of the same name who had signed the petition that had once kept James Burbage out of Blackfriars; but times had changed and Robinson was resigned to living next door to a playhouse.

The purchase of the Blackfriars property was perhaps the most complicated of Shakespeare's many complicated purchases. He paid for it in part by taking out a £60 mortgage, and both the purchase and the mortgage involved not only Shakespeare but also three trustees whom he had taken into the transaction with him. One of these trustees, almost inevitably, was John Heminges. The second was John Jackson, another London friend, who was probably the man of the same name to whom Thomas Pope willed a diamond ring. The third was William Johnson, vintner, who is chiefly interesting because he was William Johnson of the Mermaid Tavern. This is Shakespeare's only documentary connection with the famous tavern, which incidentally seems to have been a quiet and well-run house.

The reason Shakespeare went to the complication of taking three trustees into the purchase with him was so that the property could never be claimed by Anne Shakespeare under her dower rights as his wife. Such a precaution would not have been necessary in Stratford, where there was no provision for a wife's inheritance of her husband's property, but in London it had "been observed for a custom . . . that when any citizen of London dieth, his wife shall have the third part of his goods." When Shakespeare died, a third share in the Blackfriars property would normally have gone to his wife; instead, he arranged it so that it went into the hands of the three trustees who owned the property in joint tenancy with him; and after his death they handed it over to two other trustees, Thomas Greene's brother John and a Stratford man named Matthew Morris, so that it could be held in entail by Shakespeare's eldest daughter Susanna.

As Shakespeare's will shows, he was determined to leave all his property intact to a single male heir, and he did not want the land he had protected so carefully to be dissolved into alien hands. It was not improbable that his widow would marry again after he died; most widows of the period did, especially when they owned property, and men as unlike as Richard Field and Philip Henslowe got their business start in this fashion. In this case, whatever Anne Shakespeare had inherited as dower right might conceivably have been claimed by her new husband, and it was evidently to avoid any such complication that Shakespeare chose three trustees to go into the Blackfriars purchase with him, as a means of protecting the estate.

Shakespeare had an excellent example of the difficulties that could occur when a widow inherited property and then re-married in the case of his friend, Augustine Phillips. When Phillips died at his country home in Mortlake in 1605, Anne Phillips inherited his shares in the Globe, which had unfortunately been assigned to the actors in such a way that they could be willed like ordinary property, and therefore could be, in Cuthbert Burbage's bitter phrase, "dissolved to strangers." Phillips' widow married a Mortlake man named John Witter who "riotously spent, wasted and consumed" his wife's property and then refused to support either her or the children. When Anne Phillips died, it was not her husband who paid for the burial; it was John Heminges. But John Witter sued Heminges on the Globe shares, which he claimed were his. Witter said he owned "a sixth part of the said galleries, ground and gardens of the Globe playhouse," and it was not until 1620, after both Heminges and Condell had been involved in a long and expensive litigation, that the courts vindicated them completely and ordered Witter to refrain from any further suits. The whole trouble started when Anne Phillips inherited her husband's property and then remarried; and John Heminges would have been in full sympathy with Shakespeare's desire to avoid future complications when he acted as one of his three trustees in the Blackfriars purchase.

Three months after the Blackfriars transaction, the King's Men presented at the Globe what was evidently their most elaborate production of the year. It was a new play by William

Shakespeare that was given the production title of *All Is True* but which later appeared in the First Folio as *Henry VIII*.* The play is not one of Shakespeare's best, since it was chiefly a pageant designed to glorify the birth of Queen Elizabeth and gave him very little room for characterization. But there was a great deal of room for pageantry, and the King's Men made the most of it.

A contemporary spectator reports that the play was "set forth with many extraordinary circumstances of pomp and majesty, even to the matting of the stage; the knights of the Order, with their Georges and Garters, the guards with their embroidered coats, and the like." Rushes were normally used on the stage to protect the actors' costumes, since strips of matting were very expensive, but the King's Men were evidently determined to have the best of everything for Shakespeare's new play. Since the play was realistically costumed, the expenses that were assumed in this department must have been enormous. A single scene like the coronation of Anne Boleyn had an array of earls, dukes, bishops, judges and so on, each one clothed in a replica of his real robe of office that was correct down to the last coronet and the last insigne.

The play was ready for showing on the 29th of June, 1613. The last play that had been shown at the Globe had been a comedy, and the actor who entered as the Prologue to Shakespeare's new play pointed out that the Globe audience, those "first and happiest hearers," must now prepare to listen to

* At the end of the 18th century it was suggested that this play was a collaboration. By that time a theory had arisen that Shakespeare was incapable of writing a bad line, and since the play is uneven, Dr. Farmer suggested that Ben Jonson wrote part of it. In the 19th century, James Spedding acted on a chance suggestion from Tennyson and offered John Fletcher as the collaborator instead, and this theory became so popular it subsequently hardened into accepted fact. What Spedding offered as internal evidence of his position has been demolished by recent investigations and there was never any external evidence in support of the idea of Fletcher's collaboration. John Heminges and Henry Condell brought out the First Folio while Fletcher was still alive, and *Henry VIII* appears in the First Folio as the work of William Shakespeare.

graver and more aristocratic events. The actor who played
the Epilogue was prepared to ask for the special applause of
the women, but on that June afternoon the play never got as
far as the Epilogue.

During the first act there was an elaborate dance at Cardinal Wolsey's house in which Henry VIII first meets Anne
Boleyn, and at the King's entrance the stage directions call for
hautboys. These instruments had a rather shrill and reedy
sound, and to give greater impressiveness a theatre company
sometimes used a combination of trumpets and cannon fire
instead. Cannons had been fired from the thatched roofs of
the theatres for years and so far nothing had happened, but
on the 29th of June the law of averages caught up with the
Globe. The thatch on the south side ignited, smouldered and
then blew into a flame, and in less than two hours the whole
structure had burned to the ground. It was the most spectacular fire London had known since the burning of St. Paul's
steeple, and two ballads on the great event were entered in
the Stationers' Register the next day. No one was hurt, in
spite of the fact that there were only two narrow doors to
take care of what must have been a capacity crowd, and the
absence of casualties speaks well for the orderly nature of the
Globe audience.

The men who owned the Globe were the wealthiest group
of actors in London, and by the following spring they were
able to have it "new builded in a far fairer manner than before." John Heminges was evidently responsible for the details of the financing and he sent each member a preliminary
request for money towards the rebuilding, which he raised to
a higher sum when the cost of the new structure became apparent. Shakespeare owned a fourteenth interest in the Globe
at the time, which would have brought his share of the expense to about a hundred pounds.

When Shakespeare died in 1616 he must have disposed of
his holdings in both the Globe and the Blackfriars theatre,

since they are not mentioned in his will. It may be that he disposed of his Globe holdings after the theatre was burned because he did not wish to reinvest in a new building. But the Globe was an excellent income property and a safe way to invest money, and it is more likely that Shakespeare disposed of his shares before he died because he did not wish to repeat Phillips' mistake of allowing theatre shares to be inherited by outsiders. As an actor, he knew how difficult it was to operate a theatre when outsiders could assume part of the control, and his friend John Heminges was involved in still another court suit at about this time on this same subject. When William Sly died, his share had gone back to the company since he had no wife and had been reassigned to a brilliant young actor, William Ostler. Ostler died in 1614 and his share went to his wife Thomasina, who also happened to be John Heminges' daughter. Heminges withheld the share and his daughter twice brought suit against him. Thomasina was rather quick to turn to the law for redress and during the same period she brought suit against Sir Walter Raleigh's son for insulting her, but she seems to have had a legitimate grievance against her father. John Heminges was normally a man of the utmost probity in his business dealings, but he evidently felt that the welfare of the theatre and the continued smoothness of its operation were more important than his daughter's legal rights. The inheritance of theatre shares by outsiders had proved to be a disastrous policy from the first, and Shakespeare was probably wise to dispose of his holdings in both theatres before he died.

During the same month of June in which the Globe theatre burned, there was a flurry of excitement in Stratford in which the central figure was Shakespeare's elder daughter, Susanna Hall. There was a young man named John Lane, who belonged to a well-to-do family in town and whose sister had married a brother of Thomas Greene, and this John Lane accused Susanna Hall not only of having "the running of the reins" in Dr. Hall's household but of carrying on an affair with Rafe Smith at the house of John Palmer. Rafe Smith was a haberdasher in his thirties, who was a nephew of Hamnet Sadler's and was living at the time with his mother on Sheep Street.

The Halls did not ignore young Lane's piece of slander. They immediately filed suit against him in the Consistory Court of Worcester and, when the defendant failed to put in an appearance, the Halls won the verdict. John Lane was excommunicated, a penalty which was not as serious as it sounds; but it would have involved Lane in some personal and business inconvenience until he succeeded in getting himself reinstated and probably taught him to hold his tongue thereafter. Susanna Hall was thirty at the time, with a five-year-old daughter, and she was not going to have her reputation in the community brought into question.

The chief quality that seems to characterize the Shakespeares in Stratford is a careful regard for their dignity and a quick eye for their rights. This was true of John Shakespeare, and it seems to have been equally true of his son and his son's daughter. Susanna Hall guarded the dignity of her name in the same spirit in which her father guarded his real estate investments. William Shakespeare was determined to leave nothing to chance and to set a double defence about the property that was destined for Susanna and her still-hoped-for son.

In 1615, Shakespeare participated in a Chancery suit to protect the property he had bought two years earlier in Blackfriars. The land he owned had been held first by the Church and then by the Crown and then by a variety of private owners, and when Shakespeare made his purchase the documents that recorded the titles in that particular section had been in the possession of Ann Bacon. When she died, Shakespeare joined the property owners of the district in a friendly suit against Matthew Bacon, her son, to produce the old documents that established their legal rights to their own property, and Matthew Bacon told the court he was quite willing to surrender the documents to anyone the court wished to name. The Blackfriars district was a fashionable one and the petition to the court starts with a baronet and works down through several esquires before it comes to "William Shakespeare, gent."

At about this same time, Shakespeare was obliged to take action to protect another of his investments—the tithes. He had already gone to law to have a revision made in the annual payments, but now the very source of the income was being threatened. William Combe had some farming land at Welcombe that he wanted to convert into pasture for cattle, and this meant that the tenant farmers who had been renting the land would pay no more tithes. Combe hoped to annoy no one by enclosing his own land for cattle, impractical as this hope turned out to be, and he was ready to make a financial adjustment with everyone who was involved in the ownership of the tithes.

William Replingham, who seems to have been acting as Combe's agent, approached both Shakespeare and Thomas Greene in the matter. Greene had acquired the other half of the Shakespeare section of the tithes one year earlier and both men would have been involved in an equal loss of income if Combe's plan went through. Replingham entered into an agreement with them both on the 28th of October, 1614, in which they were guaranteed against any financial loss because of the proposed enclosure. Combe was prepared to do the same with the Stratford corporation, which was receiving an annual fee from each holder of the tithes and would own the whole property when the lease expired in 1636, for he was sincerely anxious to have everyone in a good mood before he started putting a ditch around his property and turning the cattle in.

The town of Stratford reacted with the utmost violence to Combe's proposal. The members of the Stratford Council felt they would be traitors to their unborn children if they permitted it, and that not even the three fires that had ravaged Stratford in the past twenty years would be as destructive as the plan to enclose the common fields at Welcombe. Eventually the whole matter became a town cause and the money to fight William Combe in the courts was voted out of town revenues, with the men of Stratford in such a fury that they must have seen themselves as a modern reincarnation of St. George with William Combe as the dragon.

Combe had stated repeatedly that the town would not lose money by the enclosures and might even make an actual profit; but the root of the difficulty was not financial but emotional. For more than a generation, any proposal to enclose land in Warwickshire had aroused an almost hysterical opposition, and seven years earlier there had been an actual crusade of three thousand men, women and children who went through the county destroying whatever enclosures they could find, filling the ditches and cutting down the hedges. To the average villager, the word "enclosure" meant that some grasping landlord was taking the bread out of the mouths of innocent people by turning into pasture the little strips of communal farm land that had been theirs to rent since time immemorial. The medieval system was hopelessly impractical, since the ground could not be maintained in good condition or the breed of cattle improved as long as everything was handled communally; but this was considered beside the point, and there were many sympathetic readers for a "ballad of God's judgment showed upon a covetous encloser of common pasture," who was trodden to death by his own cattle.

The war of the enclosures put Thomas Greene in a difficult position. Like Shakespeare, he had signed the agreement with Replingham, but unlike Shakespeare, he was closely involved with the interests of Stratford and was in fact the town's legal adviser. When Greene was in London on the 17th of November, 1614, he went to see Shakespeare, who had arrived in

London the day before, and talked the matter over with him. Shakespeare said he thought that Combe did not mean to enclose beyond Gospel Bush and would not begin surveying before the following April, and Greene added the hopeful notation in his diary, "He and Mr. Hall say they think there will be nothing done at all."

The Stratford Council thought otherwise. At a general meeting held on the 23rd of December they drafted two letters, one to Shakespeare and one to Arthur Mainwaring, Replingham's cousin, who was also working with Combe. The letter to Shakespeare is not extant, but it was probably not unlike the one that was sent Mainwaring. In it the Council listed all the tragedies that would result if the enclosure were successful, since Stratford had to support seven hundred poor out of the income from the tithes and would be utterly ruined unless "Christian meditations" caused the recipient of the letter to change his mind. Greene also sent a letter of his own to Shakespeare, giving a full acount of the meeting and reinforcing the various points that had been made in the official communication.

Shakespeare seems to have ignored both letters. He took no special interest in the controversy, and since the enclosure would not hurt the town financially he probably hoped that the whole thing would blow over. Instead, tempers grew steadily worse. William Combe's brother Thomas had already told a Stratford delegation they were "curs" (it was Thomas to whom Shakespeare willed his sword) and by January William Combe himself was in a "great passion." He started ditching his property, and the Stratford Council went out and filled the ditches up again, and the harried owner of the property said they were all Puritan knaves. The case was fought out in the London courts, and after a long and expensive litigation it was finally decreed by the Privy Council that William Combe must pay a heavy fine and put the land back as it was. It was a final triumph for medievalism, but even the most determined town council could not banish the principles of modern farming forever.

The war of the enclosures was still being fought when there was a private event of some importance in the Shakespeare family. On February 10, 1616, Shakespeare's younger daughter married Thomas Quiney. Their marriage was so sudden that it took place in a prohibited season, and they were punished by the Worcester Consistory Court because they had not obtained a special license. Like her mother, Judith married in haste, although the reason for the haste is not known. Also like her mother, she married a man younger than herself, for Judith was thirty and Thomas Quiney only twenty-seven.

Thomas was a younger son of Shakespeare's old friend, Richard Quiney, and he had been running a tavern on High Street that was called "Atwood's." At about the time of his marriage Thomas traded establishments with a brother-in-law and obtained a larger tavern in a better location that was called "the Cage." It stood at the corner of Bridge Street and High Street, near the Market Cross, and it was here that Judith went to live after her marriage.

Judith's father had already made his will a month before her marriage, and he called his lawyer to New Place in March to make the necessary changes, since what was once Judith's dowry had now become a marriage portion. Since all the bequests to Judith were on the first page of the will, the whole of it did not have to be rewritten. The lawyer's clerk found he could get all the new material on the first page by writing the lines closer together at the bottom and adding two extra lines in the space at the top of the second page. Then he crossed out the lines on the second page that were not appropriate and left the third page as it was.

The will is a rough draft, full of corrections, and it has been suggested it was left in that state because Shakespeare was so ill there was no time to make a fair copy. But the lawyer in the case was Francis Collins of Worcester, and Collins was not in the habit of always making a fair copy of the wills he drew for his clients. He was an experienced lawyer who knew exactly what would stand in court, and the nine-page will he made for John Combe, two years earlier, is also full of deletions and corrections. It is improbable that Shakespeare was seriously ill when he made the alterations in his will on the 25th of March, for the first page opens with the statement that the testator is "in perfect health and memory." Collins would have used a different formula, "sound in mind but sick in body," if Shakespeare had been ill.

Shakespeare's will had one dominant, driving purpose: to leave all the property intact to a single male descendant. John Shakespeare's eldest and only surviving son was determined to fulfill his father's dream of a Shakespeare family established in perpetuity among the landed gentry of Warwickshire, and what sounds like a complicated series of bequests had a single end in view. The land had been bought; the land had been protected; and the land was to go to a male heir. It was true that at present there was no male heir, but Susanna was still a young woman and there was no reason why she might not still have a son. If she did not, her daughter Elizabeth might have a son, and if this failed also, there was still Judith.

The will opens with the bequests to Judith, the second-born. Since the property had to be kept intact Judith could not be given land and she was given instead a generous cash settlement. The money was left to her in two sections of £150 each. Part of the first section was to be paid outright and part was to be paid as soon as she surrendered her rights to the copyhold property that Shakespeare had bought on Chapel Lane from Walter Getley—a surrender that had to be made before Susanna could legally inherit this particular piece of property. The other £150 was to be paid in three years if Judith or any of her heirs were alive but otherwise was to be kept in the Shakespeare family. Her husband, Thomas Quiney, could inherit it only if he had already given his wife the equivalent of the money in land.

All Shakespeare's own land went to his first-born, Susanna. This included his residence at New Place, the cottage he had bought from Getley, the house in the Blackfriars for which John Robinson was paying rent, the two houses on Henley Street he had inherited from his father, "and all my barns, stables, orchards, gardens, lands, tenements and hereditaments whatsoever." Susanna was to have the use of the property during her lifetime and then it was to go to her eldest son. If he was not living it was to go to her second son; if the second son was not living to the third son; and the succession was carefully itemized in the will up to the "fifth, sixth and seventh sons of her body lawfully issuing." Very few wills of the period are as detailed and as insistent as Shakespeare's when it comes to the matter of entail; for if Susanna had no sons the property was to go to the sons of her daughter, Elizabeth Hall, and if Elizabeth had no sons the property was to go to the sons of Judith Quiney.

The personal bequests were thought out with as much care as the disposal of the land. Shakespeare left his only surviving sister, Joan, a life tenancy in the house she was already inhabiting on Henley Street and she was to make in return a token annual payment of twelvepence. He also left her twenty pounds in cash and all his wearing apparel, and to each of her three sons, William, Thomas and Michael Hart, he left five pounds. He left to Judith what was evidently his most valuable single piece of plate, a bowl of gilded silver, and the rest of the plate went to his granddaughter Elizabeth. He left twenty shillings in gold to his godson, William Walker, who was about the same age as Elizabeth, and ten pounds to the poor of Stratford. Thomas Combe got Shakespeare's sword, and substantial cash bequests went to the two overseers of his will, Thomas Russell and Francis Collins. He left

money for memorial rings to John and Anthony Nashe, and
to two more Stratford friends, Hamnet Sadler and William
Reynolds. He also left money for memorial rings "to my
fellows John Heminges, Richard Burbage and Henry Condell," who were the only three surviving members of Shakespeare's original company.

Shakespeare left his wife the second-best bed, which was
probably the family one since the best bed was usually kept
for visitors. When old Thomas Combe made his will, eight
years earlier, he left his son William the best bed and his wife
the second-best, but Mrs. Combe got the rest of the household
goods and Anne Shakespeare did not. All the "household
stuff" went to Dr. and Mrs. Hall, whom Shakespeare had
made his executors. Since Collins' clerk inserted the bequest
of the second-best bed above the line it has been said that
this particular bequest was an afterthought; but the key word
house in the bequest to Shakespeare's sister is also inserted
above the line, and so is the whole of the bequest to three of
Shakespeare's closest friends, Heminges, Burbage and Condell.

It is sometimes said also that Shakespeare did not need to
leave his wife any property because she automatically would
get a third of the estate as her dower right. There was such
a custom of dower right in London, and Shakespeare went
to some trouble to circumvent it when he bought the Blackfriars property. There was no such custom in Stratford, and
if there had been, the basic purpose of Shakespeare's will
could have been defeated; for, if Anne inherited, the property might not have been kept intact.

The relationship between Anne and at least one of her
daughters was very close. The brass plate on her tombstone
bears an inscription that is unusually personal for the period:
the daughter mourns that her mother gave her life while she
in return had given a tombstone. She prays that Christ will
come quickly and her mother will then rise again and seek

the stars. It was probably Susanna rather than Judith who erected the memorial, and since Susanna was now the mistress of New Place it is probable that she made her mother's years of widowhood happy and comfortable ones.

The tone of Shakespeare's will is impersonal throughout, although most of the wills of this period are personal and affectionate. Henry Condell's will speaks of his "well-beloved wife," and John Heminges asks to be buried "near unto my loving wife Rebecca." Augustine Phillips uses the same term, and Thomas Pope even includes in his affections "my loving friend John Jackson." But Shakespeare was one member of the company whose will does not show a flicker of personal feeling. Whatever his private emotions may have been about his family or his friends, he kept them to himself.

Shakespeare put his signature on each page of the will, with a "By me, William Shakespeare," on the third and last page. Francis Collins signed as a witness, and so did four Stratford neighbors that had been called in, Julius Shaw, John Robinson, Hamnet Sadler and Robert Whatcott. Shaw lived next door to New Place and that year was High Bailiff of Stratford. Sadler was the old friend for whom Shakespeare had named his dead son, and Whatcott had served as a character witness for Susanna when she brought suit for slander against John Lane.

Less than a month after the revision of his will, Shakespeare died. He was only fifty-two but he had survived all his younger brothers. Edmund, the actor, had been buried in London nine years ago, and Gilbert and Richard had died a year apart, one in February 1612 and the other in February 1613. The date of William Shakespeare's death is given on his tomb as the 23rd of April, 1616, and the parish records show that he was buried two days later. He was carried out of his home in a wooden coffin, and the great bell in the tower of the Guild Chapel, just across the way, had been repaired in time to toll for his burial.

Since he was a lay rector, Shakespeare's body was interred inside the chancel rail of the parish church. The Church of the Holy Trinity is a beautiful building, but when Shakespear died the chancel was in a state of neglect. The rain had seeped in and blotched the paint on the walls, and the windows needed glazing.

Just behind the north wall of the chancel where Shakespeare's grave had been dug, there was a room which the minister used as his study with a vault underneath that was used as a charnel house. In the crowded burial places of England, it was the custom to move old bones to the charnel house to make room for new ones, and there is a doggerel verse on Shakespeare's grave to guard against such a possibility.

> Good friend, for Jesus' sake forbear
> To dig the dust enclosed here.
> Blest be the man that spares these stones
> And curst be he that moves my bones.

Against the wall, over the grave, an elaborate monument in marble was erected. It is not known who erected Shakespeare's monument but it was probably Dr. and Mrs. Hall since Judith certainly did not have the money for so expensive a memorial. When Shakespeare's friend, John Combe, died two years earlier, he set aside sixty pounds in his will to have his monument erected in alabaster. The London mortuary sculptor who designed the monument for Combe was also hired to design the monument for Shakespeare, and he was probably paid about the same sum for his work.

Gerard Janssen turned out one of those expensive, unimaginative pieces of work that were standard with the monument makers of the period, and the best that can be said of it is that if it had been done forty years later, when English taste was inclining even more strongly to the baroque, it would have been much worse. Between two marble columns there is a half-length statue of the poet, holding pen and paper in the conventional manner to show that he had been a writer. The carving was done in limestone, chosen because it takes paint well, and the features were done conventionally by the sculptor, who left them to the painter to be made realistic. The painter made the eyes hazel, the hair auburn, the doublet scarlet, the loose gown black, and the cushion on which the hands rest green and crimson with gilt tassels. Above the figure are Shakespeare's arms carved in stone, with a skull set above them and a cherub on either side, the one with the spade symbolizing labor and the one with the inverted torch symbolizing rest. And beneath the figure is an inscription, partly in Latin and partly in English, stating among other things that in intellect Shakespeare was a Socrates and in his art a Vergil.

When Francis Beaumont died, a month before William Shakespeare, he was buried in Westminster Abbey next to Chaucer and Spenser, and an Oxford student expressed the wish that Shakespeare could have been buried there also. William Basse ended his poem on the subject by deciding that the arrangement was better as it was:

> Under this carved marble of thine own,
> Sleep, rare tragedian Shakespeare, sleep alone.

The notion of burying Shakespeare in Westminster Abbey could never have occurred to anyone in Stratford, and in any case it was undoubtedly felt that he had been given a noble and worthy monument. By 1623 the chancel had been properly repaired and painted and the windows had been glazed. The bright paint and the clean marble of the Shakespeare monument must have looked very impressive, and no one in Stratford could have known that it was a pretentious, dead memorial to a living spirit.

The Shakespeare will was as much a failure as the Shakespeare monument, for the longed-for heir never made his appearance. The Halls had only one child, and although Elizabeth Hall became Lady Bernard and died old and rich she never had any sons. Judith Quiney bore three sons and named the eldest one Shakespeare; but when Judith was buried at the age of seventy-seven she had survived all her children, and with the death of Lady Bernard in 1670 the direct line ended. The land that Shakespeare had carefully amassed and fiercely protected went to strangers, and only a routine piece of mortuary sculpture remained to show that the greatest man in England had once walked the streets of Stratford.

Stratford had failed in its memorial to Shakespeare, but London did better. Shakespeare had never concerned himself with the safety of his plays, and it may be that he thought they were less valuable than the land. But his fellow actors thought otherwise, and seven years after his death they reared him their own kind of monument. It was the complete edition of his plays and is known as the First Folio.

Chapter 14

THREE years after Shakespeare's death, Richard Burbage was buried in London. He died in March, 1619, which was also the month of the death of Queen Anne, and Middleton scolded the Londoners for keeping all their grief for Burbage.

> When he expires, lo! all lament the man,
> But where's the grief should follow good Queen Anne?

Among those who mourned Burbage deeply was the Earl of Pembroke, who confessed to a friend more than two months later that he stayed away from a play that was being shown for the French ambassador, which "I . . . could not endure to see so soon after the loss of my old acquaintance Burbage."

Now that Shakespeare and Burbage were dead, the only two actors that remained of the original Chamberlain's company were John Heminges and Henry Condell. They stood at the head of the King's Men, and when a new royal patent was granted to the company at the beginning of the next reign, John Heminges was the first name on the list and Henry Condell the second.

Both men had had a lifetime of experience in the theatre, and Heminges, in particular, had become what might be called the dean of the London stage. The year before Burbage died, the London companies banded together to negotiate with the Master of the Revels and it was John Heminges they chose to act as their agent. He had served his own company as business manager since the beginning of the century, and had been responsible for the collection and disbursement of thousands of pounds; and the work must have been well done, for in all those years there is no record of any lawsuit within the company or the complaint of any actor against him.

His closest friend in the theatre seems to have been Henry Condell, and those two neighbors and good citizens were still living in St. Mary Aldermanbury, where they were serving as parish trustees, the year that Burbage died. When the actors were in trouble, it was to these two men they usually turned. When Alexander Cooke, who had once been Heminges' apprentice, died in 1614 he left the money for the bringing up of his "poor orphans" in the hands of Heminges and Condell; and when John Underwood, another actor in the company, died a widower ten years later, he made Condell one of the executors of his will, Heminges one of its overseers, and left the care of his five children to his "loving and kind fellows."

When Heminges and Condell gathered the plays of Shakespeare together in the First Folio, they did it with the same kind of love that made them willing to care for the orphaned children of their fellow actors. "We have but collected them, and done an office to the dead, to procure his orphans guardians; without ambition either of self-profit or fame; only to keep the memory of so worthy a friend and fellow alive as was our Shakespeare."

No better men could have been chosen to be the guardians of Shakespeare's children, for Heminges and Condell were the only two men in London who knew by personal experience what plays Shakespeare had written. It is not quite certain that Henry Condell was with the Chamberlain's company when it was formed; but John Heminges was, and he saw each script as soon as Shakespeare was finished with it for the sixteen years during which Shakespeare wrote for the company. He had discussed the scripts with Shakespeare, worked over the casting and the staging, and had acted them with him; and Shakespeare's plays were kept so constantly before the public that John Heminges would have had no reason to forget even the earliest of them.

This intimate, professional knowledge of Shakespeare's scripts was essential for anyone who planned to make a collected edition of the plays, for only the plays of his middle period were available in good printed editions and even here the list was not complete. His earlier plays had mostly been printed anonymously, if at all, and two of them were in corrupt texts that had never been corrected. As for the great series of plays he had written in the reign of James, none of these was in print except what was evidently an unauthorized edition of *King Lear*.

By the time King James came to the throne, the publishers openly coveted the name of Shakespeare on their title pages, since, as the publisher of the unauthorized quarto of *Othello* remarked, "The author's name is sufficient to vent his work." The King's Men refused to release Shakespeare's plays for publication and so the publishers took the next best course: they printed other plays that had been successful at the Globe and issued them as Shakespeare's. In 1605, Nathaniel Butter published *The London Prodigal*, "as it was played by the King's Majesty's Servants. By William Shakespeare." In 1608, Thomas Pavier published *A Yorkshire Tragedy*, "acted by his Majesty's Players at the Globe. Written by W. Shakespeare." And in 1609, Henry Gosson published *Pericles*, "acted by his Majesty's Servants, at the Globe on the Bankside. By William Shakespeare."

No outsider could have found his way about in so confused a situation. It took a man as experienced as John Heminges, who had worked with Shakespeare and his scripts ever since the company had been formed, to bring order out of chaos and produce a collection of the plays that could be trusted.

A final touch of confusion was supplied the year Burbage

died by Thomas Pavier, who decided that he would bring out a collected edition of Shakespeare's plays. Pavier held the copyright to the corrupt quarto text of Shakespeare's *Henry V* and to equally corrupt texts of the second and third parts of the trilogy of *Henry VI*. He added to the list *A Midsummer Night's Dream* and *The Merchant of Venice*, which had not been republished for nineteen years and on which he evidently felt the copyright had expired. He brought two other publishers into the venture, Arthur Johnson, who held the copyright on a corrupt text of *The Merry Wives of Windsor*, and Nathaniel Butter, who had published the unauthorized version of *King Lear*. To all these he added two Globe successes, *A Yorkshire Tragedy* and *Pericles*, and since he held the copyright on *Sir John Oldcastle* he added that also. This was the play that Drayton and three more of Henslowe's playwrights had written at the turn of the century, for a rival company, but Pavier evidently felt that the London reading public had short memories and he had no hesitation at all in attributing its authorship to William Shakespeare.

Pavier was not a printer but a publisher, and to print the collection he chose a reputable Londoner named William Jaggard. The two were close friends, for Jaggard made Pavier the overseer of his will and had done printing for him back in Elizabeth's reign. Jaggard had one of the most successful printing establishments in London, and he would have had no difficulty in turning out the rather thick quarto volume that Pavier had planned.

The volume was not issued. Instead, each of the quartos was printed to be sold separately, with individual title pages, and with the exception of one group that had evidently already gone to press, all the quartos were given false dates. It was only recently discovered by experts, working with the watermarks on the paper, the kind of type used and other technical evidence, that these dates were faked and all the quartos were issued from Jaggard's press in 1619.

In the introduction to the First Folio, Heminges and Condell spoke bitterly of the fact that Shakespeare's plays were appearing in "stolen and surreptitious copies, maimed and deformed by the frauds and stealths of injurious imposters," and it was almost certainly Pavier's edition to which they were referring. But the King's Men had a better weapon than words. They turned to the Lord Chamberlain of England, who happened to be Burbage's good friend, the Earl of Pembroke; and on the third of May, 1619, the Earl sent a letter to the Stationers' Company ordering that none of the plays in the possession of the King's Men was to be printed without their consent. Three years later two more unauthorized quartos of Shakespeare's plays were issued, and the Earl of Pembroke later sent the Stationers' Company another letter reinforcing his order.

It was not the wish of the King's Men to keep Shakespeare's plays out of the hands of the reading public. What they wished to do, as Heminges and Condell said, was to present them "absolute in their numbers as he conceived them." But this was not a very easy thing to achieve from the practical publishing point of view, for there were thirty-six plays in all. This was far too many plays to present in a quarto edition, and the only solution was the heavy expense of printing them in folio.

Folios were normally reserved for dignified books on history and theology and medicine and were not associated with ephemeral popular productions like plays. The only writer who had dared to issue his plays in a folio edition was Ben Jonson, who published what he called his "Works" the year that Shakespeare died; and although he had also included masques and poems, he had undergone a certain amount of ridicule for dignifying his plays with so august a title. Jonson had not included all his plays but only those which he felt especially merited the attention of posterity, and in any case he had achieved a rather unusual eminence in literary circles, for a playwright, and was so respected for his learning that both Oxford and Cambridge had presented him with honorary degrees.

Heminges and Condell knew very well that a folio edition of all Shakespeare's plays would be a risky venture. Shakespeare did not have Jonson's lofty reputation in cultured circles, and even Jonson's folio had not sold particularly well. In general, the kind of people who could afford to buy large folio volumes were not in the habit of reading popular plays. When Sir Thomas Bodley started his beloved library at Oxford at the beginning of the century, he said it would bring "scandal" to the library if any playbooks were admitted, and that it was highly undesirable that "such kind of books should be vouchsafed a room in so noble a library." Sir Thomas was as careful to banish books of this kind as he was to get seasoned wood for the shelves and benches, and the First Folio was only admitted to the Bodleian Library by accident. It was sent there because the Stationers' Company had made an agreement by then to supply the library with one copy of every book printed by its members.

It was a hazardous venture to print thirty-six plays in folio, and it would not be surprising if Heminges and Condell had some trouble in finding a printer. Certainly, if they could have had their choice of any printer in London, it is not likely they would have chosen the one who actually printed the First Folio. For this was William Jaggard, who had already printed in 1619 the Pavier collection that Heminges and Condell had denounced as "stolen and surreptitious."

William Jaggard was in general a reputable printer and it was only when he was dealing with Shakespeare's work that he became at all unethical. It was Jaggard who had issued *The Passionate Pilgrim* in 1599 as Shakespeare's, although only one fourth of the poems in the book were his, and the book had rewarded Jaggard by selling so well that a third edition was called for in 1612. Jaggard padded out this third edition by blandly adding some poetry from Thomas Heywood's book, *Troia Britannica,* which he had printed for Heywood three years earlier. Heywood obliged him to cancel Shakespeare's name on all the remaining title pages, and Jaggard had to issue the rest of the edition without that potent name to help the sales of the book. Six years later he printed Pavier's collection, which attributed plays like *Sir John Oldcastle* to Shakespeare, and although Jaggard showed few scruples in his use of Shakespeare's name he showed a kind of dogged devotion to the name itself.

When Heminges and Condell began to collect Shakespeare's plays for the folio edition, they ignored the three plays, *Sir John Oldcastle, A Yorkshire Tragedy* and *Pericles,* that Pavier had attributed to him, and they also ignored the bad texts that Pavier had used. They found only three quarto texts they could use without any changes at all, and even when an authorized quarto was in print they did not invariably use it. In the case of *Hamlet,* it might have been better if they had, but in general they showed excellent judgment in choosing their texts for publication. Eighteen of the plays had never been put into print at all, and for these Heminges and Condell used the scripts that had been carefully stored as the property of the King's Men.

Heminges and Condell were not acquainted with the technicalities of the publishing business and they probably had very little to do with getting the selected scripts in condition for the printer. The editor who did this work for the First Folio is unknown. It could not have been William Jaggard, for he had been blind since 1612. It might conceivably have been his son Isaac, who was made a freeman of the Stationers' Company at the early age of eighteen, the year after his father went blind, so that he could help him in the business; but it is probable that Isaac was chiefly concerned with the production rather than the editorial end of the business. When Ben Jonson's folio was published, he did his own editorial work, with such loving care that hardly a comma went un-scrutinized, and Heminges and Condell expressed regret that Shakespeare had not been alive to do the same. "It had been a thing, we confess, worthy to have been wished, that the author himself had lived to have set forth and overseen his own writings."

The editor of the Folio lost his enthusiasm for the task long before he had gone through all thirty-six of the plays. The book opened with *The Tempest*, which was probably chosen for that position because it had never been published and could be trusted to attract the eye of a casual purchaser, and *The Tempest* was edited with some care. The stage directions were rewritten to make them easier to read, and the play was complete with locale and the names of the characters. As the editor advanced in his gigantic task, he began to omit the names of the characters and the locale, even when there was plenty of room for the information, and he forgot to rewrite the stage directions. Information intended for the eye of the prompter began to creep into the text, and the names of obscure members of the company like Tawyer and Sincklo and Jack Wilson were accidentally handed down to posterity. The proof reading was not carefully done, and the quotations from foreign languages in particular are full of mistakes; and the paging of the three sections of the book is so bad that in *Hamlet* page 156 leaps to page 257 and follows from there. Jaggard was often careless about page numbers, but in the First Folio he outdid himself.

The Folio had been planned for publication in 1622, and the London edition of the catalogue of the Frankfort book fair carried an announcement of it: "Plays written by Mr. William Shakespeare, all in one volume, printed by Isaac Jaggard, in folio." But there was a delay at this point and William Jaggard turned his press over to other books instead. One of these he was in a hurry to get printed, since it involved a private feud he was having with that quick-tempered member of the Office of Heralds, Ralph Brooke. But Jaggard also printed other, shorter books before he turned back to Shakespeare's, and the delay may have been caused by lack of money. When the Folio was finally published at the end of the following year, the description it bore in the Frankfort catalogue had been changed and it was now listed as having been printed by Edward Blount. Blount was not a printer but a publisher, and it looks as though the book had been refinanced in the interim.

Blount was a rather distinguished member of the profession who had once been a friend of Christopher Marlowe's, and he brought two colleagues of his into the venture with him. The Folio states on the last page that it was printed "at the charges of W. Jaggard, Ed. Blount, J. Smithweeke and W. Aspley," so that what had evidently been Jaggard's own venture in the beginning had now become a syndicate. Blount's name appears with Isaac Jaggard's on the title page, and together they made a joint statement of ownership when they made their copyright entry in the Stationers' Register on the eighth of November, 1623. But Blount's seems to have been the dominant position, since he was able to transfer the copyrights involved as though they had been his own property when he gave them to another publisher seven years later.

An artist had to be commissioned to make the usual portrait of the author to serve as the frontispiece, and it was probably Heminges and Condell who were responsible for selecting him, since they knew, much better than anyone else involved in the venture, what their "friend and fellow" looked like. They gave the commission to a commercial artist in his early twenties named Martin Droeshout, and he gave them a stiffly correct portrait in the usual three-quarter view. If they had been able to pay more they could probably have found a more talented artist, for while the art of painting was in general at a low ebb in England there was some good work being done by portraitists. On the other hand, Ben Jonson states that the portrait was a good likeness, and at least Droeshout refrained from crowning the brow with laurel leaves and adding symbolic figures of Comedy and Tragedy. The drawing is stiff but it is straightforward and unencumbered.

It was the custom of the period to preface nearly every book, however trivial, with a series of poems from fellow writers praising the author's work. When Ben Jonson published his folio edition it opened with nine commendatory pieces in English and Latin, and when the Beaumont and Fletcher folio was published, there were thirty-six contributions and nearly every poet in England was represented. There are only four commendatory poems in the front of the Shakespeare folio, for Shakespeare did not have quite the literary standing of either Jonson or Fletcher and it may also be that Heminges and Condell did not know many poets.

The one poet the two actors knew intimately was Ben Jonson. They had acted in all six of the plays that Jonson had written for the King's Men and had worked with him in the theatre for a period that covered thirteen years. Jonson was also a close friend of Shakespeare's, and the fact that he was now the most prominent figure in English letters made him the ideal man to write a commendatory address for the volume.

Jonson wrote eighty lines "to the memory of my beloved, the author, Master William Shakespeare, and what he hath left us." He was a warm-hearted and generous man and moreover he had loved Shakespeare, and for once he was willing to forget the differences of opinion they had had on the subject of rules. He could not resist mentioning that Shakespeare had "small Latin and less Greek," but he went on to say that only the greatest of the Greek dramatists could match him and that he had outsoared all his contemporaries. He then made a statement about Shakespeare that was consistently ignored for the rest of the century, during which it was decided that Shakespeare was a child of nature who went around warbling his untutored lays and was quite without conscious art. Jonson was an experienced writer and he knew that no artist works entirely from the promptings of "nature."

> Thy art,
> My gentle Shakespeare, must enjoy a part . . .
> For a good poet's made, as well as born.

Jonson's tribute as a whole is both beautiful and intelligent, and although his praise of Shakespeare may have seemed extravagant to the average literary gentleman of the period, the judgment of posterity has shown that Jonson was not exaggerating.

Heminges and Condell then approached Leonard Digges, a learned writer whose father had been a great mathematician. The Digges family lived in the same parish as Heminges and Condell, and Digges probably wrote his own poetical tribute as an act of friendship. Unfortunately he started off in his first line by flatly contradicting Jonson. "Poets are born, not made." He then went on to say that it was no effort at all for Shakespeare to contrive a play, a matter on which Shakespeare alone knew the truth. He then said that Shakespeare never borrowed from foreign languages, never gleaned anything from other writers, and, as a final touch of complete misinformation, that he invented all his own plots. All this was indirectly aimed at Jonson, and then Digges attacked Jonson openly by saying that any of Shakespeare's characters, Falstaff or Iago or Malvolio or Beatrice, brought in more money for the King's Men than any of the plays Jonson had written for them.

There seems to be no doubt that this offering of Digges was intended for use in the First Folio, but Heminges and Condell could not open the volume with an attack on Jonson. Instead, they evidently asked Digges for something a little more conservative and he gave them twenty-two lines thanking Shakespeare's "pious fellows" for giving his plays to the world and expressing the conviction that the plays would outlast the Stratford monument. A few pretentious lines were supplied by Hugh Holland, whom the learned William Camden grouped with Shakespeare as one of the "pregnant wits" of the day, and another poet who may have been James Mabbe wrote eight more on the same idea of an actor reappearing before his public.

The choice of a patron for the book had been obvious from the first, for no one had done more for the King's Men than William Herbert, Earl of Pembroke. It had been at his house at Wilton, twenty years earlier, that the King's Men had made their first appearance before James, and since his appointment as Lord Chamberlain in 1615 he had protected the company against unauthorized publications of Shakespeare's plays. He had loved Richard Burbage so well he could not "endure" to see a play two months after his death, and he had looked with favor both upon Shakespeare and on his plays.

The Earl of Pembroke had a younger brother, Philip, Earl of Montgomery, who was also a patron of arts and letters. The two men came of a line that had always been interested in the theatre, for their father had been the patron of an acting company and their mother was the Countess of Pembroke who had tried to raise the level of English drama in the 90's.

The ten actors who later issued the Beaumont and Fletcher folio thanked the Earl of Montgomery for his "constant and diffuse goodness" to them, and said they had been inspired to dedicate the book to him because he and his brother had been chosen as the patrons of "the flowing compositions of the then expired sweet Swan of Avon, Shakespeare." They said they were only following the lead of the men who dedicated the Folio of Shakespeare's plays to that "most noble and incomparable pair of brethren," William Herbert, Earl of Pembroke, and Philip Herbert, Earl of Montgomery.

Heminges and Condell approached the two earls in the

respectful manner that had to be employed in the seventeenth century. The dignity of their rank was much "greater than to descend to the reading of these trifles." Nevertheless, the two earls had liked the plays when they were acted.

> . . . We have but collected them, and done an office to the dead, to procure his orphans guardians; without ambition either of self-profit or fame; only to keep the memory of so worthy a friend and fellow alive as was our Shakespeare, by humble offer of his plays to your most noble patronage . . . What delight is in them may be ever your Lordships', the reputation his, and the faults ours, if any be committed by a pair so careful to show their gratitude both to the living and the dead as is
>
> Your Lordships' most bounden,
> *John Heminges*
> *Henry Condell*

The rather muted tone in which the two actors addressed the two earls changed considerably in the address which they sensibly entitled, "To the great variety of readers." Heminges and Condell had been working for over thirty years before a great variety of audiences at the Rose, the Theatre, the Curtain, the Globe and the Blackfriars, and they knew two things. The first was that Shakespeare's plays could be enjoyed by a great many different kinds of people, and the second was that every audience should be ready to pay the price of admission. Anyone was free to pass judgment on the plays in the Folio, but first he must buy the book. "Read and censure . . . but buy it first." "Whatever you do, buy."

The actors continued their address to the reader with a statement of regret that the author had not lived to publish his own work, and a condemnation of the corrupt editions in which some of his plays were circulating. Then they went on to describe what Shakespeare's scripts had looked like when the actors received them from his hand. "His mind and hand went together; and what he thought, he uttered with that easiness, that we have scarce received from him a blot in his papers. But it is not our province, who only gather his works and give them to you, to praise him. It is yours that read him . . . Read him, therefore; and again and again; and if then you do not like him, surely you are in some manifest danger not to understand him." The language is not as poetic as Jonson's contribution, but there was never a truer statement about William Shakespeare.

At the end of the eighteenth century it suddenly occurred to James Boswell, son of the biographer, that Heminges and Condell did not write this address because some of the phrases are similar to some that Ben Jonson once used elsewhere. Boswell made this discovery by what he called decomposing the address, and a better name for the process could hardly be found. A great many scholars have since agreed with Boswell, although there is another group that prefers to give the credit to Edward Blount. Nevertheless, there is no reason of any kind why Heminges and Condell should not have done what they said they did. They were not illiterate men. Heminges' own son, whom he had named William, became a playwright; and when John Heminges died and left five pounds to his grandson Richard it was with the specific instruction the sum should be used "to buy him books."

There is only one current book review that is now extant on the First Folio. It was written, evidently at about the date of publication, in a manuscript book that belonged to the Salisburys and had been composed by someone who knew both actors since it was addressed "To my good friends Mr. John Heminges and Henry Condell."

> To you that jointly with undaunted pains
> Vouchsafed to chant to us these noble strains,

How much you merit by it is not said,
But you have pleased the living, loved the dead . . .

There is no question the volume "pleased the living," for a
second edition was required within the decade. Nor is there
any question that the two men had showed Shakespeare their
love and gratitude in the one way that would have been
worthy of him. Instead of a memorial of stone they made
him one of his own words.

Heminges and Condell grew old and died and were buried
near each other in the parish church of St. Mary Aldermanbury. The Puritans came into power and closed every playhouse in England. The last of Shakespeare's descendants died
and the direct line became extinct. But Shakespeare's plays
went on being read, and in every generation there was an increasing number of people who loved him. Heminges and
Condell had wished him "such readers" and given him the
chance to get them. Every year their number increased, and
they have now built a monument to him that extends over
the whole of the world.

Appendix 1

The Sonnets

A YEAR or two before Shakespeare retired from the theatre, a London publisher brought out a book called *Shakespeare's Sonnets*. The book was entered in the Stationers' Register on the 20th of May, 1609, and it was evidently on sale a short time later.

The publisher was Thomas Thorpe, a minor figure in the London book trade, and since he had neither a press nor a retail outlet he arranged to have the book printed by George Eld and sold through the book shops of William Aspley and John Wright. These two men were well established in the business and probably welcomed the chance to sell a new book by as popular a writer as William Shakespeare. The price of the *Sonnets* was fivepence, as Edward Alleyn noted on the back of a business letter when he bought a copy the year of its publication and entered it under "household stuff."

In spite of the popularity of Shakespeare's name the book did not sell especially well, since a second edition was not called for until more than thirty years later. If the book had been published in the 90's, at the same time as *Venus and Adonis* and *The Rape of Lucrece*, it would probably have sold as well as either of them and gone through several editions. Everyone was reading sonnets in the 90's, but there was a very different literary atmosphere in London fifteen years later.

Many efforts have been made to find a single, connected story in the sonnets, but no arrangement has ever been found that will reveal one. They seem to have been written over a considerable period of time and under a variety of circumstances, and there is even a religious sonnet and two that were evidently suggested by the town of Bath.

Nevertheless, while there is no single story, the majority of the sonnets are addressed to a man, and the tone is the usual one for the Renaissance and glorifies the idea of friendship between men. As John Lyly once put it, "The love of men to women is a thing common and of course; the friendship of man to man infinite and immortal." The Renaissance used the violent, sensuous terms for friendship between men that later generations reserved for sexual love, and when Portia spoke of "the bosom lover of my lord" she did not mean herself but one of Bassanio's men friends. Shakespeare's use of a term like "master-mistress" sounds abnormal to the ears of the twentieth century, but it did not sound so at the end of the sixteenth.

Although all the sonnets in the book cannot be linked together, the first twenty at least form an unbroken sequence. The poet is addressing his young and beautiful friend, imploring him to marry so that his loveliness will not die with him but will be bequeathed to a son. He can expect to achieve immortality because of the sonnets that are being addressed to him,

> But were some child of yours alive that time,
> You should live twice,—in it and in my rime.

The idea that a poet could confer immortality on his beloved though his writing is one of those Renaissance commonplaces that keep occurring and recurring in the sonnets that were written in the sixteenth century. Shakespeare used the idea repeatedly throughout the whole of the *Sonnets* and found a dozen ways of saying the same thing:

> So long as men can breathe, or eyes can see,
> So long lives this, and this gives life to thee.

This was the idea that Thomas Thorpe picked up and used in the dedication to the *Sonnets*. It was the custom for the poet to write his own dedication, but in this case, since the book was obviously unauthorized, Thorpe had to do it himself, and he dedicated it to the man who had inspired the sonnets and to whom Shakespeare had promised immortality. "To the only begetter of these ensuing sonnets, Mr. W. H., all happiness and that eternity promised by our ever-living poet wisheth the well-wishing adventurer in setting forth, T. T."

Not all the sonnets are addressed to a man. Some are addressed to a woman, and some to no one in particular. But enough of them are addressed to a single man to whom the poet promises immortality to make the dedication seem a reasonable one to the average reader. Moreover it gave the whole book a tone of respectability and authenticity, since Mr. W. H. presumably had given the manuscript collection to Thorpe and, if he had also inspired the sonnets, their authority was assured.

There is no contemporary evidence as to the identification of this Mr. W. H. One member of the book trade had these initials, and it has been suggested that he collected the sonnets for Thorpe and Thorpe was thanking him in the dedication. But this is not what the dedication says. Whether or not Thorpe was speaking the truth is another matter, but he clearly wished the reader to believe that the man to whom the book was dedicated was the man who had inspired the writing of the sonnets.

Towards the end of the eighteenth century, Edmund Malone thought he had found a clue to the identity of Mr. W. H., having noticed that in the twentieth sonnet, which serves as the climax to the first group, the word *Hues* is printed with a capital and in italics. In a later sonnet there is an extended pun on the word *Will*, and Malone combined these two points and suggested that the object of Shakespeare's affections was a young man named William Hues or Hughes. This theory holds up well until the reader looks through the original printing. Then he finds that nearly a score of words in the sonnets are printed in the same way, capitalized and in italics. *Statues* is printed that way in sonnet 55, *Satire* in sonnet 100, *Autumn* in sonnet 104, *Informer* in sonnet 125, and so on; and what Malone hoped was some kind of a secret message from Thorpe is nothing but the occasional inconsistency of the printer.

The imaginary William Hughes was never, in any case, a very popular candidate for the honor of having inspired the sonnets. He would have been a commoner, and by the nineteenth century it was generally agreed that so great a man as William Shakespeare could not have consorted with less than lords. In 1817 it was suggested that Mr. W. H. might be Henry Wriothesley, Earl of Southampton, and in 1832 it was suggested that he might be William Herbert, Earl of Pembroke. Scholars were divided about evenly in support of the two men, although in the case of Southampton the initials had to be reversed before they would fit.

The only documentary connection that can be established between Shakespeare and the Earl of Southampton is the fact that Shakespeare dedicated two narrative poems to him in 1593 and 1594, just before he joined the Chamberlain's company. The only documentary connection that can be established between Shakespeare and the Earl of Pembroke is that Shakespeare and his company played at the Earl's residence in 1603 and that the First Folio was dedicated to him because of the many "favors" he had shown both to Shakespeare and to other members of the company. All other relationships between Shakespeare and either of the earls belong in the realm of conjecture only.

This conjecture, however, began with the Restoration and developed rapidly. By the beginning of the nineteenth century Shakespeare was pictured as being on intimate terms with Southampton, or with Pembroke, or with both, and it required only a slight extra leap of the imagination to see one of the earls as the beloved object of the sonnets. By this time Shakespeare was not thought of as an actor but as a kind of demigod, and even the greatest of lords should have been glad to be intimate with him. Conjecture hardened so completely into actuality that it was decided that Mary Fitton, who had borne the Earl of Pembroke an illegitimate child in 1601, must be the dark-haired woman in the sonnets who comes between the poet and his friend; and such is the power of legend over fact that many people who know almost nothing else about Shakespeare have heard that he was in love with Mary Fitton.

At the base of this whole romantic structure stands the lone fact that Thomas Thorpe dedicated the sonnets to a Mr. W. H. and this happens also to be the fact that demolishes it. For Thomas

Thorpe, who is the sole authority for the initials, puts in front of them the title "Mr." and this was not a title used for earls. The rigid social distinctions of the seventeenth century were a serious matter in their own day, however unimportant they may seem now, and the publishers were the last people in England to forget them.

When Thomas Thorpe wanted to address an earl, who in this case actually happened to be the Earl of Pembroke, this is how he did it:

> To the Right Honorable, William, Earl of Pembroke, Lord Chamberlain to his Majesty, one of his most honorable Privy Council, and Knight of the most noble order of the Garter, etc. Right Honorable—It may worthily seem strange unto your Lordship, out of what frenzy one of my meanness hath presumed to commit this sacrilege, in the straitness of your Lordship's leisure, to present a piece . . . in this scribbling age, wherein great persons are so pestered daily with dedications . . . Pardon my presumption, great Lord, from so mean a man to so great a person . . .
>
> Your Lordship's humble devoted T. T.

Again Thorpe was writing a dedication, in this case because the author himself had died, and he wrote this dedication to the Earl of Pembroke the year after he dedicated *Shakespeare's Sonnets* to Mr. W. H., the commoner.

Very little can actually be said about the sonnets. There is no proof of the date of composition, the order of composition, or the reasons for composition, and even if the identity of Thorpe's Mr. W. H. could be discovered it could not be proved that the publisher was speaking the truth when he claimed him as the poet's inspiration. It is probable, although not certain, that most of the sonnets were written in the middle years of the 90's, when the craze for sonneteering was at its height in England. Some of them certainly were composed before the end of the decade, since two of them were published in 1599 in *The Passionate Pilgrim*, and the year before Francis Meres had mentioned Shakespeare's "sugared sonnets among his private friends."

Many attempts have been made to interpret the sonnets as

autobiographical, and no doubt the desire to discover something about Shakespeare's private life is legitimate enough. But each reader finds a different story in the sonnets and reaches a different conclusion, and perhaps it is just as well. No single theory can safely be formed about them, and in the meantime William Shakespeare remains securely in possession of his privacy.

Appendix 2

The Legends

THERE was no attempt to record the facts of Shakespeare's life until the Restoration, and by then it was found that almost no information was available.

Thomas Fuller published a book in 1662 which he called *The History of the Worthies of England*. He divided the book into counties, and under the heading of Warwickshire he included a short account of William Shakespeare. Fuller had exact information on some of his "worthies," like Ben Jonson. He had no exact information on Shakespeare, and short as the account was, he was obliged to pad it with references to Martial, Ovid, Plautus, Heraclitus and Democritus. His chief information about Shakespeare was that "his learning was very little" and that he used to have "wit combats" with Jonson. He was not even certain of the date of Shakespeare's death and left a space for the information to be filled in later. But at least it could be said of Thomas Fuller that he did not invent anything, and it could be wished that other writers of the period had followed his example.

At about this same time a Stratford vicar named John Ward was filling a series of fifteen manuscript volumes with notes on sermons, anecdotes, medical recipes and any other stray pieces of information that interested him. It occurred to Ward that he should have read the works of his great fellow townsman and he wrote a reminder to himself in one of the volumes: "Remember to peruse Shakespeare's plays, to be much versed in them, that I may not be ignorant in that matter." He also jotted down some random notes on Shakespeare's life, and thus made the first attempt at what might be called a biography.

Since Ward was a Stratford man, most of his exact information centered around Shakespeare's daughters. He knew there were two of them, and that one had married Dr. Hall and was the mother of the present Lady Bernard. He does not mention the other daughter, Judith, by name, but she was still living when he wrote his notes and he speaks of her in another connection. Judith Quiney was in her late seventies and died in 1662, so that there was probably no opportunity to ask her about her father; and this is the whole of Ward's knowledge about William Shakespeare:

> I have heard that Mr. Shakespeare was a natural wit, without any art at all; he frequented the plays all his younger time, but in his elder days lived at Stratford, and supplied the stage with two plays every year, and for it had an allowance so large, that he spent at the rate of £1,000 a year, as I have heard. Shakespeare, Drayton and Ben Jonson had a merry meeting, and it seems drank too hard, for Shakespeare died of a fever there contracted.

Although Ward was writing nearly half a century after Shakespeare's death, it might be hoped that he had acquired a piece of authentic information about the drinking party. It was true that Ben Jonson was a friend of Shakespeare's and that he was a heavy drinker. It is also true that Michael Drayton, although he was not a heavy drinker and was in fact famous for his sobriety, was a Warwickshire man and later a patient of Dr. Hall's, and he may very well have been a friend of Shakespeare's and a frequent visitor at New Place. But Ward's trustworthiness as a biographer collapses when he states that Shakespeare spent at the rate of a thousand pounds a year. This preposterous sum destroys any possible respect for Ward as a biographer, and if the story of the drinking party rests on no better basis than this it remains both unproven and unprovable.

The next attempt to write a biography of Shakespeare was made about twenty years later. Anthony Wood the noted antiquarian, was doing research for a book, and a friend of his named John Aubrey undertook to help him by compiling manuscript notes on some of the people involved. The more Aubrey worked on his own series of biographies the more excited he became, until he finally announced with enthusiasm, "I believe never any in England were delivered so faithfully and with so good authority."

Aubrey was reliable enough when it came to describing his own family, and it is on good authority that the reader learns that the eyes of the author's mother are at present a little sore and that the author himself once had the measles. But Aubrey is not so reliable when it comes to describing events of the past, although his intentions are obviously excellent. He gives an account, for instance, of a castle near Newbury that was once the home of an individual he calls "Sir" Geoffrey Chaucer. The fact that Chaucer used to sit under a special oak outside this castle is proved by the fact that the oak was eventually cut down, and Aubrey heard the whole story from an attorney who attended the Star Chamber trial of the wretch who had thus offended against literature. It is not stated where Aubrey's "able attorney" got all this information in the first place, since Chaucer was not a knight and did not own Dunnington Castle or any other.

In his account of Shakespeare, Aubrey showed the same good intentions and the same trusting willingness to believe any story that came his way. He filled a whole page with information on Shakespeare that he had gathered together, recording it slightly uphill in his slanting hand, and as a further mark of respect he drew a small laurel wreath in the left margin. It was not lack of good intentions on Aubrey's part that made his account so poor; it was lack of information.

Aubrey started off briskly and inaccurately by stating that Shakespeare's father was a butcher. He brought up his son in the same trade, and there was another butcher's son in town who was just as clever as William. "This William, being naturally inclined to poetry and acting, came to London I guess about eighteen," not a very good guess since the twins were born in Stratford when Shakespeare was twenty-one.

Aubrey makes some vague remarks about the virtues of Shakespeare as an actor and playwright, and then continues with some stories he has picked up. He says that a constable lived on the road from London to Stratford, and that Shakespeare used him as the model of the constable in *A Midsummer Night's Dream.* Aubrey is quite undeterred by the fact there is no constable in this play, for a friend of his, a Mr. Howe, knew the original of the character well. Another story that Aubrey found was that an "old rich usurer" of Stratford named Combe was to be buried and Shakespeare wrote a mocking rhymed epitaph for his grave. It is true there was once a rhyme about usury on John Combe's grave but it is unlikely it was put there by that landed country gentleman, William Shakespeare, whom John Combe remembered in his will. Aubrey also states that Shakespeare left a yearly income of two or three hundred pounds "to a sister." The sister is presumably Joan Hart; but Shakespeare left her twenty pounds, and his total cash estate was not more than £350.

For a brief period during the making of his notes, Aubrey had access to a man who could have given him some information about the old days in the theatre before the Civil War. He had the good fortune to meet old William Beeston, whose father, Christopher Beeston, had been an apprentice of Augustine Phillips and had acted briefly with Shakespeare's company before he joined a rival organization. Aubrey was tremendously excited at meeting old Mr. Beeston, although he did not quite catch the name, and he made a note in his book on the first of September, 1681: "I have met with old Mr. — who knew all the old English poets, whose lives I am taking from him; his father was master of the — playhouse." In time Aubrey discovered the man's name and wrote a memorandum to himself that Mr. Beeston lived at Hog Lane in Shoreditch and must be consulted for particulars on the lives of both Shakespeare and Jonson. The next note of Aubrey's on the subject is a sad one: "Old Mr. Beeston . . . died at his house in Bishopsgate Street Without, about Bartholomew-tide, 1682." The man whom Dryden had called "the chronicle of the stage" was no more, and Aubrey was left to get his theatrical information from men as unreliable as Sir Edward Shirburn, who gave him the astonishing information that Ben Jonson had killed "Marlowe, the poet, on Bunhill, coming from the Green-Curtain playhouse." A statement of this kind is unfortunately typical of the state of Restoration information on the Elizabethans, and it results from a telescoping of the fact that Marlowe died a violent death, that five years later Jonson killed an actor named Gabriel Spencer in a duel, and that there was a playhouse named the Curtain which had been erected on the Curtain estate long before the days when green curtains were used in the theatres.

Aubrey managed to get one piece of information about Shakespeare from old William Beeston before he died: the statement that Shakespeare "had been in his younger years schoolmaster in the country." This statement would have more value if it had come from a more direct source than the son of one of the Queen's Men, or if it could have been transmitted by someone less careless than Aubrey. It is not likely that Shakespeare could have been a "master" of a school in his early twenties, since this was an office that was handled under a rigid system of licenses from the Worcester diocese, whether the applicant wished to teach in a public school or in a private family, and almost invariably required university training. Shakespeare may have assisted a schoolmaster or done some informal teaching before he went to London, but since no documentary evidence survives there is no way of knowing.

Elsewhere in his huge collection of biographies, Aubrey wrote down the life of the late Poet Laureate of England, Sir William D'Avenant. Before Sir William changed the spelling, the name had been Davenant, and his father owned a tavern near High Street in Oxford which had often been honored with the presence of William Shakespeare. The eldest son, Robert, who later became a parson, remembered that when he was a child Shakespeare had "given him a hundred kisses," and Shakespeare was such a close friend of the family that the second son, William, was probably named for him. The Davenants had seven children, whom they brought up with great care, and they were evidently a devoted couple; when John Davenant died during his term as mayor of Oxford, a contemporary elegy attributes his death to the loss of his wife a fortnight earlier.

Sir William D'Avenant was only ten years old when Shakespeare died, but he liked to feel that he had received Shakespeare's mantle as a dramatist. He liked to be called the swan of Isis as Shakespeare was called the swan of Avon, and announced that he wrote with the "very spirit" of Shakespeare. When he was slightly drunk and with sympathetic companions, D'Avenant was not above reinforcing his claims as a writer by hinting rather broadly that he was actually Shakespeare's son. D'Avenant lived in a casual age and was careless enough in his own affairs, for "he got a terrible clap of a black handsome wench that lay in Axeyard, Westminster"; but it was quite another thing to call his mother a whore, even though at the time he was being "pleasant over a glass of wine." Although Aubrey was a born gossip he disliked this particular story and crossed it out in his manuscript so that it would not get into print; but his precaution was not sufficient and in the next century the respectable Mrs. Davenant was firmly established in the popular mind as an adulteress.

The next writer to attempt a biography of Shakespeare was Nicholas Rowe, who brought out a six-volume edition of Shakespeare's plays in 1709 and prefaced it with a life of the poet. Rowe's biography was the first to get into print, since the work of both Ward and Aubrey had remained in manuscript; and Rowe did his best to make the account reliable. He even consulted the famous actor, Thomas Betterton, for information about Stratford, and Betterton admired Shakespeare so deeply that he had made a special trip into Warwickshire to collect biographical data. Unfortunately, Betterton was not familiar with the uses of old documents, and although he inspected the Stratford register he thought Shakespeare was one of ten children, since he did not know there were two Joans instead of one and accidentally added three children from a different Shakespeare family in Stratford. Betterton was even more careless when he came to Shakespeare's own children, since he thought that Judith was the oldest and that Hamnet was a girl. As for John Shakespeare's occupation, the "butcher" had now become a dealer in wool and trained his son in the same business.

Rowe had heard the popular story of Shakespeare and the thousand pounds, but according to Rowe's information the money had been given to him by the Earl of Southampton. Even to Rowe this seemed an exceedingly improbable sum, and he said that he would not have ventured to mention it, "if I had not been assured that the story was handed down by Sir William D'Avenant." It would be difficult to find a more unreliable witness than Sir William D'Avenant, and the story is chiefly interesting because it marks the beginning of the long association between Shakespeare and Southampton in the minds of all subsequent biographers.

Shakespeare must have received a handsome sum from Southampton in return for dedicating two successful books to the earl just before he turned back to writing for the stage, but any other "marks of favor and friendship from the Earl of Southampton" belong in the realm of conjecture. The instinct to connect Shakespeare with an earl was evidently the same one that made the seventeenth century persist in calling Chaucer a "knight," and as Shakespeare's reputation grew the impulse to link him with lords grew with it. Each writer amplified the statements of his predecessors, and by the end of the nineteenth century it was almost an article of faith that Shakespeare had been a close personal friend of Southampton's and intimately concerned with all his doings.*

Nicholas Rowe did his best with the various stories that had

---

* A poem was published in 1594, written in praise of a constant wife. It was published just after *The Rape of Lucrece*, and a verse preceding the poem announces that the heroine of the poem, a lady named Avisa, is more chaste even than Lucrece. The introduction of the poem is interesting because it is the first mention of Shakespeare's name as a narrative writer. He is one of the "brave poets" who have written of chaste women.

The poem, which was called *Willobie His Avisa*, continues with an account of various assaults made on the lady's impregnable virtue. Various suitors try to tempt her, among whom is a Frenchman named D.B. and an Englishman named H.W. According to the poem itself, H.W. stands for Henry Willoby; but since he had a friend named W.S. it was suggested in the twentieth century that W.S. was William Shakespeare and H.W. was Henry Wriothesley, Earl of Southampton. It seems safe to say that such a suggestion could never have been made, since it had no support in the poem itself, if it had not been for the many generations of scholars who had worked to connect Shakespeare with the Earl of Southampton. By the twentieth century, Shakespeare towered so far above all his contemporaries that it seemed natural to assume that no other W.S. had ever existed, although the initials were actually so common that, in the single year of 1597, Richard Burbage was intimately associated in his profession with three men who had those initials: William Sly, William Shakespeare and William Smith.

come his way, although he had no way of judging whether or not any of them were true. He repeated the story of the doggerel verses on John Combe's tomb and added that "the sharpness of the satire is said to have stung the man so severely, that he never forgave it"—an embellishment to the story he would have omitted if he could have seen John Combe's bequest to Shakespeare in his will. He told the story of Queen Elizabeth commissioning *The Merry Wives of Windsor*, which he got from a contemporary of his, and added another story to the effect that Ben Jonson was "altogether unknown" until Shakespeare persuaded his fellow actors to produce one of Jonson's plays. It is a pretty story, but Jonson's first production with the Chamberlain's Men was in 1598, and by that time his work for Henslowe was so well known that Francis Meres listed him as one of "the best for tragedy."

But the most popular story that Rowe brought before the public was the deer-stealing story. This had first been written down by the Rev. Richard Davies of Gloucestershire, who inherited a collection of manuscript biographies from a friend of his and made several additions to them before he himself died in 1708. The original manuscript biography on Shakespeare was of no interest but the Rev. Davies improved it by two startling additions. One was that Shakespeare had died a Papist. The other one, delivered in a single breathless sentence, was that Shakespeare was "much given to all unluckiness in stealing venison and rabbits, particularly from Sir —— Lucy, who had him oft whipped and sometimes imprisoned, and at last made him fly his native country to his great advancement, but his revenge was so great that he is his Justice Clodpate, and calls him a great man, and that in allusion to his name bore three louses rampant for his arms."

Rowe was able to improve on the story, for he knew that "Sir —— Lucy" must be Sir Thomas Lucy of Charlecote, and that "Justice Clodpate" would be Justice Shallow of *The Merry Wives of Windsor*. He did not know that the Lucy family did not have a deer park in the sixteenth century, a piece of information that destroys the whole story, and he was in fact so pleased with the deer that he abandoned the Rev. Davies' "rabbits" entirely.

Rowe made quite a vivid little story out of the deer-stealing in which Shakespeare indulged after his marriage. "He had, by a misfortune common enough to young fellows, fallen into ill company, and amongst them, some that made a frequent practice of deer-stealing engaged him with them more than once in robbing a park that belonged to Sir Thomas Lucy, of Charlecote, near Stratford. For this he was prosecuted by that gentleman . . . to that degree that he was obliged to leave his business and family in Warwickshire for some time and shelter himself in London." Later on in his biography, Rowe added that Shakespeare had made Falstaff "a deer-stealer, that he might at the same time remember his Warwickshire prosecutor under the name of Justice Shallow; he has given him very near the same coat of arms."

The subsequent vitality of the story has been extraordinary. Some of this may be attributed to eighteenth-century love of gossip, but most of it comes from the little circumstantial touch about Justice Shallow and the twelve luces on his coat of arms. Sir Thomas Lucy bore three luces on his coat of arms, and therefore he must have been the model for Justice Shallow, and therefore the deer-stealing story must be true. No one was deterred by the fact that the comic characterization of Shallow has nothing in common with Sir Thomas Lucy, soldier and gentleman, or that Shakespeare gave respectful prominence to an ancestor of his, Sir William Lucy, in *Henry VI*. Nor was anyone deterred by the fact that the luce, a fresh water pike, appears on many of the arms of the period, from the Gascoigne family to the company of London fishmongers, and from Justice Gardiner to the Earl of Northampton, who actually had the "twelve luces" that are given to Shallow. Sir Charles Percy quartered three luces on his coat of arms because one of his ancestors had married into the Lucy family, and Sir Charles once actually compared himself to Shakespeare's Justice Shallow. But Sir Charles was not thinking of coats of arms, but of characterization. Justice Shallow and his colleague, Justice Silence, had been so popular on the London stage that they had become a kind of byword for rustic justices of the peace; and Sir Charles had been so busy with country matters that he wrote ruefully to London: "If I stay here so long in this fashion, at my return I think you will find me so dull that I shall be taken for Justice Silence or Justice Shallow."

A few other legends about Shakespeare grew up in the course

of the eighteenth century. The story that had the longest life was supposed to have originated with D'Avenant and consisted of the theory that when Shakespeare first came up to London he held horses for the customers outside the theatres. This story was then expanded into a tale that he organized a collection of other young horse-holders who were known as "Shakespeare's boys."

At the end of the eighteenth century, Edmund Malone made the first determined effort to disentangle fact from legend in Shakespeare biographies. Malone was the first, and one of the greatest, of the real Shakespearian scholars, and Malone said frankly that he did not believe the horse-holding story. Nor did he believe the deer-stealing story, since, as he pointed out, Sir Thomas Lucy had no deer. Nor did he believe a great many other stories that were currently circulating about Shakespeare. In fact, said Malone bitterly, Nicholas Rowe had made eleven statements about Shakespeare's life and eight of them could be proven to be false.

Malone had very great influence as an editor, but he had almost none from the biographical point of view. Although he tried to remove the legends about Shakespeare he had nothing to offer in their place, and the legends took root again at once and flourished as though they had never been disturbed. There is nothing like a colorful story for surviving, no matter how unsupported its basis may be; and if a story is both colorful and disreputable, its immortality is practically assured.

Appendix 3

The Canon

HENRY CONDELL died in 1627, four years after the publication of the First Folio. That same year the actors at the Red Bull attempted to produce some of Shakespeare's plays, and John Heminges, acting for the King's Men, forced them to discontinue the practice. Heminges was the active head of the company, in spite of his age, and the following year he was still serving in the difficult and responsible position of paymaster.

John Heminges died in 1630, two years before the second edition of Shakespeare's plays was published. His authority as an editor was unquestioned and the second folio contained the same thirty-six plays as the first. The only difference was the addition of three new commendatory poems, one of them written by a promising young student at Cambridge named John Milton.

A decade after the second folio was published, the Puritan revolution forced the closing of all the theatres in England. Most of the actors enlisted in the Royalist forces, and after King Charles was executed they did what they could to earn a living, putting on a few plays secretly or attempting another profession. John Lowin, who had been a member of the King's Men and is listed in the First Folio as one of the actors in Shakespeare's plays, tried to succeed as an innkeeper, and when he died "his poverty was as great as his age."

The last threads with the old Elizabethan world of the theatre were snapped during the period of the Puritan Commonwealth, and when Charles II came to the throne of England in 1660 he ruled in what was a different world. The Restoration theatre had nothing whatever in common with the Elizabethan one, and it was during the Restoration that the third folio of Shakespeare's plays was published.

The third folio was believed to be such an improvement over its predecessors that the Bodleian Library disposed of its copy of the First Folio and bought the new edition of 1664 instead. At least it could be said that the Restoration reader got more for his money, since "seven new plays, never before printed in folio" were added. These included the three plays that Pavier had attributed to Shakespeare in 1619, *A Yorkshire Tragedy*, *Pericles* and *Sir John Oldcastle*, and four other plays that had been attributed either to Shakespeare or to "W.S." in early quartos: *The London Prodigal*, *Thomas Lord Cromwell*, *The Puritan Widow* and *Locrine*.

In assigning only seven more plays to Shakespeare, the publisher of the third folio was actually showing great restraint, since Volume One of the King's own collection of Shakespeare's plays consisted of *Fair Em*, *Mucedorus*, and *The Merry Devil of Edmonton*. The truth was that no one during the Restoration knew what Shakespeare had written and what he had not, and as soon as the authority of Heminges and Condell was ignored there was no limit to the number of early plays that could be attributed to him. The fourth folio, which was published in 1685, also included the seven extra plays, and so did Nicholas Rowe in his handsome illustrated edition at the beginning of the eighteenth century. But the later editors of the eighteenth century removed them again and went back to the original canon.

The best play of the seven was *Pericles*. Ben Jonson called it a "mouldy" old tale and deplored its popularity, but it nevertheless has some vigorous and effective writing in it. When Edmund Malone was preparing his excellent edition of Shakespeare's plays at the end of the eighteenth century, Dr. Richard Farmer persuaded him to include *Pericles*, and it is largely because so great an editor as Malone sponsored the play that it has been accepted into the Shakespeare canon by nearly every editor since.

If Malone had been content merely to add plays to the canon, very little harm would have been done. Unfortunately, Malone had so little respect for the authority of Heminges and Condell that he began to take away plays they had included, and it was Malone who started the disintegration of the canon that worked such havoc in the next hundred years.

Malone was a careful, intelligent editor, and perhaps his only fault was his inability to understand that John Heminges had also been a careful and intelligent editor and had possessed the further advantage of working intimately for nearly two decades with the author himself. Malone evidently thought of his predecessor as an elderly figure who had lived in a rather barbaric age, and Heminges' careful selection of plays for the First Folio merely served in Malone's eyes as a starting point for speculation.

The play on which Malone chiefly focussed his attention was *Henry VI*. This was an old-fashioned play even by later Elizabethan standards, and from the eighteenth-century point of view it was difficult to believe that a writer as great as Shakespeare could ever have written it.

The trilogy of *Henry VI* divides into three parts and is listed in the First Folio in that manner. But when the second and third parts were first printed in 1594 and 1595, not long after they were written, they were called *The First Part of the Contention between the Houses of Lancaster and York* and *The True Tragedy of Richard, Duke of York.* They were published at the end of the plague period, after the actors returned to London from their long exile in the country, and like most of the play quartos that appeared on the market at that time, they were badly printed from corrupt texts that the actors had reconstructed out of their memories for country playing. When the actors could not remember the lines of a play, they often interpolated lines they remembered from some other play. There were omissions, paraphrases and dislocations, with lines either appearing in earlier scenes than the author had intended or else omitted entirely. Prose was frequently turned into verse, which was easier to memorize, long speeches were chopped down to a few lines, and the author's brief stage directions were lavishly expanded.

In Malone's day there was one standard explanation to cover all bad texts of Elizabethan plays. It was believed that they were always the result of a shorthand version that had been made illegally at a regular performance by some member of the audience and then sold to an unscrupulous printer. Thomas Heywood had some trouble of this kind with his plays, and Heywood's complaint against shorthand pirates was frequently quoted. But Malone realized that the state of the texts in Shakespeare's two quartos could not be blamed on corruption through shorthand, since shorthand could not turn prose into verse or place a line earlier than its author had intended.

The solution to the problem was available to Malone if he had wished to accept it. Richard Brinsley Sheridan had written a play called *The Duenna*, which had not been printed, and each group of country actors who produced the play and had no authorized script built up the lines piecemeal from memory. The variations between these corrupt texts and Sheridan's original were the same as the variations between the two quarto texts of *Henry VI* and the original that was printed in the First Folio. This was pointed out to Malone, but by that time he had formed a theory of his own to account for the differences in the text and refused to be dislodged from it.

Malone's theory was a rather complicated one. Its basis was that the Folio version was not the original. The two original plays were the quarto versions, which had been written by different playwrights entirely, and Shakespeare had merely altered them somewhat here and there and then claimed them as his own. In searching for a likely candidate for the original authors, of whose existence he was now convinced, Malone lighted on Robert Greene. Greene had attacked Shakespeare in 1592, and what could be a more likely reason than that Shakespeare had stolen Greene's plays, and Greene, to use Malone's words, "could not conceal the mortification he felt"? Either Greene had written both the quarto plays, or Greene had written one and Peele the other. At any rate, Shakespeare had not written them; he had merely rewritten them slightly, and it was for this reason that Greene attacked him as young "Shake-scene." Malone's theory did not find much support in his own day, and men like Tyrwitt and Steevens and Dr. Johnson united to point out the various flaws in it. But Malone was determined to vindicate Shakespeare from the charge of having written any poor plays and he refused to abandon his position.

Malone could not use the same technique on the first part of *Henry VI*, since there was no corrupt early text of that particular play and it made its first appearance in the First Folio. Instead, Malone stated that the play should not have been admitted to the First Folio at all, since Shakespeare could not have written more than a scene or two in it. Heminges and Condell must have included it either because they were old and forgetful or because they felt it rounded out the series. Malone was rather proud of the fact that he had, as he put it, "vindicated Shakespeare from being the author of *1 Henry VI*" and then he also set out to vindicate him from being the author of *Titus Andronicus*.

Malone might have gone on rearranging the canon indefinitely, since there was no limit to the number of speculations that could be advanced as soon as Heminges and Condell were dismissed as careless and untruthful. But Malone died, leaving his life of Shakespeare to be seen through the press by Boswell's son and his theories to be amplified by the scholars of the nineteenth century.

The nineteenth century was the age of the Romantic Revival, when Shakespeare was exalted into a demigod. It was easy to agree that a demigod could never have written a bad line, and the enormous advantage of Malone's theory was that it made it possible to attribute every piece of less than perfect work in the First Folio to some other writer. Many plays were removed from the canon entirely and those that remained were carefully examined, inch by inch, so that all the good lines could be attributed to Shakespeare and the bad lines to someone else. A play was not a play to the scholars of the nineteenth century; it was a collection of lines, and each line could be scrutinized and divided up and attributed, on what was called internal evidence, to various contemporary playwrights. As the Shakespeare idolatry spread, so did the conviction that every second-rate line in the First Folio could by care and application be traced to someone else.

All this work was well intentioned and its basis was a reverence for Shakespeare. But the scholars failed to notice what a curious picture of the man himself they were building from it. The portrait they constructed out of a desire to honor him was that of a man who opened his career as a plagiarist, stealing Greene's lines and dishonestly passing them off as his own, and who spent most of the rest of his career either revising his own lines or rearranging and interpolating those of other people until he could hardly be said to have written any of his own plays at all. Add to this the fact that the Restoration legends of the butcher's son and the deer-stealing were still flourishing unchecked, and it was natural that many people found it hard to reconcile the strange being that was called "William Shakespeare" with the author of the plays.*

The trouble with the scholars was not a lack either of intelligence or of good intentions. It was only that they tried to stand too close to the problem and were consequently unable to get a reasonable perspective on it. When the first crack was made in the structure that had been erected, it came, naturally enough, through a piece of research that had nothing to do with Shakespeare at all. Walter W. Greg was studying the quarto edition of Greene's play, *Orlando Furioso*, which was published at the end of the plague period at the same time as the two quartos of Shakespeare. A fragment of Greene's original script for the play had survived in an actor's prompt copy, and Dr. Greg was able to show that the errors in the quarto had been caused by what he called "memorial reconstruction." The text was corrupt because it had been reconstructed from memory by country actors.

This theory of memorial reconstruction was applied to some of the corrupt Shakespeare quartos, like the first edition of *Romeo and Juliet*, and it was found that it accounted satisfactorily for the dislocations and alterations in the text. The test was not at first applied to the two quartos of *Henry VI*, since it was believed that Greene's attack on Shakespeare established these quartos as original texts rather than as corrupt copies. But Greene's state-

---

* Many people felt almost relieved when Delia Bacon took the final logical step in 1857 and suggested that the plays of Shakespeare were written by someone else entirely. Delia chose Sir Francis Bacon for the honor. Later candidates to be suggested have been the Earl of Oxford, Sir Edward Dyer, the fifth Earl of Rutland, the sixth Earl of Derby and even the Countess of Pembroke, who worked as part of a syndicate and supplied womanly touches here and there. This respect for the literary value of noble birth is impressive in its unanimity but a little hard to explain logically, since the most learned of Elizabethan dramatists was a bricklayer, and the most poetic, next to Shakespeare, was the son of a cobbler.

ment was finally reexamined and it was realized that he was attacking Shakespeare as an actor turned writer and not as a plagiarist; and at this point the whole of Malone's argument collapsed.

It is easy enough, looking back, to see why this mistaken approach to Shakespeare's plays came into existence and why it lasted as long as it did. The destruction of the theatres in 1642 did more than create a physical gap in the history of the English stage. It created a mental gap also, and the men who stood on the near side of the chasm looked back at the Elizabethan theatre with the eyes of aliens. Nearly all of them, consciously or unconsciously, shared the conviction that the common theatre of the people was not a suitable place of residence for England's greatest poet, and they tried to pull him away from the earth that had given him life. They made him lord of the schoolrooms and the libraries, but they took him away both from his profession and from the daily life of his own century.

It was done in all love and respect, for no group of men ever honored Shakespeare more vehemently than the scholars of the nineteenth century. But the cause of truth was not served, and it is fortunate that in the recent years of the twentieth century a more reasonable approach to one of the greatest men in the world is at last beginning to find favor.

Selected Bibliography

JOHN CRANFORD ADAMS, *The Globe Playhouse: Its Design and Equipment*, Cambridge: Harvard University Press, 1942.

JOSEPH QUINCY ADAMS, *Shakespearean Playhouses*, Boston: Houghton Mifflin Company, 1917.

PETER ALEXANDER, *Shakespeare's Henry VI and Richard III*, Cambridge: Cambridge University Press, 1929.

PETER ALEXANDER, *Shakespeare's Life and Art*, London: James Nisbet and Company, Ltd., 1939.

EDWARD ARBER, editor, *A Transcript of the Registers of the Company of Stationers of London, 1554–1640*, 5 volumes, London, 1875–1894.

JOHN AUBREY, *Brief Lives*, edited by Andrew Clark, 2 volumes, Oxford: Clarendon Press, 1898.

CHARLES SEARS BALDWIN, *Renaissance Literary Theory and Practice*, New York: Columbia University Press, 1939.

T. W. BALDWIN, *William Shakspere's Small Latine & Lesse Greeke*, 2 volumes, Urbana: University of Illinois Press, 1944.

E. A. B. BARNARD, *New Links With Shakespeare*, Cambridge: Cambridge University Press, 1930.

W. P. BARRETT, editor, *Present Remedies Against the Plague*, Shakespeare Association Facsimiles, no. 7, London, 1933.

WILLIAM BARRETT, *The History and Antiquities of the City of Bristol*, Bristol, 1789.

CHARLES READ BASKERVILLE, *The Elizabethan Jig and Related Song Drama*, Chicago: University of Chicago Press, 1929.

FRANCIS BEAUMONT AND JOHN FLETCHER, *Comedies and Tragedies Written by Francis Beaumont and John Fletcher, Gentlemen*, London: Humphrey Moseley, 1647.

GERALD EADES BENTLEY, *The Jacobean and Caroline Stage*, 2 volumes, Oxford: Clarendon Press, 1941.

THOMAS BIRCH, *The Court and Times of James the First*, 2 volumes, London, 1848.

THOMAS BIRCH, *Memoirs of the Reign of Queen Elizabeth*, Volume II, London, 1754.

FREDERICK S. BOAS, *Christopher Marlowe*, Oxford: Clarendon Press, 1940.

FREDERICK S. BOAS, *Shakespeare and the Universities*, Oxford: Shakespeare Head Press, 1923.

M. C. BRADBROOK, *Elizabethan Stage Conditions*, Cambridge: Cambridge University Press, 1932.

TIMOTHY BRIGHT, *A Treatise of Melancholie*, New York: Columbia University Press, 1940. (Facsimile Text Society.)

C. F. TUCKER BROOKE, editor, *The Shakespeare Apocrypha*, Oxford: Clarendon Press, 1918.

C. F. TUCKER BROOKE, "Shakespeare's Moiety of the Stratford Tithes," *Modern Language Notes*, 1925.

GEORGE BUCK, "The Third University of England," appendix to Stow's *Annales*, London, 1631.

Calendar of State Papers, Domestic Series, of the Reigns of Elizabeth and James I, 11 volumes, London: Longmans, Green and Company, 1865–1872.

WILLIAM CAMDEN, *Annales, the True and Royall History of the Famous Empresse Elizabeth*, London, 1625.

WILLIAM CAMDEN, *Britain, Or a Chorographicall Description of the Most Flourishing Kingdomes, England, Scotland and Ireland*, London, 1610.

WILLIAM CAMDEN, *Remaines Concerning Britain*, London, 1657.

LILY B. CAMPBELL, *Scenes and Machines on the English Stage During the Renaissance*, Cambridge: Cambridge University Press, 1923.

J. L. CARDOZO, *The Contemporary Jew in the Elizabethan Drama*, Amsterdam: H. J. Paris, 1925.

JOHN CHAMBERLAIN, *Letters*, edited by Norman Egbert McClure, 2 volumes, Philadelphia: American Philosophical Society, 1939.

EDMUND K. CHAMBERS, *The Elizabethan Stage*, 4 volumes, Oxford: Clarendon Press, 1923.

EDMUND K. CHAMBERS, *William Shakespeare; A Study of Facts and Problems*, 2 volumes, Oxford: Clarendon Press, 1930.

ROBERT CHAMBERS, *The Life of King James the First*, 2 volumes, Edinburgh, 1830.

EDWARD P. CHEYNEY, *A History of England from the Defeat of the Armada to the Death of Elizabeth*, 2 volumes, New York: Longmans, Green and Company, 1914 and 1926.

ARTHUR MELVILLE CLARK, *Thomas Heywood*, Oxford: Basil Blackwell, 1931.

ALBERT COHN, *Shakespeare in Germany in the Sixteenth and Seventeenth Centuries*, London, 1865.

J. PAYNE COLLIER, *Memoirs of the Principal Actors in the Plays of Shakespeare*, London: Shakespeare Society, 1864.

ARTHUR COLLINS, *Letters and Memorials of State*, 2 volumes, London, 1746.

G. H. COWLING, *Music on the Shakespearian Stage*, Cambridge: Cambridge University Press, 1913.

HARDIN CRAIG, *The Enchanted Glass*, New York: Oxford University Press, 1936.

JOHN W. CUNLIFFE, *The Influence of Seneca on Elizabethan Tragedy*, New York: G. E. Stechert and Company, 1925.

PETER CUNNINGHAM, *Extracts from the Accounts of the Revels at Court in the Reigns of Queen Elizabeth and King James I*, London: Shakespeare Society, 1842.

SAMUEL DANIEL, *The Whole Workes of Samuel Daniel Esquire in Poetrie*, London, 1623.

JOHN ROCHE DASENT, editor, *Acts of the Privy Council of England*, new series, vols. 14-32, London: Eyre and Spottiswoode, 1897–1907.

W. ROBERTSON DAVIES, *Shakespeare's Boy Actors*, London: J. M. Dent and Sons, Ltd., 1939.

THOMAS DEKKER, *The Non-dramatic Works of Thomas Dekker*, edited by Alexander B. Grosart, 5 volumes, London, 1884–1886.

WILLIAM DUGDALE, *Origines Juridiciales*, London, 1671.

O. JOCELYN DUNLOP, *English Apprenticeship and Child Labour*, London: T. Fisher Unwin, 1912.

MARK ECCLES, *Christopher Marlowe in London*, Cambridge: Harvard University Press, 1934.

LEWIS EINSTEIN, *The Italian Renaissance in England*, New York: Columbia University Press, 1935.

WILLARD FARNHAM, *The Medieval Heritage of Elizabethan Tragedy*, Berkeley: University of California Press, 1936.

ALBERT FEUILLERAT, editor, *Documents Relating to the Office of the Revels in the Time of Queen Elizabeth,* Louvain: A. Uystpruyst, 1908.

JEFFERSON BUTLER FLETCHER, *Literature of the Italian Renaissance,* New York: The Macmillan Company, 1934.

EDGAR I. FRIPP, *Master Richard Quyny,* London: Oxford University Press, 1924.

EDGAR I. FRIPP, editor, *Minutes and Accounts of the Corporation of Stratford-upon-Avon,* 3 volumes, Oxford: Dugdale Society, 1921.

EDGAR I. FRIPP, *Shakespeare, Man and Artist,* 2 volumes, London: Oxford University Press, 1938.

EDGAR I. FRIPP, *Shakespeare Studies,* Oxford: Oxford University Press, 1930.

EDGAR I. FRIPP, *Shakespeare's Stratford,* London: Oxford University Press, 1928.

THOMAS FULLER, *The History of the Worthies of England,* London, 1662.

PHILIP GAWDY, *Letters,* edited by Isaac Herbert Jeayes, London: J. B. Nichols and Sons, 1906.

VIRGINIA GILDERSLEEVE, *Government Regulation of the Elizabethan Drama,* New York: Columbia University Press, 1908.

ISRAEL GOLLANCZ, editor, *Studies in the First Folio,* London: H. Milford, 1924.

GODFREY GOODMAN, *The Court of King James the First,* 2 volumes, London, 1839.

STEPHEN GOSSON, *The Schoole of Abuse,* edited by Edward Arber, Westminster: Constable and Company, 1895.

JOSEPH WILLIAM GRAY, *Shakespeare's Marriage,* London: Chapman and Hall, Ltd., 1905.

ROBERT GREENE, *Life and Complete Works,* edited by Alexander B. Grosart, 15 volumes, London, 1881–1886.

WALTER WILSON GREG, *Dramatic Documents from the Elizabethan Playhouses,* 2 volumes, Oxford: Clarendon Press, 1931.

WALTER WILSON GREG, *The Editorial Problem in Shakespeare,* Oxford: Clarendon Press, 1942.

WALTER WILSON GREG, *Two Elizabethan Stage Abridgements: The Battle of Alcazar and Orlando Furioso,* London: Oxford University Press, 1922.

J. O. HALLIWELL-PHILLIPPS, *Outlines of the Life of Shakespeare,* 2 volumes, London: Longmans, Green and Company, 1886.

ALFRED HARBAGE, *Shakespeare's Audience*, New York: Columbia University Press, 1941.

JOHN HARINGTON, *Nugae Antiquae*, 3 volumes, London, 1792.

WILLIAM HARRISON, "An Historical Description of the Island of Britain," in Volume I of Holinshed's *Chronicles*, London, 1587.

ALFRED HART, *Stolne and Surreptitious Copies*, Melbourne: Melbourne University Press, 1942.

GABRIEL HARVEY, *Works*, edited by Alexander B. Grosart, 3 volumes, London, 1884–1885.

WILLIAM CAREW HAZLITT, editor, *English Drama and Stage Under the Tudor and Stuart Princes*, London, 1869.

PHILIP HENSLOWE, *Henslowe Papers*, edited by Walter Wilson Greg, London: A. H. Bullen, 1907.

PHILIP HENSLOWE, *Henslowe's Diary*, edited by Walter Wilson Greg, 2 volumes, London: A. H. Bullen, 1904–1908.

PAUL HENTZNER, *A Journey Into England*, Reading: T. E. Williams, 1807.

CHARLES H. HERFORD, *Studies in the Literary Relations of England and Germany in the Sixteenth Century*, Cambridge: Cambridge University Press, 1886.

THOMAS HEYWOOD, *Dramatic Works*, 6 volumes, London, 1874.

HAROLD NEWCOMB HILLEBRAND, *The Child Actors*, 2 volumes, Urbana: University of Illinois Press, 1926.

RAPHAEL HOLINSHED, *The Whole Volume of Chronicles*, London, 1587.

J. LESLIE HOTSON, *Shakespeare Versus Shallow*, London: Nonesuch Press, 1931.

C. M. INGLEBY, editor, *Shakespeare and the Enclosure of Common Field at Welcombe*, Birmingham, 1885.

EDWARD JACOB, *The History of the Town and Port of Faversham*, London, 1774.

P. ROWLAND JAMES, *The Baths of Bath in the Sixteenth and Early Seventeenth Centuries*, Bristol, 1938.

BEN JONSON, *Ben Jonson*, edited by C. H. Herford and Percy Simpson, 8 volumes, Oxford: Clarendon Press, 1925–1947.

F. M. KELLY, *Shakesperian Costume for Stage and Screen*, London: Adam and Charles Black, 1938.

W. P. M. KENNEDY, *Elizabethan Episcopal Administration*, 3 volumes, London: A. R. Mowbray and Company, Ltd., 1924.

GEORGE LYMAN KITTREDGE, *Witchcraft in Old and New England,* Cambridge: Harvard University Press, 1929.

M. M. KNAPPEN, *Tudor Puritanism,* Chicago: University of Chicago Press, 1939.

THOMAS KYD, *Works,* edited by Frederick S. Boas, Oxford: Clarendon Press, 1901.

WILLIAM LAMBARDE, *An Alphabetical Description of the Chief Places in England,* London, 1730.

KATHLEEN LAMBLEY, *The Teaching and Cultivation of the French Language in England During Tudor and Stuart Times,* Manchester: Manchester University Press, 1920.

ERNEST LAW, *Shakespeare as a Groom of the Chamber,* London: G. Bell and Sons, 1910.

WILLIAM J. LAWRENCE, *Pre-Restoration Stage Studies,* Cambridge: Harvard University Press, 1927.

K. M. LEA, *Italian Popular Comedy,* 2 volumes, Oxford: Clarendon Press, 1934.

B. ROLAND LEWIS, *The Shakespeare Documents,* 2 volumes, Stanford: Stanford University Press, 1940.

M. CHANNING LINTHICUM, *Costume in the Drama of Shakespeare and His Contemporaries,* Oxford: Clarendon Press, 1936.

THOMAS LODGE, *Complete Works,* 4 volumes, Glasgow, 1883.

ANDRÉ HURAULT, sieur de Maisse, *Journal,* edited by G. B. Harrison, London: Nonesuch Press, 1931.

EDMUND MALONE, *The Life of William Shakespeare,* London, 1821.

EDMUND MALONE, *The Plays and Poems of William Shakespeare,* Volume VI, London, 1790.

JOHN MANNINGHAM, *Diary,* edited by John Bruce, Westminster, 1868.

JOHN MARSTON, *Works,* edited by A. H. Bullen, 3 volumes, London: John C. Nimmo, 1887.

BALDWIN MAXWELL, *Studies in Beaumont, Fletcher and Massinger,* Chapel Hill: University of North Carolina Press, 1939.

FRANCIS MERES, *Palladis Tamia, Wits Treasury,* New York: Scholars' Facsimiles and Reprints, 1938.

FYNES MORYSON, *Shakespeare's Europe,* London: Sherratt and Hughes, 1903.

RICHARD MULCASTER, *Elementarie,* edited by E. T. Campagnac, Oxford: Clarendon Press, 1925.

THOMAS NASHE, *Works*, edited by R. B. McKerrow, 5 volumes, London: A. H. Bullen, 1904–1910.

J. E. NEALE, *Queen Elizabeth*, New York: Harcourt Brace and Company, 1934.

BERNARD H. NEWDIGATE, *Michael Drayton and His Circle*, Oxford: Shakespeare Head Press, 1941.

JOHN NICHOLS, *Progresses and Public Processions of Queen Elizabeth*, 3 volumes, London, 1823.

JOHN NICHOLS, *The Progresses of King James the First*, 4 volumes, London, 1828.

EDWIN NUNGEZER, *A Dictionary of Actors and of Other Persons Associated with the Public Representation of Plays in England Before 1642*, New Haven: Yale University Press, 1929.

The Pilgrimage to Parnassus with the Two Parts of the Return from Parnassus, edited by W. D. Macray, Oxford: Clarendon Press, 1886.

THOMAS PLATTER, *Thomas Platter's Travels in England, 1599*, translated and edited by Clare Williams, London: Jonathan Cape, 1937.

ALFRED W. POLLARD, *Shakespeare Folios and Quartos*, London: Methuen and Company, 1909.

ALFRED W. POLLARD, *Shakespeare's Fight with the Pirates*, Cambridge: Cambridge University Press, 1920.

WILLIAM RENDLE, *Old Southwark and Its People*, Southwark, 1878.

GEORGE FULLMER REYNOLDS, *The Staging of Elizabethan Plays at the Red Bull Theatre, 1605–1625*, London: Oxford University Press, 1940.

WILLIAM BRENCHLEY RYE, *England as Seen by Foreigners*, London: John Russell Smith, 1865.

REGINALD SCOT, *Discovery of Witchcraft*, London, 1651.

MATTHIAS A. SHAABER, *Some Forerunners of the Newspaper in England, 1476–1622*, Philadelphia: University of Pennsylvania Press, 1929.

WILLIAM SHAKESPEARE, *Mr. William Shakespeare's Comedies, Histories and Tragedies*, London: Isaac Jaggard and Ed. Blount, 1623.

WILLIAM SHAKESPEARE, *The Poems*, edited by Hyder Edward Rollins, Volume 22 of the New Furness Variorum, Philadelphia: J. B. Lippincott Company, 1938.

WILLIAM SHAKESPEARE, *Romeo and Juliet*, a facsimile of the first quarto by Charles Praetorius, London, 1886.

WILLIAM SHAKESPEARE, *The Sonnets*, edited by Hyder Edward Rollins, Volumes 24 and 25 of the New Furness Variorum, Philadelphia: J. B. Lippincott Company, 1944.

Shakespeare and the Theatre by members of the Shakespeare Association, London: Oxford University Press, 1927.

Shakespeare's England, 2 volumes, Oxford: Clarendon Press, 1932.

C. J. SISSON, *Lost Plays of Shakespeare's Age*, Cambridge: Cambridge University Press, 1936.

C. J. SISSON, editor, *Thomas Lodge and Other Elizabethans*, Cambridge: Harvard University Press, 1933.

J. S. SMART, *Shakespeare, Truth and Tradition*, New York: Longmans, Green and Company, 1928.

G. GREGORY SMITH, editor, *Elizabethan Critical Essays*, 2 volumes, Oxford: Clarendon Press, 1904.

J. E. SPINGARN, *Critical Essays of the Seventeenth Century*, Volume I, Oxford: Clarendon Press, 1908.

J. E. SPINGARN, *A History of Literary Criticism in the Renaissance*, New York: Columbia University Press, 1920.

MARY SUSAN STEELE, *Plays and Masques At Court During the Reigns of Elizabeth, James and Charles*, New Haven: Yale University Press, 1926.

DUKE OF STETTIN-POMERANIA, *Diary of the Journey of Philip Julius, Duke of Stettin-Pomerania, Through England in the Year 1602*, Transactions of the Royal Historical Society, new series, Volume VI, London, 1892.

CHARLOTTE C. STOPES, *Burbage and Shakespeare's Stage*, London: Alexander Moring, Ltd., 1913.

CHARLOTTE C. STOPES, *Shakespeare's Environment*, London: G. Bell and Sons, Ltd., 1914.

CHARLOTTE C. STOPES, *Shakespeare's Warwickshire Contemporaries*, Stratford-upon-Avon: Shakespeare Head Press, 1907.

JOHN STOW, *Annales, or a Generall Chronicle of England*, with additions by Edmund Howes, London: Thomas Meighen, 1631.

JOHN STOW, *The Survay of London*, with additions by Anthony Munday, London: George Purslowe, 1618.

PHILIP STUBBES, *The Anatomie of Abuses*, London, 1583.

JOHN STYRPE, *Life and Acts of John Whitgift*, 3 volumes, Oxford: Clarendon Press, 1822.

R. H. TAWNEY AND EILEEN POWER, *Tudor Economic Documents,* 3 volumes, London: Longmans, Green and Company, 1924.

EDWARD ANDREWS TENNEY, *Thomas Lodge,* Ithaca: Cornell University Press, 1935.

WILLARD THORP, *The Triumph of Realism in Elizabethan Drama, 1558–1612,* Princeton: Princeton University Press, 1928.

ROBERT RICHARD TIGHE AND JAMES EDWARD DAVIS, *Annals of Windsor,* 2 volumes, London, 1858.

E. M. W. TILLYARD, *The Elizabethan World Picture,* London: Chatto and Windus, 1943.

E. M. W. TILLYARD, *Shakespeare's History Plays,* New York: The Macmillan Company, 1946.

Victoria History of the Counties of England. A History of Warwick, Volume III, Oxford: Oxford University Press, 1945.

VICTOR VON KLARWILL, editor, *The Fugger News-Letters,* second series, London: John Lane, 1926.

VICTOR VON KLARWILL, *Queen Elizabeth and Some Foreigners,* London: John Lane, 1928.

CHARLES WILLIAM WALLACE, "The First London Theatre," *University of Nebraska Studies,* 1913

CHARLES WILLIAM WALLACE, "Shakespeare and His London Associates," *University of Nebraska Studies,* 10, 1910.

SEDLEY LYNCH WARE, *The Elizabethan Parish in Its Ecclesiastical and Financial Aspects,* Baltimore: Johns Hopkins Press, 1908.

FOSTER WATSON, *The Beginnings of the Teaching of Modern Subjects in England,* London, 1909.

FOSTER WATSON, *The English Grammar Schools to 1660,* Cambridge: Cambridge University Press, 1908.

ANTHONY WELDON, *The Court and Character of King James,* Westminster, 1820.

ROGER WILBRAHAM, *The Journal of Sir Roger Wilbraham, 1593–1616,* edited by Harold Spencer Scott, Royal Historical Society Publications, series 3, number 4, London, 1902.

EDWIN ELIOTT WILLOUGHBY, *A Printer of Shakespeare. The Books and Times of William Jaggard,* London: Philip Allen and Company, Ltd., 1934.

EDWIN ELIOTT WILLOUGHBY, *The Printing of the First Folio of Shakespeare,* Transactions of the Bibliographical Society of London, Supplements 8–10, London, 1932–1935.

ARTHUR WILSON, *The History of Great Britain, Being the Life and Reign of King James the First,* London, 1653.

Shakespeare *of London*

F. P. WILSON, *The Plague in Shakespeare's London*, Oxford: Clarendon Press, 1927.

RALPH WINWOOD, *Memorials of Affairs of State in the Reigns of Queen Elizabeth and King James*, 3 volumes, London, 1725.

ALEXANDER MACLAREN WITHERSPOON, *The Influence of Robert Garnier on Elizabethan Drama*, New Haven: Yale University Press, 1924.

HENRY WOTTON, *Reliquiae Wottonianae*, London, 1672.

LOUIS B. WRIGHT, *Middle-class Culture in Elizabethan England*, Chapel Hill: University of North Carolina Press, 1935.

Index

Index

A.B.C. and Little Catechism, The, 14
Absalom, 72
Accedens of Armory, see Legh, Gerard
Act of Uniformity, 9
acting companies:
 Admiral's, 75, 106, 122, 130, 131, 135, 147, 150, 162, 170, 174, 213, 219, 246, 257
 Chamberlain's, *see* Shakespeare's company
 Derby's, 98n.
 Hunsdon's, *see* Shakespeare's company
 King's Men, *see* Shakespeare's company
 Leicester's, 22, 24, 25
 Pembroke's, first company, 98, 98n., 106, 136; second company, 192, 193, 205
 Prince's Men, 257, 265, 269
 Queen's Men (Queen Anne), 257, 265, 269, 284, 285, 291, 293, 349; (Queen Elizabeth), 137, 173, 219, 262
 Strange's, 86, 95, 98, 106, 122, 123, 127, 239
 Sussex's, 98n., 136
 Warwick's, 22, 24
 Worcester's, first company, 24; second company, 257
acting companies, boy, 102, 131, 230-233, 284, 303
 Children of the Chapel Royal at Blackfriars, first company, 102, 207, 230; second company, 230-231, 232, 265, 289

Paul's Boys, first company, 102, 107, 231; second company, 231, 232
acting companies, provincial, 22, 91, 194
actors' apprentices, 54-55, 86, 126-127, 160, 161, 325, 348
actors, as buyers of plays, 74, 78, 80, 93, 131, 152, 156, 191; as dancers, 88-89, 160, 161n., 178, 213-214; as musicians, 161, 161n.; attacks on 34, 54, 54n., 55, 80-81, 83-84, 191, 218, 225-226, 245 (*see also* theatre, opposition to); on tour, *see* touring; restrictions on, 22, 34-35, 104, 105, 137, 192, 193; training required, 86-91, 160
actors, boy, 86, 160-161, 178, 232, 272
actors, foreign, 61, 96, 194-195
actors, hired, 91, 159, 164, 166, 194
actresses, 194-195
Addenbrooke, William, 299
Admiral's company, *see* acting companies
admission prices, 58, 67, 69; in the theatre, 26-27, 28, 37, 214, 291
Adonis, 116
advertising, 33, 66-67, 112, 137, 167
Aegiale, 170
Aesop, 81, 83
Africa, 62, 72
Agincourt, Battle of, 219, 221
Alchemist, The, see Jonson, Ben
All Is True, 309
Allen, Giles, 36, 206, 208, 211
Alleyn, Edward, 89, 91, 106, 127, 213, 239, 246, 261, 339; as an actor, 43,

375

Alleyn, Edward—*Continued*
  75, 88, 92, 106, 122, 127, 128, 158,
  161, 183-184, 261
Alleyn, Mrs. Edward, 106, 127
Allot, Robert, 169
All's Well That Ends Well, see
  Shakespeare, plays
ambassadors, 144, 145, 150, 261, 289,
  324; *see also* Castile, Constable of
Amours of Falstaff, The, 221n.
Anne, Queen of England, 253, 257-
  258, 260, 262, 264, 265, 324
anthologies, 116, 169, 172, 216, 223,
  225
Antipholus, 101
Antonio, 176
Antony and Cleopatra, see Shake-
  speare, plays
Antony, 109, 249, 272
Antwerp, 59
Apocalypse, the, 253
Apollo, 110
Apology for Actors, An, see Hey-
  wood, Thomas
apprentices, 38-39, 56, 104, 142, 277,
  284, 301; as play-goers, 34, 38-39,
  76, 192, 284; *see also* actors' appren-
  tices
Arabia, 62
Arbactus, 159
Arcadia, see Sidney, Sir Philip
Arden, Mr., 196
Arden, Agnes, 50
Arden family, 7, 45, 184-185
Arden, Forest of, 13, 216
Arden, Mary, *see* Shakespeare, Mary
Arden of Faversham, 196-197
Arden, Robert, 7, 9, 50
Ariel, 293
Ariosto, Lodovico, 101; *Orlando Fu-
  rioso*, 112
Aristotle, 71, 72
Armada, Spanish, 56, 65, 122, 183, 190,
  214
Armado, 103
Armin, Robert, 255-256
Art of English Poesie, The, 112
Arundel, Earl of, 69
As You Like It, see Shakespeare,
  plays

Asia, 72, 75
Aspinall, Alexander, 189
Aspley, William, 332, 339
atheism, 82, 108
Atlas, 83
Atwood's tavern, 316
Aubrey, John, 347-350
audiences, 22, 23, 26, 28, 37-41, 70, 75-
  76, 89-90, 149, 151, 271; at Shakespeare's plays, 41, 63, 83, 93, 94, 95,
  97, 102, 103, 156, 162-163, 168-169,
  173-174, 216, 219, 221, 229, 233, 246,
  268, 271, 272, 273, 281-282, 287, 291,
  309-310, 336; penny public, 26-27,
  28-29, 37, 38-39, 119-120, 227;
  writers' contempt for, 27, 39, 79,
  109, 110, 283, 284, 285-286, 287-288,
  (*see also* Jonson, Ben). *See also*
  apprentices *and* women.
Augusta, 105
Autolycus, 292
Avisa, 351n.
Avon river, 1, 12, 198, 199, 335, 350
Axeyard, 350

Babington Conspiracy, 68
Babylon, 71, 75
Bacon, Anne, 312
Bacon, Delia, 360n.
Bacon, Sir Francis, 360n.
Bacon, Matthew, 312-313
Badger, George, 47
Baker, Mr., 280
"Baker, cousin," 297n.
ballads, 65, 68, 69, 136, 169, 253, 310,
  314
Bank Croft, 13
Bankside, the, 213, 256, 269, 326
Banqueting Hall, 143, 266, 293
Banquo, 274
Barbary, 62
Barker family, 279
Barker, Henry, 300
Barker, John, 279
Barnes, Barnabe, 114, 154; *The Devil's
  Charter*, 154
Barnfield, Richard, 118, 224
Barnhurst, Nicholas, 47
Barrabas, 177
Barton, Richard, 55

Bassanio, 340

Basse, William, 287, 322

Bastard of Faulconbridge, 172

Bath, 195, 197-198, 198n., 259, 340

Battle of Alcazar, The, 88

bear-baiting, 27, 36, 43, 69, 246, 263

Bear Garden, 27, 69, 236

Beatrice, 41, 216, 334

Beaumont, Mr. Justice, 283

Beaumont, Francis, 121, 283-284, 286, 287, 303-304, 322, 333; attitude towards Shakespeare, 284, 284n.; *The Knight of the Burning Pestle*, 283-284; collaboration with Fletcher, 283, 291, 303, 304, 333, 335, *A King and No King*, 303, *The Maid's Tragedy*, 303, *Philaster, or Love Lies A-Bleeding*, 291, 303

Beeston, Christopher, 348

Beeston, William, 348, 349

Belch, Sir Toby, 282

Bell inn, 26, 136, 188

Belott, Stephen, 277, 278, 301, 302

Belvedere, or the Garden of the Muses, 223, 225

Bermudas, the, 292

Bernard, Lady, *see* Hall, Elizabeth

Berowne, 103

Betterton, Thomas, 350

Bible, the, 62, 261

Biron, Marechal, 102-103

Bishop, Nicholas, 31

Bishopsgate Street, 63, 126, 136, 234, 348

Bishopsgate ward, 235-236

Bishopton, 279

Blackfriars company, *see* acting companies, boy

Blackfriars, liberty of, 111, 206, 207, 290, 302, 306, 312, 313, 318

Blackfriars theatre:
first theatre, 102, 207, 230
second theatre, under James Burbage, 206-208, 306; under Cuthbert and Richard Burbage, 208, 230, 289-290: used by boys' company, 230, 289, 291, used by Shakespeare's company, 92, 130, 288-291

Blacksmith's Daughter, The, 70

Bladud, King, 198n.

Blind Beggar of Alexandria, The, *see* Chapman, George

Blount, Edward, 332, 337

Bodenham, John, 223

Bodleian Library, 261, 329, 356

Bodley, Sir Thomas, 329

Bohemia, 204, 304

Boleyn, Anne, 309, 310

Boleyn, Sir Geoffrey, 145

"book," the, 158, 166

Boswell, James the younger, 337, 359

Bosworth Field, 172

Bott, William, 10

Bottom, 153, 176, 178

bowling, 13, 36, 60, 198, 207

boy actors, *see* actors, boy

boys' companies, *see* acting companies, boy

Bradeley, Robert, 52n.

Branch, Lady Helen, 121

Brayne, John, 29, 30

Brayne, Margaret, 30, 31

Brend, Sir Nicholas, 210, 212, 290

Brend's Rents, 212

Bretchgirdle, John, 9

Bridewell prison, 289

Bridewell school, 161

Bridge Street, 12, 316

Bright, Dr. Timothy, 228

Bristol, 22, 176, 195, 197, 198-199, 200

Britain, 275

Britannia, *see* Camden, William

broadsides, *see* ballads

Brooke, Arthur, 153-156, 160

Brooke, Henry, *see* Cobham, 8th Lord

Brooke, Ralph, 185, 332

Brooke, William, *see* Cobham, 7th Lord

Browne family, 125

Browne, George, 297

Brussels, 261

Bryan, George, 129, 161, 256

Buck, Sir George, x, 302-303

Buckhurst, Lord, 180

bull-baiting, 27

Bull, Eleanor, 107

Bull inn, 70, 136, 137

Bunhill, 348

Burbage, Cuthbert, 31, 32, 43, 125, 126, 127, 208-209, 210, 211, 235, 290, 308; mention of Shakespeare, xi, 92, 209, 289

Burbage, Elizabeth (Mrs. Cuthbert), 55, 127

Burbage, Ellen (Mrs. James), 29, 31, 210

Burbage family, in the "war of the broomsticks," 31; in the dismantling of the Theatre, 210

Burbage, James, as an actor, 25, 26, 36, 128; as a theatre builder and manager, see Blackfriars theatre and the Theatre; temperament, 29, 30, 31, 43, 59, 206; death, 208

Burbage, Richard, as an actor, 43, 126, 128-129, 130, 160, 203, 208, 215, 225, 269, 271, 303; in Shakespeare's plays, 43, 128, 172, 212, 217, 265, 266, 276; as a theatre owner, see Blackfriars theatre, Globe theatre financing, and the Theatre; as a company member, 129, 131, 146, 152, 255, 256, 257-258, 269, 290, 351n.; apprentices, 126, 160; as a painter, 306; relation to Pembroke, 259, 324, 328, 335; relation to Shakespeare, 43, 218, 276, 306, 319; private life, 31, 124, 130, 235, 245; death, 125, 324

Burbage, Winifred (Mrs. Richard), 55

Burghley, William Cecil, Lord, 115, 226, 251, 275

Butt Close, 12

Butter, Nathaniel, 326, 327

Cade, Jack, 96

Cage tavern, 316

Cambises, 23

Cambridge, town of, 226

Cambridge, university of, 16, 56, 63, 64, 73, 74, 79, 102, 115, 193, 248, 281, 329, 355; relation to the theatre, 72, 73, 74, 116, 149, 193, 226 (see also theatricals, amateur)

Camden, William, 16, 84, 185-186, 202, 203, 249, 335; relation to Shakespeare, 185-186; Britannia, 186

Canaries, the, 216

canon, disintegration of the, xi, 94n., 309n., 356-361

Canterbury, 1, 6, 51, 74

Canterbury, Archbishop of, see John of Stratford or Whitgift, Dr. John

Capulet, Lord, 161, 162, 170

Carew, Richard, 224

Carter Lane, 66, 188

Castile, Constable of, 262-264

casting, 158-159

Catholicism, 4, 5, 9-10, 19, 46-47, 66, 102, 205, 251

Catiline's Conspiracies, 70

Catullus, 224

Cecil, Robert, later Viscount Cranborne, 115, 251, 257, 258

Cecil, William, see Burghley, Lord

censorship, 65-66, 113, 139, 157, 192-193, 201, 231, 247-248, 289

Ceres, 285

Chamberlain, Lord, 123, 137, 138, 140, 150, 190-191, 256, see also Hunsdon, Lords and Pembroke, 3rd Earl of

Chamberlain's company, see Shakespeare's company

Chancellor, Lord, 300

Chancery Lane, 177

Chapel, Children of the, see acting companies, boy

Chapel Lane, 189, 244, 298, 317

Chapel Street, 47

Chapel Street ward, 189

Chapman, George, 14, 93, 121, 133, 229, 231, 232, 265, 267, 275, 282, 286, 287, 288, 289; The Blind Beggar of Alexandria, 170; The Iliad, 133

Chalecote, 352, 353

Charles I, as prince, 260; as king, 355

Charles II, 355, 356

Chaucer, Geoffrey, 15, 16, 58, 59, 63, 73, 100, 101n., 177, 224, 229, 239, 263, 281, 287, 322, 347, 351

Cheshire, 185

Chettle, Henry, 84, 85, 86, 91, 132

Children of the Chapel Royal, see acting companies, boy

children's companies, see acting companies, boy

China, 62

Index

Choice of Valentines, The, see Nashe, Thomas
Chorus, use of, 218, 219
Christ's Hospital, 149
Christ's Tears Over Jerusalem, see Nashe, Thomas
"Chronicle of Cambridge Cuckolds, A," 74
Chronicles, see Holinshed, Raphael
church law, 10, 50, 52, 195, 235
Church of the Holy Trinity, 9, 11, 52, 296, 321
churches, *see under individual listings*
Churchyard, Thomas, 97
Chute, Mr., 218
Cicero, 145
Cinthio, Giraldi, 266
Civil War, 295, 348, 355
classical theory, 71-72, 79, 109, 110-111, 227, *see also* Jonson, Ben
Clement's Inn, 149n.
Cleopatra, 109, 249, 272
Clerkenwell, 138, 139, 157, 264, 265, 269, 302
Clink, liberty of the, 210, 211, 236-237, 277
Clink prison, 240
"Clodpate, Justice," 352
Clopton, Sir Hugh, 1, 12, 187, 298
Clopton Pew, 187, 279
Clutterbook, Ferdinando, 235
Clytemnestra, 24
coat of arms, 48, 112, 245, 246, 353, *see also* Heralds, Office of, *and* Shakespeare, John *and* William (private life)
Cobham, Henry Brooke, 8th Lord, 174
Cobham, William Brooke, 7th Lord, 191
cock fighting, 69
collaboration, *see* plays, collaboration on
College of Heralds, *see* Heralds, Office of
College of Physicians, 105
Collegiate Church, 279
Collins, Francis, 316-317, 318, 319, 320

Combe family, 243, 300
Combe, John, 243, 298, 300, 317, 321, 348, 352
Combe, Thomas the elder, 319
Combe, Thomas the younger, 300-301, 315, 318
Combe, Mrs. Thomas, 319
Combe, William the elder, 243, 300
Combe, William the younger, 300, 313-315, 319
Comedy of Errors, The, see Shakespeare, plays
Comedy of the Most Virtuous and Godly Susanna, The, 24
commonplace books, 20, 117, 169
Commonwealth, Puritan, 160, 355
companies, *see* acting companies *or* Drapers', Stationers' *or* Watermen's Company
Complaint of Rosamund, The, see Daniel, Samuel
Condell, Elizabeth, 55, 125, 127, 128, 320
Condell, Henry, as company member, 125, 130, 255, 256, 289, 290, 324, 325; relation to Heminges, 125, 308, 325; relation to Shakepeare, 126, 128, 134, 319; as joint editor of First Folio, 125, 134, 156, 259, 309n., 325, 328-330, 331, 332-338, 356, 357, 359; private life, 125, 127-128, 130, 245, 277, 320; death, 338, 355
Consistory Court, 51, 52, 312, 316
Constantinople, 62
control of theatres, *see* theatre, opposition to
Cooke, Alexander, 126, 325
Cooke, Rebecca, 126
Cooke, Robert, 46, 46n., 47, 184, 185
Cope, Sir Walter, 257
Cope, William, 62
copyrights, 111, 118, 120, 327, 332
Cordelia, 276
Coriolanus, see Shakespeare, plays
Cornelia, see Kyd, Thomas
Cornelia, 109
Cornwallis, Thomas, 60
Corporation, *see* Stratford Council
Cosin, Dr., 52

costume, theatrical, 67, 140-141, 142, 163-166, 214, 219, 226, 261, 265, 282, 309; handling of, 138-139, 142, 193, 265
Cotswold Hills, 245
Council, see London, Privy or Stratford Council
Counter prison, 240
Court of Chancery, 182
Court of Common Pleas, 241
Court of Queen's Bench, 181, 182
Court of Record, 11, 299
Court of Requests, 301
Covell, William, 224
Coventry, 182, 201, 259
Cowley, Elizabeth, 124
Cowley, Richard, 124, 216, 255, 256
Cranborne, Viscount, see Cecil, Robert
Cressida, 65
Crosby, Sir John, 234
Crosby Place, 234
Cross Keys inn, 25, 136-137
Cross Keys inn, 25, 136-137
Crosse, Henry, 245-246
cue sheets, 78, 158, 360
Curle, Mr., 218
Curtain theatre, 42, 73, 124, 126, 130, 169, 206, 269, 349
cutting of plays, see plays, cutting of
Cymbeline, see Shakespeare, plays
Cynthia's Revels, see Jonson, Ben

dancing, 33, 38, 88-89, 146, 147, 148, 169, 291, see also actors as dancers
Daniel, Samuel, 109, 117, 121, 205, 250; The Complaint of Rosamund, 117; Philotas, 250
Danter, John, 136, 169, 171
Danzig, 199
Darby, Robert, 52n.
Datchet, 222
Datchet Mead, 222
Dauphin of France, 24
Davenant, John, 349
Davenant, Mrs. John, 349, 350
Davenant, Robert, 349
Davenant, William, see D'Avenant, Sir William
D'Avenant, Sir William, 349-350, 351, 354

Davies, Sir John, 134
Davies, Rev. Richard, 352
Day, John, 132; The Isle of Gulls, 289
dedications, 66, 113-114, 116-117, 248, 259, 335-336, 343
Dekker, Thomas, 121, 132, 232, 261, 275, 286; Satiromastix, 232
Democritus, 345
Denmark, 129, 253
Denmark, Christian IV, King of, 264
Denmark, Frederick II, King of, 129
Dennis, John, 221n.
Derby, 5th Earl of, see Lord Strange
Derby, 6th Earl of, 360n.
Derby's company, see acting companies
Dethick, Sir William, 185
de Vega, Lope, 79
de Velasco, Juan Fernandez, see Castile, Constable of
Devil's Charter, The, see Barnes, Barnabe
Diana, 163
Digges family, 334
Digges, Leonard, 334-335
Dixon, Thomas, 189
Dogberry, 176
Dolly, 127
Donat, the, 15
doubling, 22-23, 89, 97, 106, 159
Dover, 195-196
Dowgate, 82
Drake, Sir Francis, 238
drama, general survey, 23-24, 57, 69-78, 200, 274-275, 282-283, see also plays, stage, theatre and individual dramatists
Drapers' Company, 42
Drayton, Michael, 132-133, 174, 205, 261, 286, 327, 346; Heroical Epistles, 133; Poly-Olbion, 133
Droeshout, Martin, 332-333
Dryden, John, 348
Duenna, The, see Sheridan, Richard Brinsley
Dulwich College, 246, 306
Dumaine, 103
Dunnington Castle, 347
Dyer, Sir Edward, 360n.

Earl Godwin and His Three Sons, 132, 133

Edinburgh, 255

education, 13-20, 73, *see also* London, educational facilities

Edward VI, 11, 241

Egypt, 275

Eld, George, 339

Elector Palatine, *see* Frederic of Bohemia

Elizabeth, Stuart, princess of England, 260, 302, 303, 304, 305

Elizabeth Tudor, Queen of England, accession, 4, 8; at Greenwich, 142-143; at Kenilworth, 21; at Norwich, 97, 144; at Richmond, 252; characterization, 60, 67, 143-146, 198, 222, 248, 250-252, 261, 268; as a writer, 99, 145-146, 254; relation to Essex, 247-248, 250; relation to the theatre, 60, 137, 145-146; relation to Shakespeare's company, 138, 143, 144-145, 191, 250, 252; relation to Shakespeare, 121, 221n., 222, 258, 309, 352; death, 252

Elsinore, 129, 161

enclosure controversies, 240, 313-316

England's Helicon, 223

England's Joy, 167

England's Parnassus, 169, 223

Ephesus, 101

Epilogue, use of, 41, 310

Epistles, see *Tully's Epistles*

Essex conspiracy, 248-250, 258

Essex, county of, 208, 211

Essex, Earl of, 115, 218, 247-250

Esther and Ahasuerus, 136

Euphues, see Lyly, John

Euripides, 71

Evans, Henry, 230, 231, 232, 289, 290

Evans, Thomas, 290

Eve, 67

Every Man in his Humour, see Jonson, Ben

Every Man out of his Humour, see Jonson, Ben

Evesham, 188

excommunication, 50, 312

Fair Em, 356

fairs, *see individual listings*

Faithful Shepherdess, The, **see** Fletcher, John

Falstaff, Sir John, 171, 173-174, 203, 219, 220-222, 282, 334, 353

Famous Victories of Henry the Fifth, The, 173

Farmer, Dr. Richard, 309n., 356

Fastolf, Sir John, 174

Faversham, 196-197

fencing, 60, 61, 67, 87, 167, 169

Fenner, Edward, 250

Field, Henry, 56, 111

Field, Jasper, 56

Field, Nat, 232, 304

Field, Richard, 56, 102, 111-112, 118, 207, 308

Finsbury Fields, 36, 41

First Folio, *see* Folio, First

First Part of the Contention Between the Houses of Lancaster and York, The, 357

Fish Street, 132

Fitton, Mary, 342

Flanders, 61

Fleet Street, 66, 150

Fletcher, John, 156, 283, 286, 287, 288, 304, 333; collaboration with Beaumont, *see* Beaumont, Francis; conjectural collaboration with Shakespeare, 309n.; *The Faithful Shepherdess*, 283, 304

Fletcher, Lawrence, 239, 255, 256, 263

Florence, 275

Florio, John, 40, 114

Folio, First, 84, 94n., 125, 126, 128, 133-134, 136, 256, 259, 287, 309, 309n., 323, 325-326, 328-338, 342, 355, 356, 357, 358, 359

folios, second, 355; third, 356; fourth, 356

Fontainebleau, 24

Fool, the, 276

"Forces of Hercules, The," 86

Forman, Dr., 292

"Fortune my foe," 136

Fortune theatre, 213, 231, 238, 269

France, 61, 65, 97, 102, 109, 221, 277

France, Queen of, 289

Francisco, 81

Frankfort fair, 91, 331
Frederic of Bohemia, 304
Freeman, Thomas, 286
French, teaching of, 18, 62-63
French theatre, 42, 96
Friar Lawrence, 162
Frias, Duke de, *see* Castile, Constable of
Frizer, Ingram, 107, 179
Frobisher, Sir Martin, 238
Fuller, Thomas, 345; *The History of the Worthies of England*, 345

gardens, 62, 106, 187, 297, 298
Gardiner, Justice William, 135, 353
Garnier, Robert, 109, 214, 259
Garter inn, 222
Garth, Richard, 62
Gascoigne family, 353
gatherers, 28, 31, 123-124, 130, 168
Gaunz, Joachim, 176-177
George inn, 30, 208
Gerarde, John, 62
Germany, 41, 105, 190
Getley, Walter, 244, 317, 318
Gilbourne, Samuel, 126
Gl' Ingannati, 217
Glaucus, 110
Globe Alley, 212
Globe theatre, financing, 209-210; location, 210, 210n., 236-237; erection, 211; date of opening, 213, 236; division of shares, *see* shares, theatre; performances at, *see* Shakespeare's company; closed by plague, 269, 290; burning and rebuilding, 310
Gloucester, 22, 23
Gloucestershire, 189, 352
Golden Age, The, *see* Heywood, Thomas
Goldsmiths' Row, 122
Gorboduc, 72
Gospel Bush, 315
Gosson, Henry, 326
Gosson, Stephen, 70, 102
Gough, Robert, 124
Gower, John, 239
Gowry, 274
Gowry, Earl of, 274

Gowry House, 274
Gracechurch Street, 26, 136
grammar schools, *see individual listings*
"Graves, cousin," 297n.
Gray's Inn, 147, 148, 149, 150, 303
Greece, 74
Greek language, 17, 112, 145, 214, 333
"Green-Curtain" theatre, 348-349
Greene, Anne, 297
Greene, John, 307
Greene, Letitia, 297
Greene, Robert, 77, 78, 79, 80-84, 91, 102, 174, 180, 193, 204, 291, 358; attack on Shakespeare, 83-85, 92, 97-98, 104, 358, 360-361; death, 82, 104, 107; *Greene's Groatsworth of Wit*, 82-84; *Orlando Furioso*, 78, 360
Greene, Thomas, 297-299, 307, 311, 313, 314-315; relation to Shakespeare, 297, 297n., 300, 314-315
Greene, William, 296-297
Greene's Groatsworth of Wit, *see* Greene, Robert
Greenhill Street, 7
Greenwich, 142, 143, 147, 264
Greg, Dr. Walter W., 360
Gresham College, 63, 234
Gresham, Sir Thomas, 59, 63, 234
Greville, Sir Edward, 240-241, 242, 278
Greville, Sir Fulke, 241, 249
Grooms of the Chamber, *see* Shakespeare's company as the King's Men
guild buildings, *see* Stratford
Guild of the Holy Cross, 13
guildhalls used as theatres, 22, 26, 193, 197, 199
Gullio, 224-225
Gunter's, 249

Hal, Prince, *see* Henry V
Hall, Edmund, 44
Hall, Edward, 220
Hall, Elizabeth, 296, 301, 317, 318; as Lady Bernard, 323, 346
Hall, Emma, 44
Hall, Dr. John, 295, 299, 311, 312, 315, 319, 321, 346

Index

Hall, Susanna, *see* Shakespeare, Susanna

Hall's Croft, 296, 297, 299

Hamlet, old play of, 136, 227, 276

Hamlet, see Shakespeare, plays

Hamlet, 128, 171, 227-229, 230, 232, 272, 275, 276

Hampton Court, 260, 261, 264

handwriting, 6, 14, 64, 84, 132, 188, 297, 347

Harrison, John, 112, 113, 118, 120

Hart, Joan, *see* Shakespeare, Joan

Hart, Michael, 318

Hart, Thomas, 318

Hart, William the elder, 242

Hart, William the younger, 318

Harvey, Gabriel, 18, 96, 108, 174, 229

Hathaway, Anne, *see* Shakespeare, Anne

Hathaway, Bartholomew, 50, 53

Hathaway, Richard, 50, 53

Hatton, Lady, 265

Haughton, William, 132

Hebrew language, 112, 176

Hecuba, 227

Helen of Troy, 71

Heminges, John, as an actor, 203, 215, 271, 289, 303, 333; as a company member, 125, 131, 152, 209, 255, 256, 290; position in company, 125, 324-325, 355; as business manager, 125, 262, 263, 290, 302, 310, 325, 355; in company law-suits, 308, 311; apprentices, 126, 325; neighbors, 209, 210, 334; services to friends, 308, 325; relation to Condell, 125, 325; relation to Shakespeare, 126, 128, 134, 307, 308, 319, 325-326; as editor of the First Folio, 125, 134, 156, 259, 309n., 325-326, 328-330, 331, 332-338, 355, 356, 357, 359; private life, 125, 127-128, 245, 277, 320, 337; death, 338, 355

Heminges, Rebecca, 125, 126, 128, 320

Heminges, Thomasina, *see* Ostler, Thomasina

Heminges, William, 337

Henley Street, 7-8, 12, 19, 47, 48, 182, 241, 296; Shakespeare houses: east, 7-8, 10, 12, 44, 45, 242, 318, middle,

44, 53, 242, 318, west, 44, 182-183

Henry IV, see Shakespeare, plays

Henry IV, 173, 220, 247

Henry V, see Shakespeare, plays

Henry V, 70, 173, 218-219, 220, 247

Henry VI, see Shakespeare, plays

Henry VI, 94, 104

Henry VII, 185

Henry VIII, see Shakespeare, plays

Henry VIII, 145, 187, 260, 310

Henry of Navarre, 66, 102

Henry Stuart, prince of England, 257, 260, 304-305

Henslowe, Philip, 42-43, 122, 162, 239, 308; diary, 95, 132, 273; relation to actors, 43, 122, 130, 150, 163, 194, 257; relation to Alleyn, 43, 106, 122, 127, 183-184; relation to writers, 43, 132-133, 202, 231, 327, 352; as a theatre owner: the Fortune, 213, 238, the Rose, 42, 95, 105, 199, 210, 211

Heraclitus, 345

heraldry, 64n.

Heralds, Office of, 7, 11, 45, 46, 46n., 47, 184-185, 332

Herbert, Philip, *see* Montgomery, Earl of

Herbert, William, *see* Pembroke, 3rd Earl of

Hercules, 212, 293

Herne's Oak, 222

Hero and Leander, see Marlowe, Christopher

Heroical Epistles, see Drayton, Michael

Hertford, Lady, 265

Heywood, Thomas, as an actor, 93, 121, 129; as a writer, 93, 121, 130, 233, 257, 265, 267, 284, 285, 286, 288, 291, 293, 358; relation to Shakespeare, 285, 286-287, 330; *An Apology for Actors,* x; *The Golden Age,* 285; *The Rape of Lucrece,* 285; *The Silver Age,* 285; *Troia Britannica,* 285, 330

Hiccox, Lewis, 242

High Street, Bath, 197; Oxford, 349; Stratford, 55, 316; Windsor, 222

hired men, *see* actors, hired

History of the Worthies of England,
  The, see Fuller, Thomas
history plays, 69-70, 94, 161n., *see also*
  individual titles
Hoby, Sir Edward, 150
Hog Lane, 77, 348
Holborn, 68
Holinshed, Raphael, 94, 95, 220, 272,
  273, 276; *Chronicles,* 94-95, 98, 172,
  272
Holland, 302
Holland, Hugh, 335
Holofernes, 103, 178
Holy Trinity, Church of the, *see*
  Church of the Holy Trinity
Holywell Lane, 42
Holywell, liberty of, 36
Holywell Street, 124
Homer, 71
Horace, 9
Horestes, 23
hornbooks, 14
Horseshoe Court, 239
Hotspur, 284
Howard, Charles, Lord, 122
Howe, Mr., 348
Howes, John, 105
Huband family, 279
Huband, Ralph, 279
"Hues, William," *see* Hughes, William
"Hughes, William," 341-342
Huguenots, 277
Hunsdon, George Carey, 2nd Lord,
  191, 198, 207
Hunsdon, Henry Carey, 1st Lord,
  122, 137-138, 190-191
Hunsdon's company, *see* Shakespeare's company
Hunt, Simon, 19
Hyde, John, 32

Iago, 334
Iliad, The, see Chapman, George
Illyria, 216
impresa, 305-306
Indians, 61-62
Indies, 62
"Inganni," *see* Gl' *Ingannati*
Inner Temple, 72, 149, 283, 303

inns, 12, 41, 65, 195, 196, 197; *see also*
  individual listings
Inns of Court, 72, 76, 79, 99, 147-149,
  149n., 200, 228, 281
inn-yards, used as theatres, 25-26, 27,
  28, 35, 136-137, 193, 197, 227, 234
Insatiate Countess, The, 282-283
Ireland, 61, 94, 190, 218, 248
Iris, 226
Isis river, 350
Isle of Dogs, The, 192-193, 202, 204
Isle of Gulls, The, see Day, John
Israel, 276
Italian theatre, 27, 61, 70, 101, 103,
  140, 194, 217
Italy, 61, 65, 293

Jackson, John, 307, 320
Jaggard, Isaac, 330, 331, 332
Jaggard, William, 223, 285, 327, 329-
  330, 331-332
James I, King of England, as James
  VI of Scotland, 253-254, 274; accession, 253-254; coronation, 258; at
  London pageant, 261; at Oxford,
  261, 268; characterization, 205, 254,
  260, 261-262, 264-265, 267-268, 273-
  274; as a writer, 253-254; attitude
  toward witchcraft, 273; relation to
  the theatre, 254-255, 264, 267-268,
  281; relation to Shakespeare's company, 255, 257, 259, 260, 264, 268,
  269, 274, 290, 335; relation to Shakespeare, 121, 267-268, 274
Janssen, Gerard, 321-322
Java, 62
Jenkins, Thomas, 19
Jeroboam, 276
Jerusalem, 108
Jesuits, 19
Jew, The, 70
Jew of Malta, The, see Marlowe,
  Christopher
Jews, 176-177
Joan of Arc, 95-96
John of Stratford, 1
Johnson, Arthur, 327
Johnson, Henry, 211
Johnson, Joan, 278
Johnson, Dr. Samuel, 358

Johnson, William, 307
Jonah, 91
Jones, Inigo, 205, 265, 267, 268
Jones, Richard, 91
Jonson, Ben, private life, 193, 199, 202, 204-205, 258, 349; as an actor, 92, 193; as a playwright, 92-93, 130-131, 175, 180, 193, 201-205, 215, 231-232, 286, 289, 352, 36on.; masques and pageants, 121, 261, 265, 328; folio edition of works, 202, 275, 328, 329, 330-331, 333; attitude toward classics, 16, 18, 202, 215, 270; attitude toward audiences, x, 216, 217, 233, 283, 287, 288; relation to other writers, 18, 204-205, 232, 283, 284n., 286, 287, 334; relation to Shakespeare's company, 193, 203, 206, 232, 257, 269-271, 303, 333, 352; relation to Shakespeare, 202, 203-205, 206, 215, 270-271, 287, 332-334, 345; conjectural relation to Shakespeare, 309n., 337, 346, 352; miscellaneous references, 14, 212, 259, 287, 300, 345, 348-349, 356; *The Alchemist*, 303; *Cynthia's Revels*, 231-232; *Every Man in his Humour*, 92, 202, 203, 205, 206, 275; *Every Man out of his Humour*, 215-216; *Poetaster*, 232; *Sejanus*, 92, 269-270; *Volpone*, 271
Jove, 212, 285, 291, 293
Juliet, 153, 155, 156, 160, 162, 163, 169, 170, 171
Julius Caesar, see Shakespeare, plays
Julius Caesar, 195, 215
Juvenal, 82

Kempe, William, 129, 145, 146, 152, 159, 161, 170, 171, 209, 216, 221, 225, 255, 257
Kenilworth, 21
Kent, 183, 193, 195
King and No King, A, see Beaumont, Francis
King at Arms, 46
King John, see Shakespeare, plays
King Lear, old play of, 276
King Lear, see Shakespeare, plays
King Lear, 64n., 198n., 276; in Shakespeare's play, 128, 171, 212, 276
King's Bench prison, 240
King's Men, see Shakespeare's company
Knell, William, 219
Knight of the Burning Pestle, The, see Beaumont, Francis
Kremzow, 40, 68
Kyd, Thomas, 14, 76, 108-109, 180, 287; *Cornelia*, 108, 109; *The Spanish Tragedy*, 76, 78, 98, 108, 202, 225, 284

Lambert, Edmund, 181, 182
Lambert, John, 182
Lancashire, 246
Lancaster, Henry of, see Henry IV
Lane, John, 311-312, 320
Lane, Richard, 300
Laneman, Henry, 42, 73
Langley, Francis, 42, 122, 124, 135
Latin, 9, 15-17, 18, 20, 48, 54, 63, 79, 102, 110, 112, 144, 145, 186, 254, 279, 295, 322, 333
Launce, 175
Lavinia, 99, 100
law courts, 37, 48, 69; see also individual listings
law schools, see Inns of Court and individual listings
Leadenhall, 63
Lear, see King Lear
Lee, Anne, 135
Legh, Gerard, 64n.; *Accedens of Armory*, 64n.
Leicester, 273
Leicester, Earl of, 21, 22, 24, 103
Leicester's company, see acting companies
Lepanto, 253
Levison, William, 209
liberties, 35-36, see also individual listings
liberty of the Clink, see Clink, liberty of the
licensing, of actors, 22, 25, 35, 197; of books, 84, 98n., 111; of gaming houses, 60; of marriages, 51-52, 316; of play scripts, 35, 157, 158; of printers, 56; of schoolmasters, 349;

licensing—*Continued*
of theatres, 209; of travellers, 3, 195; of watermen, 237
lighting, *see* stage lighting
Lily, William, 15, 16, 20
literary theories, *see* classical theory
Lives, see Plutarch
Locrine, 356
Lodge, Thomas, 77, 78-79, 81, 91, 107, 110, 111, 216, 258; *Rosalynde,* 216; *Scilla's Metamorphoses,* 79, 110
Lodge, William, 107
Lombard Street, 59
London, general description, 58-69; trade, 29-30, 37, 59, 62, 66, 176; government, *see* London Council; overcrowding, 37, 56, 59, 105; educational facilities, 17-18, 62-67, 147, 149; recreational facilities, 60, 62, 67-71, (*see also* theatres, bear-baiting, *etc.*); used as background of plays, 275. *For streets, churches, districts, etc., see individual listings.*
London Bridge, 27, 42, 58, 68, 199, 234, 237
London Council, 34-35, 38, 43, 59-60, 67, 104, 105, 137
London Prodigal, The, 223, 326, 356
Longaville, 103
Longueville, Duc de, 102
lotteries, 30, 209
Louis, *see* Dauphin of France
Love's Labour's Lost, see Shakespeare, plays
Love's Labour's Won, 179
Love's Martyr, 120
Low Countries, 65
Lowin, John, 355
Lucrece, see *Rape of Lucrece, The*
Lucrece, 116, 117, 118, 286, 351n.
Lucy family, 352
Lucy, Sir Thomas, 352-353
Lucy, Sir William, 353
Ludgate Hill, 290
Lyly, John, 102, 107, 230, 231, 340; *Euphues,* 102

Mabbe, James, 335
Macbeth, see Shakespeare, plays
Macbeth, 273

Macbeth, Lady, 292
Machiavelli, Niccolo, 61
Maid Lane, 210n., 237
Maiden-Head inn, 242
Maid's Tragedy, The, see Beaumont, Francis
mail service, 26, 183-184
Mainwaring, Arthur, 315
Malone, Edmund, 341, 354, 356-359
Malvolio, 216, 217, 282, 334
Manners, Francis, *see* Rutland, 6th Earl of
Manningham, John, 217-218, 292
Margaret, Queen, 96, 97
Market Cross, 12, 19, 182, 316
Market Street, 21
Markham, Gervase, 113
Marlowe, Christopher, 16, 52n., 74-76, 77-78, 98, 193, 200, 202, 287, 332; as a playwright, 74-76, 78, 84, 172, 175, 360n.; as a free-thinker, 77, 82, 84, 108; relation to Greene, 83-84; death, 107-108, 179, 348-349; *Hero and Leander,* 78; *The Jew of Malta,* 177; *Tamburlaine,* 74-76
Marlowe, John, 6, 51
Marprelate, Martin, 282
Marshalsea prison, 192, 193, 199, 240, 241, 247
Marston, John, 200-201, 205, 231, 232, 282, 289, 297; *Pygmalion's Image,* 201; *The Scourge of Villainy,* 201
Martial, 345
Mary Stuart, Queen of Scots, 250, 253
Mary Tudor, Queen of England, 4, 9, 10, 238, 241
masques, 121, 150, 260, 265, 267, 303
Massacre of St. Bartholomew, 277
Massinger, Philip, 304
Master of the Revels, *see* Revels, Master of the
Masters in Chancery, 31
Mauley, Lord, 185-186
Mayenne, Duc de, 102
Measure for Measure, see Shakespeare, plays
medieval influences, 2-4, 15, 45, 58, 59, 177, 243, 244
Menaechmi, see Plautus

Menelaus, 24

Merchant of Venice, The, see Shakespeare, plays

Merchant Tailors' school, 17, 76

Mercury, 226

Mercutio, 155, 166, 172

Meres, Francis, 178-180, 224, 343, 352; *Palladis Tamia,* 178-180

Merlin Ambrosius, 197

Mermaid tavern, 307

Merry Devil of Edmonton, The, 303, 356

Merry Wives of Windsor, The, see Shakespeare, plays

Metamorphoses, see Ovid

Middle Temple, 217, 297

Middleton, Thomas, 275, 324

Midsummer Night's Dream, A, see Shakespeare, plays

Milan, 231

Miles, Ralph, 31

Miles, Robert, 31

Milton, John, 281, 355

miracle plays, 23, 139

Mirror for Magistrates, The, 172

Mirror of Monsters, A, 54n.

monopolies, 167

Montgomery, Philip Herbert, Earl of, 259, 306, 335, 336

Moorgate, 58

morality plays, 23-24

More, Sir Thomas, play on, 131-132

Morris, Matthew, 307

Mortlake, 245, 259, 308

Mountjoy, Lord, 113

Mountjoy, Christopher, 277, 278, 301, 302

Mountjoy, Mrs. Christopher, 277, 301, 302

Mountjoy, Mary, 277, 278, 301

Mucedorus, 284, 356

Much Ado About Nothing, see Shakespeare, plays

Mulcaster, Richard, 17, 18, 20, 76

Munday, Anthony, 102, 131

music, 33, 38, 63, 64, 146, 161; in private theatres, 231; in public theatres, 161, 161n., 310

Nashe, Anthony, 301, 319

Nashe, John, 280, 301, 319

Nashe, Thomas, of Stratford, 301

Nashe, Thomas, 77, 78, 80, 81, 82, 83, 84, 95, 102, 108, 113-114, 129, 136, 191, 192-193, 204; *The Choice of Valentines,* 78, 115; *Christ's Tears over Jerusalem,* 108

Navarre, Henry of, see Henry of Navarre

Navarre, King of, 103

New Place, purchase of, 186, 187, 197, 242-243; description of, 187, 298; social position of, 186-187, 279, 298; guests at, 295, 296-297, 346; see also Shakespeare, relation to Stratford

Newbury, 347

Newgate, 82, 139

Newington, 42, 135

Newington Butts theatre, 42, 135, 136

news pamphlets, 65-66, 102

North, Sir Thomas, 112, 214

Northampton, Earl of, 295, 353

Northamptonshire, 242

Norwich, 97, 144

Nottingham, 181

Nuremberg, 41

nurse, Juliet's, 155-156, 159, 162, 170

Oberon, 21

Office of Heralds, see Heralds, Office of

Office of the Revels, see Revels, Office of the

Old Stratford, 279

Oldcastle, Sir John, 173-174

Ophelia, 212

opposition to the theatre, see theatre, opposition to

Orlando, 78

Orlando Furioso, see Ariosto, Lodovico *or* Greene, Robert

Orleans, 96

Ostler, Thomasina, 311

Ostler, William, 232, 311

Othello, see Shakespeare, plays

Othello, 128, 276

Ovid, 16, 78, 100, 110, 115, 225, 345; *Metamorphoses,* 16, 225, 285

Oxford, Earl of, 102, 180, 230, 360n.

Oxford, town of, 12, 226, 349

Oxford, university of, 56, 64, 73, 79, 102, 225, 261, 329; graduates of, 9, 19, 73, 79, 178, 286, 287, 295, 322; relation to the theatre, 72, 74, 149, 226, 268 (*see also* theatricals, amateur)

pageants, 8, 21, 67, 121, 126; for James, 258, 261
Painter, William, 153, 155
painters, 140, 141, 142
Palladis Tamia, see Meres, Francis
Pallas, 260
Palmer, John, 312
Papal Secretary, 251
Paris, 42
Paris Garden, liberty of, 237
Parliament, 60, 67, 235, 251, 260, 281, 299; Acts of, 2, 22
Parnassus plays, 73-74, 116, 224-226
Passionate Pilgrim, The, 223, 329-330, 343
patronage, of actors, 22, 122, 137-138, 256-257, 269; of writers, 102, 113-114, 116-117, 259, 335, *see also* dedications
Paul's Boys, *see* acting companies, boy
Pavier, Thomas, 326-328, 330, 356; collection of plays, 327, 328, 329, 330
Pearce, Edward, 231
Peascod Street, 222
Peele, George, 14, 78, 83, 358
Pembroke, Mary, Countess of, 109, 214, 259, 335, 360n.
Pembroke, William Herbert, Earl of, 259, 260, 265, 267, 306, 335, 343; relation to Shakespeare's company, 259, 324, 328, 335, 336, 342; relation to Shakespeare, 259, 335, 336, 342; conjectural relation to Shakespeare, 342
Pembroke's company, *see* acting companies
Percy, Sir Charles, 248, 249, 353
Pericles, 326, 327, 330, 356
Peter, 159, 170, 171
Petrarch, Francis, 61
Philaster, see Beaumont, Francis

Philip II, King of Spain, 9
Phillips, Anne, 124, 128, 308
Phillips, Augustine, as an actor, 129, 203; as a company member, 209, 250, 255, 262, 263, 308; apprentices, 126, 161, 348; relation to Shakespeare, 126; private life, 124, 128, 239, 245, 308; will, 126, 161, 256, 311, 320
Phillips, Elizabeth, see Quiney, Elizabeth
Philomela, 100
Philotas, see Daniel, Samuel
"Phoenix and the Turtle, The," see Shakespeare, poems
Pickering, Sir John, 235
"Pig," see Pyk, John
Pistol, 75
plagues, 10, 54, 104-105, 192, 258; effect on theatre activity, 104, 105-107, 109, 122, 135, 137, 259, 269, 290, 357
Platter, Thomas, 213-214, 218
Plautine comedy, 101, 203, 217
Plautus, 17, 72, 79, 101, 104, 179, 293, 345; *Menaechmi*, 101, 147, 217
play-bills, 167
plays, collaboration on, 131-132, 133, 174, 232, 289, 304, 327; *see also* Beaumont, Francis
plays, cutting of, 106, 157-158, 194, 230
plays, prices paid for, 118, 130-131, 132, 202
plays, printing of, 78, 107, 109, 154, 283, 288, 291, 304, 328, 356; *see also* quartos, corrupt *and* Shakespeare, plays, publication of
"plot," the, 166
Plutarch, 145, 214, 271; *Lives*, 112, 214
Poetaster, see Jonson, Ben
Polonius, 275
Poly-Olbion, see Drayton, Michael
Pompey and Caesar, 70
Pope, the, 81
Pope, Thomas, 124-125, 126, 129, 159, 161, 209, 239, 245, 256, 307, 320
Popham, J., 250
Porter, Henry, 132, 163

Portia, 41, 340
Portia, wife of Brutus, 109
Portugal, 61
Prague, 176
Prescott, Richard, 265
Price, Michael, 182
printing of plays, see plays, printing of
printing trade, 33, 56, 65, 111-112; see also Stationers' Company and names of individual printers
prisons, see individual listings
prisons, actors in, 192, 246, 289
prisons, writers in, 77, 193, 201, 202, 204-205, 289
Privy Council, 56, 108, 122, 145, 147, 176, 189, 190, 191-193, 195, 197, 207, 208, 247, 248, 274, 315
Prologue, use of, 143, 168, 174, 309
prompt books, see "book," the
prompter, 90, 158
properties, see stage properties
Proserpine, 285
Prospero, 293
Protestantism, see religion
Psalms, the, 253
publishing, see printing trade
Puck, 178
pulpit influence, 9, 33
punctuation, 17
Puritan Widow, The, 356
Puritanism, 33-34, 46-47, 53-55, 160, 192, 254, 280-282, 338; in Stratford, 280, 295-296, 298, 315; attacked by actors, 55, 282; see also theatre, opposition to
Puttenham, George, 18
Pygmalion's Image, see Marston, John
Pyk, John, 127
Pyramus, 153, 178

quartos, corrupt, 78, 107, 118, 169, 170, 326, 327-328, 357-358, 360: Hamlet, 226, Henry V, 222, 327, Henry VI, 327, 357-358, 360-361, Merry Wives of Windsor, 222, 327, Orlando Furioso, 78, 360, Romeo and Juliet, 169-170, 360
Queen's Men, see acting companies

Quiney, Adrian, 6, 48, 56, 184, 188, 241-242
Quiney, Elizabeth, 49, 53
Quiney family, 48, 49, 187
Quiney, Judith, see Shakespeare, Judith
Quiney, Richard the elder, 48, 49
Quiney, Richard the younger, 48-49, 52, 53, 187-188, 240, 241, 278, 316; relation to Shakespeare, 187-188, 278
Quiney, Shakespeare, 323
Quiney, Thomas, 316, 318

Rabson, Henry, 196
Raleigh, Sir Walter, 62, 311
Rape of Lucrece, The, see Heywood, Thomas or Shakespeare, poems
Raphael, 101
recusancy, 9, 46, 77
Red Bull theatre, 269, 285, 286, 291, 355
Reformation, the, 5, 13, 33, 35, 73, 239, 279
rehearsals, 87, 139-140, 154, 158, 166-167, 265
religion, 4, 5, 9-10, 14, 64, 66, 105, 183, 195, 235; see also atheism, Catholicism, church law, Jews, pulpit influence, Puritanism, recusancy and Reformation
Repentance of Mary Magdalene, The, 23
Replingham, William, 313, 314, 315
Restoration, the, xi, 342, 345, 349, 356, 360
Return from Parnassus, The, see Parnassus plays
Revels, Master of the, 138-139, 324; see also Buck, Sir George and Tilney, Sir Edmund
Revels, Office of the, 138-143, 163, 190-191, 256-257, 264, 265, 302, 324; rental of costumes and properties, 26, 142
revenge tragedy, 76, 227-228
Reynolds, William, 280, 319
Rice, John, 126
Richard, King, play on, 150
Richard II, see Shakespeare, plays

Richard II, 172-173, 247, 248, 263
Richard III, see Shakespeare, plays
Richard III, 172, 173, 217, 218, 220, 234
Richardson, John, 51
Richmond, 252
Roberto, 82
Roberts, James, 167
Robinson, John (of London), 306, 318
Robinson, John (of Stratford), 320
Roche, Walter, 19
Rogers, John, 280
Rogers, Philip, 299
Roman theatre, x, 27, 76, 99
Rome, 74, 272
Romeo, 153, 155, 162, 163, 166, 169, 170, 171, 224
Romeo and Juliet, see Shakespeare, plays
Romeo and Juliet, ballad on, 169
Rosalind, 41, 160, 216
Rosalynde, see Lodge, Thomas
Rosamund, 117
Rose theatre, 42, 95, 98n., 105, 122, 124, 170, 199, 210, 211, 236, 239
Rowe, Nicholas, 350-353, 354, 356
Rowington, Manor of, 244
Rowley, William, 304
Royal Exchange, the, 58-59, 63, 199, 200
Russell, Lady, 207
Russell, Thomas, 301, 318
Russia, 66
Rutland, county of, 180
Rutland, Francis Manners, 6th Earl of, 305-306
Rutland, Roger Manners, 5th Earl of, 360n.
Rye, 196

Sadler, Hamnet, 55, 189, 312, 319, 320
Sadler, Judith, 55
St. Anne's church, 207
St. Bartholomew's fair, 199
St. George, 5, 8, 314
St. Helen, church of, 234-235; parish of, 234-235, 236
St. James' fair, 199
St. John's, Clerkenwell, 139

St. John's Hall, 74
St. Lawrence's church, 145
St. Leonard's parish, 124, 125, 235
St. Mary Aldermanbury, church of, 338; parish of, 125, 325
St. Mary Overy, 239
St. Mary's House, 297, 299
St. Olave, church of, 278, 301; parish of, 277
St. Paul's Cathedral, 58, 66, 249, 264, 310
St. Paul's churchyard, 30, 66, 88, 112
St. Paul's school, 15; *see also* Paul's Boys
St. Savior, church of, 236, 239-240, 256; parish of, 124, 239
Salisbury, 259
Salisbury family, 337
Salisbury, Sir John, 120
Sallust, 285
Samson, 70
Sandells, Fulke, 51
Sara, 127
satires, 201, 202, 215
Satiromastix, see Dekker, Thomas
Saxony, Duke of, 129
Saye, Lord, 96
schools, *see under individual listings*
Scilla, 110
Scilla's Metamorphoses, see Lodge, Thomas
Scoloker, Anthony, 229
Scotland, 61, 94, 255, 257, 260, 275
Scourge of Villainy, The, see Marston, John
Sejanus, see Jonson, Ben
Seneca, 72, 76, 99-100, 101, 109, 136, 145, 179
Senecan drama, 76, 99-100, 136, 214, 227, 269-270
"Shake-scene," 83, 98, 358
Shakespeare, Anne (sister), 44
Shakespeare, formerly Hathaway, Anne (wife), 49-55, 297, 307-308, 316, 319-320
Shakespeare, Edmund (brother), 44, 239-240, 320
Shakespeare, Gilbert (brother), 12, 44, 244, 320

Index

Shakespeare, Hamnet (son), 55, 183, 184, 277, 350

Shakespeare, Henry (uncle), 1, 182, 243

Shakespeare, Joan (first sister), 8, 9, 44, 350

Shakespeare, later Hart, Joan (second sister), 44, 242, 318, 348, 350

Shakespeare, John (father),
private life: arrival in Stratford, 1; as a glover, 2, 6, 12; marriage, 6-7; ability to write, 6; religion, 9-10, 46; coat of arms, 11-12, 45-47, 48, 184-185; as a landowner, 7-8, 45, 47, 181-182, 317, *see also* Henley Street, Shakespeare houses; relation to William Shakespeare, 52, 53, 182, 184; services to friends, 6, 111, 182; law suits, 49, 181-182, 241; fines, 3, 48; death, 242
public life: ale-taster, 4; capital burgess, 4; constable, 4-5, 8, 89; affeeror, 5, 48; chamberlain, 5-6, 9; alderman, 10; High Bailiff, 11, 21, 45, 46n., 48, 185; justice of the peace, 11, 45, 185, 186; Chief Alderman, 48; trips to London, 48; departure from Council, 46-47, 49, 181; final service to Council, 241-242

Shakespeare, later Quiney, Judith (daughter), 55, 183, 316, 317-318, 320, 321, 323, 346, 350

Shakespeare, Margaret (sister), 8

Shakespeare, formerly Arden, Mary (mother), 7, 8, 9, 10, 11, 45, 181, 182, 184-185, 186, 296

Shakespeare, Richard (grandfather), 48, 243

Shakespeare, Richard (brother), 44, 320

Shakespeare, later Hall, Susanna (daughter), 53, 183, 295-296, 297, 307, 311-312, 317, 318, 319, 320, 321, 346

Shakespeare, William, life in Stratford,
birth, 8, 44-45; baptism, 9, 10; childhood, 12-13; education, 13-21; religion, 10; handwriting, 14, 132; marriage, 49-55; birth of children, 53, 55; date of leaving town, 56-57; coat of arms, 184-186; retirement 92, 293-294, 297-298; property: New Place, *see* New Place, land bought from Combes, 243-244, 300, Getley copyhold, 244, 317, 318, tithes, 278-279, 300, 313; efforts to protect property, 242-243, 300, 307-308, 312-313, 317; relation to Stratford as owner of New Place: malt survey, 189-190, highway list, 299; enclosure controversy, 188, 313, 314-315; law suits. 182, 188, 299; loan to Quiney, 187-188; as a godfather, 10, 296; as a member of the gentry, 242, 243, 245, 278-280, 301, 317; attitude toward Stratford, 188-189, 299, 312, 315; friends in Stratford, *see individual listings;* will, 132, 242, 301, 307, 316-320, 323, 348; death, 8, 320; burial, 279, 320-321; monument, 321-322

Shakespeare, William, life in London,
personal: arrival, 56-57; lodgings, 54, 124, 125-126, 234-236, 277-278; as a taxpayer, 126, 235-236; placed under bond, 134-135; relation to Mountjoys, 277-278, 301-302; *impresa*, 305-306; Blackfriars purchase, 306-308, 312-313, 318, 319; temperament, 84-85, 134, 154, 204, 205, 270

in the theatre: as an actor, 83-85, 86-93, 129, 154, 159, 183, 185, 203, 269-270, 289, 294, 335; training as an actor, 15-16, 17, 86-91; attack by Greene, *see* Greene, Robert; defense by Chettle, 84-85, 86, 91; advantage of being an actor, 93, 131, 156, 288; Manningham anecdote, 217-218; as a company member, 123, 128, 255, 256, 262-263: advantage of being a member, 123, 129-131, 133-134, 156-157, 158, 171, Groom of the Chamber, 262-264, income, 130-131, 235, 245, 246, in Court records, 52n., 83, 129, 146, theatre

Shakespeare, William—*Continued*
shares, Blackfriars, 289-290, 310-311, theatre shares, Globe, 209, 212, 310-311
For relation to Elizabeth, James, Jonson, Pembroke *and* Southampton, *see individual listings. See also* Burbage, Condell, Heminges *and* Shakespeare's company.

Shakespeare, William, legends about, apprenticeship, 347, 350, 360; deer-stealing, 352-353, 354, 360; religion, 352; teaching school, 349; horse-holding, 354; drinking party, 346; income, 346, 348, 350-351; doggerel on Combe, 348, 352; theft of Greene's play, 358, 359-360; relation to Mrs. Davenant, 350; relation to Mary Fitton, 342; relation to "William Hughes," 341. *For conjectural relation to* Jonson, Pembroke *and* Southampton, *see under individual listings.*

Shakespeare, William, contemporary references to as a writer,
anonymous, 118, 121, 351n.; Barnfield, 118, 224; Basse, 287, 322; Beaumont, 284n.; Camden, 186, 335; Carew, 224; Chettle, 84; Condell, *see* Heminges *below;* Covell, 224; Davies, 134; Digges, 334-335; Drayton, 286; Freeman, 286; Harvey, 229; Heminges, 134, 156, 325, 328, 331, 332, 336-337, 338; Heywood, 286-287; Holland, 335; Jonson, 203-205, 215, 270, 287, 333-334; Mabbe, 335; Meres, 178-180, 224, 343; *Parnassus* plays, 116, 224-225; Scoloker, 229; Webster, 286; Weever, 224

Shakespeare, William, as a playwright,
success with the public, *see* audiences at Shakespeare's plays; attitude toward publication, x-xi, 120, 288; speed of composition, 92-93, 156, 203, 337; length of plays, 157, 230; characterization,

155-156, 171, 172, 173-174, 177, 215, 216, 221, 229, 272; use of sources, 153-154, 292: popular fiction, 204, 216, 266, 267, 291, old plays, 171-172, 227-228, 276, Brooke, 153-156, Holinshed, 94-95, 172, 220, 272-273, Plutarch, 214, 271-272; influence of Italian theatre, 101, 103, 173, 175, of Lyly, 102, of Marlowe, 98, of Plautus, 101, 293, of Seneca, 99-100; attitude toward classical theories, 100, 101, 203-204, 227, 270, 272, 292, 293; freedom as a playwright, 19, 41, 57, 67, 100-101, 119-120, 121, 129-130, 133, 134, 171, 203, 270, 281; conservatism, 146, 153, 175-176, 216, 284-285, 291-292; use of stock characters, 103, 155-156, 173, of clowns, 175-176, of bawdry, 41, 146, of puns, 102, of old plots, *see above,* use of sources; inaccuracies, 95-96, 97, 204; attitude toward history, 98, 220, 247; lack of interest in realistic backgrounds, 153, 176, 216, 275; refusal to point a moral, 154-155, 172, 276; conjectural collaboration, 131-132, 309n., 359-360. *See also* canon, disintegration of.

Shakespeare, William, plays,
All's Well That Ends Well, 146, 267
Antony and Cleopatra, 134, 161n., 271-272
As You Like It, 175, 216
Comedy of Errors, The, 101-102, 110, 147, 150, 161n., 179, 203, 215, 267, 293
Coriolanus, 271, 272
Cymbeline, 162n., 212, 291, 292
Hamlet, 19, 43, 93, 226-230, 232, 246, 330, 331
Henry IV, 150, 173-174, 179, 220, 284, 303
Henry V, 218-219, 220-221, 267, 327
Henry VI, 84, 94-98, 100, 172, 179, 220, 291, 327, 353, 357-359, 360
Henry VIII, 161n., 309, 309n., 310

Index

Shakespeare, Wm., plays—*Continued*
Julius Caesar, 88, 213, *214-215*, 218, 230, 270, 271, 303
King John, *171-172*, 179
King Lear, 43, 154, 196, *275-277*, 326, 327
Love's Labour's Lost, *102-104*, 175, 178, 179, *257-258*, 267
Macbeth, 212, *272-273*, 274, 292
Measure For Measure, *266-267*
Merchant of Venice, The, 175, *176-178*, 179, 267, 327
Merry Wives of Windsor, The, *221-222*, 266, 327, 352
Midsummer Night's Dream, A, 21, *178*, 179, 327, 348
Much Ado About Nothing, 124, *216*, 222, 303
Othello, 43, 264, *265-266*, 278, 303, 326
Richard II, *172-173*, 179, 247, *248-250*
Richard III, 172, 179, 225, 276
Romeo and Juliet, *152-171*, 175, 179, 191, 192, 360
Taming of the Shrew, The, 136, 179
Tempest, The, 134, 161n., 291, *292-293*, 303, 331
Timon of Athens, 161n., *271*
Titus Andronicus, *98-100*, 101, 110, 136, 162, 169, 179, 359
Troilus and Cressida, 288
Twelfth Night, 175, *216*, 217, 292
Two Gentlemen of Verona, 175, 179, 217
Winter's Tale, The, 291, 292, 303
For plays attributed to Shakespeare, see *Locrine, The London Prodigal, Pericles, The Puritan Widow, Sir John Oldcastle, Thomas Lord Cromwell* and *A Yorkshire Tragedy*.
publication of plays: in quarto, 110, 136, 169, *170-171*, 179, 191, 222, 247, *287-288*, 326, 327 (*see also* quartos, corrupt); in folio, *see* Folio, First *and* folios.

Shakespeare, William, poems,
"Phoenix and the Turtle, The," 120
Rape of Lucrece, The, *116-118*, 119, 121, 179, 224, 229, 285, 339, 351n.
Sonnets, xi, 120, 179, *339-344*
Venus and Adonis, *110-116*, 117, 118, 119, 120, 179, 201, 224, 229, 339
For poems attributed to Shakespeare, see *The Passionate Pilgrim*.
publication of poems: in anthologies, 116, 117, 169, 223; by Field, 56, *111-112*; by Harrison, 118; by Jaggard, 223, *329-330*; by Thorpe, 120, 339, *340-343*

Shakespeare's company, personnel, *124-126*, 129, 232, 239, *255-256*, 325, 355; professional standing, 122, *128-129*, 138, 171, 246, 250, 256; members as householders, 55, *124-128*, 239, 246, 320; relation to each other, *123-124*, 125, 128, 194, 210, 256, 325; ownership of theatres, *see* shares, theatre; relation to Shakespeare, 123, 128, 129, 133, 134, 156, 167, 171, 204, 209, *289-290*, 323, 325, 336; attitude toward publication of Shakespeare's plays, *133-134*, 158, *170-171*, 222, 323, 326, 328. *For members of the company and for relation of the company to Elizabeth, James, Jonson and Pembroke, see individual listings.*
as the Chamberlain's company: date of organization, *122-123*, 128; theatres used, Cross Keys, *136-137*, Curtain, 206, Globe, *see* Globe Theatre, Newington Butts, *135-136*; productions at Court, 123, 138, 143, *146-147*, 191, 222, 250, 252, 258, at Inns of Court, 147, 148, 150, 217, in private houses, 150, on tour, 136, *183-184*, *193-199*; production of plays other than Shakespeare's, 136, *202-203*, 215, *227-228*, 232, 274, 333, 352; production of Shakespeare's plays, 88, 136, 147, 150, 173, 191, *213-217*, *218-219*, 222, 258, 288, first production of *Romeo and Juliet*, 152, *157-168*, difficulty over *Rich-*

Shakespeare's company—*Continued*
ard *ll*, 247-250; rivalry with boys'
company, 232; parodied in *Parnassus* plays, 225; relation to the
Lords Hunsdon, 122-123, 137-138,
191

as Lord Hunsdon's company, 191

as the King's Men: date of organization, 255; theatres used, *see*
Blackfriars *and* Globe; productions at Court, 154, 257, 260, 264,
265-267, 278, 285, 293, 302-303,
304, in private houses, 258, 259,
335, on tour, 259, 290; production
of plays other than Shakespeare's,
154, 223, 269-270, 271, 274, 291,
303, 326, 333, joint production
with Queen's Men, 285; production
of Shakespeare's plays, 154,
257-258, 264, 265-267, 272, 276,
278, 291-292, 293, 302-303, 309-
310; as Grooms of the Chamber,
262-264

Shallow, Justice, 149n., 352, 353

shares, actors', 91, 123-124, 233

shares, theatre: Blackfriars, 288, 289-
290, 310-311; Globe, 209-210, 255,
289, 308, 310-311; law suits over,
124, 308, 311

Shaw, Julius, 320

Sheep Street, 312

Sheffield, Thomas, 143

Sheridan, Richard Brinsley, 358; *The
Duenna*, 358

Shirburn, Sir Edward, 348

Shoreditch, 59, 124, 125, 149, 208, 210,
234, 348

Shoreditch Road, 126, 136

shorthand, 357-358

Shottery, 50, 51

Shylock, 176-177

Sidney, Sir Philip, 72, 78, 103, 109,
162, 186, 200, 227, 229, 259, 272;
Arcadia, 229, 259

Silence, Justice, 353

Silver Age, The, see Heywood,
Thomas

Silver Street, 277

Sincklo, John, 331

Sir John Oldcastle, 133, 174, 327, 330,
356

Sly, William, 125, 129, 255, 256, 290,
311, 351n.

Smith, Rafe, 312

Smith, Sheriff, 249

Smith, William (of Stratford), 6

Smith, William (of Waltham Cross),
210-211, 351n.

Smithfield, 69

Smithweeke, John, 332

Snitterfield, 1, 7, 12, 48, 55

Socrates, 322

Soer, Dorothy, 135

Somerset House, 262, 263, 264

sonneteering, 103, 343

Sonnets, see Shakespeare, poems

Sophocles, 72

Southampton, Henry Wriothesley,
Earl of, 113-115, 248, 258; relation
to Shakespeare, 114, 116-117, 118,
119, 120, 342, 351; conjectural relation to Shakespeare, 342, 350-351,
351n.

Southwark, 27, 36, 42, 104, 124, 125,
126, 135, 149, 210, 235, 236-240, 245,
269, 277. *For theatres, streets, districts, etc., see individual listings.*

Spain, 62, 94, 190, 262, 264, 277

Spanish Tragedy, The, see Kyd,
Thomas

Spedding, James, 309n.

spelling, xii, 52n.

Spencer, Gabriel, 349

Spenser, Edmund, 78, 186, 202, 224,
287, 322

stage directions, 79, 331, 357

stage effects, 23, 75, 91, 291, 293; in
atrocity scenes, 87-88, 96-97, 98-99

stage levels, 28, 86-87, 96, 212

stage lighting, 142-143, 231, 266

stage machinery, 28, 142, 212, 226

stage properties, 26, 28, 88, 96-97, 140,
141, 142, 162

stage scenery, 101, 140, 268; lack of,
72, 162-163

Star Chamber, 69, 190, 280, 290, 347

Stationers' Company, 111, 112-113,
150, 167, 328, 329, 330

Stationers' Hall, 112, 113, 150, 201

Stationers' Register, 111, 118, 222, 288, 310, 332, 339

Steevens, George, 358

Stonehenge, 197

Stow, John, 59, 84

Strand, the, 258

Strange, Lord, later 5th Earl of Derby, 86, 122, 123, 127, 239

Strange's company, *see* acting companies

Stratford, relation to London, 1, 48, 55-56; general description, 1, 2-6, 12-13; charter, 11, 13, 241; town laws, 2-4 (*see also* Stratford Council); fires, 182-183, 187, 314; fairs, 21, 241; pageants, 8; plays, 21-24, 280; attitude toward plays, 24, 53-54, 280. *For houses, streets, etc., see individual listings.*

Stratford bridge, 1, 12, 187

Stratford Council, 4, 10, 19, 22, 46-47, 48, 49, 187, 279, 280, 298, 313-314, 315

Stratford grammar school, 13, 14-17, 19-20

Stratford guild buildings, 4, 19, 22, 280; chapel and garden, 5, 10, 13, 137, 320

Stratford, parish of, 50, 51, 279

Stratford register, 8, 50n., 183, 350

Street, Peter, 210, 211, 212, 213

Stringer, Thomas, 50

Stuarts, *see under first names*

Sturley, Abraham, 278

Suffolk, Duke of, 96, 97

Surrey, county of, 245, 259

Surrey, Sheriff of, 236

Sussex, county of, 193

Sussex, Earl of, 98n., 113

Sussex's company, *see* acting companies

Swan inn, 12

Swan theatre, 42, 87, 122, 124, 135, 192, 199, 239

Symons, Thomas, 235

Talbot, Lord, 95

Tamburlaine, see Marlowe, Christopher

Tamburlaine, 75

Taming of a Shrew, The, 136

Taming of the Shrew, The, see Shakespeare, plays

Taranto, 101

Tarleton, Richard, 87, 129, 145, 255, 256, 262

Tarleton's Jests, 255

Tarquin, 116

Tawyer, William, 331

Taylor, John, 5

Tempest, The, see Shakespeare, plays

Temple, Sir Thomas, 298

Tennyson, Alfred, Lord, 309n.

Terence, 17, 72, 79, 134

Tetherton, William, 299

Thames river, 27, 37, 42, 56, 67, 142, 199, 210, 211, 212, 213, 222, 236, 237, 249, 277

Theatre, the, under James Burbage: date of erection, 25, 29; design, 26-29; financing, 29-30; location, 36, 124, 126; difficulties with lease, 32, 206; difficulty with the Braynes, 30-31; mortgages, 29, 32; management policy, 27, 29, 37, 73; attacks on, 32-35, 38; plays shown at, 70. Under Cuthbert and Richard Burbage: difficulties with lease, 208; dismantling, 208-209, 210-211

theatre, opposition to: by the clergy, 32-33, 105, by local residents, 207-208, 290, 306, by the London Council, 34-35, 38, 104, 137, 191-192, 197, by the Privy Council, 192-193, 197, 226, by the Puritans, 33-34, 38, 54, 54n., 55, 254-255, 281, 355, by the Stratford Council, 280, by the universities, 149, 226

theatres, architecture of, 214 (*see also* Globe *and* the Theatre); food served in, 28, 168, 214; private residences used as, 26, 150, 258, 259; *See also* guildhalls, inn-yards *and* names of individual theatres.

theatres, private, *see* acting companies, boy

theatricals, amateur, 17, 72, 73-74, 76, 99, 103, 147-148, 193, 224-225, 226, 268, *see also* masques

Thisbe, 153, 178

Thomas Lord Cromwell, 356
Thorpe, Thomas, 339, 340-341, 342-343
Thyestes, 100
Tichfield, Baron of, *see* Southampton, Earl of
Tilney, Sir Edmund, 139, 149, 157, 158, 209, 263, 264-265, 302
tilt-yard shows, 67
Timon of Athens, see Shakespeare, plays
tithes, 278-279, 300, 313-315
title pages, 92, 98, 98n., 112, 169, 191, 222, 226, 326, 330, 332
Titus Andronicus, see Shakespeare, plays
Titus Andronicus, 99, 136
Titus Andronicus, ballad on, 136, 169
Tobias, 12
Tolzey, the, 199
Tooley, Nicholas, 126-127
touring, abroad, 24, 88, 91, 129; in England, 21-24, 25, 91, 92, 105-106, 122, 127, 136, 183-184, 193-199, 259, 290
tournaments, 263, 305-306, *see also* tilt-yard shows
Tower of London, 68, 69, 226
Townley family, 246
translations, 61, 66, 76, 99, 109, 112, 145, 153, 214, 253, 285
trap doors, 28, 90, 96, 100, 212
Trinity College, 99
Troia Britannica, see Heywood, Thomas
Troilus, 65
Troilus and Cressida, see Shakespeare, plays
Troy, 227
True Tragedy of Richard, Duke of York, The, 98, 357
Tudors, *see under first names*
Tully's *Epistles*, 48
Turkey, 71
Turks, 70
Turner, Dr., 217
Turnhout, Battle of, 274
Twelfth Night, see Shakespeare, plays

Two Gentlemen of Verona, **see** Shakespeare, plays
Tybalt, 166
Tyler, William, 6
Tyrwitt, Thomas, 358

Underhill family, 187
Underhill, Hercules, 242-243
Underhill, William, 242
Underwood, John, 232, 325
unities, the, 71-72, 101, 120, 202, 204, 227, 270, 292, 293
universities, *see* Cambridge *or* Oxford
usury, 70, 176

Vautrollier, Thomas, 56, 112
Venice, 176
Venus, 116, 118, 286, 305
Venus and Adonis, see Shakespeare, poems
Vere, Sir Francis, 274
Verges, 124
Vergil, 71, 322
Verona, 163, 176
Vice, the, 23
Viola, 216
Virginia, 62
Vittoria, 194
Volpone, see Jonson, Ben

"W.H., Mr.," 341-343
Walker family, 10, 296
Walker, Henry (of London), 306
Walker, Henry (of Stratford), 240, 296, 299
Walker, William, 10, 296, 318
Waltham Cross, 210
Wapping, 67
"war of the theatres, the," 232
Ward, Rev. John, 345-346, 350
Wars of the Roses, 94, 94n., 96, 98, 172
Warwick, Anne, Countess of, 244
Warwick, Earl of, 22, 24, 241, 244
Warwick, town of, 20, 182, 243, 295
Warwick's company, *see* acting companies
Warwickshire, 1, 7, 21, 45, 52, 132, 185, 280, 286, 298, 314, 317, 345, 346, 350, 353

watermen, 237-239
Watermen's Company, 238
Watson, Mr., 72
Watson, Thomas, 77, 78
Wayte, William, 135
Webster, John, 285-286, 288; *The White Devil*, 285
Weever, John, 224
Welcombe, 242, 243, 279, 313, 314
Westminster, 37, 69, 181, 241, 350
Westminster Abbey, 69, 191, 234, 322
Westminster school, 202
Whatcott, Robert, 320
Whateley, Anne, 52
Whateley, George, 47
Whetstone, George, 292
White Devil, The, see Webster, John
White Greyhound book shop, 112, 113, 118
White Lion prison, 240
Whitechapel, 30
Whitehall, 140, 143, 191, 250, 251, 258, 263, 266, 276, 278, 291, 293, 305
Whitgift, Dr. John, as Bishop of Worcester, 51, 52; as Archbishop of Canterbury, 45, 51, 104, 111, 201, 252
Wilbraham, Sir Roger, 33
William the Conqueror, 7, 218
Willingson, Goodwife, 125
Willis, R., 22
Willobie His Avisa, 351n.
Willoby, Henry, 351n.
Wilmcote, 7, 181
Wilson, Jack, 331
Wilson, Robert, 132
Wilton House, 259, 335

Wiltshire, 197, 241, 259
Winchester, Bishop of, 210, 236
Winchester House, 237, 239, 240
Windsor, Castle of, 221; town of, 222
Wingfield, Sir Edward, 113
Winter's Tale, The, see Shakespeare, plays
witchcraft, 253, 273, 292
Wit's Commonwealth, 178
Wittenberg, 227
Witter, John, 308
Wolsey, Cardinal, 310
women, position of, 40-41, 61, 149; as play-goers, 39-41, 75, 99, 146, 218, 222, 310
Wood, Anthony, 346-347
Woodland, the, 13
Worcester, Bishop of, see Whitgift, Dr. John
Worcester, diocese of, 51, 52, 312, 316, 349
Worcester, Earl of, 24, 257
Worcester, town of, 49, 317
Worcester's company, see acting companies
Worcestershire, 189
Wright, John, 339
Wright, Peter, 266
Wriothesley, Henry, see Southampton, Earl of

York, Duke of, 97, 98
York Herald, 185
York, Richard of, see Richard III
Yorkshire Tragedy, A, 223, 326, 327, 330, 356

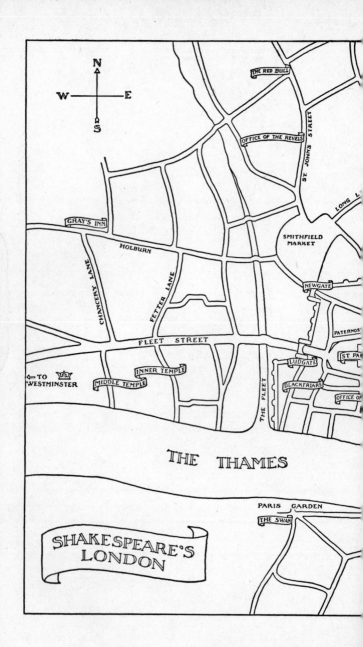